YOURS TO COMMAND

THE LIFE AND LEGEND OF TEXAS RANGER CAPTAIN BILL MCDONALD

HAROLD J. WEISS, JR.

Number 5 in the Frances B. Vick Series

UNT PRESS
University of North Texas Press
Denton, Texas

10 9 8 7 6 5 4 3 2 1

Permissions:
University of North Texas Press
1155 Union Circle #311336
Denton, TX 76203-5017

The paper used in this book meets the minimum requirements of the American National Standard for Permanence of Paper for Printed Library Materials, z39.48.1984. Binding materials have been chosen for durability.

Library of Congress Cataloging-in-Publication Data

Weiss, Harold J.
Yours to command : the life and legend of Texas Ranger Captain Bill McDonald / Harold J. Weiss, Jr.
p. cm. -- (Frances B. Vick series ; no. 5)
Based on the author's Ph. D. thesis, Indiana University, 1980.
Includes bibliographical references and index.
ISBN 978-1-57441-260-4 (cloth : alk. paper)
1. McDonald, William Jesse, 1852-1918. 2. Texas Rangers--Biography. 3. Peace officers--Texas--Biography. 4. Texas--History--1846-1950. 5. Frontier and pioneer life--Texas. I. Title. II. Series: Frances B. Vick series ; no. 5.
F391.M142W456 2009
363.28--dc22
[B]

2009002367

Yours to Command: The Life and Legend of Texas Ranger Captain Bill McDonald is Number 5 in the Frances B. Vick Series

Permission has been given to reprint all or part of the following article by the author:
"The Texas Rangers and Captain Bill McDonald in General—And the Conditt Murder Case in Particular," *South Texas Studies* 9 (1998): 52–70. Reprinted with permission of the Division of Social and Behavioral Sciences, Victoria College, Victoria, Texas.

To those who cared: Mom and Dad
Oscar Osburn Winther
Martin Ridge

Contents

Illustrations and Maps

Photo Gallery Number Three—After Chapter Fifteen

Preface

The historiographical map of the operations of the Texas Rangers is covered with accounts that either chronicle dates and events or narrate the adventures of intrepid Rangers. A dominating theme in these works has been the image and reality of a Ranger as a citizen soldier in the nineteenth century, as seen, for example, in the Ranger and military careers of John S. "Rip" Ford, John C. "Jack" Hays, and Benjamin "Ben" McCulloch. In order to broaden the scope of Ranger history, however, historians need to examine more fully the passage from the life of a Ranger as a citizen soldier to the operations of a Ranger carrying out investigative and administrative duties of police work within an organizational structure. This changing scene from the nineteenth to the twentieth centuries, as portrayed in the life and times of Texas Ranger Captain William J. "Bill" McDonald of Company B, is the focus of this book.

The personality and career of "Captain Bill" show the varied aspects of law enforcement in American culture. In one sense, McDonald, better than the other Ranger captains of his generation, embodied the thoughts and actions of the Rangers as citizen soldiers, from handling mobs and strikers to being seen as a gun-wielding, heroic individual who heightened his popular image with showmanship qualities. In another sense, however, McDonald became a career-minded peace officer with an Anglo-Saxon cultural heritage; functioned as the head of a police force who carried out administrative and investigative duties, from collecting evidence to writing reports, within an organizational framework; and performed as a policeman with a law and order mentality and an ability to solve crimes and track criminals. All this took place, moreover, in a Texas undergoing economic and political change, from being crisscrossed by railroad lines to having to deal with the age-old question of the relation of government to society. The merging of the belief of the intrepid Ranger with the idea of a constable Ranger in a changing Texas is one of the keys in understanding Ranger history for two hundred years.

Past writings about the life and times of Bill McDonald do not adequately cover the complexities of his careers inside and outside law enforcement. McDonald's official biographer, Albert Bigelow Paine, in a well-known study played up the actions of McDonald in Ranger events and played down the role of the Ranger organization and the other members of Company B. Other writers, such as Mike Cox, Eugene Cunningham, Wayne Gard, Tyler Mason, Walter Prescott Webb, and Robert Utley, sketched dates, events, and character traits and told wild and woolly stories about Captain Bill. To paraphrase the satire of Finley Peter Dunne about Theodore Roosevelt at the turn of the 1900s, the book about McDonald that emerged from these works should be entitled: "Alone in Texas."

Since McDonald left few private papers for posterity, this biography reexamines his professional career. The human quest for an ordered society is age-old. In the United States at the turn of the twentieth century scores of public and private police officers patrolled the towns and countryside in their search for those who broke the law. The balancing of order and disorder, moreover, became more complicated when an industrialized America through its mass media created a national audience who entertained themselves with tales of Robin Hood bandits and detective heroes in dime novels, pulp magazines, and silent films. Into this scenario of real-life adventures and action-oriented stories in the popular culture about the exploits of outlaws and lawmen rode Bill McDonald.

By the late nineteenth century in America, criminal acts, like murder and robbery, were carried out in various ways. At times outlaw gangs formed and violence-prone mobs moved about. Secretive groups even created fear in a community by killing those they disliked. To combat such conspiracies, vigilantes rode and hanged those who committed offenses against the social order. Then law officers had to arrest the members of a lynching party for operating outside the scope of the law. Equally troublesome for the Rangers were the feuds between individuals and families. Feudists sought revenge through violent attacks at a given time and place. Captain Bill gained a reputation as a peace officer who could stand up to feudists, lynchers, and mob assassins.

A work of this magnitude is the result of the efforts of many people. The initial impetus for this book came from the study of the Texas Rangers, Captain McDonald, and intergovernmental relations in two seminars conducted by the late Professor Oscar Osburn Winther at Indiana University at Bloomington. At the same time encouragement to pursue this topic also came from the late Professor Chase C. Mooney. The credit for the turning of a seminal idea into a study of the life and times of a Ranger captain, however, must go to the late Professor Martin Ridge, who guided a dissertation on this subject through its various revisions. In addition, my gratitude must be extended to the late Professor Donald F. Carmony, who, as second reader, made useful suggestions, and to the other members of the dissertation committee at Indiana University: late Professors Maurice G. Baxter and John F. Stoner.

It would be impossible for me to list all the names of individuals and organizations that made contributions to the research and writing of a manuscript carried on for several decades. On my field trips to Texas, assistance provided by those in charge of county courthouses, town libraries, the state archives, and the other research centers, especially the Center for American History at the University of Texas at Austin, proved to be invaluable. A special thanks must go to the staff who guided me through the papers of the Ranger service at the Archives Division of the Texas State Library: John Anderson, Tony Black, Donaly E. Brice (a topnotch researcher), and the quiet, smiling woman at the photocopying machine. In addition, Professors Larry D. Ball, Stephen L. Hardin,

Ben Procter, Gary L. Roberts, Paul Spellman, and the late Barry Crouch, and historical consultants and authors, David A. Clary, David Johnson, Robert Utley, and John P. Wilson, shared their knowledge with me about western history and, more specifically, outlaws and lawmen in Texas and the Old West. A personal debt is also owed to the late Professor Lamar L. Kirven and his wife, Dr. Jamesanna E. Kirven, whose hospitality on my trips to Austin can not be repaid; to the members, especially John Boessenecker, Mike Cox, Robert DeArment, Gary Fitterer, Rick Miller, and Chuck Parsons, of the Wild West History Association for their willingness to share their research and findings; to Darlene Hopkins and Lynne Weber for their typing expertise; to my daughter, Bonnie Tompkins, for her computer knowledge; and to my parents who, although their schooling was limited, encouraged and supported my educational pursuits while they were alive. Yet, after all is said and done, any errors of fact or faulty interpretation are my own.

Jamestown Community College, New York
Harold J. Weiss, Jr.
"G. T. T."

PART ONE

EMERGENCE OF A RANGER CAPTAIN

But one thing seems clear to everyone who returns from field work: other people are other. They do not think the way we do. And if we want to understand their way of thinking, we should set out with the idea of capturing otherness.

—Robert Darnton, *The Great Cat Massacre and Other Episodes in French Cultural History.*

In this role, "Captain Bill" . . . mixed the gun-toting image of a frontier lawman with the savvy of a modern police investigator.

—Harold J. Weiss, Jr., "Organized Constabularies: The Texas Rangers and the Early State Police Movement in the American Southwest."

More than any other captain, he was a showman, a colorful character, a self-promoter who reveled in notoriety.

—Robert Utley, *Lone Star Justice: The First Century of the Texas Rangers.*

Ever threatened, often shot, his gray eyes never lost their steadfast courage, and one by one he "nailed" the "bad men," discouraged lawlessness, put a stop to killing and stealing, and generally "cleaned up" until "wild and woolly" Texas came to be as uninterestingly peaceful as a Connecticut community on Sunday.

—Denver *Post*, Oct. 10, 1909.

Chapter 1

BILL MCDONALD, THE HISTORICAL RECORD, AND THE POPULAR MIND

A lone rider, sitting easily in the saddle of his dusty horse, travels across the plains toward a small, new town with muddy streets and lively saloons. He wears a tattered, wide-brimmed hat, a loose-hanging vest [with a tin star], a bandanna around his neck, and one gun rests naturally at his side in a smooth, well-worn holster. Behind him, the empty plains roll gently until they end abruptly in the rocks and forests that punctuate the sudden rise of towering mountain peaks.[1]

The life and times of Texas Ranger Captain William Jesse "Bill" McDonald, better known as "Captain Bill," can be viewed from several vantage points: first, the ins and outs of crime and violence in the trans-Mississippi West in the late 1800s; second, the operations of the Texas Rangers in theory and practice inside and outside the Lone Star State; third, the ambiguous nature of McDonald as a lawman in thought and deed; and fourth, the never-ending folk tales built around the exploits of the fabled Captain Bill.

One difficulty with the historical literature about the life and times of Bill McDonald is the reliance by writers on the information provided by Albert Bigelow Paine, McDonald's official biographer. Although Paine interviewed the Ranger captain, he failed to search for and use effectively official records. He also erred in not verifying his data and in downplaying the activities of those who served under McDonald in Company B. The result was a romantic story with flowery language that contained factual inaccuracies and misleading statements.

Captain Bill (1852–1918) lived at a time when the United States was undergoing vast changes during the Gilded Age. The settlement of western lands by people of all creeds and colors led to warfare with Indian tribes, brought new states into the union, and made terms like "cowboy" and "gunfighter" popular expressions. In addition, agricultural machinery and railroad lines transformed the rural landscape and allowed for the production and transportation of crops and cattle to feed a growing population. Equally important, industrial firms discovered the processes needed to make steel and refine oil, which helped to create modern urban centers complete with skyscrapers, cars, telephone lines, and big-city police departments. The populace also found new ways to enjoy leisure time, from reading comic strips to enjoying spectator sports to watching silent films, like the *Great Train Robbery*. As events would show, such changes in lifestyles created a more complex network of police forces to combat a mobile underworld in Texas and the nation.

BADMEN OF THE OLD WEST

Violent criminal acts in the trans-Mississippi West varied in number and kind in time and space. Many settlers in the western lands, especially in farming, family-oriented communities, with their church steeples and bells summoning the faithful, cared more about building a new life for themselves in a hostile physical environment than about robbing or killing their neighbors or the strangers who happened to pass their way. Peace officers in Texas and other western areas had to spend much time and effort handling minor criminal offenses: rounding up drunks, stopping fistfights, investigating petty thievery, and arresting those charged with disorderly conduct. These undramatic violations of the rules of society made some westerners afraid; others, though, still believed that they lived in law-abiding communities with the bad element under control. Westerners did try to structure society to function in an orderly way.

One historian noted that "frontier violence has infinitely greater appeal to the reader than frontier calm."[2] In the pecking order of western crime and violence, the bank-and-train robber and the gunfighter gained the most notoriety. Many individuals have seen the actions of Old West bandits and gunmen as something more than criminal in nature. Such misdeeds were just boyish pranks; done to defend one's honor; carried out to attack the oppressors of the common folk; executed to help foment a revolution. In western America a violent frontier heritage has meant glorifying the holdups and gun battles of such desperadoes as Sam Bass, the Texas Robin Hood, and John Wesley Hardin, a feared gunman in the Lone Star State. Many times lawmen carved an appropriate epitaph on the tombstones of these shootists: hold an inquest and bury the body.

Crime and violence in the trans-Mississippi West by the turn of the twentieth century, in the view of some, was more than dramatic—it was pervasive. One expert examined lethal violence in three counties located in three different areas, Arizona, Colorado, and Nebraska. In these places, 977 homicides occurred in the four decades after 1880. Multiple factors, particularly transient males, alcohol, guns, and ethnic and racial tensions, brought about high levels of violent actions. Other writers have also tried to make sense out of the endless number of killings found here and there in the western lands. One attempt—called the Western Civil War of Incorporation—tied together the isolated incidents of mayhem into a grand theory. The move by the monied interests to form a market economy in the late 1800s was opposed by small farmers, ranchers, and unionized workers. Both sides used gunmen. Forty-two violent showdowns took place between the opposing forces in the seventy years after 1850. From this violent era came the popular images of the "conservative mythical hero" (like Wyatt Earp) and the "dissident social bandit" (a la Jesse James).[3]

In the wake of the desperado, came the western lawman. To some, the peace officer with a badge and a six-shooter just "mopped up the outlaw."[4] In reality, his jurisdiction covered vast stretches of land, and he was a law officer who handled outbreaks of disorder in the towns and countryside, arrested those who committed crimes, and carried out judicial orders. While doing this, his badge of authority might read marshal or ranger or sheriff or special agent or another apt designation. As one authority perceptively noted, "Some modern nations have been police states; all, however, are policed societies."[5]

Old West policing jurisdictions appeared in many forms. Some of these lawmen and their posses became effective members of governmental police agencies, from town constables to county sheriffs to United States marshals. Others with a bent for corralling badmen entered the field of private law enforcers, as, for example, private detective agencies, the security forces of the railroads, and Wells Fargo shotgun riders and special agents. In addition, military forces, state and federal, assisted civil authorities in preserving law and order until otherwise instructed. The state police movement in the early West, whether legendary Texas Rangers or their counterparts in Arizona, New Mexico, and elsewhere, played a minor-but-vital role in this complex machinery of law enforcement. The spread of western police agencies was a major achievement for a democratic citizenry.[6]

TEXAS RANGERS: FORMED AND REFORMED

In the mechanism of western law enforcement the Texas Ranger, singly or in groups, played a memorable role. Through revolution, statehood, and the rise of an urban Texas, the operations of the Rangers can be divided into three different periods: 1823–1874, 1874–1935, and 1935 onward. In the first stage ranging companies sporadically took the field to fight for family and community against Indian tribes and Mexican nationals. These citizen-soldier Rangers were organized in the closing months of 1835 in the midst of the Texas Revolution and had developed traditions and procedures that were well entrenched by the time McDonald became a captain. Although the word "ranger" was first used by Stephen Austin in his colony as early as 1823, the expression "Texas Rangers" gained more credence in informal sayings than formal statutes in the nineteenth century. After 1874 the state of Texas established a permanent Ranger organization and authorized the officers and the rank and file to act as peace officers. Their existence as law officers under the control of the governor and the adjutant general lasted until the Great Depression of the 1930s when they were combined with other crime fighting units and made a part of a Department of Public Safety.[7]

Established in 1874, the mounted Frontier Battalion, in which Bill McDonald would one day serve, consisted of six companies of seventy-five men each under the control of the adjutant general and the governor. Each Ranger officer, an important term in future legal disputes, had "all the powers of a peace officer" and had the "duty to execute all criminal process directed to him, and make arrests under capias [writ] properly issued, of any and all parties charged with offense against the laws of this State." Men joining the Frontier Battalion supplied some of their own equipment, like horses and an "improved breech-loading cavalry gun" bought from the state by each Ranger at cost. In turn, the state government furnished some supplies, such as ammunition. Pay for officers and privates in the various companies ranged from $125 per month for major to $100 each for captains, $50 for sergeants, and $40 for privates.[8]

As a Ranger officer (1891–1907), McDonald understood the law-and-order mandate to patrol the frontier lands and the settled regions within the borders of Texas. Unlike county sheriffs and town marshals, the Rangers quelled public disturbances and investigated those who committed felonies and misdemeanors throughout the state. On some of McDonald's stationery the heading read: "Texas State Rangers."[9]

The dividing line between such statewide authority and undesirable interference in local affairs by the Rangers in McDonald's era was difficult to ascertain. At one point Private Carl T. Ryan informed Captain Bill from Sanderson in southeastern Texas that upon the request of the local sheriff he had closed the saloons on Sunday as the law required. Ryan did not like this job—"some are kicking and some wants us to close them"—and thought this duty belonged to local peace officers.[10] McDonald responded by telling Ryan to "let the local authorities attend to such matters, that our duties were to look after criminals and larger game."[11] In this reaction the adjutant general concurred: "Our force has no business interfering with anything local," he noted, "such interference might cause us considerable annoyance."[12]

By McDonald's day the "mounted constables" of the Frontier Battalion had the authority, weapons, organizational knowhow, and charismatic leaders to be effective in the field.[13] Walter Prescott Webb once wrote that a Ranger leader "must have courage equal to any, judgment better than most, and physical strength to outlast his men on the longest march or the hardest ride."[14] Yet few captains in the Ranger service approached this ideal picture, as many officers sometimes misjudged their adversaries, sometimes faltered in the face of the enemy, and sometimes pulled back from the violent side of human nature, even within themselves. More likely, as one historian noted, a person in charge of a ranging company in the field "made his own rules based on the immediate situation, educated guesses, and simple instinct."[15] Some Ranger officers, however, did have charisma and became famous through self-reliance and persistence in times of crises. By the opening of the twentieth century Captain McDonald's fight for law and order resulted in public acclaim for himself and the Rangers under his command.

From the laws of Texas and court decisions, state and national, came the authority of the Texas Rangers to make arrests, hold prisoners, and use deadly force. As peace officers, the Rangers could legally arrest Texans with or without warrants, and, equally important, could use "all reasonable means" in taking lawbreakers into custody. Furthermore, peace officers also had the right to commit justifiable homicides in preventing a series of crimes from taking place on Texas soil: arson, burglary, castration, disfiguring, maiming, murder, rape, robbery, or theft at night. In addition, in Texas and other states in the 1900s, judges forged a new doctrine of self-defense. They "changed the English common-law tradition, which required one to retreat before defending oneself, to the American legal doctrine of self-defense, by which one could stand one's ground and fight. Thus, Texans and their police forces in McDonald's day had ample legal authority to use violent means."[16]

By the late 1800s another controversial part of the operations of the Frontier Battalion was its use of weapons in chasing outlaws and controlling feudists and mobs. Through experimentation with various small arms the Rangers found the guns that fitted their needs. Of the different types of Colt six-shooters, they preferred the "version known as the Classic Peacemaker in .45 caliber with a seven-and-a-half-inch barrel."[17] In addition, although some members of the Frontier Battalion used the Sharps long gun, Rangers ultimately switched to the popular 1873 Winchester rifle that used .44 caliber ammunition. McDonald himself carried a Colt revolver, a Winchester rifle, and a shotgun for crowd control. The heavily armed peace officers of Texas had sufficient firepower to carry out a running fight with outlaws.[18]

Yet the Texas Rangers were not exceptional shootists in Old West gunfighting lore. Only one Ranger of note—Captain John R. Hughes—appeared in the list of the premier gunmen of that violence-prone era.[19] At the other end of the spectrum stood Captain Samuel A. McMurry. He had the embarrassment to report to his superiors that his holstered pistol went off and the bullet struck him in the leg. The Ranger officer thought that someone must have hit the hammer while a crowd of people gathered around him.[20]

The individuality of a Texas Ranger can not be separated from the organization within which he operates. In the command structure, orders and the power to carry them out flowed downward: from the governor's office to the adjutant general and his staff, including the battalion quartermaster, to the field captains and those in charge of subcompanies located here and there. At the top of this pyramid stood the governor who had the final word in executing the laws of the state. Captain Bill served as a company commander in four different gubernatorial administrations. No governor since the early days of statehood approached the status of James S. Hogg in Texan politics. Hogg, capable and heavy-set, served as governor for two terms in the early 1890s. He was followed in the governor's mansion by three state leaders known for conservatism: Charles A. Culberson (1895–1899), Joseph D. Sayers (1899–1903), and Samuel W. T. Lanham (1903–1907).[21]

At the apex of the pyramid structure the adjutant general's office kept track of budgetary expenses, investigations of criminal cases, and the movement of the Rangers throughout the state. In two decades of service McDonald and the rank and file of Company B served under four adjutant generals: Woodford H. Mabry (1891–1898), Alfred P. Wozencraft (1898–1899), Thomas Scurry (1899–1903), and John A. Hulen (1903–1907). During his captaincy McDonald followed directives from central headquarters and acknowledged his instructions by ending some of his letters with the phrase, "Yours to command."[22] Too often Texan writers have underplayed an important point about captains in the Frontier Battalion: they took orders from their superiors.

Within this organizational structure the individuality of a Texas Ranger was highly valued. Centralized police work had to be meshed with the Ranger tradition of duty, initiative, and the ability to outlast opponents. Therefore, field officers in the Frontier Battalion in their police operations had much freedom of action within the bounds of the laws of the state and the traditions of the service. This process covered the whole scope of Ranger life, from the selection of recruits to carrying out scouting missions to investigating acts of crime and violence. McDonald's recognition of this method of operation came when he ended a letter to the adjutant general early in his captaincy with the words, "Write occasionally."[23] Captain Bill knew that a loose hierarchical structure, fostering decentralization of authority, characterized the Ranger organization.

Although the individuality of a Texas Ranger was highly prized in organizational channels, the conduct of men in charge of subcompanies sometimes created problems. In one case McDonald's sergeant, W. J. L. Sullivan, was in charge of a detachment of Rangers from two different companies at San Saba. At one point Sullivan informed Captain John H. Rogers that all orders to the men at the encampment must be sent through him.[24] Captain Bill disagreed and wrote that Sullivan was becoming too "dictatorial."[25] The Ranger sergeant then apologized to the adjutant general and Rogers and noted in a more humble letter that he was worried about his "authority" over his "little sub-company."[26]

For companies and subcompanies the collection and use of information became a powerful tool in their law enforcement operations. To aid in the capture of desperate characters, the adjutant general's office compiled a *List of Fugitives from Justice*, sometimes called "Bible Number Two," from information received from local sheriffs. In turn, Rangers used this "Black Book" in the pursuit of lawbreakers. Captain Bill and his fellow Rangers then filed lengthy reports with their superiors about their daily activities against crime and disorder.[27]

PATHWAYS TO UNDERSTANDING: "MCDONALDOLOGY"

Too often the life of Bill McDonald has been seen as an either-or equation. On the one hand, his admirers have described him as a hell-bent, two-gun Sir Galahad, whose heroic deeds in eliminating crime and disorder make him stand as tall as the brave Texans of revolutionary fame. These hero worshipers have viewed Captain Bill as an extraordinary manhunter and a hard-nosed detective in the mold of Sam Spade. On the other hand, McDonald's detractors have portrayed him as a pompous peace officer, who accepted questionable information, precipitated violence, hungered for publicity, and related tall tales that cast himself as the central figure in the stories. One Texan noted that McDonald's fertile imagination "ran riot." "To be accurate," this person concluded, "the old-timers of Southwest Texas did not consider Bill McDonald a Ranger Captain at all."[28] Each of these depictions contains some element of the fact; neither, however, presents a truthful portrait of McDonald.

Another complicating aspect in the study of the life and times of Bill McDonald has been the historical view that he was a one-dimensional man. One historian concluded that the Ranger captain was "an uncomplicated man, unwilling—or unable—to view life in complex form. To him no shades of gray existed. People were either good or evil, right or wrong, scoundrels or honest individuals."[29] Yet McDonald, like his fellow captains, to use an analogy, was both a hedgehog and a fox. Like the single-mindedness of the hedgehog, Captain Bill strove to enforce law and order. Like the multifaceted fox, he used varying techniques of police work, from tracking criminals to collecting evidence, to collar lawbreakers and put them behind bars. In the chapters to follow McDonald and the men under his command become many-sided figures.[30]

One of the first steps in knowing McDonald as a person and as a Ranger captain is to gain a bird's-eye view of his thoughts and actions:

1. "*Four Great Captains*": Bill McDonald and the other three members of the "Four Great Captains"—J. A. Brooks, John R. Hughes, and John H. Rogers—became faithful public servants. Of the four, McDonald was the flamboyant Ranger and Hughes was the best gunman. Brooks and Rogers, in the words of the dean of Ranger historians, were "dependable, intelligent, and wise in the ways of criminals."[31] As a prominent Christian Ranger, Rogers even carried his Bible with his guns.
2. *Company Commander*: At the bottom of the chain of command in the Frontier Battalion the captains and other officers shouldered the administrative tasks. Such assignments ranged from setting up and maintaining company headquarters and

subcompany stations to hiring and firing personnel, purchasing equipment and supplies within budgetary allocations, and assigning Rangers to details to scout and investigate crimes. Once Captain Bill showed his annoyance with the paperwork involved with such duties. He wrote the battalion quartermaster that when a mistake appeared in a bill submitted to the Ranger command post, he would "take it as a favor" if the quartermaster would correct the error rather than sending the form back to him to be redone.[32] McDonald served under several quartermasters, including W. H. Owen, G. A. Wheatley, and, especially, Lamartine P. "Lam" Sieker, who twice served in this post after 1885.[33]

3. *Motto:* "No man in the wrong can stand up against a fellow that's in the right and keeps on a-comin'."[34] From this succinct creed in the psychology of law enforcement, Bill McDonald can be seen as either a picturesque anachronism or a primitive prototype of the modern Texas Ranger. To be sure his skill in subduing a troublemaker—what one writer called his "suddenness"—stood McDonald in good stead against bullies, gunmen, or a riotous assemblage of persons.[35] "If you wilt or falter he will kill you," Captain Bill insisted, "but if you go straight at him and never give him time to get to cover, or to think, he will weaken ninety-nine times in a hundred."[36] McDonald had courage. But this exercise of applied psychology against an adversary surely put too much emphasis on his indomitable will. And Captain Bill never entertained the notion that he was bulletproof.
4. *Peace of the Community*: During his years as a law officer, Bill McDonald was a firm believer in upholding law and order. He proved to have a remarkable ability to stand up to and face down a disorderly crowd. Carl T. Ryan, a member of Company B, once said, "I used to tell him, Cap, you're going to get all of us killed, the way you cuss out strikers and mobs." " 'Don't worry, Ryan,' " he would reply. " 'Just remember my motto.' "[37]

In this peacekeeping role Captain Bill and other Rangers gained a reputation as gun-wielding riot busters.

5. *Feuding Parties*: In the search for order those engaged in the ranging service tried to work with local authorities in handling bloody feuds before and after the American Civil War. The members of the Frontier Battalion especially used different intervention techniques, which ranged from keeping factions apart, confiscating weapons, and protecting witnesses, to moving about to try to deter violent showdowns and make feudists believe they should be someplace else. Sometimes Captain Bill and other Rangers did quiet things temporarily. Most of the time, though, they could do little about the root causes—like family disputes, personal grudges, political and economic clashes, and mob outbursts—that lay behind the ongoing feuds scattered around the Texas landscape.
6. *Manhunter*: Whether on horseback, on foot, in a buckboard, or on a train, McDonald was relentless in the pursuit of lawbreakers. This dogged pursuit coupled with his knack of disarming and guarding those taken into custody became the hallmarks of his operations as a Ranger captain. In doing so, McDonald attempted to avoid the use of large posses and running gun battles. Yet he knew enough to call upon the men under his command for assistance when the odds against the Rangers were too great.[38] McDonald's courage was usually tempered by a degree of common sense.
7. *Shootist*: Bill McDonald was an expert with firearms, but the historical record belies his public image as a deadly gunfighter. He brought in prisoners alive, rather than dead. His makeup did not include being trigger-happy. "I never was a killer," Captain Bill confided to his official biographer. "Some fellows seem to want to kill, every chance they get, and in a business like mine there's plenty of chances. But I never did want to kill a man, and I never did it when there was any other way to take care of his

case."[39] McDonald did participate in a few gunfights, but his reputation as a gunman rested upon his easily demonstrated marksmanship, his flair for using his weapons to overawe his opponents, the publicity given his several violent encounters with Texan badmen, and the fanciful stories woven around his exploits for the gullible public.

8. *Criminal Investigator*: Captain Bill knew that criminal cases could not be solved without the patient collection and analysis of evidence and the interrogation of those taken into custody. He talked with people as soon as he arrived at the scene of a crime. He also searched for evidence when he saw some questions that needed to be answered and interrogated witnesses and suspects in an effort to obtain what he required. McDonald even offered protection to those who gave him information in order to quiet their fears of reprisals. Yet he perfected the art of the manhunt more than the techniques of criminal investigation.
9. *Detective*: In the nineteenth century the practices employed by detectives gained a foothold in England, France, and the New World. Before and during McDonald's captaincy the word "detective" began to appear in Ranger records.[40] The Rangers viewed detective work in two ways. For one thing, state authorities saw detectives as undercover agents who used disguises and other covert activities to gain access to the criminal underworld. For another thing, state officials defined the word "detective" to mean a person skilled in the handling of evidential facts furnished by witnesses or derived from objects found at the scene of a crime. Both detection methods would be used by Captain Bill and the Rangers under his command. Especially praiseworthy was McDonald's ability to use physical evidence, like handprints found at the scene of a crime, to help him solve a mystery.[41]

Yet there were limitations to McDonald's investigative skills, which resulted from his own personality and the culture of his times. He had a tendency to accept hearsay evidence, and his perception of the criminal personality prevented him at times from carrying out investigations of illegal acts with an open mind. Moreover, McDonald was not always able to overcome the racial and cultural prejudice against blacks and Hispanics that permeated societal relations at the turn of the century. "Captain Bill, it may be remembered," wrote his official biographer, "does not mince his words. A white man who has committed a crime is, to him, always a 'scoundrel,' or worse, openly. A black offender, to him, is not a negro, or a colored man, but a 'nigger,' usually with pictorial adjectives."[42]

Bill McDonald had little time or interest in learning more about the science of detection. He did not look into or write about the use of physical measurements for identification championed by Alphonse Bertillon. Nor did he witness the initial developments in fingerprinting in Europe and America. By the end of his life McDonald did own a car, use a typewriter, send telegrams, and make telephone calls. But other Old West lawmen, not Captain Bill, were more involved with the newer aspects of the fact-finding process. McDonald was a first-rate tracker of fleeing fugitives; but he was not a detective of the first rank.[43]

10. *Minority Groups*: To some historical writers Bill McDonald was a "committed lawman as well as an arrant racist."[44] Surely he baited lawbreakers by calling them degrading names. Even more to the point, McDonald would be called, by modern standards, a bigot in his beliefs about minority groups. Throughout history racism has involved notions about superiority and persecution. McDonald did not want to tyrannize minority citizens, but he did want them to follow orders and obey the law. Ever since childhood in the Old South, Captain Bill had ambivalent feelings about blacks, which carried over to his career as a peace officer. On the one hand, he could castigate black offenders. On the other hand, he

could protect black prisoners from third-degree beatings and mob vengeance. To some, McDonald was not a lawman worthy of emulation. To others, his bigotry was counterbalanced by his strong belief in law and order and by his lack of a killer instinct.

11. *Company B in the Wider World*: As a captain of an organized body of Rangers, McDonald spent much time, as did the prominent sergeants of Company B, James M. "Grude" Britton, William J. McCauley, and W. J. L. Sullivan, in working with officials on the three levels of government. These public servants included army officers, county sheriffs, district attorneys, federal marshals, judges, mayors, and town police forces. In this complex network Rangers had to deal with Texas as a separate identity and as part of the federal system of government.

Such interactions tested McDonald's decision-making ability and resulted in both cooperation and conflict among all parties concerned. Captain Bill, who opposed having his men do "low down ungentlemanly things," discharged Rangers for drunkenness, insubordination, and lack of judgment in the use of firearms.[45] With some new enlistments McDonald once admitted that he could "boast of having a sober company & one that is not gambling & drinking all the time."[46] The Ranger captain also agreed with his superiors that the members of Company B should not cross the Rio Grande or the boundaries of another state or territory except to carry out the extradition of fleeing fugitives. Unofficially the rank and file of the company moved into Oklahoma to pursue outlaws with or without the assistance of peace officers in that territory and to take a short cut to Greer County while that place was still part of Texas. At one point McDonald did acknowledge in a monthly report that a Ranger detachment chased horse thieves through Greer County into Oklahoma. But they did not make any arrests since they crossed the "line" and were "out of the state."[47] In carrying out his duties Captain Bill learned when to come on—and when to back off.

CAMPFIRE TALES

For a myth to be popular, it must reflect society. It must illuminate shared beliefs of the common folk. In the late 1800s in Texas the tradition of the fabled Ranger had passed to a new generation: that of Captain Bill. Seen as Canadian Mounties without uniforms, Russian Cossacks on horseback, McDonald and his fellow Rangers captivated the American public through daring exploits in song and story.

The uplifting nature of the story of the legendary Ranger in the late nineteenth century results from its simplicity: a white hat takes on a black hat. In this morality play Bill McDonald played a key role. His easily remembered macho deeds would be turned into memorable tales about the law enforcement operations of the Texas Rangers.

In the Ranger Valhalla McDonald holds an honored place. Some authors see him as a super peace-officer Ranger. "Perhaps the best known Ranger of all," one person concluded, "was Captain Bill McDonald. The mention of his name, as one writer stated it, 'made the pulses of good Texans beat quicker and the feet of outlaws move faster.' "[48] Other chroniclers stress that McDonald carried out his duties wherever needed: "Is it a riot in a lumber camp?—McDonald and his men are hurried thence. Is it a chase for horse thieves or lynchers?—McDonald and his men are on the scene. Is it a patrol of range fences?—McDonald is in it."[49] One day this omnipresence got embedded in the Texan psyche.

Possibly the only tale that the public can recall about the Texas Rangers is the singular action by McDonald, which resulted in the "one-Ranger-one-riot" story. Years ago Webb aptly summarized it:

> He was responsible for the story, now a worn-out chestnut, about the call for a company of Rangers to quell a mob. When a lone Ranger got off the train—Bill McDonald, of course—there was vigorous protest from the citizen committee at his inadequacy to control the situation. "Well, you ain't got but one mob, have you?"

> he inquired sweetly. Though there is some basis for the story, there is no basis for anyone's ever telling it to a Texas Ranger because each one has had to laugh at it a thousand times.[50]

Historical writers have differed about the setting for this particular anecdote. They usually have applied this yarn to the happenings in either the Reese-Townsend feud at Columbus or a violent act in a Texan town like Abilene or a prizefight in Dallas.[51] The only extant historical source for these accounts is the information that McDonald gave to his official biographer.

Most suited to the purpose of the "one-Ranger-one-riot" story would be Paine's statement about McDonald, mobs, strikers, and prizefights. Paine wrote:

> At other points McDonald or his Rangers quieted the strikers and prevented trouble of various kinds. Usually Captain Bill went alone. It was his favorite way of handling mob disorders, as we have seen. It is told of him in Dallas how once he came to that city in response to a dispatch for a company of Rangers, this time to put down an impending prize-fight.
>
> "Where are the others?" asked the disappointed Mayor, who met him at the depot.
>
> "Hell! aint I enough?" was the response, "there's only one prize-fight!"[52]

This unforgettable anecdote can not be found in the records of the Ranger service (although McDonald did intervene in prizefights in El Paso and Galveston). To numerous individuals, however, a memorable tale that reflects the inner spirit of being a Texan should be repeated and not questioned. In Texas lore the indomitable Captain Bill became the embodiment of the positive traits of the Rangers. These attributes included standing your ground and doing your lawful duty to the best of your abilities against feudists, lynchers, and rioters.

Besides the "one-Ranger-one-riot" story, two other factors helped to create McDonald's legendary image. First, a future chapter about preventing a prizefight in El Paso in 1896 describes a tall tale that McDonald forced William Barclay "Bat" Masterson to swallow his pride and back off from a violent showdown. Second, and more important, in the aftermath of the raid on Brownsville in 1906, a US Army investigator on the scene reflected on the mythical beliefs of the common Texans in McDonald's ability to stand and fight when he wrote, "It is said here he [McDonald] is so brave he would not hesitate to 'charge hell with one bucket of water.' "[53] Yet in real life Captain Bill did not harbor a death wish; and he did not want to take part in an Armageddon. One can even contemplate that in the final battle between good and evil the implacable McDonald would only charge hell at the head of a large force of Rangers—armed with buckets.

The mythical aspects of the lives of Captain McDonald and his fellow Rangers left an imprint on those who created Wild West Rangers in the pop culture of the early 1900s. One of these hell-bent Rangers was Jim "Lone Wolf" Hatfield who served under Captain "Roaring Bill" McDowell. In a short story in a pulp magazine, Hatfield had cat-like moves and could charge through a hail of lead by dodging the bullets. He was known as the Ranger who "would charge hell with a bucket of water." Yet Hatfield also had the ability to use markings on a shell and a damaged firing pin in a weapon to solve a crime. When he stopped a revolt from happening on the border, the novella ended with these words:

> "It shore beats hell," said the sheriff, "one Ranger bustin' up a rev'-lution single-handed, all by hisself."
>
> "Well," chuckled the Lone Wolf, "you just had one revolution!"[54]

The legendary McDonald still chases outlaws and desperados in Wild West fiction. For some, crossing the line between history and fiction captures the essence of society at a given time and place. For others, however, such literary strokes entangle the historical record and regional folklore.

THE UNFOLDING STORY

Although capable and flamboyant, the flesh-and-blood McDonald could not live up to the public's adulation of the fabled Captain Bill. In reality McDonald was not only an action detective but also carried out the humdrum work of running encampments and writing reports. While carrying out these duties the Ranger captain, although pulling his weapons and firing, did not kill anyone. Contrary to public opinion—and the beliefs of some historical writers—no notches appeared on his guns. Just as important, during McDonald's tenure as officer in charge of Company B, only one Ranger was killed in the line of duty. And that did not mean the rank and file of this company shot first.

In the pages to follow the complexities of McDonald's lifestyle will be examined. This comprehensive study is the first biography of Bill McDonald published in a hundred years. It differs from previous writings about the Ranger captain in several ways. For one thing, records have been looked at in order to shed new light upon his financial dealings and bankruptcy as a grocer in Mineola. Next, the major events in his career as a Texas lawman have been studied through archival holdings. This research has produced a more balanced narrative, filled with McDonald's own words. In carrying out his duties as a crime fighter in hectic day-to-day operations, Captain Bill foreshadowed the modern era of policing. His ability as a detective has been underplayed by historians ever since. And lastly, McDonald's role as state revenue agent at the end of his life, particularly his interaction with circuses and Buffalo Bill's Wild West Show, needs amplification as a memorable event and spectacle.

By McDonald's day, Texas had become known as a place where things happen. The interaction among the native inhabitants, Spanish colonists, and Anglo pioneers was chronicled by early Texan historians. They tried to collect information by studying documentary sources. Yet they viewed events in a subjective way—through the enduring beliefs of the "Promised Land," the "Agrarian Ideal," and the "Great-Man Thesis."[55] A philosopher once noted that the hero in history can be seen either as an "event-making man" or as an "eventful man" (who happened to be in the right place at the right time to become famous).[56] To some, Bill McDonald, either through careful thought or sheer luck, had a foot in each philosophical camp.

ROMANTICIZING McDONALD AND THE RANGERS

A Pictorial Essay

We fought [the Indians] for full nine hours before the fight wis o'er;
The sight of dead and woundit I nivir saw before;
Five thousan' gallant rangers that ivir left the West
Lay buriet by their comrades, and peace shall be their rest.

—Kenneth S. Goldstein, "'The Texas Rangers' in Aberdeenshire."

His is a tale unended. Still riding down the years
Come the hoofbeats of the Ranger and his stalwart form
appears . . .
Though dark may be the danger, he has no care for that,
Riding on into the future in his tall—white—
hat.

—"The Ranger" in William B. Ruggles, *Trails of Texas.*

Captain Bill McDonald is a wild and wily Ranger,
Kind enough to folks at home but stern to any stranger.
Down upon the pampas plains of wide and woozy Texas,
Captain Bill kerswats the azure in its solar plexus.
Nary such another man from Galveston to Dallas;
Wears a bent Damascus blade where most men wear a gallus;
Wears a bucket on his head—for thats his chief kerswatter;
Bill would charge all hell, they say, with a single pail o' water!

—"The Texas Terror" in Washington *Post*, Jan. 18, 1907.

A Texas Ranger in the popular press. This illustration has become the classic image of the Texas Ranger in fact and fiction in antebellum Texas. The caption for this sketch quoted a "gentleman" thus: "Ben McCullough's Texas Rangers [*sic*] are described as a desperate set of fellows. They number one thousand half savages, each of whom is mounted upon a mustang horse. Each is armed with a pair of Colt's navy revolvers, a rifle, a tomahawk, a Texan bowie-knife, and a lasso." In their military struggles with American Indians and Mexican nationals, soldier-Rangers gained a national reputation for ragtag appearances and fierce-fighting abilities. Yet this oft-reproduced drawing rooted in western and Texan folklore resembles too much the way people envisioned mountain men in the wilds of the American West. The illustrator had taken into account the colorful stories about pioneers moving westward that appeared in the national media in the middle of the 1800s. The legendary fighter-Ranger had surfaced in the world of print. (*Harper's Weekly*, Vol. 5, 1861, p. 430.)

QUELLING A LYNCHING MOB AT WICHITA FALLS.

"Boys, have you still got the prisoners?"

In the late 1800s the soldier-Ranger passed into history. A new Ranger emerged who carried badges to investigate crimes and chase outlaws. In the above illustration the artist gave his version of Ranger Captain McDonald as a riot buster. An outnumbered Ranger making a stand against an angry mob has been one of the recurring themes in the McDonald saga in the popular press. These real-life Rangers embellished in song and story even had their counterparts in the world of fiction. The foremost made-up lawman-Ranger thrilled audiences for decades: the adventures of the Lone Ranger. As developed by George Trendle and Fran Striker for radio in the 1930s, the masked man and Tonto, his faithful companion, fought for justice in the Wild West through duty, fair-play, and courage. Yet Captain Bill, whether in reality or fictionalized formats, was no model for the Lone Ranger. (ALBERT BIGELOW PAINE, *CAPTAIN BILL MCDONALD, TEXAS RANGER: A STORY OF FRONTIER REFORM*, 211.)

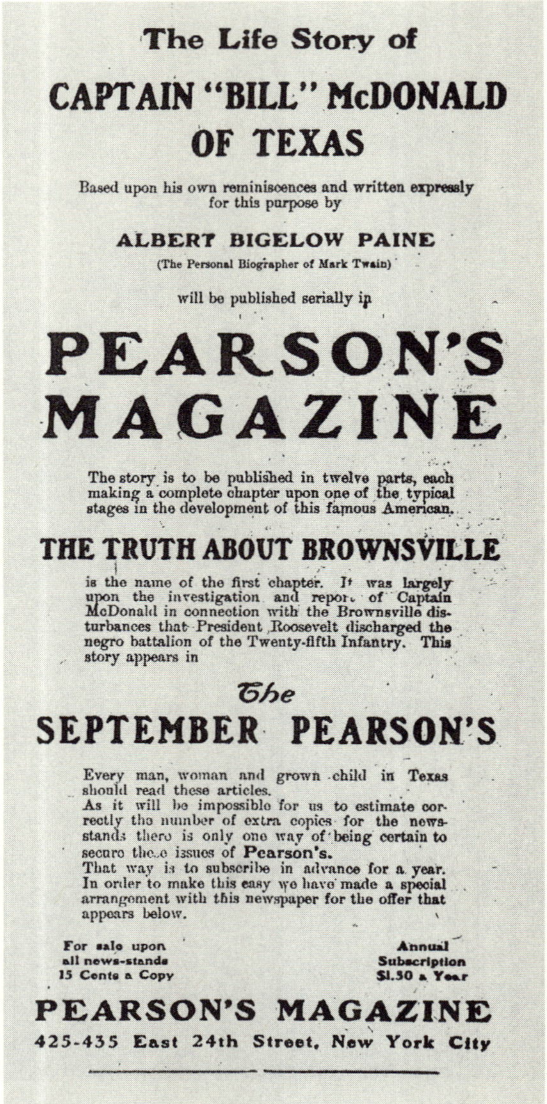

During his lifetime Bill McDonald made friends with Edward M. House, a political advisor to Democrats in Texas and the nation. House was instrumental in obtaining the services of Albert Bigelow Paine to write a biography of Captain Bill, published in 1909. Before this happened excerpts of Paine's work appeared in *Pearson's Magazine.* With these stories McDonald's image changed from regional hero to national icon. Decades later House also got Tyler Mason to write a wild-and-woolly book about McDonald that was published in 1936. Some of these tales appeared the year before in the popular magazine *Liberty*. In addition, House sent for Captain Bill to be a bodyguard to Woodrow Wilson in the presidential election of 1912. By the time McDonald passed away, he had gained a reputation as an action-oriented lawman inside and outside the Lone Star State. This fact differentiated him from the other Ranger captains of his generation. For further analysis of these events, see Chapter 15. (Colorado *Citizen*, Aug. 27, 1908.)

Bill McDonald—the real McCoy. This photograph of an aging McDonald shows his most striking facial features: protruding ears, a straight-as-an-arrow nose, and deep-set eyes that stare at you in a piercing way. His picturesque face raises the question: Which became more memorable—the real-life icon or the legendary figure? (COURTESY TEXAS STATE LIBRARY AND ARCHIVES COMMISSION.)

The Fitzsimmons-Maher prizefight (1896) and the hybrid Ranger. McDonald, the other Ranger captains, and their companies moved to El Paso to stop this event from being staged on Texas soil. This cartoon can be seen in two different ways: as a caricature of life along the border held by easterners; and as a belief system that only a new creature—a frightening mix of a Ranger and a Mexican bandido—would be able to referee the contest. In the late 1800s some people saw boxing in terms of athletic skills. Other segments of the society, though, viewed pugilistic encounters (both bareknuckle and glove) as a blood sport that needed to be outlawed. The violent nature of prizefighting equaled that of other vicious entertainment, as, for example, bullfighting and cockfighting. (NEW YORK *WORLD*, FEB. 12, 1896.)

FROM PICTORIAL IMAGERY TO WORD PAINTING: INVENTIVE MESSAGES FROM RANGERS IN THE FIELD

One of the hallmarks of the legendary Rangers as peace officers was their ability to write terse reports. These laconic communications, more imaginary than real, have been quoted in popular literature about American law enforcement to illustrate their masculine courage, quick-triggered summary justice, and primitive methods of gathering information. Once James D. Dunaway, who served under Captain McDonald, supposedly wired a classic message to his superiors: "I am shot all to pieces. Everything quiet." At another time a "nameless Ranger" was quoted as saying, "We had a little shooting and he lost." McDonald even put together a brief telegram which ended with the words, "Everybody disarmed; everything quiet." The alleged report of a Ranger quoted in a work on criminal investigation said it all:

NAME Big Nose Smith

CRIME Homicide

DISPOSITION Mean as hell, had to shoot him

First quotation: Sterling, *Trails and Trials of a Texas Ranger*, 360;
Second quotation: Gillett, *Six Years with the Texas Rangers*, xiv–xv;
Third quotation: *Paine, McDonald*, 370;
Fourth quotation: John J. Horgan, *Criminal Investigation* (New York: McGraw-Hill, 1974), 154.

Chapter 2

THE MAKING OF A TEXAS LAWMAN

. . . a Texas Ranger could ride like a Mexican, trail like an Indian, shoot like a Tennessean, and fight like a devil.[1]

To grasp the inner workings of the world of Texas Ranger Captain Bill McDonald, one must move in a westerly direction across the Atlantic Ocean to the New World and a place called Texas. Since ancient times humans have sailed westward and marched inland to find fame and fortune and build an orderly society under God.[2] This restless force in the cultures of Europe and America—that migrating impulse that has been called the "M-Factor" in American history—was captured in those haunting lines by Stephen Vincent Benet:

> Americans are always moving on.
> It's an old Spanish custom gone astray,
> A sort of English fever, I believe,
> Or just a mere desire to take French leave,
> I couldn't say. I couldn't really say.[3]

This restless temper brought McDonald's Scottish ancestors from Europe to America. The methods of fighting crime used by Captain Bill resulted from his contacts with people and cultures in the Old South and the Lone Star State. As a youth he grew up in antebellum Mississippi. As a young man he took part in the westward migration to Texas. All these experiences helped to mold the character and shape the career that made McDonald a lawman of note in the United States at the turn of the twentieth century.[4]

Bill McDonald is probably unrepresentative of many lawmen, but his varied career makes him an unusually useful figure for the study of American western history. He upheld and broke the law on different occasions, and he worked at both the lowest and the highest levels of law enforcement, from deputy sheriff to Texas Ranger to United States marshal. He traveled over vast areas in Texas and the surrounding territories in the pursuit of criminals, particularly the Texas Panhandle, No Man's Land (Oklahoma Panhandle), the Cherokee Outlet, and nearby areas of Oklahoma. These regions were so little populated and had such opportunities for economic advancement that they were a true frontier environment. There was no aspect of the changing criminal justice system of the Southwest that McDonald did not encounter, and he left his mark on judges, lawyers, and jailers.

In the fullness of his maturity, McDonald was almost the protean figure out of which the stereotype of the western peace officer in folklore and fiction evolved. Slim, wiry, somewhat large-boned, erect, and generally well-proportioned, McDonald was tall for his day, roughly six feet in height. His head seemed somewhat small for his large angular frame, and he kept a mustache as did many law officers of his generation. His face was weather beaten; his lips were thin; and his prominent, narrow-bridged nose—straight with flaring nostrils—gave him a dignity of expression that offset his hollow cheeks, protruding ears, and steel blue-grey eyes that lay hidden, recessed in his skull. He appeared at once disarming and inept, and only the stern gaze and his graceful movements betrayed the latent threat he posed to potential offenders. Fading photographs do an injustice to this striking figure of a western lawman whose physical makeup was an asset in his contacts with the criminal world.[5]

MCDONALD'S SOUTHERN ROOTS

Two points about the early life of "Bill Jess" McDonald are clear: he was not a Texan by birth, and he did not grow up with a desire to join a police force. McDonald was born on September 28, 1852, in Kemper County, Mississippi. His parents, Enoch McDonald and Eunice Durham McDonald, like so many other planters on the southern frontier, were of Scottish ancestry. They could boast of a heritage that sometimes aligned them with the forces that had struggled to preserve order and independence in both Scotland and America. McDonald's father and mother also grew up in Jacksonian America, with its deep-seated faith in rough-hewn heroes, lively politicos, and westering masses. By way of North Carolina (the Durhams) and Georgia (the McDonalds), the parents of Bill Jess entered Mississippi when that area still offered promise for financial success.[6]

The McDonalds, Enoch and Eunice, were cotton planters. Their plantation (or farm as some called it) nestled on the good black loam of Mississippi at a time when rural interests dominated the affairs of the state. The main house of the McDonald plantation, built of logs and boards, would have been dwarfed by a Monticello or one of the many stately plantation homes of the Caroline tidewater. Yet this same homestead, in the words of one relative, was a "good farm," valued at $1,500 in 1850. Eight years later Enoch enriched himself by selling 400 acres for $1,600. To work the land and care for horses, cows, and oxen, a small force of slaves lived on the premises. Although Paine in his classic study used the figure of "half a hundred slaves," the exact total was much smaller: six blacks in the 1850 census and eight blacks ten years later (three males and five females ranging in ages from fifty-five to thirteen). In this antebellum setting Enoch and Eunice raised two children: Bill Jess and his older sister Mary.[7]

Bill McDonald was reared in the semi-isolation of this plantation society. His formal education, for example, was irregular because the local schoolhouse also served as a church or a meeting place when one was needed. His practical education differed little from that of most rural youth of the antebellum era. At an early age he learned to swim, fish, ride, shoot, hunt deer and raccoons, and track game in the woodlands. The wilderness held no fear for him, and the self-reliance so frequently evident among frontier farmers and adventurers of an earlier generation was steadily instilled within him. Moreover, to many southerners hunting was more than a violent sporting event, more than a feeling of camaraderie with your fellow hunters. It also developed a mindset in McDonald's day which stressed the danger and excitement of the chase, domination of man over beast, and an appreciation of the place of both humans and animals in an orderly state of nature. This vigorous upbringing in mind and body became a valuable asset in McDonald's future manhunts as a lawman.[8]

One other occurrence in the formative years of Bill Jess affected his later work as a peace officer. He grew up among blacks who worked his father's plantation. McDonald played with black slaves, was served by them, ordered them about, was disciplined by them, and even hunted them with bloodhounds by himself or with others when runaway slaves needed to be caught. These everyday interactions between whites and blacks left an imprint on the psyche of the future Ranger captain.[9]

In retrospect, McDonald's childhood experiences made him view black individuals in contradictory ways. Black children learned by doing; so did Bill Jess. Black children liked to play, swim, and fish; so did Bill Jess. At times McDonald approached plantation blacks in work and play with gestures of goodwill. Yet these personal contacts took place within a master-slave environment. One gave orders; and the other obeyed. Throughout his lifetime, however, McDonald's paternalistic attitudes did not include a cruel, inhuman streak. He wanted black lawbreakers to give up and follow orders. He did not want to waylay them and wantonly shoot them down.

The values and folkways of the McDonald plantation mirrored those of the larger southern society of which they were a part, particularly the attitudes of frontier Mississippi. This was a hierarchical society of Indians, slaves, Scotch-Irish pioneers, and established planters. Its leading spokesman was Jefferson Davis, who represented in the nation's capital the views of the new planter gentry. In many ways it symbolized the mixture of newly acquired wealth and slaves and the myth of a patrician cavalier of the Old Tidewater South. Davis and his constituency had a preoccupation with the protection of agriculture and slave labor below the Mason-Dixon line. They also had an exaggerated sense of hospitality and honor as well as romantic ideas about womanhood, dueling, and public service. Moreover, antebellum southerners sought in their community life order and stability. The effects of these values were everywhere present in the behavior of the plantation gentry who attempted to replicate what they thought were the ways of plantation owners of the richer and established slaveholding states of the East. The symbols, slogans, and shibboleths of this society, as events would show, deeply influenced McDonald's youth.[10]

The earliest tragedies of Bill McDonald's life came with the dissolution of that society. Lincoln's election, southern secession, and the firing on Fort Sumter brought a crisis in American institutions. In Mississippi Confederate sentiment was strongly entrenched. Davis led the Confederacy; the Stars and Bars flew atop the state capital; and Mississippi's whites eagerly enlisted and steadfastly served in Confederate armies.

Enoch McDonald joined the Fortieth Mississippi Infantry. He held the rank of major and served as a regimental staff officer. If he demonstrated any attachment to the Union, it was not conveyed to his family, for there is no recollection among family records other than of dedicated service to the Lost Cause. That young Bill Jess loved and missed his father is attested to by a family story that tells how he walked miles to share some time with his father at an encampment. At the end of the trip the lad had his first encounter with a train, got scared by the sound of a locomotive, caught up with his startled father on the drill field, and had to have his mother come to the railroad junction and take him back home. The death of Major McDonald in a frontal assault at the Battle of Corinth in October 1862 was a devastating loss to his family.[11]

In the years that followed, the blight of the Civil War spread over the South. Ruin and poverty followed in its wake. The battles fought in Mississippi disrupted governmental functions, laid waste to the land, scattered blood relatives in various directions, and put large numbers of Confederate soldiers in their graves. By the time of Appomattox, many southern families had been destroyed and many southern women confronted a serious problem of rebuilding family life.

EARLY DAYS IN EAST TEXAS

Eunice McDonald, widowed and left with young children, was faced with managing a plantation, preserving a family, and surviving in a vanquished country. She went about these tasks with an indomitable will. Although Enoch McDonald left no will upon his death, Eunice still kept her properties together (three farms with a gin house on one of them) and provided for her family through working the land. Former slaves continued to stay with her. At the end of the Civil War she even sold a crop of cotton at twenty-five cents per pound. Then Eunice made a momentous decision. She decided to move her family to Texas in 1866 or 1867 (the parties involved differ on the exact date). Here she would keep house for her bachelor brother, Thomas Durham, who owned a farm near the town of Henderson in Rusk County. Within a year or two, the sickly Thomas passed away, with his homestead being bought by another brother, D. D. Durham. To get to Texas the McDonalds took a "public conveyance" through Shreveport, Louisiana, and Eunice "paid" for the trip.[12]

Besides bringing her family to Texas, Eunice McDonald played another important role in the affairs of the McDonald-Durham clan. She acted as a banker. For years she loaned money with interest to her children and other relatives. Although Paine in his celebrated study stressed that the McDonalds lived in a state of poverty after the Civil War, that was not the case. Before she left Mississippi Eunice sold lands and stock to various people and kept some property to rent. She also allowed at least one piece of real estate, probably the remnants of the plantation that her husband had built, run down after the war and worth a few hundred dollars, to go to the state for taxes. Thus, Eunice brought with her to Texas $1,000 in gold, more or less. She continued to have monies sent to her from Mississippi and she received some land and stock when her father died in that state in the 1870s. Although Eunice visited Mississippi during that decade, she had already become a Texan.[13]

Bill McDonald's youth ebbed away in those early years when the family lived in East Texas. His mother continued to be a homemaker. Although she bankrolled family members, Eunice had no desire to fight for women's rights. At the same time, though, she was no weary and forlorn female living in a man's world. She liked being a woman of means. She enjoyed the give-and-take with family members. Eunice just wanted to be left alone by those outside her family circle.

Bill McDonald moved to East Texas without entering an alien world. Through the centuries this region, with its well-watered lands and forests, became home to people of different creeds and colors. These included Indians, Spanish-Mexican colonists, southern pioneers with a Celtic heritage, and black individuals held in or freed from slavery. Confederate dead were buried in the ground. In this new environment McDonald's formal schooling continued off and on. He also found time to hunt coon and other game with dogs, but increasingly his life was taken up with farm chores and the hard work of splitting wood. The opportunities and mode of life available to the son of a Mississippi plantation owner were lost. What remained for McDonald was not the heritage of the lesser southern gentry, but that of the violence of war, reconstruction, and a society with southern and western lifestyles. In the pages to follow the need for McDonald and his Rangers to confront crime and violence in the eastern portions of the state will be explored. As a restless youth, he began his search for fame and fortune in Rusk County.[14]

In retrospect the history of Texas can be viewed from several vantage points: as a region, as a process of settlement, and as a political state. Before the people came, there was the land. Travelers to the area called Texas have been struck by the contrasts in climate and geography. From the humid coast and pine forests of East Texas to the dry plains of West Texas, Texans of all stripes have seen the land as a wilderness to explore and conquer and as a garden to cultivate and enjoy. For some, an appreciation of nature arose from their efforts; for others, a belief developed, as one army officer put it: "If I owned hell and Texas, I would rent Texas out and live in hell!"[15]

For thousands of years humans have called Texas their homeland. In this area three civilizations rose and fell. First came the Indians who spread southward throughout the New World from their base in Asia. In Texas the inability of the Indian tribes like the buffalo-hunting Comanches to unite and plan strategy together for long periods of time was a decisive disadvantage when they came into conflict with the Hispanics and Anglos. The Spanish intrusion into Texas northward from Mexico, with their missions, presidios, and economic enterprises, brought about settlements at Nacogdoches, San Antonio de Bexar, and places in between. In turn, these outposts succumbed to land-hungry, Anglo-American pioneers.[16]

Anglo Texas, even in the 1800s, was first and foremost a state of mind. The unique image of the state and its inhabitants, the "mystique" of Texas as one historian called it, is more than a braggart's tall tale. The "mystique" arose during the period of settlement, in the struggles for independence and nationhood, and in the conflict of cultures that followed. The bases for the myth-making since these early days were several larger-than-life heroes and noteworthy events: the stand at the Alamo against the forces of Antonio López de Santa Anna; the Texas Rangers riding into the jaws of death in their struggles with Indians and Mexicans; and the guiding hand of Samuel "Sam" Houston who led Anglo Texas in its march from revolution to statehood. Texans were repeating a unifying experience that Americans as a whole had known during the emergence of the United States.[17]

The cultures of the slave South and the new West met in Texas. The Anglo-American settlers, the initial "Old Three Hundred" and other pioneers, who followed Stephen F. Austin into Mexican Texas in 1821 and after, came for the most part from the trans-Appalachian South. These early settlers turned areas of East Texas into a slave-oriented, agricultural society dominated by Protestant churches. In the years before and immediately after the Civil War southern planters from Georgia and Mississippi crossed the Mississippi River into Texas without entering an alien social order. This planter class made Texas quite different from other frontier states. But a trickle of hunters, trappers, traders, and squatter frontiersmen also wandered into Texas from Missouri and Arkansas in the formative years. In addition, redneck yeoman farmers from Alabama and Tennessee pushed inland in Texas in an attempt to get away from the slave plantations in the eastern portions of the state. Squatting on land at the edge of the frontier, these self-reliant settlers lived in rustic poverty, hunting, planting corn and sweet potatoes, and building dog-runs: log cabins with open corridors between the two rooms. Their lives were hard, monotonous, and at times dangerous, because Texas had a strife-ridden Indian frontier.[18]

Violence was endemic in Texas and the southern states, for as one wag noted, they were "below the Smith and Wesson line." Texans needed to be familiar with the use of firearms because of the hazards of living in semi-isolation and close to the frontier. Moreover, most of them were southerners, already schooled in the chivalric code that called for personal satisfaction if any affront, real or imagined, was sensed in interpersonal relations. Such thoughts and actions led Texans and other southerners to engage in duels, feuds, and rough-and-tumble fights. In Texas too slavery had brought a debasement of human values, an emotional environment ripe for outbursts of racial hatred, and a tradition of lynching that extended beyond blacks to anyone who seemed to violate the mores of the community. Texans considered themselves law-abiding, but they did not see a contradiction in an individual claiming the freedom to revenge a personal wrong through bloodshed. In fact, a distorted sense of southern masculinity argued that a person who refused to wipe out an insult with violence "ain't no man."[19]

No one reaching maturity in Texas could escape from this environment of violence, especially during Radical Reconstruction and its military occupation of the state by Union troops. And Bill McDonald was almost victimized by it. He came close to becoming a killer on the run. Lawlessness and violence against black Texans in the Reconstruction era took place for several reasons. Throughout the state blacks wanted to take charge of their lives and vote the Republican ticket. Declining crop prices also forced white landowners to cut costs, which made it difficult for blacks to earn a living.[20]

Revengeful thoughts led to multiple murders. At the start of April 1869, Colonel Peter Green stopped at a cabin near Henderson in Rusk County to get something to eat. Here Green, who was intoxicated and abusive, was seized by several blacks, taken outside, and hanged from a hickory tree. In turn, a relative, Charles Green, and others took five blacks involved in the crime from the county jail and strung up their prisoners on shade trees in the town square in retaliation. Soon after, federal soldiers arrived and investigated. They eventually arrested Green, who was charged with murder, and placed him in the military stockade at Jefferson.[21]

According to his official biographer, young Bill Jess became involved in this terrifying incident. The McDonalds and the members of the Green clan were related. The arrest of the killers of Peter Green did not quiet the fury of these Texans, who resented the northern bluecoats and the black males associated with them. McDonald may not have been a part of a mob that stormed the jail and lynched the blacks, but he certainly participated with Charles

Green in a running gun battle with the soldiers at Henderson. The shootout ended when the bluecoats, holed up in a courthouse, captured and disarmed Green as he attempted to enter the building. McDonald then decided to give ground and try to form a rescue party. The troops, however, moved Green from the town before the rescue gang could act. Later McDonald was taken prisoner while "nosing" about the stockade holding Green. At the military trial that followed, Green was sent to prison. McDonald was defended by David B. Culberson, a well-known Texas lawyer and later a prominent politician. The boy escaped conviction and a jail sentence. But more important, because unlike John Wesley Hardin and William P. Longley, who in the aftermath of the rebellion turned to lawlessness, McDonald shunned outlawry. Nor did he develop a taste, as did some westerners, for mixing banditry with the work of a peace officer—moving between the two at will.[22]

TEXAS AS PART OF THE WEST

During the decade following the Civil War most Texans were concentrated in a region east of a line drawn approximately from Fort Worth to San Antonio. Beyond this line lay a narrow belt of land—sprawling north and south in Central Texas—inhabited perhaps by one person per ten square miles. The vast areas of West Texas were virtually devoid of white and Mexican settlers. The Texas Panhandle, the northernmost counties of the state, too, was almost without white settlements. In succeeding decades, northwestern Texas, the place where McDonald's Rangers had their early encounters with badmen, would become a destination for immigrant trains, with ranchers and farmers moving in and changing the nature of the region.[23]

In post-Civil War Texas the imprint of western culture had begun to make the state less southern in outlook. A number of far-reaching events helped to create a new Texas. Anglo men, women, and children moved into the arid lands of West Texas with their dry farming techniques. The rise of the cattle kingdom resulted in longhorns being driven on trails to markets outside the state. In art and literature the cowboy joined the fur-trader, the lumber-jack, and the prospector in shaping the popular West. At the same time federal troops and Texan forces found unsouthern ways of battling Comanches on the plains. In everyday life lariats, boots, and Stetsons became fashionable items. In folk music one could hope for a better fate than to die on the "lone prairie" and be buried in a "little grave": "Where the coyotes howl and the wind blows free." From Fort Worth to Forts Griffin and Davis and beyond, West Texas had become a distinctive region—one of many in the American West. [24]

Each generation of historical writers tries to reassess the mode of life in the western states and territories. To some, their viewpoint remains fixed upon the traditional story championed by the Turnerian school of history. In brief, white pioneers hacked their way through woods and moved across plains to build a new society through heroic actions against those who opposed their advance. To others, like the adherents of the "New Western History," the conquest of the western lands resulted in destroying the environment, slaughtering Indians, and persecuting minority inhabitants. Westerners—even Texans—carried out both heroic acts and villainous deeds in their search for their identity.

The tenets of the "New Western History" provide insights into the patterns of existence in the trans-Mississippi West. One conviction stresses the importance of place in everyday affairs. The intermingling of different groups in the western regions brought about a pluralistic society, with women becoming active players in the ongoing drama. The newer historians of the western lands also emphasize the adverse impact of civilization and progress on Indians, blacks, and the environment. Transient miners, for example, could pan for gold and dig for minerals one day, and leave behind tin cans and other trash the next morning. Then, too, US troopers had the unenviable duty to protect Indians from whites and whites from Indians. In carrying out their research, the new-faith writers have challenged the traditional story of triumphal pioneers moving across a romantic western landscape from east to west. Yet early-day westerners—in order to survive and keep their humanity—carried rifles in one hand and Bibles in the other, without becoming schizophrenics.[25]

Bill McDonald lived to take part in this passage of frontier lifestyles to regional patterns of existence in the American West. As the decade of the 1870s opened, McDonald decided to become a businessman. He entered, with funds borrowed from his mother, Soule's Commercial College in New Orleans in 1871. Then, after graduation and a short interlude of teaching penmanship (with his own stylish handwriting on display), McDonald borrowed money from relatives and purchased a ferry-store business at Brown's Bluff on the Sabine River in Gregg County. He operated this enterprise for about a year before seeking other economic opportunities.[26]

TUMULTUOUS YEARS IN MINEOLA

McDonald's move to Mineola in Wood County as a grocer by the summer of 1873 was a key step in shaping his future. Organized in the 1850s, Wood County, at the western end of the piney woods in northeastern Texas, had nearly 7,000 residents by the time McDonald arrived. Economic activity centered around farming, raising livestock, lumbering, and constructing railroads. The coming of the rail lines in the 1870s led to the rise of Mineola as a population center. For a few years McDonald witnessed the incorporation of the town and the building of houses and businesses, with potbellied stoves inside and hitching posts outside.[27]

From Henderson to Longview to Mineola in East Texas, three families—the McDonalds, the Durhams, and the McCauleys—supported each other, personally and financially. The maiden name of McDonald's mother was Durham; and Bill's sister, Mary, married J. H. McCauley. In 1873 McDonald and his partner, M. L. Durham, operated a grocery firm—called W. J. McDonald & Company—in

Mineola. McDonald borrowed money from his mother to start the business. She allowed her son, however, to make decisions and run the store as her agent. In the summer of 1876, E. G. Carter took over Durham's interests. In his official biography Paine wrote that McDonald's business "venture was a success." But trouble was coming, as the owners tried to balance stock purchases, sales, and debts. Two basic problems existed: selling goods on credit and continually borrowing funds, especially from J. H. McCauley.[28]

Business activities in Mineola, despite the new construction and gung-ho attitudes, were risky, and McDonald at times was on the verge of bankruptcy. John H. Newsom, pioneer farmer, justice of the peace, and a clerk in McDonald's business venture, mentioned that in the first month of 1877 McDonald faced financial troubles. To his chagrin Newsom had invested several hundred dollars in the business. McDonald wished to keep the sum for a longer period of time, but Newsom wanted it returned, since he doubted that McDonald realized how close to failure he really was. But the dealer in foodstuffs and household supplies knew he was going broke.[29]

The firm of W. J. McDonald & Company became insolvent in the fall of 1877. In popular terms McDonald was "embarrassed." The debts totaled $18,000; assets, including goods, notes, and real estate (excluding two homesteads), amounted to $16,000. On September 1 of that year, fifteen creditors, who sought $13,712, met and agreed with McDonald to accept the total amount of assets in payment for all debts owed by the company. But other creditors refused to go along with this solution. Before that happened, goods and property were turned over to a receiver. He sold some, while other merchandise went, at a sacrifice, in a sheriff's sale. McDonald took back stock worth about $2,000. The returned staples, in his words, were "mostly damaged."[30]

For some time Bill McDonald wanted to do two things. First, he needed to pay off local creditors. Second, he had a heartfelt desire to redeem the notes held by three relatives: Eunice McDonald (his mother), J. H. McCauley (his brother-in-law), and M. L.

Durham (his uncle). McCauley even loaned his relative cash, a hack, and a wagon. McDonald recorded the debts owed family members in private ledgers and not in the accounts of his business. This procedure surprised creditors when the grocery firm went under.

The beleaguered grocer found the resources to pay off several creditors, who included Durham and Newsom. By the end of 1877, McDonald signed over to McCauley the deeds for several pieces of real estate: a block of five lots and a group of two lots with improvements. In order to receive a clear title to the group of two lots, McCauley gave McDonald $900 to pay off B. F. Read & Company. The next year McCauley shifted all the deeds for these properties to Eunice McDonald for a sum of money, since he himself had financial problems in Gregg County.[31]

Several court cases resulted from the collapse of McDonald's financial world.[32] The most bitter and long-lasting lawsuits were filed by W. A. Dunklin & Company. At the end of 1877 this firm obtained a judgment in the district court of Wood County for $1,375 against McDonald's grocery business. The following year Dunklin & Company received titles to all the pieces of real estate previously mentioned. Yet the ownership and possession of the lots remained in question.

Dunklin & Company again took McDonald, his mother, and his brother-in-law to court in the summer of 1879. Judge John C. Robertson of the Seventh Judicial District of Texas kept granting continuances until the end of May 1882. At this point a jury awarded the block of five lots in Mineola to Dunklin & Company, while McDonald and his relatives kept the group of two lots with improvements. The plaintiffs in this case then moved for a new trial. When this motion was rejected by the judge, the lawyers for Dunklin & Company appealed the decision to a higher court. In the summer of 1885, the Texas Supreme Court reaffirmed the decision of the lower court. McDonald's economic travails had ended.[33]

Despite the accumulation of debts and cash-flow problems in the 1870s, McDonald and his relatives were not poor people.

Eunice McDonald, as previously noted, brought a large sum in gold with her when she came to Texas. Later she told lawyers that where she got her money was "nobody's business." Eunice also said that no one had ever called upon her to pay taxes on her funds.[34] Her brothers were also not penniless. They migrated from the South to Texas before McDonald's mother. M. L. Durham, a farmer, had the most wealth. At the start of the 1860s in Rusk County, he had in his possession real estate, twelve black slaves, and other property worth thousands of dollars.[35] Another brother of means was D. D. Durham. This farmer moved from the county of Rusk to Gregg County where he lived and died.[36] This family network proved effective during trying times.

Bill McDonald followed this family tradition. During the 1870s he found funds to purchase land and buildings and pay taxes, county and state. He even owned cattle, hogs, horses, and mules. At the start of the next decade McDonald reported to county assessors that his cash on hand totaled $940.[37] This happened, in part, because he purchased goods on credit in 1879 and opened a mercantile business in a storehouse located on the aforementioned group of improved lots in Mineola. Again McDonald's mother provided some funds and allowed her son to run the enterprise.[38]

In retrospect, McDonald as a businessman gave cogent answers to questions posed by lawyers about the collapse of his grocery firm. Yet his financial transactions were too complex. This prevented McDonald from easily refuting charges of fraud. One inescapable conclusion resulted from looking at the record: McDonald needed to find a new occupation. And he had to make his way in the world without borrowing a lot of money from his mother (who moved away to live with her daughter).

As his economic woes increased, Bill McDonald still maintained his social position in the community. He became active in the cultural life of Mineola and built McDonald Hall, probably the first opera house in the town. R. H. Bruce, an old-time owner of opera establishments in Mineola, reminisced that in 1877 he heard *Blind*

Tom performed in McDonald Hall.[39] Perhaps the dramatic aspects of an operatic performance were more entertaining to McDonald than the musical score. At least his expanding cultural horizons allowed Mineola to keep pace with the construction of opera houses in other towns in the Old West.

More important than Bill McDonald's cultural efforts on behalf of the townspeople was his relationship with James S. Hogg, county and district attorney after 1878, and McDonald's desire to carry out law-and-order duties in Mineola and Wood County. The friendship between McDonald and Hogg proved tempestuous. They differed sharply over politics, even supporting different candidates in a congressional race. Furthermore, McDonald never quite forgave Hogg for prosecuting him and others for concealing firearms. The weapons were uncovered when McDonald assisted in the arrest of individuals for disturbing the peace. Yet Hogg introduced McDonald to his future wife, and, later as governor of Texas, Hogg appointed McDonald a captain in the Texas Rangers.[40]

On January 13, 1876, McDonald married Rhoda Isabel Carter (1858–1906). One writer described her as a "young woman with fine nerve and force of character."[41] Her parents came to Texas from Tennessee. E. G. Carter, the father of the bride and a prominent attorney in Wood County, owned real estate and other property of considerable value. He even invested in McDonald's grocery firm. The 1880 census listed Rhoda as a housekeeper and Bill as a businessman dealing in groceries and dry goods.[42] The newly married couple would never have any children.

Bill McDonald and his wife lived apart for long periods of time. This happened because McDonald liked to move around the countryside in search of outlaws and gunmen. In this peacekeeping role, he excelled. Why did the budding entrepreneur join a police force?

In his early life a threefold sequence seemed to plague his footsteps. On the one hand, his restless nature and his need to move westward across the northern part of Texas made him pursue a number of occupations outside the field of police work. On the other hand, repeated business reverses may be partly responsible for his periodic desire to turn to law enforcement for a living. Moreover, the more he carried out the duties of a peace officer, the more he realized that his background and makeup—his years in the outdoors and the southern imprint on his character—made him well-qualified to chase desperadoes. McDonald enjoyed manhunts; he delighted in the publicity generated by his actions as a lawman; and he took to heart his sworn duty to uphold law and order.

For more than a decade, Bill McDonald, while attempting to succeed as a businessman and a rancher, held several different jobs as a peace officer. His official biographer related that McDonald's first appointment as a lawman was his selection as a deputy sheriff of Wood County after an episode involving a local bully named George Gordon. Gordon came into Mineola with a bulldog that attacked and injured McDonald's "prized pointer." When McDonald threatened to shoot the bulldog, Gordon promised to keep his animal at home. Having overawed the bully, McDonald decided to apply for a commission as a deputy sheriff of Wood County in order to protect the community from Gordon and "others of his kind." Later, Gordon went on a drinking spree and brandished a six-shooter in Mineola, and McDonald forcibly disarmed, arrested, and jailed him. Much humbled, Gordon paid a fine the next day.[43]

Local historians, however, pointed out that when McDonald became a town hero, he was serving in Mineola as a deputy to City Marshal George Reeves.[44] McDonald's official biographer admitted that the two lawmen worked together to suppress disorder in Mineola when the railroad brought in men to cut timber for ties. At one point McDonald even stood beside Reeves with his gun drawn and used sharp words to stop a mob from interfering with the removal of a drunken tieman from a boarding house to the jail.[45] In taking such actions, maybe McDonald carried a town or county badge, maybe not. Maybe he just became part of the system inherited from England of citizens being called upon to aid police officers in the discharge of their duties.

Whether Bill McDonald acted as an assistant marshal of Mineola is debatable, but no question exists over the fact that he served as a deputy sheriff of Wood County. McDonald tracked criminals in flight to avoid prosecution. But most of his work was quite mundane—guarding prisoners and collecting fines—tasks long associated with a sheriff's office. Still, he first gained notoriety as a western lawman in his role as a deputy sheriff.

Under orders from Sheriff F. P. Dowell from 1881 to 1883, Bill McDonald carried out assignments for local courts in Wood County. He guarded, boarded, fed, and transported county prisoners, even before jails were built in some towns. Indeed, he served as a member of a committee to investigate and report on the establishment of jails at two different locations. For conducting this undramatic but necessary police work the court compensated him: the smallest recorded sum paid for handling prisoners—$4.50—and the largest sum—$83.60. He was not reimbursed, however, for such items as handcuffs and leg-irons. McDonald, also, collected the small fines—not always successfully—levied by the judge and gave reports of such monies to the court for approval. At one point he earned a small sum of money for summoning a jury.[46] These mundane duties as a deputy sheriff did not fit a man of McDonald's restless nature, and he moved frequently and changed jobs in the years to come.

Bill McDonald early learned some of the dilemmas associated with the powers of the local police. As a deputy sheriff of Wood County, he went into Smith County to locate and capture some outlaws. Using a shotgun he wounded one desperado, but the outlaws escaped, as he was led into following a wrong set of footprints. Some public officials, alleging that he had exceeded his authority by crossing over into another county and attempting an illegal arrest through violent means, demanded that McDonald be disciplined and prosecuted for his actions. But District Attorney Hogg quieted the matter by informing the grand jury that he would refuse to prosecute. He also reinforced the bond of friendship between himself and McDonald.[47]

KEY MOVE: ACROSS NORTH TEXAS TO QUANAH

Mineola's declining business prosperity in the early 1880s convinced McDonald to pull up stakes and seek new opportunities. He and his wife drove a herd of cattle across northern Texas into Wichita County. Organized in 1882, a year or two before the McDonalds arrived, it was a growing community of hunters, ranchers, wagon freighters, and railroaders. The population expanded tenfold during the decade. McDonald established lumber yards in Wichita Falls and Harrold and invested in cattle, but he soon abandoned commerce for ranching. He had to protect his business accounts and herds with tough talk and armed action. At one point he assisted a town marshal in subduing a drunken, disorderly person. McDonald told the peace officer, "Give me the keys to the calaboose, and the' won't be no need of a posse."[48]

Bill McDonald, however, grew restless again and continued to move in a westerly direction across northern Texas. In the mid-1880s he took his cattle and moved to Hardeman County at the southeast edge of the Texas Panhandle, where he settled on some land near Wanderers Creek. Organized in 1884, Hardeman County developed at a slow pace because of Indians and a lack of transportation. The population expanded from 50 in 1880 to 3,904 in 1890. But the coming of the railroad lines helped to solve the settlers' problems.[49]

As Anglo pioneers pushed westward into Hardeman County, the town of Quanah, named after the famed Comanche chief Quanah Parker, became a railroad-market center and the county seat. In 1890 the population of the town stood at 1,477 inhabitants. Before that year state officials put a Ranger station at Quanah. From this central location in North Texas, Rangers could more easily send out scouting expeditions. Surrounded by ranch and farm lands, this growing gateway to the Panhandle region McDonald and Rhoda affectionately called their permanent home.[50]

His official biographer wrote that McDonald moved to Hardeman County and the town of Quanah in 1885. Yet the county tax rolls do not list any property owned by the McDonalds until 1887. In that year acreage, animals, a town lot, and miscellaneous items were recorded. For more than two decades, either as a resident or a nonresident, they continued, off and on, to accumulate wealth in that region. At times Bill and Rhoda had separate listings in the tax rolls. In addition, in 1891 they held titles to a considerable amount of real estate: several lots in the town and 2,593 1/2 acres in the countryside. On this land McDonald put cattle, hogs, horses, and mules (with goats added in 1895).[51] He and his wife saw themselves as ranchers and not as farmers.

McDonald's new ranch was situated on the border of the Texas Panhandle. This region covers the northernmost twenty-six counties of the state (as shown on the map). These local forms of government, most of which appeared in the closing decades of the 1800s, are arranged in five tiers. The upper row of counties is sandwiched between the counties of Dallam and Lipscomb. The bottom rung consists of six counties flanked by Childress and Parmer. The area contains 25,610 square miles and borders Oklahoma and New Mexico. Most important, the Texas Panhandle is part of the land mass known as the Great Plains. The impact of the plains environment on early Anglo-American settlers was best expressed by one who knew:

> Like an ocean in its vast extent, in its monotony, and in its danger, it is like the ocean in its romance, in its opportunities for heroism, and in the fascination it exerts on all those who come fairly within its influence. The first experience of the plains, like the first sail with a "cap" full of wind, is apt to be sickening. This once overcome, the nerves stiffen, the senses expand, and man begins to realize the magnificence of being.[52]

In McDonald's generation the majority of the settlers in the Panhandle were Anglo Americans, with some Spanish-speaking inhabitants and a few blacks. Cattle outnumbered sheep—a triumph of Anglo-American ranchers over Mexican-American sheepmen—

and the railroads, particularly the Fort Worth & Denver City Railway and its subsidiary company, the Texas Townsite Company, built tracks through the area, developed townsites, and contributed to the population growth. Indeed, cattlemen in this region encouraged the expansion of agriculture, unlike other places in the Old West. And a pattern emerged of people living along the major lines of transportation. By the opening of the twentieth century, the population of the Panhandle had increased dramatically, with the area reaching northward from McDonald's ranch having one to ten persons for each square mile.[53]

Soon after his arrival in Hardeman County, Bill McDonald officially entered law enforcement. For several years he served as a deputy sheriff of Hardeman County, as a Special Texas Ranger (including circumstances and interests outside the regular Ranger companies), and as a federal deputy marshal. In each capacity he perfected the techniques of police work and made important contributions to the peace and stability of the community. As a horseback lawman, McDonald was always ready to assist cattlemen's associations, like the Texas Cattle Raisers Association, in their attempts to combat criminal activities. One historical writer noted that McDonald "examined hides with particular skill at detecting brand alterations."[54] In the cattle country of the Old West, the Texas Rangers as peace officers made their mark:

> . . . there is glamor in the names
> Of the men who made the Rangers, as the record still
> proclaims:
> The lifter left the cattle and the outlaw hid his gat
> When they thought about the rider in the tall—white—
> hat.[55]

McDonald was an active deputy sheriff during the reign of Sheriff James M. Allee in Hardeman County (with the county seat still at Margaret). In the local court records of 1887 and 1888, where McDonald's name first appeared, the new deputy carried out assignments long associated with a sheriff's office. He fed and guarded prisoners. For this work McDonald was paid small amounts of money, which ranged from a low of $5.40 to a high of $20.15 (if his accounts were correctly made out). At one point Deputy Sheriff McDonald opened a session of the commissioner's court. He also carried out an assignment from that court to procure a lot in Quanah to build a jail.[56] The "well-intentioned" sheriff, in the words of an annalist, was "understaffed for the extent of both petty and serious crime."[57]

The heroic image in the McDonald saga had its origins in his role as a deputy sheriff. From Wood County to Hardeman County he chased lawbreakers, took part in shootouts, and learned to handle bullies and mobs with tough talk and a commanding presence. In the late 1880s Quanah was a boom town, with settlers, railroaders, and ne'er-do-wells working and carousing together. Deputy Sheriff McDonald walked the streets of Quanah and disarmed more than once a town troublemaker. In enforcing gun-control laws, McDonald, in the words of one person, even "took a pistol from a boy last night with a wooden barrell [*sic*]." A more formidable opponent, though, appeared in the form of John Davidson.[58]

A McDonald-Davidson clash was inevitable. A chronicler described the latter as a "loud, proud, and clannish individual, often boisterous and sociable, sometimes quick-tempered, and invariably well armed."[59] In 1887, trouble followed the footsteps of McDonald, Davidson's clique, including his brother, and Pat Wolforth, an upstanding local resident. At one point Wolforth fired two shots at Davidson and another person in a saloon. Later Wolforth fired warning shots as Davidson and his followers stalked him. At other times McDonald quickly disarmed Davidson more than once, even after he carried a lawman's badge from Wilbarger County. Then McDonald and Davidson and his crowd had encounters inside and outside a saloon, with the deputy sheriff hitting one of them with a piece of wood. In the end, a drunken Davidson was arrested by another peace officer of Hardeman County for pistol-whipping individuals, while his brother was taken into custody by the Rangers for horse theft.[60]

ON THE PATH TO BEING A RANGER OFFICER

In order to enhance his ability to go after lawbreakers far and wide, Deputy Sheriff McDonald rode with the Rangers of Company B, called the "boys," under the command of Captain Samuel A. "Soft Voice" McMurry. From the end of 1886 through 1888, McDonald (initially spelled "McDonnell" by one Ranger) interrelated with McMurry's men in several ways.[61] Both the Rangers and the sheriff of Hardeman County needed each other in order to make their jobs easier. Thus, the "boys" turned over prisoners to McDonald to be housed in a local jail. Sometimes this arrangement ended in failure. Once, a Ranger handed over a Texan under arrest to McDonald. While the authorities were finding a judicial officer, the alleged horse thief hit the deputy sheriff and escaped. McDonald then fired at the fleeing fugitive to no avail. At this point in his career McDonald was a "strong-minded and competent lawman, but hardly the infallible figure of legend and myth."[62]

More in tune with McDonald's personality were his manhunts, in conjunction with McMurry's Rangers. He joined the members of Company B on long, hard rides in all kinds of weather. The goal was simple: to get the lay of the land and seek out and arrest those committing crimes. McDonald, as a local peace officer, and the Ranger rank and file took into custody horse thieves, rowdy individuals, and other lawbreakers on the run. McDonald even rounded up prostitutes and had them pay fines.[63] At one point the deputy sheriff and the Rangers pursued a suspected murderer to Cottle County and returned without making an arrest after traveling 200 miles.[64] Still at large, too, was the most notorious gang of outlaws in North Texas.

Deputy Sheriff McDonald and McMurry's men made a determined effort to bring to justice a band of thieves. These badmen were led by Bill and Bood Brooken (or Brookin), described as "two wild and crazy brothers."[65] Hiding in the rough terrain along the Wichita River, the Brooken gang stole horses and ultimately committed violent acts. These outlaws trafficked in stolen stock between the counties of Hardeman, Greer, and Wilbarger. Local lawmen and the Rangers searched high and low for the Brooken gang. Sometimes they made contact, sometimes not. Once McDonald got mad when, as a member of a posse, he could not convince the other peace officers to act decisively enough to stop these outlaws from escaping. As recorded, McDonald snapped, "Do you suppose they are going to wait and hold an afternoon tea when we arrive?"[66] By the middle of 1888, the Brooken brothers, nevertheless, had been captured, jailed, convicted, and sent to prison.[67]

His official biographer maintained that McDonald relentlessly pursued the Brookens like a "hound on the trail." This doggedness ended with the capture of Bood and the forcing of his brother to flee to Mexico before being taken into custody.[68] This scenario is more fiction than reality. As a researcher concluded, "It is more likely that Sheriff [W. N.] Barker [of Wilbarger County] and Captain McMurry provided the resolve and forces that finally terminated the Brooken gang—not Bill McDonald."[69] Yet McDonald had developed a "new persona—the avenging angel of the Hardeman frontier."[70]

In 1889 and 1890, Bill McDonald was an active Special Texas Ranger. These state peace officers came from the ranks of cattlemen, local lawmen, ex-Rangers, and other Texans. Such specials, serving without pay, augmented the small number of Rangers in the regular companies. They scouted, made arrests, recovered stolen property, and reported to their superiors. At the end of the 1890s, Ollie Perry, a former member of McDonald's company and a local lawman, applied for a commission as a Special Ranger. On the application he noted that this badge would allow him to chase lawbreakers across county lines without going through "so much trouble." And he added he would also "feel safer."[71]

As a Special Ranger, Bill McDonald could ride with the men of Company B or work on cases himself. Years later McDonald wrote that he "worked with the rangers as a special in Capt. McMurrays [*sic*] co. & we worked a great deal in Greer county as his co was stationed at this place [Quanah] & it was only eight miles to the line of Greer co. & there were many hard characters in that county & frequent scouts were made in fact not a month passed but what the rangers scouted in Greer co."[72] In 1889 Special Ranger McDonald not only arrested and turned over to authorities in Hemphill County a person charged with carrying a pistol, but also earned Attorney General Hogg's praise (and advice about earning fees) for his efforts to prevent illegal cutters from taking timber from school lands at Clarendon, Donely County, in the southeastern part of the Panhandle.[73] In the same year McDonald even stopped a gun battle between two sheriffs by seizing their shotguns.[74] For McDonald the stage was set to play a larger role in Ranger affairs.

By 1891 Bill McDonald held another lawman's badge—that of "Deputy U. S. Marshal," as printed on his letterhead stationery. As a federal deputy marshal under George A. Knight of the Northern District of Texas, McDonald, accompanied at times by another lawman, Lon Burson, went into No Man's Land (Oklahoma Panhandle), the Cherokee Outlet, and nearby areas in Oklahoma to search for and arrest lawbreakers. This criminal element committed horse and cattle thefts and highway robbery. "The general plan," according to one analysis, "was the same in all. The early morning hour; the hack and the Winchester; the surprise attack, and the pleasant drive home with the guests duly handcuffed and shackled; these were features common to each episode. Though conducted against desperate men, it was a bloodless warfare. Nobody was killed—scarcely a gun was fired."[75]

At this time Deputy Marshal McDonald used an interesting technique for tracking fugitives. He learned to assume other identities—at one time passing himself off as a fruit-tree salesman on horseback to collect information about crimes and criminals. In his travels he chatted about his dislike for the law and about the fictitious crimes he had committed. He not only collected orders for fruit trees that would never be filled, but also pried out of outlaws in conversations information about their crimes, their associates, and the locations of stolen property. McDonald was becoming aware that the process of gathering facts is the key in carrying out criminal investigations.[76]

Bill McDonald's ability to join state and national police forces bothered some Texas sheriffs. In 1889 McDonald obtained arrest warrants from a district attorney in Roberts County and served them on a number of citizens for illegal cutting and hauling timber. The local sheriff disliked this process, as he was not informed and he lost his fees. The sheriff raised the question with state officials: Can McDonald who claimed to hold federal and state badges "usurp my authority"? The answer was that Special Ranger McDonald had the power to serve process and take bond.[77] In mentioning this episode Captain McMurry said that officials in this county were in "ill humour."[78]

Bill McDonald's unorthodox methods did raise questions among people concerned with law enforcement. A story is told that he went to see James Hogg, then governor of Texas, and asked for an appointment to the vacant post of captain of Company B of the Texas Rangers. McDonald did not bring any recommendations, but Hogg had available a pile of letters from his days as attorney general of the state, which took McDonald to task for his methods—harassment, enforcement of nonexistent laws, and inhumane detention of prisoners. His critics insisted that McDonald, armed with a Ranger's badge, was more a menace than an aid to society. "That's so, Jim," McDonald answered in defense. "I do put 'em in box-cars when there ain't a jail; the way I used to do back in Mineola—you recollect, when the jail was full—and I lariat 'em out with a chain and a post when there ain't a box-car handy; but I don't reckon they're innocent."[79] Hogg preferred to believe that the letters came from lawless elements and interpreted them as the best endorsements McDonald could have. He appointed him a Ranger captain. But the episode may be apocryphal.[80]

A less romantic view of McDonald's appointment as a captain in the Texas Rangers can be derived from a letter McDonald wrote to Hogg on December 12, 1890:

> It has been suggested to me by many friends in the Panhandle that I apply for the position of Captain of the ranger force provided there is an appropriation made for their sustenance. Knowing the duties of the office, & acquainted with the country, & having been engaged in the work think I can keep things quiet on the border. Should this meet with your favorable approbation would like to have your influence. If a petition will be necessary I can get a large one at the proper time. I know you are bothered a great deal with applications & I hate to ask this favor but will be under many obligations for your kindness if you will assist me in this matter.[81]

This statement indicates far more practical reasons on Hogg's part to appoint McDonald to the vacancy left by the resignation of Captain McMurry. Special Order Number One by Adjutant General William H. Mabry confirmed McDonald's appointment as captain of Company B, effective February 1, 1891. McDonald assumed command of a company of Rangers that consisted of a dozen men, with Thomas Platt as sergeant. Platt would soon leave the service and be replaced as sergeant by another member of the company—James M. "Grude" Britton. McMurry, who characterized Britton as "cool conservative & brave," recommended the Ranger private to the adjutant general as a good candidate for the captaincy. Indeed, Britton did apply for the position, enclosing a supporting petition signed by the members of Company B and numerous prominent citizens and public officials of Amarillo and Potter County, but Governor Hogg preferred to appoint a friend instead.[82]

At the time of his appointment, McDonald was over thirty-eight years old. He was an aging lawman who could no longer be called one of the "boys" of Company B. Yet his life in the outdoors since childhood and his experiences as a local, state, and national police officer prepared him better than many younger men to understand the role of a Ranger in Texan society. One acquaintance expressed the view that McDonald, a "cool, fearless, efficient and conscientious officer," was qualified for the position because of his "experience" and "good judgment."[83] As a Ranger captain, McDonald stood ready to investigate crimes and maintain order in reality. His words and actions, furthermore, would be retold in romantic yarns about hell-bent Rangers by those sitting around campfires.

Chapter 3

CAPTAIN BILL AND COMPANY B IN THE PANHANDLE

Suppose you saw in yesterdays news of my escapade with the pickpockets at Ft Worth. I am awful sore yet from running. They both made fight but I finally made them submissive [after they robbed an "old man."][1]

Bill McDonald led an active personal as well as professional life. As a rancher and a victim of crime, he showed resiliency and a dogged determination. At one point a newspaper reported, "Captain W. J. McDonald, farmer, Capt. State Rangers, was touched by a pickpocket, who obtained $50 cash and $300 diamond pin."[2] In addition, like many ranchers, he could do little about his cattle being stolen from his ranch near Quanah. While McDonald was away on police business, which often happened, his wife and a few hired hands were at times defenseless against rustlers who sought plunder and revenge by swooping down on his herds, making off with his cattle, and causing "Bill Jess" to "cuss a blue streak."[3] McDonald tried hard to achieve economic success at ranching. He even attempted to raise goats, but they became a nuisance and were finally freed to run wild.[4] McDonald was also one of the first settlers in Hardeman County to grow wheat, and he promoted a successful irrigation scheme. He dammed Wanderers Creek. For a while he became a rancher-farmer.[5]

Religion played a role in Bill McDonald's lifestyle. Both organized religious groups and the abstinence factor prevalent in nineteenth-century Protestant culture attracted his attention. As an adult living in Mineola, McDonald was baptized by W. D. Powell, a Baptist preacher whose flock also included James Hogg.[6] In developing his religious beliefs McDonald benefited from his experiences and became a church-going person. His official biographer noted that he did accompany his wife to church in Quanah and called himself a "brother-in-law to the church."[7] At the end of his life McDonald also said to a friend, "I am now a devout Christian, a member of the Presbyterian Church, and attend Sunday School every Lord's Day."[8] In addition, McDonald joined the Masonic Lodge. In early December 1892 he attended as a delegate, with other officers of the law, ranchers, farmers, businessmen, and professional people, the meeting of the Grand Lodge, Ancient Free and Accepted Masons, in Houston, Texas.[9] Equally important, Captain Bill got rid of the immoral habits of his generation. In his early life in and out of the Rangers, McDonald liked to chew tobacco, use a pipe, drink bourbon, play poker and faro, and cuss when needed. Yet his official biographer who knew him in his declining years made a telling point: he did not drink; he did not smoke; and he did not use any stimulants, even coffee or tea.[10] As McDonald once wrote, "I have long since quit all my bad habits."[11]

Before and after his appointment as a Ranger captain, Bill McDonald was active in Texan politics. In the gubernatorial election of 1890 he chaired the Hardeman County Democratic Convention, which endorsed the candidacy of Jim Hogg. The Hardeman Democrats resolved "to take with them their winter clothes" to the state convention assembled in San Antonio in August and "if necessary, stay until November 7 to secure" the nomination for Hogg.[12] In 1892, McDonald supported his old friend Hogg's bid for reelection. In the bitter contest between Hogg and George Clark for the Democratic gubernatorial nomination at the convention in Houston in August 1892, which Hogg won, rumors were spread that Clark's forces would try to pack the meeting. The convention met in the huge "car stable" or "car shed"—a building with one side not walled in order to move streetcars in and out. McDonald and a crew of men erected a fence across the open space with a small gate to allow official delegations to enter the floor of the convention. The next day, Clark's supporters, who had planned to pack the session but were now held back by the barrier, hurled epithets and worse—shoes, umbrellas, and other objects—at McDonald's guards.[13]

McDonald provided less spectacular support of the Hogg candidacy in the Panhandle region before and after the convention. In several letters to the adjutant general, the Ranger captain gave his succinct, partisan analysis of Hogg's chances of carrying the Panhandle in the nominating process and the subsequent election: "There is going to be a bitter fight in the gubatorial [*sic*] race in the Panhandle and while it will be close I think we will snow the Clark crowd under."[14] Clark, supported by Republican voters and followers who had bolted the Democratic party, did indeed lose the gubernatorial election in 1892, although county by county the race was close in the Panhandle. McDonald was a highly visible figure in Texan politics, and for years—for both personal and professional reasons—he served as a sergeant at arms at Democratic gatherings throughout the state.[15]

Governor Hogg, a controversial politician who steered a course between the conservative Democrats and the Populists, threw his political support behind the creation of a state commission to regulate the railroads. Hogg, who developed a sense of law and order as he progressed in his legal career from the prosecution of the criminal element on the county level to state attorney general, believed that unbridled corporate wealth, especially railroad financiers, restricted the freedom of the citizens of Texas. The rapid construction of railroads in the state after the Civil War enabled Texan farmers to move from subsistence to commercial agriculture, contributed to the growth of the lumber industry, and allowed police officers to move rapidly from one part of the state to another in pursuit of lawbreakers. The establishment of a railroad commission stands as one of the significant achievements of the Hogg years.[16]

During his two administrations as governor, Hogg often found his state in conflict with the federal government regarding many issues. Among these were the enfranchisement of blacks (which Hogg favored), federal bounties for sugar growers (which he opposed), funds from the national government for harbor improvements (which he wanted), improved relations with Mexico along the border (which he desired), and the constitutionality of the Texan law setting up the railroad commission (which the United States Supreme Court declared valid).[17] But Hogg was irked by the actions of United States marshals and federal receivers, especially for the railroads, and he in his initial message to the legislature declared:

> In her independent autonomy, Texas should be sovereign and free in the management of her own domestic affairs. Cordially and with pride she claims and feels an interest in the Federal Union as one of its important members. In all the powers delegated to it, she cheerfully joins, to the end that the general government may be honored and respected within its legitimate sphere. In the administration of her own affairs she expects and demands recognition and respect.[18]

Such sentiments were not uncommon among people on the national scene and within the states in the late 1800s. At times McDonald himself could view the scope and operation of the American federal system from this vantage point. As time would show, he had to face such intergovernmental questions in his dealings with federal lawmen and military chiefs within and without the Lone Star State.

The problems of citizen McDonald were quite different from those of Captain McDonald. The pages to follow describe how he faced administrative and operational dilemmas. As senior officer he had to take the lead in resolving organizational and personnel issues within Company B. These knotty points ranged from establishing a headquarters to selecting recruits and obtaining supplies. He also faced the question of how best to deploy the company to combat crime and violence in the Texas Panhandle. To solve these problems, Captain Bill had to work with other law enforcement officers as well as public officials. McDonald proved successful at this, earning a reputation as an able officer who could be depended upon in a time of crisis.

Although Bill McDonald spent much of his time in the early 1890s with the Rangers of Company B and local public officials in the Panhandle, he became increasingly involved with federal officers. Relations between the Ranger captain and law enforcement officials of the national government took two forms: exchange of information and collaboration on manhunts, particularly with federal marshals and army units, and the extradition of fugitives who fled to foreign countries. In a fugitive case with another nation in the mid-1890s, for example, McDonald waited patiently in Mexico with his prisoner in a jail for extradition papers and actions by slow-moving Mexican authorities. When the papers arrived in improper form, he wired the governor of Texas to send a copy to the secretary of state of the United States for his certification.[19] McDonald learned early in his captaincy that bureaucratic red tape made the wheels of justice turn slowly.

Captain Bill also worked with authorities in the other states in the American Union. These encounters dealt with the exchange of information and cooperation in tracking down outlaws and the interstate rendition of fugitives fleeing from justice. The spread of information and cooperation on manhunts in McDonald's day between the Rangers and public officials in Oklahoma and New Mexico became routine operations. Especially important would be the use of the Rangers' "Bible Number Two" by lawmen outside Texas. At one point McDonald requested that his superiors in Austin send the "Fugitive List" to a county sheriff in South Dakota.

This local peace officer, an old acquaintance of Bill, thought that several fugitives from Texas were hiding in his state.[20] Yet the relations between Company B and the authorities in the surrounding states and territories were less important in number and kind than the contacts between the Rangers and local units of government in the Lone Star State.

FIRST YEAR—1891

In 1891 McDonald took charge of Company B, Frontier Battalion, which was stationed at Quanah in order to patrol the Panhandle region and Greer County.[21] The Frontier Battalion consisted of the newly created Company E, under Captain J. S. McNeel at Alice; the Rangers in Company D at Alpine, commanded by Captain Frank Jones; Company F at Cotulla, with Captain J. A. Brooks in charge; and McDonald's Company B. Captain Lamartine P. Sieker, battalion quartermaster, was at central headquarters in Austin. From December 1890 through November 1891 McDonald and his men traveled 11,613 miles, conducted fifty-two scouting missions, arrested 140 lawbreakers, and assisted judges, jailers, and other authorities and citizens seventeen times. Sixty-one of these persons taken into custody by Company B were charged with murder or assault or horse and cattle thefts or other robberies. The company's records noted that no criminals were killed or injured and no Rangers were wounded or slain in the line of duty. W. H. Mabry, the newly appointed adjutant general, observed in his report that the Rangers, as peace officers, carried out duties, such as transporting prisoners and witnesses from place to place, for which the state would otherwise have had to reimburse local sheriffs.[22]

During the first few months of McDonald's captaincy, a dozen Rangers stood ready to follow orders. Important cogs in the operations of Company B in 1891 and years after would be Sergeant Britton and Privates William J. McCauley (who was first added to the payroll as a teamster) and W. J. L. Sullivan. A Special Ranger of note listed in the muster rolls and assigned to the company by the adjutant general was Ira Aten, famed ex-Ranger sergeant from previous gubernatorial administrations. For their work in investigating crimes and making arrests, captains earned $100 a month; sergeants, $50; privates, $30; and specials served without pay. Keeping expenses within budgetary sums approved by the state legislature became an important function of the officials at central headquarters in Austin.[23]

At the start of McDonald's captaincy Adjutant General Mabry revoked the commissions of the Rangers serving without pay. At the same time he issued, with the authority of the governor, new regulations for the appointment of Special Rangers. First, the applicant had to submit a printed form obtained from the state which gave pertinent personal data, the oath of office, and recommendations by two upright citizens. Second, Special Rangers would still receive no pay from the state. Third, appointees were to be assigned to a regular company of the Frontier Battalion and carried on the rolls as "Absent on special duty, serving without pay." Fourth, monthly reports of arrests and related information and current addresses of the specials would be submitted by letter to both the company officer in charge and the adjutant general's office. Failure to comply with any of these rules would subject the Special Ranger to dismissal from the service.[24]

One of the first duties that McDonald had to perform as the newly appointed officer in charge of Company B was to take inventory of the equipment and supplies. Following orders he reported to the adjutant general on the public property turned over to him by his predecessor: one wagon, one harness set, two mules, some .45 caliber revolver and .44 caliber Winchester shells, and a quantity of rations. McDonald pointed out that one mule was quite old and of little service and that the balance of the equipment and supplies were usable, except for several guns not yet collected and listed in the inventory. One weapon turned out to be "rusty," and the other two proved to be "misplaced or stolen." McDonald notified the quartermaster at the Austin headquarters that because of the lack of storage facilities the rations on hand had been left at the place where they had been purchased and that the company needed canteens and utensils for cooking. He also asked Quartermaster Sieker to get him some printed letterhead paper, which he would pay for himself if necessary. In addition, he requested three more mules (one for wagon use and two pack mules with saddles), a cover for the wagon, four tents (the old ones were discarded before McDonald assumed command), and a copy of the rules and regulations of the current Ranger organization. In the last recorded message to Mabry on the needs of Company B, the new captain ended by saying: "Write occasionally."[25]

Particularly important for the operation of Company B were the pack mules. In their scouting, manhunts, and investigative work in the Panhandle and Greer County and assignments elsewhere in the state when necessary, movement over the countryside by McDonald's Rangers took place on horseback or in railroad cars. Pack mules accompanied horseback expeditions or jumped a few feet with the horses from the door of a railroad car to start their journey. Loaded with tinware the mules made a frightful noise galloping over the landscape. "That infernal racket seemed to jar the nerve of a criminal," McDonald said, "for I never knew a pack-mule charge where the men we wanted seemed to have either spunk enough to put up a good fight or sense enough to get away."[26]

In a series of communications Battalion Quartermaster Sieker instructed McDonald in the ins and outs of running a Ranger operation in the field. On the needs of Company B Sieker told the Ranger captain in quick succession—to charge the state for stationery and postage as incidental expenses; to purchase camp equipment and list such items, like forks, pans, and plates, as public property on reports; to look into the most economical way of buying mules and a cover for the wagon and report such information to central headquarters; to record the markings of all state mules; and to watch for two pack saddles and four tents being shipped to the

Ranger captain.[27] Sieker also informed McDonald that state property could be condemned and sold by central command if the captain in the field got two individuals to inspect and report under oath that such property could no longer be used and should be condemned.[28] In addition, the battalion quartermaster had no qualms in returning payment vouchers to McDonald for clarification and telling him to use railroad passes only for official business as the state pays half the fare. Finally, Sieker pointed out that McDonald's payrolls and monthly reports must be done in triplicate and his ration returns in duplicate. These records must be filed in several different places.[29] As an administrator Captain Bill had much to learn.

McDonald's initiation as officer in charge of Company B came in January 1891 when Indians were reported to be on a rampage near Salisbury, along the Fort Worth & Denver City Railroad in northeastern Hall County. Panic spread through the Panhandle. Signs of Indians of unknown origins were reported from everywhere. McDonald, thinking at first that the Ranger rank and file of the company were playing a joke on their new captain, decided to take action as a steady stream of news about the Indian raid, especially from railroad officials, reached him at his quarters in the Panhandle. A trainmaster twice telegraphed the Ranger captain that 100 Indians or so were setting fire to buildings and killing people. McDonald kept the Austin headquarters informed about the contents of these messages and his course of action.[30] Governor Hogg even wired back that he should give the inhabitants protection, arrest the marauding parties, and call upon the military at Childress if it were needed.[31]

Although it seemed impossible that Indian raiders could have reached inland as far as Hall County without being noticed, McDonald and his men with horses and equipment boarded a train and proceeded to Salisbury. Upon arrival they questioned the inhabitants and scouted the region. They discovered that more than one person had reported Indians nearby; a woman even mistook some rowdy cowboys, who had killed a steer, for nameless Indians. As rumors spread a settler and his son, hearing yells and seeing fires, fled on horseback and caused a panic. Since no Indians could be found, the sudden terror soon disappeared. The "hoax," as McDonald called it, was over.[32] Later his superior wrote the Ranger captain that he quelled the raid so "effectively" there remained no "glory" for the adjutant general.[33]

McDonald and Company B now settled down to routine work. As an Amarillo newspaper commented at one point, "the Captain was all business."[34] In the day-by-day police operations, a Ranger sometimes lost contact with a criminal case after the initial investigation and arrest. At other times he appeared in court with a person taken into custody and accompanied the convicted individual through the gates of the prison. In February 1891 a local judge called McDonald and one of his men to Claude in Armstrong County. The Ranger captain was to protect an accused murderer from a mob, and at the request of the sheriff, who was carrying out a magistrate's order for custody and removal of the killer, he accompanied the county peace officer and the prisoner to a jail in Fort Worth.[35] In the months to follow Captain Bill and the rank and file of Company B received judicial orders and traveled hundreds of miles to take individuals charged with crimes—even a sheriff accused of murder—from one Panhandle county to another for trial and safekeeping.[36] This was a conventional chore for McDonald and his Rangers, who often communicated with local sheriffs and judges, appeared as witnesses at trials, took charge of and guarded prisoners, and preserved the peace.[37]

Those involved in the administration of justice in past generations realized that crimes can be viewed by individuals in different ways. Criminal activities in Texas and elsewhere ranged from misdemeanors and lesser felonies, such as disturbing the peace and larcenous activities, to serious felonies like murder. Furthermore, some highly publicized cases of notorious desperadoes carried regional and national overtones. At one point, for example,

McDonald went after two pickpockets and subdued them.[38] Other minor offenses that Company B had to deal with included defacing public property, drunkenness, fighting, and carrying a pistol. To some officials, though, such crimes paled in significance to other criminal activities that McDonald's Rangers investigated. These more eventful violations of the law appeared in records as assault and battery, bribery, embezzlement, forgery, and rape. The monthly reports of Company B for 1891 showed numerous arrests of Texans for committing misdemeanors and felonies.[39]

Chasing thieves was an important part of McDonald's work during his first year as captain of Company B. From burglaries to highway banditry and train robberies, the list of stolen property amounted to financial losses not easily handled by hard-working people: cattle, horses, money, watches, and other goods. Some thieves, however, did not keep their ill-gotten gains, as they were taken into custody by the Rangers and local police officers. At one point two Rangers pursued and captured at the Texas border two burglars who had robbed a depot in Amarillo. McDonald himself successfully tracked and caught two outlaws charged with cattle and horse theft. To help him, McDonald reluctantly enlisted the aid of an unsavory character, who was in cahoots with a band of robbers. In March 1891 Captain Bill had in his custody two thieves captured by several Rangers, one arrested in Potter County and charged with train robbery, the other taken into custody in Hartley County and turned over to the sheriff of DeWitt County, where the crime was committed. At the end of 1891 one report even read that two Rangers "went to Childress & went with the sheriff after robbers supposed to be the Dalton brothers." McDonald once wrote that on a scouting expedition after thieves and Mexican bandits in the Panhandle, the Rangers had "no pack mule" and had to hire a "buggy to carry some provisions."[40]

Even Special Rangers attached to Company B took part in the recovery of stolen property. At the end of May 1891, Ira Aten complied with orders for the appointment of Special Rangers and sent his monthly report to the adjutant general. In the letter Aten stated that he made no arrests, but he traveled 140 miles in five days and recovered four stolen horses that outlaws had abandoned near the boundary of New Mexico. The former sergeant noted that once horses stolen in Northwest Texas were run into New Mexico and sold recovery was difficult.[41]

A commonplace procedure in the operations of the Texas Rangers was to extradite fugitives who crossed state borders. One of McDonald's more complex extradition cases occurred in the summer of 1891. On June 20 the Ranger captain and Sergeant Britton traveled to Ouray County in Colorado to get Charles Marlow charged with murder in Young County, Texas. Armed with the proper papers from the Colorado governor, the Rangers asked the local sheriff to assist them in taking Marlow into custody or authorize them to do the same. Then a series of unusual events took place. On June 24 the Rangers and the sheriff went to Ridgeway and met with Charles and his brother, George Marlow. The Marlows were armed and said that they would die before being arrested. George Marlow also claimed that he was a federal deputy marshal for U. S. Marshal George Knight of the Northern District of Texas and that he was holding his brother as a witness in cases for a U. S. court in that state. At the same time Marshal Knight wired McDonald that the Marlow brothers were being held under federal process and that state officers would be in "serious trouble" if they interfered. In turn, the governor of Colorado wired the local sheriff that he had "no authority" to remove Marlow from the custody of a federal marshal. Although the governor of Texas telegraphed McDonald to challenge the "right" of George Marlow to hold his brother as a witness and to get the sheriff to arrest the fugitive, Captain Bill and his sergeant returned to Texas "empty handed" and disgusted by the end of the month after traveling 1560 miles. The actions of the chief executive of Colorado and the possibility of a violent showdown with the Marlows and their friends stopped the Rangers from taking further action.[42] Governor Hogg even wired the head of the state of Colorado that the "attempted intimidation" by Marshal Knight was "unwarranted" and a "menace to the ends of justice."[43]

During the last six months of 1891 Bill McDonald received requests from local officials to station Company B in other places in the Panhandle. McDonald did dispatch some Rangers to Greer County and sent others to guard the sheriff of Hall County, who had murdered a newspaperman. He also contemplated sending two Rangers each to Hartley and Potter counties. In these places judicial officials and others were worried about criminal activities. The adjutant general, however, thought it was unwise to divide the company. In late 1891, although a detachment of Company B did remain in Potter County, McDonald told a judge in Hartley County that scattering his command around the Panhandle was "not a good idea." The Ranger captain emphasized that the financial resources of Company B were so limited he would not run up any more bills for the state than necessary and that he would dispatch a Ranger or two to Hartley County if local officers would shoulder the expenses.[44]

The troubles in the county of Hartley made Captain Bill write a special report. With a keen understanding of local affairs, he described the political machinations of county officials. In a series of elections, appointments, and secret meetings, especially over the creation of Dallam County, some officers of Hartley County took bribes and threatened to kill those who stood in their way. For several months at the end of 1891, Rangers of Company B, including Britton, McCauley, McDonald, and Sullivan, went to Hartley County off and on to make arrests, guard prisoners, and keep the peace.[45]

One solution to the problem of too few Rangers for too much territory in Northwest Texas was to move the headquarters of Company B from Quanah. Early in December 1891, Adjutant General Mabry informed McDonald that the growth and development of the Panhandle region meant he should move his command "further West." Mabry wrote that the Ranger captain should consider in his selection of a new station the area to patrol and protect, the location of transportation and communication facilities, and the need for water, grass, and timber. Of the three sites mentioned by the adjutant general, McDonald selected Amarillo, Potter County, the heart of the Panhandle.[46]

Pursuant to instructions, Captain Bill made arrangements with the Fort Worth & Denver City Railroad for the transportation of men, horses, and equipment (which saved the state some money) and moved Company B to a new base camp in Amarillo on December 18, 1891. Though wood was scarce on the plains and had to be hauled for miles, the Rangers purchased lumber and nails to build shelters for themselves and the mules and horses. Stables for the animals were especially important for protection against the severe winds of the Panhandle winter. McDonald returned to Quanah on occasion for business and personal reasons, but he agreed with his superiors that Amarillo was the best place for the "protection of the west."[47]

Started by merchants and ranchers at the end of the 1800s, Amarillo became a railroad depot and a commercial center for the surrounding region. The population of the town went from 482 in 1890 to 1,442 by 1900. Although incorporated in 1892, Amarillo did not have a city government until 1899. Municipal affairs, therefore, were in the hands of county officials and the Texas Rangers for some time.[48]

During this first year as officer in charge, McDonald had to deal with the hiring and firing of the rank and file of Company B. Although outsiders believed that the Rangers lacked discipline and order, that was not always the case. When Captain Bill faced serious personnel problems within his command, he discharged four men, John Bracken, Frank Coy, Bill Neely, and John Platt, for drunkenness, insubordination, and lack of judgment in the carrying of firearms.[49] The Ranger captain also dismissed George Adamson for "running a saloon and having so much outside business."[50] By the end of 1891 with other resignations and new appointments,

Company B was a more sober and efficient organization, consisting of McDonald, one sergeant, a teamster, and twelve privates, a total of fifteen Rangers.[51]

SECOND YEAR—1892

During the second year of McDonald's tour as a Ranger captain, the Frontier Battalion consisted of Company B, now stationed at Amarillo, Captain McNeel's Rangers that were located at Alice, and Companies D and F, which had been moved to Marathon and Realitos respectively. Despite these shifts, the work habits of the Rangers remained basically the same. They scouted and tried to locate lawbreakers, guarded jails, and attended court sessions. McDonald especially had to pay attention to crime and violence in the counties of Greer and Hartley. In doing so, the Ranger captain and his men had to deal with George Knighten who became a fugitive from justice. At the same time McDonald had to endure the misfortunes of Ranger W. L. Evans, who was mistaken for an outlaw. The summary sheet of the operations of Company B in 1892 contained three important blank spaces: no one arrested for murder, no criminals killed, and no Rangers slain in the line of duty.[52]

Bill McDonald continued to be an active field commander. Within the ranks of Company B during 1892, he selected new recruits, discharged Collie Taylor for drunkenness, and promoted A. M. Lewis to corporal. At the same time Captain Bill personally arrested lawbreakers for embezzlement, fighting, forgery, swindling, theft of cattle and horses, and threatening to kill someone (after the person resisted arrest and stood off a constable). In order to do this, McDonald carried out his usual duties, from going on scouts to guarding jails and attending court sessions. His dogged attitude especially earned him praise. On one manhunt he pursued a horse thief through Wilbarger and Greer counties. After the arrest, the Ranger captain brought his prisoner to Quanah and turned him over to the sheriff. Most troubling to McDonald during

1892 was his failure to extradite George Knighten from the Cherokee Strip. The Rangers had chased this accused murderer off and on for months.[53]

More than once local authorities requested that W. J. L. Sullivan be one of the Rangers dispatched to their areas.[54] In one letter Sullivan was characterized as an "energetic and efficient" peace officer who was "untiring in his efforts to bring offenders to Justice."[55] During 1892 the Ranger private did join scouting expeditions and make arrests in a number of Panhandle counties. Yet the enigmatic Sullivan also penned a note to the adjutant general requesting that he assist him in whatever way possible in obtaining a position as a "river guard" on the Rio Grande. Sullivan said that he wanted a "larger salary" for one thing and that he was "by no means tired" of being a Texas Ranger.[56]

The extant records of Company B for the year 1892 show that McDonald received requests for Ranger assistance from residents of several Panhandle counties. For several months judges and sheriffs sought the aid of the Ranger service to maintain law and order in their bailiwicks. In February a detachment of four Rangers reported to the county judge of Sherman County. Although the judge wanted the peace officers to "keep down any trouble," the Rangers "found things quiet." After three days the ranging force scouted through five counties looking for several badmen.[57] In March the sheriff of Potter County requested assistance at a session of the district court. Since the jail was "unsafe," members of Company B "guarded prisoners & assisted in serving criminal process" for several weeks.[58] In May a state district judge contacted McDonald and reported that in an upcoming trial in Memphis, Hall County, some of the relatives and friends of the prisoner might attempt to free him. The judge concluded that as a "precautionary measure" Rangers should be present during the trial, which was later changed to another county. Captain Bill and some of his men removed the said prisoner from the jail in Quanah to the courtroom in Memphis.[59] Such everyday police work—more humdrum than dramatic—by the officers and the rank and file of Company B left an indelible imprint on the administration of justice in northern Texas.

Crime and violence in two counties—Greer and Hartley—especially worried Captain McDonald. Both the sheriff and a judicial official in Greer County believed that local law officers were unable to handle the criminal element—especially cattle rustlers—in a county with so much territory and so many new inhabitants. Leaving Sergeant Britton in charge at Amarillo, McDonald and four Rangers moved into Greer County. On the evening of April 15, 1892, they reached Mangum, the county seat. Information from the sheriff indicated that thieves were working along the line with the Oklahoma Territory. McDonald and his men rode about thirty miles to the border. He reported to the adjutant general that "everything on the line passed off quietly though many are of the opinion that the presence of the rangers had much to do with that." By the end of April McDonald had returned to Quanah, leaving the other Rangers on the border between Greer County and the Oklahoma area. A month later this detachment of Company B under Corporal Lewis, with the criminal atmosphere in Greer County having been "purified," as McDonald put it, made a scout for rustlers through Cottle and nearby counties.[60]

The doings of George Knighten troubled Captain Bill and the Rangers under his command. At the start of 1892, Knighten was under arrest for assault. Then during the summer of that year authorities in Hartley County summoned Rangers to assist the sheriff and protect the courts and citizens. At the end of June Knighten was again arrested and indicted for "perjury & illegal voting." In turn, the enraged Knighten shot and killed a member of the grand jury that brought the indictment. Two Rangers in the town of Hartley, one in a drugstore and the other in the courthouse, did not find out about the killing soon enough to stop the murderer from taking a horse and escaping across the prairie. In an attempt to head off the killer, Britton, Lewis, Sullivan, and other members of Company B rode toward the border of New Mexico from different directions.

In one report McDonald said that the Rangers followed Knighten "into New Mexico but failed to find him." At the same time the local judge and district attorney began the process of obtaining requisition papers from the governor in order to return the murderer to the state of Texas if needed. In October McDonald and Britton even went to the Cherokee Strip in Kansas with requisition papers for Knighten. But he "made his escape." During that fateful summer Captain Bill wrote the adjutant general that the murder was a "cold blooded & premeditated affair" and that "everything was quiet" in the town of Hartley after a personal inspection.[61]

A controversial aspect in the organization of some western areas was the location of the county seat. The issue of the establishment of a county seat or its relocation has usually been settled by peaceful means through political elections and judicial decisions. Sometimes the dispute over the location of county government, however, ended in the forcible removal of records from one town to another, in injury or death to the combatants, and in the use of the state militia to keep order. Before and after McDonald became a Ranger captain, Company B was involved in disputes over the locations of county seats in the Panhandle. Early in his captaincy, McDonald received requests, as happened in the summer of 1892 from Moore County, to send Rangers to maintain law and order during an election to decide a county seat location. In early July of that year Corporal Lewis and three Rangers arrived in Dumas in Moore County. They would be present "at the organization of the county where trouble was expected."[62]

A serious yet amusing episode in the operations of Company B occurred in the summer of 1892. McDonald gave Ranger W. L. Evans time off to accompany a prominent citizen of Amarillo on a trip to Colorado and New Mexico. Evans was to hunt fugitives, while his companion hoped to recover his health in the higher elevations of the mountain states. Unfortunately, the two were mistaken for California robbers, arrested by a sheriff in the New Mexico Territory, and detained in Taos in the month of July. Evans wrote McDonald about his predicament, explaining that he showed his credentials to the "thick skulled Mexican Sheriff" to no avail. He also said that this county lawman prevented him from seeing a lawyer to obtain a write of habeas corpus. The jailed Ranger even contacted Governor Hogg, noting that the "avaricious" sheriff wanted the reward money of several thousand dollars. Evans wanted the chief executive of Texas to immediately obtain his release. In turn, Hogg wired McDonald for information—"what about him & his case."[63]

Captain Bill sent word to both the Ranger private and the New Mexican sheriff. He also notified central headquarters about the situation and his concern that the two Texans were being held "without any warrant or lawful reason." In addition, McDonald telegraphed the governor that Evans had been "arrested on suspicion without cause." This contentious affair came abruptly to an end when Sergeant Britton received word that Evans and his companion were set free on July 14, 1892. Later an embarrassed McDonald reprimanded Evans for his poor judgment, but kept him in the Ranger service.[64]

THIRD AND FOURTH YEARS—1893 and 1894

During 1893 the companies of the Frontier Battalion underwent changes in leadership. McDonald still commanded Company B quartered at Amarillo and Captain Brooks remained in charge of Company F with its headquarters moved back to Cotulla. But Company D, stationed at Ysleta, was taken over by John Hughes from Captain Jones and Company E, still located at Alice, passed from the hands of Captain McNeel to John Rogers. Both Jones and McNeel ended their Ranger careers in controversy. The latter did not willingly leave the ranging service. For various reasons the adjutant general sought the removal of McNeel (effective at the end of December 1892). When it happened, the captain influenced the rank and file of his company to resign en masse. Even worse, the popular Jones and several of his Rangers chased outlaws along the border in West Texas. In the pursuit in the summer of 1893, they accidently crossed the ill-defined line and took part in a gun battle inside Mexico, with the result that Jones was shot and killed. From these events the "Four Great Captains"—Brooks, Hughes, McDonald, and Rogers—came together and ably presided over the fight against crime and disorder.[65]

A summary of the law enforcement work of Company B over a two-year period after 1892 showed few dramatic changes from previous years. The Rangers scouted, chased felons, and dealt with local police officers and judges. In 1893 McDonald nearly died in a gunfight (but not in the line of duty) and had to endure the repercussions from a violent act committed by a member of his company outside the state of Texas. In 1894 the Ranger captain protected railroads against train robbers, pursued the Bill Cook gang, and received orders to intervene in labor-management disputes. The lack of violent deaths in Company B was striking: no persons involved in criminal activities were killed and no Rangers were shot in the line of duty.

During the early 1890s Company B under Captain McDonald was the only Ranger company that engaged outlaws without casualties on either side. This happened not because the rank and file shot first; but because McDonald impressed upon his men the need to investigate crimes without bloodshed. McDonald's career as a Ranger captain was sandwiched between the violent eras in Ranger history through the 1880s and the dark days in Ranger annals for a decade after 1910 during the Mexican Revolution (when border turmoil with rebels and bandits resulted in Hispanics being repressed and executed, called "evaporations," by Rangers, local lawmen, and others who took the law into their own hands).[66]

McDonald continued to face problems as a police detective and administrator in the two years after 1892. Among these were opposition to the stationing of a Ranger force in Amarillo and the conduct of criminal investigations in the Panhandle region. Equally important, Captain Bill had to deal with the constant need to make arrangements for equipment and supplies for the Ranger rank and file. He also had to handle the demands—sometimes excessive—by central headquarters for reports and letters describing company activities. Being a harried Ranger captain became an occupational hazard.[67]

Early in 1893 McDonald counteracted the criticism of his company and the Frontier Battalion by naming in his dispatches to the adjutant general the persons who were critical of the men of Company B headquartered at Amarillo and stationed in Higgins. In addition, he gathered petitions to demonstrate the widespread support for the work of the Panhandle Rangers, went personally to Austin to seek support for the ranging service among state legislators and other public officials, and urged his friends to write letters of support to these state authorities. At one point Captain Bill wrote that some "disgruntled citizens of Amarillo are a little disappointed because they cant control the management of the rangers." At another time the adjutant general told McDonald to "hurry up" those letters and petitions in support of Ranger appropriations in the state legislature.[68]

Responding to criticism coupled with the problem of coping with the internal needs of Company B limited the amount of time that Bill McDonald could put into police work. He wrote often to the battalion quartermaster and his superiors in Austin about the purchase of supplies and equipment, especially the need for new tents at Amarillo and Higgins. McDonald also talked about the payment of bills for the use of horses in the locale around Quanah when it became impossible to get mounts from Amarillo in time to pursue outlaws. In turn, G. A. Wheatley, who succeeded Sieker as battalion quartermaster in February 1893, stressed the need to obtain bids from merchants for the purchase of supplies before the appropriations for the battalion were exhausted. In addition, Wheatley had no problem questioning McDonald's expense statements and returning his monthly forms to record the number of scouts and the distances traveled in the correct manner. At least the staples in the diet of the Rangers had become fixed. For some time foodstuffs included beef, bacon, beans, potatoes, rice—and pickles.[69]

During his third year of service Captain Bill still found time to carry out his investigative duties. He rode on scouts. He assisted sheriffs in guarding prisoners. And he personally made arrests of lawbreakers for adultery and bigamy, assault, and carrying a pistol and attempting to shoot someone. In July 1893 McDonald and Private Robert McClure took into custody several parties charged with stealing cattle and fighting in a courtroom. At the same time the commander of Company B promoted Sullivan to corporal and hired replacements for departing rank-and-file members. One failure, though, still appeared in the records of the operations of the company. George Knighten had not been captured. Was he in Texas, in Arkansas, in Louisiana? Rangers continued to chase him in those places, but, as McDonald noted, "he has so many relatives & friends it is a hard matter to catch the scoundrel."[70]

In his reports to Ranger headquarters in Austin in 1893, McDonald realized that the counties in and around the Panhandle, especially Hartley, Lipscomb, and Hardeman, next to the lands of New Mexico, Oklahoma, and the disputed county of Greer, were havens of refuge for outlaws. These desperadoes could commit crimes, hide out in the rugged terrain, and cross the state line at will. The worse thing that could happen for law enforcement in these regions would be to have local lawmen turn to crime themselves. In July McDonald reported that Rangers of Company B had arrested as a cattle thief a county sheriff from the Oklahoma Territory.[71] A few months earlier the sheriff of Hartley County was taken into custody by Panhandle Rangers and housed in the Amarillo jail for stealing several thousand dollars of county funds. Sergeant Britton assumed temporarily the duties of the office of sheriff upon the insistence of the local judge, district attorney, and other residents. McDonald did not object to this course of action—the need and "no pay in the office to speak of" weighing heavily in his decision.

As Britton stayed on longer than anticipated, correspondence between the Ranger captain and the adjutant general indicated that the latter did not like Britton's dual role. After Mabry wrote a letter to the judge in that locality, McDonald notified his superiors in June that Britton had turned in his resignation (not the first time) as sheriff of Hartley County.[72]

As the year 1893 came to a close, Bill McDonald was involved in a controversial murder case. Ranger Thomas M. "Red" O'Hare (or OHare) of Company B was arrested for killing a Cheyenne Indian named Wolf Hair near the town of Cheyenne in Roger Mills County, Oklahoma Territory, on November 20, 1893.[73] As reported in a newspaper account of the murder trial a year later, O'Hare had scared Wolf Hair with his weapons and drunken statements. The Indian left Cheyenne with his wagon as fast as he could. O'Hare then got on his horse and went after Wolf Hair to get him to return to a store and finish his trading. When O'Hare caught up with Wolf Hair, the Indian climbed off his wagon, according to the Ranger's story, grabbed O'Hare's rifle, which was lying in front of him across his saddle, and pulled the trigger. O'Hare returned the fire with his revolver and killed Wolf Hair with a bullet in the head. Afterwards, the Ranger private turned himself in and townspeople went out to take care of the body.[74]

Upon hearing of O'Hare's arrest, Captain Bill wired the news to central command in Austin. Noting his concern that unknown Indians might storm the jail, he asked for permission to go to Cheyenne (located near the Texan border). The adjutant general telegraphed back that the Rangers as peace officers had "no business" being "outside of Texas." O'Hare had to depend on the courts and other public officials in the Territory for protection. McDonald then informed Mabry that the Ranger private left Texas and entered the Oklahoma area against his "instructions" and without his "authority."[75]

In communications with his superiors Captain Bill stressed that the rank and file of Company B had "positive orders" to stay out of the Oklahoma Territory. But O'Hare of "his own accord" decided to answer the call for assistance in the capture of outlaws (some wanted in Texas) from peace officers on both sides of the border. Since McDonald was involved as a witness in several cow theft cases, Sergeant Britton was in Fort Worth, Corporal Sullivan was at Lampasas testifying at a murder trial, and A. A. Neely, who was next in line, went to Hartley to assist the sheriff, O'Hare took charge of the detachment at Higgins, Lipscomb County, near the Texas-Oklahoma border. McDonald feared that he would be blamed for the tragic affair, and he told the battalion quartermaster that the incident was not his "fault."[76] Although the Ranger captain had previously called O'Hare one of his "best men," he now had to make a command decision. The adjutant general approved McDonald's suggestion to remove O'Hare from the ranging service at the end of 1893. For Mabry the reason for this action was clear—"disobedience of orders."[77]

As Private O'Hare lost his Ranger commission, a dramatic event took place that could have ended McDonald's career as officer in charge of Company B. Captain Bill became involved in a shootout with Sheriff John P. Matthews of Childress County (see Chapter 4). McDonald survived the gun battle. But the recuperation from his serious injuries hindered his ability to be an effective company commander at the start of the next year. At one point the battalion quartermaster noted that the monthly report of Company B for December 1893 had not been filed. If McDonald was not "well enough" to do it, he wrote, then Sergeant Britton should complete the paperwork.[78]

Troubles still plagued the detachment of Company B stationed at Higgins. Believing that McDonald was "disabled," B. M. Baker, judge of the Thirty-first Judicial District, contacted the adjutant general's office in January 1894. He criticized the conduct of some Rangers in Lipscomb County (but not McDonald himself). A few of the ranging force, the judge emphasized, "have not been conservators of the peace, but law breakers." This element has been "productive of bad feeling among the people and consequently of great harm, at least for the present." Judge Baker recommended that the Rangers be removed from the area.[79]

The adjutant general responded in several ways. He notified Captain Bill about the judge's complaint. He ordered Sergeant Britton to recall to company headquarters the detachment located at Higgins. And he told Judge Baker that he regretted what had happened. The adjutant general even thought about moving Company B from the Panhandle to another place in the state.[80]

Even before the judicial complaint was made, McDonald sent Sergeant Britton to Higgins to investigate a disturbance between Ranger Arthur Jones and Frank McPherson, a local resident under indictment for breaking jail and helping a cattle thief to escape. When in Higgins the Rangers attended a dance and afterwards went to a saloon. In his report Britton stated that someone took Jones' hat and in a conversation about this among Jones, McPherson, and others, McPherson struck Jones and reached for his gun. Before the Ranger could be stopped, he fired a shot "without doing any damage." Then, before McPherson could shoot, Private McCauley "threw down on him," seized his weapon, and the row was over. Both Britton and McDonald saw the incident in terms of a plot by the local criminal element to make the Rangers look bad.[81]

The interplay among Baker, Mabry, and McDonald continued for some time. After a talk with Britton about the circumstances of the case, Judge Baker modified his critical stand. Yet Baker still believed that better qualified members of Company B (like the Ranger sergeant) should be headquartered at Higgins in order to handle the outlaws along the border between Texas and the Oklahoma Territory. In turn, McDonald stressed to his superiors that he would dismiss any subordinate for drunkenness and improper behavior. Yet he believed that the citizens who supported law and order in Higgins also backed the Rangers stationed there and that Judge Baker was "mistaken" in his position. Although the adjutant general read Britton's report, his previous order about the removal of the detachment stood. At the end of January 1894 four members of Company B moved the Ranger outpost in Lipscomb County back to the base camp at Amarillo. At the same time Mabry decided to keep McDonald's company in northern Texas. Letters to the adjutant general's office criticizing and praising the actions of the Rangers in the Panhandle would come and go. Months after this affair, for example, a lawyer in the Panhandle wrote state authorities that he supported the stationing of Company B in that area to help local officers in "ferreting out crime, and capturing criminals." This Texan also added that the officers of Company B have "maintained a rigid discipline of their men."[82]

1894—A CONTINUING SAGA: LABOR, OUTLAWS, AND TRAINS

As Bill McDonald recovered from his wounds, the Rangers under his command rode out of camp in all directions. By horse or rail the members of Company B scouted throughout the Panhandle in 1894 for cattle and horse thieves. More than a dozen rustlers were taken into custody. Equally important, the Rangers grappled with several law enforcement problems. They took a proactive stand and protected trains on several railroad lines in order to stop attacks by outlaw gangs. At one point in this preventive deployment newly appointed Private C. B. Fullerton guarded "one passenger coach" on a railroad from Austin to Taylor in central Texas in "expectation of an attempt to hold up the train." In addition, McDonald and his men became enmeshed in labor-management disputes at Thurber and took part in a massive manhunt for a gang of desperadoes led by William Tuttle "Bill" Cook. Although McDonald himself made few arrests, he did make a number of organizational decisions. He promoted Sullivan to the rank of sergeant at the start of April (after Britton's resignation). Captain Bill also returned to writing his own monthly reports by the end of the year, rather than sending to his superiors monthly statements from each member of Company B.[83]

A perplexing duty in Ranger chronicles occurred when the officers and the rank and file of the Frontier Battalion became involved in labor-management disputes. Such happenings at the turn of the twentieth century especially took place in coal mining, oil drilling, and the running of the railroads. The actions of the Rangers in these hot spots were either lauded or condemned by the public. More often than not the Rangers sided with the owners of the companies. Yet they did sit down and listen to the workers talk about their grievances. The interplay between the members of the ranging companies and the business world mirrored societal trends in an industrial-urban America.

By the late 1880s Thurber had become an important bituminous-coal-mining town in Erath County in North-Central Texas. Into this region moved paternalistic company officials, union organizers, especially from the Knights of Labor, and miners with different ethnic and racial backgrounds. The Texas & Pacific Coal Company, led by Robert D. Hunter, dominated the scene. Hunter has been described as an "opportunistic entrepreneur, fierce competitor, and autocratic employer." The population of the village went from 978 people in 1890 to 2,559 residents in 1900. Most of the males located in the area at the turn of the century identified themselves as coal diggers. Their lives, with the Italian nationality predominating, can be summed up thus: "A large non-English-speaking population of predominantly southern and eastern European extraction labored in Thurber's mines and resided in drab company housing in ethnic enclaves filled with Old World atmosphere."[84]

For nearly fifteen years a struggle occurred between the coal operators who sought order and a nonunion environment and the miners who wanted better living conditions. In order to ensure more tranquility Hunter erected a "six-foot, four-wire barbed fence that enclosed the nine-hundred-acre tract." The workers saw this barrier as a "symbol" of his "control over them." In troubled times the coal company could call for assistance from private forces and local and state officials. Several times the Rangers entered the area to uphold law and order: Captain McMurry and the men in his command in 1888–1890; McDonald and the rank and file of Company B in 1894;

and still more Rangers under Captain Rogers in 1903. To translate orders about protecting property, keeping the peace, and carrying out even-handed justice, into a course of action became a bedeviling task for the Frontier Battalion.[85]

One of the reasons for the unrest in the Thurber mines in 1894 was the economic depression that had engulfed the country. In this atmosphere Hunter reduced the tonnage rate paid to miners from $1.15 to $1.00. Yet McDonald indicated that the coal diggers still received a decent wage and prices for goods in the company store were not exorbitant. A focal point in the troubles between the workers and the owners of the company were the activities of several individuals who ran a saloon just over the county line in Palo Pinto County. The miners got boisterously drunk at this place, as they were attracted to the establishment through leaflets proclaiming free beer during certain hours. Since absenteeism increased after these drinking sprees, the employer retaliated by firing anyone found in a drunken stupor. The saloon keepers and a person from the mines in the Indian Territory kept stirring up the workers against the company. A number of them even met in the Knights of Labor hall in Thurber. For some time these disgruntled individuals called for a strike, spread the word that the mines would be dynamited, and proclaimed that the officials of the company would be physically assaulted.[86]

Although the Texas & Pacific Coal Company had hired an undercover agent or two to investigate the threats, the president of the company finally requested that the adjutant general appoint five Special Rangers to be stationed in the coal fields. Hunter provided a specified list (including former sergeant Britton) who could aid in the maintenance of law and order. Instead, McDonald and Captain W. H. Owen went to Thurber to investigate. Their presence helped to counteract the feeling that Governor Hogg would not intervene.[87]

On June 7 Adjutant General Mabry sent Captain Bill his orders. In his investigation, McDonald should dispense justice in an impartial way without a lot of publicity. The Ranger captain should also "preserve the peace without arbitrary actions towards the men because they may be strikers."[88] The next day McDonald wired his superior from Thurber that everything was "quiet" and that he would write a "report at the very earliest moment."[89] On June 11 the adjutant general transmitted a confidential message to McDonald. Mabry noted that Governor Hogg did not want to use the power of the state to "intimidate workmen whose wages may be below what justly can be paid them as living wages." The adjutant general again stressed that McDonald and Owen must collect the "facts," stop "lawless acts," and "quietly" meet with those who might take up arms.[90]

Captain Bill played his usual role in these affairs: meet with all parties concerned, collect information, and make sure all participants understand that law and order would prevail. On June 10 McDonald sent a letter to headquarters explaining in general terms the situation at Thurber. Two days later Adjutant General Mabry wired back that the report was "not satisfactory," as it did not go into "particulars" enough to enlighten state officials in Austin.[91] The Ranger captain then forwarded a more detailed statement, endorsed by Owen, which the adjutant general accepted. McDonald aptly described the two problems in the coal region. He noted the cut in the tonnage rate by the company, which was offset, according to him, by paying the miners in cash rather than time checks and by selling goods in the company store at cheap prices. He also talked about the charges and countercharges between the coal operators, the miners, and the saloon owners across the county line. To counteract this, McDonald and Owen met with diggers from the different pits and stressed that "no lawlessness would be tolerated." Their presence removed the workers' fears that the mines would be blown up. Their actions quashed any possibility of a violent upheaval.[92] Hunter praised Captain Bill as a "brave and efficient officer" who prevented "bloodshed."[93]

When Hunter and McDonald asked for more Rangers to be sent to Thurber, the adjutant general refused. Yet Sergeant Sullivan remained in the area and late in June he arrested a person for "threatening to blow up the coal mines." Sullivan and other Rangers in the closing months of 1894 also went to Thurber and surrounding areas looking for train robbers. For whatever reason, the members of Company B kept abreast of events that could lead to disorder in the coal region.[94]

More important for the operation of the Texas & Pacific Coal Company would be Hunter's desire to obtain commissions as Special Rangers attached to Company B for two individuals employed by the coal-digging firm: Sterling Price and William Lightfoot. A former Ranger standing six-feet-five-inches tall, Price received his commission as a Special Ranger in late 1893. In the last two months of that year he reported twelve arrests for crimes ranging from larceny and disturbing the peace to assault, indecent exposure, and sending obscene literature through the mails.[95] Commissioned a Special Ranger in 1894, Lightfoot (with some help) took into custody in three months nineteen people for assorted crimes, including carrying a pistol and assault and murder. Following procedures Price and Lightfoot turned over their prisoners to the sheriff or the town police force. Such Special Rangers not only took part in maintaining law and order but also protected the interests of the coal company.[96]

In the summer of 1894 Captain Bill and his men had to deal with another labor-management crisis. They faced the impact on Texas of the strike by the American Railway Union under Eugene V. Debs against the Pullman Palace Car Company. In the states in Middle America disruption and violence brought the intervention of federal troops to protect the delivery of the mails. In Texas Captains Brooks, Hughes, McDonald, and their Rangers worked the "lines all the way from Galveston through Fort Worth to the Red River." In July a detachment of Company B left Amarillo for Gainesville and Temple to help guard trains and railroad property. McDonald himself traveled to Wichita Falls because of unrest among the workers of the railroad. He and the sheriff went to a meeting of the strikers and "advised them not to attempt to violate the law by burning or destroying property or intimidating others who wanted to work." The railroad laborers decided to end the strike but the company "refused to take them back."[97]

Captain McDonald and the rank and file of Company B also had to pursue and capture train robbers. For years outlaws tried to loot the express cars on trains in Texas, sometimes with success, sometimes not. On October 19, 1894, four outlaws, including Sam Baker and Ben Hughes, forced a section crew to pull spikes and spread rails in order to stop a train of the Texas and Pacific Railroad near Gordon in Palo Pinto County. In the robbery the thieves escaped with thousands of dollars from the express car. Local posses pursued and Hunter notified McDonald about the holdup. By train and horseback the Rangers moved to the scene of the crime. Sergeant Sullivan took a detachment and scoured several counties looking for the bandits. He had no "luck" in finding them, although he did arrest one person for aiding the outlaws. McDonald himself went to the Indian Territory, since he believed that Ben Hughes would head that way to be with his brother. More important than the Rangers would be the pursuit of the train robbers by deputy United States marshals, including ex-Ranger Sergeant Britton. In a gun battle they wounded and captured Ben Hughes in early 1895. Later a second bandit surrendered at his house without incident and a third turned himself in to the federal lawmen. Brought back to Texas from the Indian Territory, the trio of train robbers were charged and jailed in Dallas. The determination of the cases against them, though, can not be determined. In time, Baker would be shot and killed in a dispute about a business deal. But the Hughes brothers, in and out of prison for other crimes, died from old age in the middle of the 1900s.[98]

In the closing months of 1894 outlawry associated with the shipments of money on the railroads worried Captain Bill. In retrospect he took two actions. In December in a preventive mode Rangers of Company B rode on and guarded trains of two different rail companies. At the same time McDonald's superiors ordered him to chase bandits who robbed trains at Fort Worth and other places. In these endeavors the rank and file of Company B had to move around and remain on guard. The Ranger captain once reported to central command: "There was a large sum shipped today and it was generally thought that the train would be robed [*sic*] but they failed to show up."[99]

In the waning days of 1894 the Rangers under the command of McDonald encountered the Bill Cook gang. This band of outlaws, some of whom had Indian blood, terrorized parts of the Southwest. These marauding desperadoes robbed banks, stages, and trains, as they moved from the Oklahoma and Indian Territories through northern Texas into the lands of New Mexico. The Oklahoma federal marshals, Indian police, McDonald and the men of Company B, and local peace officers in the New Mexico Territory exchanged information about the movements of the Cook gang. Their cooperation prevented the outlaws from finding a safe place to hide. Meanwhile, law enforcement officials on all levels of government engaged in a series of manhunts, sometimes together, sometimes separately, which ultimately resulted in the capture of Bill Cook and his followers.[100]

After returning from their search for the Gordon train robbers, Sergeant Sullivan and his Ranger detachment learned that suspicious armed men were camped near Bellevue in Clay County. In the subsequent manhunt the Rangers surrounded a house in the middle of November. When those inside opened fire, Sullivan and his men emptied their Winchesters and six-shooters. This gunplay forced the desperadoes to climb into a loft. Then Sullivan followed by McCauley broke down the door, threatened to burn down the house, and placed four members of the Cook gang under arrest: Thurman "Skeeter" Baldwin, William Farris, Jess "Buck" Snyder, and Charles Turner. The courageous members of Company B and other lawmen escorted these prisoners to Fort Smith, Arkansas, where three of them received long prison sentences for various crimes.[101]

Bill Cook himself fled across Texas into New Mexico. Tracked by Texas Sheriff Thomas D. Love and Sheriff and Deputy U. S. Marshal Charles C. Perry of New Mexico, Cook was captured in early 1895. Love, Perry, and Texas Sheriff Young D. McMurray brought the prisoner back through Texas to Fort Smith, Arkansas. After Cook pleaded guilty, Judge Isaac C. Parker sentenced Cook to prison, where he died.[102]

In his memoirs Sullivan said he also trailed Cook across Texas into New Mexico and provided Perry with valuable information. In this case the Ranger sergeant seemed to be outmaneuvered by other lawmen and exhibited a vainglorious attitude. Yet McDonald in his monthly report noted that by horse and train Sullivan and other Rangers went looking for Cook, from the town of Childress and Dickens County in Texas to Roswell, New Mexico. In the Territory local officers agreed to accompany the Rangers to where they had found Cook's horses. But these lawmen, in McDonald's words, "went contrary to [the] agreement & the sheriff caught Cook & claimed the honor . . . , which is all right as the outlaw was captured & run down by us after breaking up the larger portion of the gang near Bellevue."[103]

SUMMARY—1895 and 1896

During 1895 and 1896 the "Four Great Captains"—Brooks, Hughes, McDonald, and Rogers—remained in charge of Companies F, D, B, and E respectively, stationed in Cotulla, Ysleta, Amarillo, and Alice. From February 1895 through November 1896, Company B under Captain McDonald traveled 65,218 miles (more than any other company), arrested 184 individuals—fifty-six for horse, cattle, and other thefts, nineteen for assault and murder, forty-five for robbery and burglary, and forty-seven for minor offenses—failed forty-one times to effect arrests, carried out 223 scouts (more than the other companies), assisted civil authorities eighty-eight times, and guarded jails on eleven different occasions (far surpassing the other companies). The adjutant general's report also showed that Company B guarded railroad trains six times and apprehended five persons for robbing trains (far more cases and arrests than the other companies combined). In addition, the arrests made for robbery and burglary outstripped the other three Ranger companies. Although Company B tied Captain Hughes' company for the most arrests for horse, cattle, and other thefts, McDonald's Rangers recovered the least number of horses and cattle. Finally, although no member of Company B died in action, the rank and file put three criminals in their graves and wounded three others.[104]

Such arduous police work took its toll of Rangers and local peace officers. One sheriff said that thieves had him "dodgen like a cuting horse." For weeks McDonald carried out his duties while on crutches with a bruised foot and a sprained ankle. The ineptness of one Special Ranger during a train holdup near Childress by two nineteen-year-olds prompted McDonald to write the adjutant general that some of the specials should be removed from the service. In crossing over into Greer County by the shortcut through the Oklahoma Territory, Sullivan and other Rangers took part in a violent encounter at the end of 1895. No Panhandle Ranger was hurt except Sullivan who received a bruise on his chest when his horse fell on him. The Ranger sergeant noted, though, that "we stood our ground."[105]

As the need for the Rangers of Company B increased in the counties and towns, the adjutant general ordered a reduction in the number of privates in the spring of 1895 because of "decreased appropriations." The company would now consist of a captain, a sergeant, and six privates. For the rest of the year the personnel of Company B included McDonald, Sullivan, and Privates Jack Harwell, Arthur Jones, William McCauley, Robert McClure, Doc Neely (replaced by E. F. Connell in the fall), and Lee Queen. This small band of Texas peace officers had to cover the northern parts of the state, as they scouted, went after lawbreakers, and guarded jails and courts.[106]

During the first five years of McDonald's captaincy, he grappled with three principal questions. First, he searched for solutions to organizational and personnel problems within Company B and tried as best he could to meet the need for reports to central headquarters. Three Rangers of note—Britton, McCauley, and Sullivan—arose from the ranks of the company to assist McDonald in his endeavors. Second, Captain Bill solved to a great extent the problem of the deployment of Company B in the Panhandle to combat crime and disorder when the company's headquarters were moved to Amarillo. Finally, McDonald cooperated with local and national police agencies on both sides of the Oklahoma-Texas border to control the outlaws who roamed the area. A district attorney in the Panhandle once wrote that he "learned to love, respect, and admire this fearless officer [McDonald], who always placed duty before his own life. In those days on the frontier of Texas, it was almost worth a man's life to uphold the majesty of the law, and the five years of such experience I had in doing so teaches me the value of such men as Captain Bill McDonald."[107]

With few exceptions, the mundane criminal cases McDonald and his fellow Rangers worked on in these first years of service to the state were not the type to gain prominence in the romanticized accounts of Ranger history. They were, however, preparation for the events of the next five years, a period that would provide a legendary dimension to McDonald's life and give him even wider experience as a law enforcement officer. But first Captain Bill had to stay alive. He almost died in a blazing gunfight in the Texas Panhandle.

Chapter 4

A GUNFIGHT BETWEEN TWO GUARDIANS OF THE LAW

It was strange, indeed, that McDonald did not "happen to get killed" in those busy days of the early nineties. One of the favorite vows of tough "pan-handlers" was to shoot Bill McDonald on sight.[1]

In his investigation of criminal activities in the first half of the 1890s in the Texas Panhandle, Captain McDonald took part in a bloody gun battle. No outlaw ambushed him in cowardly fashion. No desperado had the nerve to face him in a fast-draw gunfight. Instead, McDonald found himself in the streets of Quanah in December 1893 shooting it out with a county sheriff. When the gunfire ended, Captain Bill had near-fatal wounds and the other lawman was headed for his grave.

Through the years the reasons for such clashes in the American West have been varied and complex. In the hurried atmosphere involving split-second gunplay, accidents did occur. In addition, gun-wielding peace officers held grudges, became mean, and showed violent natures, especially after drinking and carousing in saloons and houses of prostitution. The police in western America also reflected departmental infighting and societal beliefs. Burning social issues, like the struggle to suppress commercialized vice, and the antagonistic thought-patterns resulting from law officers disputing their authority to make arrests and get rewards, pushed some policemen into shootouts with each other. As the United States moved westward, lawmen at cross purposes with other lawmen could turn their jurisdictions into battlegrounds.

Captain Bill was not the only member of the Frontier Battalion who found himself in a gun battle with another lawman. The officers and rank and file of the ranging companies even pulled their side arms or other weapons and fired at each other. In 1877 "drunk and disorderly" Ranger Private W. H. Turner tried to shoot a fellow Ranger and was dishonorably discharged from the service for his conduct.[2] In 1882 Ranger A. H. S. Davenport was captured and removed from the service after he failed to pay his debts, got drunk, and tried to desert. In a chase Davenport pulled his rifle, as other Rangers fired several shots, one of which hit his horse.[3] Four years later the monthly report of Company B stated that Private Sterling Price "killed" Private George May. An argument about placing a coffee pot on a fire led to the deadly gunplay.[4] Then in 1894, Special Ranger and Deputy U. S. Marshal Baz (Bass) Outlaw, drunk and mean, shot and killed Ranger Joe McKidrict and wounded a town constable, while being gunned down himself by the same constable.[5] Such unwanted violence hampered the operations of the Frontier Battalion.

Cascading events led to the downfall of more than one Texas Ranger. A classic case occurred in 1881 at Fort Davis. Rangers Jeff Davis Milton and W. H. "Buck" Guyse of Company E went to town, got drunk, and fired their guns, even at a deputy sheriff. When Milton returned to the Ranger camp, he sobered up and took his punishment. Guyse, on the other hand, disappeared. When found by Rangers sent after him, Buck hid in rocks, opened fire, and, in turn, took a bullet in the shoulder from the weapon of a charging Ranger. After medical treatment at Fort Davis, Guyse deserted. Then the Ranger captain informed his company by special order that Rangers would be treated like criminals when they broke the law.[6]

Captain Bill had the ability to stop gunplay between local peace officers. In his service as a Special Ranger he reported to his superiors in 1889 that he stopped an armed confrontation between outgoing and incoming sheriffs in a county in the Panhandle. McDonald did this by taking away the weapons that these lawmen had—especially their shotguns. McDonald noted that he kept the outgoing sheriff from being "killed" and that "things" had become "more quiet."[7]

To the chagrin of those who have praised Bill McDonald for his ability to handle riotous situations, the Ranger captain did not keep things quiet in his troubles with a particular county sheriff. He did not resolve the numerous issues with the local lawman. Nor did he disarm his opponent before the bullets flew.

The most serious conflict in law enforcement in the Panhandle in the early 1890s occurred in a gunfight between Captain McDonald and Sheriff John P. Matthews of Childress County. The McDonald-Matthews shootout surpassed in drama and controversy other violent encounters of that era. Armed clashes between local and state officials are one of the more extreme forms of conflict in relations between governmental bodies. Such violence degrades the officers involved; it hampers the ability of police agencies to carry out their mission; and it creates a feeling of revulsion for cops in the public's mind. In the case of the McDonald-Matthews fight, the hostility between the two men from official and unofficial actions far overshadowed any failures in the structure and operation of the Ranger command post in Austin in bringing on the gun battle.[8]

One noticeable thread goes through the account of hostility between McDonald and Matthews: the actions of Joseph P. Beckham, sheriff and tax collector of Motley County, who turned to crime and became a renegade lawman. Beckham's troubles began with the struggle between the Matador Land and Cattle Company and its opponents, including the sheriff, in the spring and summer of 1893. At one point the Commissioner's Court removed Beckham, in his absence, as tax collector for failing to obtain a new bond and appointed J. L. Moore as sheriff. Upon the complaint of G. W. Cook, county commissioner, that Beckham had misappropriated county funds, an arrest warrant was issued. Moore then took Beckham into custody. In turn, Beckham and his friends disarmed the new sheriff and his deputies and charged them with unlawfully carrying arms. Both lawmen appealed to the governor for assistance, with Beckham even requesting a "company of rangers."[9]

As the governor waited for more particulars, other events of importance took place. The would-be sheriff, a few citizens, some employees of the cattle company, and Sheriff Matthews (who held a "personal grudge" against Beckham) came to town and put Beckham's deputies in jail. With Beckham in absentia, no bloodshed was spilled. But District Judge W. R. McGill, who had opposed the cattle company in removing the cattle of settlers from the range, refused to recognize Moore as sheriff and maintained that Beckham still held the office. The judge also notified McDonald to be on hand to stop any violence by armed men from the Matador Ranch. Then Judge McGill suspended Beckham, who "had done enough" to have charges brought against him, and appointed William Moses as sheriff. The county judge praised the work of McGill and Captain Bill in this affair.[10]

Beckham's tribulations continued as he fled to the Oklahoma Territory. Commissioner Cook and Sheriffs Matthews and J. S. Harkey of Dickens County went after the fugitive. Matthews even traveled to Austin to obtain extradition papers for Beckham on an assault charge from Dickens County. With the move across the state border, Matthews "got McClure to go with him." These officers not only caught up with Beckham but the Ranger private also found himself in difficulty with Matthews and the others through a charge of attempted rape of an Indian girl. McDonald went to investigate and found little substance to the charge, as events took place in daylight in a house with other individuals of both races being present. Yet McClure did hug the girl who did not protest. The local district attorney dropped the case. Soon after, Captain Bill brought McClure, a much wiser Ranger by now, back to Quanah.[11]

Before Matthews could return to the Oklahoma Territory with requisition papers for Beckham, the former sheriff was released from custody, surrendered to McClure at Quanah, and asked for protection. In taking Beckham back to Matador, the county seat of Motley County, for trial, McClure and his prisoner—who feared death at the hands of Matthews and Cook (the latter had earlier tried to shoot Beckham)—passed through the Panhandle and encountered Matthews. McDonald wrote that the sheriff of Childress County "attempted to take Beckham away from McClure." To prevent this from happening, the Ranger private armed Beckham. McClure was also assisted by another Texas sheriff, who helped to stop any bloodshed. Finally, the Ranger and his prisoner, charged with embezzlement, safely reached Matador on August 16, 1893, where McDonald was waiting. In the view of the Ranger captain, the judicial stand by McGill and the "presence of the rangers" had a "very soothing effect & the disturbing elements are very quiet."[12]

Captain Bill left Sullivan in charge of a Ranger detachment with orders that when the court session was over, he was to move out of the town and scout the area back to headquarters. On August 21, Sullivan even escorted Beckham to Fort Worth and delivered him to the sheriff of Tarrant County for safekeeping. In this charged atmosphere, a dramatic incident took place, at least in the eyes of McDonald's official biographer: "On his way back to Quanah, waiting for a train in Childress, Matthews appeared and demanded that McDonald dismiss Ranger McClure on general charges connected with the Beckham episode. McDonald mildly but firmly refused and spoke his mind pretty freely on the subject. All of which added fuel to the old resentment which Matthews nursed and nourished in his bosom for Captain Bill."[13]

The Beckham episode exacerbated already tense relations between McDonald and Matthews. The Ranger captain listed the Beckham case in the key events leading to the gunfight, and he took pains to describe and analyze the happenings in the Beckham affair to the adjutant general when they occurred during the summer of 1893. After the gun battle McDonald wrote in his monthly report, "The row here was caused on account of McClure not allowing him [Matthews] to take his prisoner away from him." In addition, a local historical writer sympathetic to Matthews quoted the sworn statement of Sheriff R. P. Coffer of Hardeman County, an eyewitness to the gunfight, to the effect that on the day of the conflict in Quanah, Matthews spoke twice with Coffer about locating Beckham who had "forfeited his bond in Childress County the week previous."[14]

McDonald did not get along with Matthews personally or professionally. Captain Bill saw the sheriff of Childress County as a "domineering" person who got "mad" when he failed to get his way, who said derogatory things about the Rangers until McDonald got "rather sore," and whose "abuse" of McDonald would have "branded" him a "coward" if he did not fight, with the result that his "usefulness" as a Ranger officer would have been over. McDonald concluded that the public viewed Matthews as the sheriff of the entire Panhandle and the Oklahoma country.[15] A lawyer from Quanah wrote the adjutant general that the trouble between Captain Bill and the sheriff of Childress County was the result of the "clash between the two men as officers" and not the result of "personal differences." Then he concluded: "It seems to have been the determination of Matthews to make the rangers odious so far as his influence extended, and to this end, his vituperations were directed against McDonald as the recognized head in this Section. As I gather from all sources, McDonald without a commission, or with it, yielding to Matthews in matters of difference in judgment, there would have been no difficulty."[16] Captain Bill knew there was one other way to avoid hostility with the sheriff of Childress County: pack up and move out of the region.[17]

In Ranger chronicles other incidents kept Sheriff Matthews and the members of Company B at loggerheads. In this saga three events stood out:

First, years before the current crisis, when Matthews worked on a ranch in the Panhandle, he and others brought a herd of cattle to Amarillo to ship on the railroad. In the town they drank and gambled. Matthews and his sidekick tried to "take by force some money away from the man who they were gambling with." Two Rangers happened to be at the scene. One Ranger got the drop on Matthews and made him leave the establishment. His companion tried to pull his gun and the other Ranger knocked him down with a blow on the head. One historical writer believed that this encounter was the "turning point" in the relations between Matthews and the Rangers.[18]

Second, Matthews resented McDonald's refusal to enlist a deputy of the Childress County sheriff in the Ranger organization and allow him to be paid by the state but be stationed in the town of Childress and remain under the control of the sheriff's office. Captain Bill wrote that Matthews "made a row" about his refusal.[19]

Third, Matthews, who felt that Texas sheriffs suffered at the hands of state officials, tried to discuss the matter with Governor Hogg during the annual sheriff's convention and later on a steamer. Hogg repeatedly attempted to pacify Matthews. McDonald, who was present, was ready, according to a newspaper account, "to protect the governor from insult by taking the fight off his hands." When Matthews and McDonald exchanged words during the steamer voyage, other lawmen moved in and prevented a tragic encounter.[20]

McDonald's official biographer depicted Matthews as a killer before he became a sheriff and as a vengeful, trigger-happy peace officer, who spread the word that he would shoot Captain Bill. Decades after the gunfight, a newspaper columnist went so far as to say, "It was McDonald who shot it out with the renegade Matthews, and all but died from the bullet wounds he received in putting this hard-bitten outlaw under the Texas sod."[21]

In retrospect, Matthews, known in his early years as John Pearce, had a flawed personality—but he still did good deeds.

Although admittedly in some type of trouble in Louisiana where he was born in 1857, the handsome and well-groomed Matthews became a respectable citizen of the Texas Panhandle. Records indicate that he resigned as sergeant major of the First Battalion Cavalry to accept the elective post of second lieutenant of the Pan Handle Cavalry in 1892. The following year he rose to the rank of captain of the same military force.[22] In addition, Matthews became the second sheriff of Childress County at the start of the 1890s. He even won reelection to that office by a majority of twenty-two votes in a three-man race in late 1892.[23] By the time he had his showdown with McDonald, Matthews had become a Texan of importance.

Matthews carried out his duties as a peace officer in a satisfactory way. He went after those who committed assaults and thefts and brought them before the bar of justice, and his manner and conduct won him the respect and admiration of A. J. Fires, a prominent Childress County lawyer and judge.[24] Matthews also took an interest in obtaining extradition papers from the governor's office for criminals who had fled Texas. The sheriff wanted the state to pay his expenses in such endeavors, but Governor Hogg wrote back that he could not honor the request because of the "limited amount" of funds for the "payment of rewards and expenses in the enforcement of the laws."[25] As Matthews' career as a lawman came to an end, his wife believed that her husband was investigating illegal activities on part of some of the Rangers when he was shot. It has been argued that Matthews went to Quanah to inform McDonald and Coffer about cattle rustling among an unknown group of Rangers and that the rank and file of Company B involved in the criminal activity had to silence Matthews.[26]

On December 9, 1893, Sheriff Matthews and several companions stepped off a train in Quanah in the morning hours. Matthews met Sheriff Coffer three times before late afternoon, twice in his office and once in a saloon. They discussed among other matters the Beckham case. Later Sergeant Britton would stress in his report to Ranger headquarters that the Matthews party came to town "drunk" and "continued" to drink during that day. But the Childress County sheriff also took a nap. In his sworn statement Coffer said that he again met Matthews, who was returning from the railroad depot. Matthews remarked that he understood McDonald thought he came down to Quanah to kill him, but that was not the case. Matthews said that he did not want a fight in Coffer's town, as he thought too highly of him to do such a thing. At that point the Hardeman County lawman maintained, "We then separated for Matthews to go to supper. I did not see him any more until a few minutes before the time of the shooting between he and Captain McDonald."[27]

After having dinner Matthews again talked with Coffer at the post office and the conversation now included a third party. A local resident, Dick Crutcher, who thought he could mediate the differences between the two antagonists, warned Matthews of the rumor that he had come to town to murder McDonald. In a sworn statement, Crutcher stated that he first saw Matthews at a store, told the sheriff about the rumor, and heard Matthews' denials. Crutcher told the Childress County peace officer to remain where he was until the matter was settled with the Ranger captain, which Matthews agreed to. Then Crutcher left to find McDonald. When he located him at the depot, he told him what Matthews had said. McDonald responded in a positive way, and told Crutcher he would accompany him to meet Matthews. But Crutcher replied by saying that McDonald should stay put and that he would go to see Matthews to settle the dispute. As Crutcher walked away, he and McDonald saw Matthews and Coffer step off a sidewalk in front of a store about sixty feet away. All parties then walked towards each other.[28]

About six o'clock in the evening on the street near the railroad depot—where many townspeople carried out the ritual of watching the train labor into the station—McDonald and Crutcher met Matthews and his companions and Sheriff Coffer. Crutcher opened the conversation by saying that now the two antagonists could settle their differences without any trouble. And Coffer agreed. Coffer, Crutcher, and McDonald noted in their reports that Captain Bill asked Matthews about the harsh words he had reportedly said about him—calling him a "damned, c— s——— s.o.b.," and saying he would shoot him "between the eyes." As Matthews tried to explain what things he had said, he raised his hand and pointed a finger toward McDonald. At this point Matthews told McDonald not to put his hand on his gun, and Coffer stepped between the two to stop a fight.[29]

Then Captain Bill from his coat pocket and Sheriff Matthews from a hip holster drew their revolvers at the same time and fired at each other in quick succession at almost point-blank range. Coffer crouched between them to get out of the way. Two of McDonald's three shots struck a "plug of tobacco" and a "book of papers" in a pocket just over Matthews' heart. The other bullet from McDonald's gun probably missed Matthews by a "hair's breath." Three shots of different caliber—Crutcher believed from parties in three different directions—were fired from behind Sheriff Matthews. One shot struck his holster and the other two bullets hit him in the back. One bullet entered the right shoulder and wound up on the left side of the neck near the collar bone. The other shot struck the lower part of the back toward the hip and paralyzed Matthews. He went down. At the same time McDonald received serious injuries. In between a miss or two Matthews and probably his companions wounded McDonald in both shoulders. One bullet followed a path from his right shoulder to open a wound on the left side of his neck. The other shot struck his left shoulder and moved downward toward his back, shattering his collar bone, puncturing a lung, and injuring his ribs. Captain Bill staggered away and sat down on a curbstone. He was alive—but barely.[30]

The question about who fired the first shot in the gunfight can not be satisfactorily answered. Of the participants, Matthews believed that McDonald fired first. The sheriff just pulled his weapon in self-defense.[31] Captain Bill initially telegraphed Austin headquarters that both went for their guns "about the same time," and then later he reported that Matthews drew first.[32] Of the eyewitnesses, Sheriff Coffer, under oath, said McDonald shot first, but in a newspaper account it was stated that Coffer was not able to tell.[33] Crutcher swore that "both pulled their pistols and began shooting."[34] Later Sergeant Britton informed central command that Matthews punctuated his talk by going for his revolver and the "shooting began."[35]

For a short time it seemed that the sheriff and the Ranger captain would recover from the wounds sustained in the gun battle. Matthews, however, died on December 30, 1893, from blood poisoning from his wound in the shoulder. A large number of people attended his funeral in Childress. Matthews reportedly "expressed a desire to shake hands" and become "friends" with McDonald before he passed away. This good-will gesture made McDonald feel better and he wrote that the "citizens of Childress seem to be well satisfied now."[36]

Captain Bill slowly recovered from his injuries. His shoulder and neck wounds healed more quickly than the injuries to his lungs and ribs. Most troublesome was the broken collar bone which took some time to knit back together. Until this happened, McDonald was forced, in his words, to "lay in one position so long it tires me very much." He stayed in bed most of the time through the early months of 1894. Near the end of January he had to have, as he wrote, his "back cut near where the ball came out." Early in February, due to a blood clot on the brain, Sergeant Britton noted that McDonald's body became "rigid," his eyes "seemed to set in his head," blindness overcame him, and his mind wandered. After this crisis passed, McDonald recovered and resumed his duties.[37]

During his recuperation Captain Bill kept in contact with other Texans. Messages of sympathy came from friends and acquaintances throughout the state. Others journeyed to his bedside in Quanah, including fellow Rangers and members of the Masonic lodge. At one point McDonald hired a nurse. Although the adjutant general realized that the Beckham case was a factor in bringing on the gunfight, Mabry took the position that the state would not pay the expenses for a doctor or a nurse. He told the Ranger captain that the conflict resulted from a "personal difficulty, not in the line of duty." And the governor agreed. At least the adjutant general looked favorably upon McDonald's recovery from his multiple injuries.[38]

Soon after the gun battle, charges were brought against the participants. The cases against Cal Dykes and D. S. Smith, two of Matthews' companions, for their part in the shootout were dismissed. McDonald appeared in court with his counsel, pled not guilty to the indictment, and posted bail. On May 16, 1894, jurors heard the evidence in the case and after due deliberation found that Captain Bill had not killed the sheriff. His defense argued that he fired in self-defense and that Matthews was killed by bullets fired by others in Quanah. This coincided with the facts of the case, more than any romantic account of the gunfight. The source of the fatal bullet remains a mystery to this day.[39]

Ironically, in this classic gunfight in a street in a western town, the two combatants might not have put any bullet holes in each other. Judge Fires observed, "McDonald was facing Matthews all the time and there was not a scratch on the front of Matthews' body."[40] In addition, no evidence has surfaced to indicate that the sheriff, from the shooting or otherwise, spun around, so that his back faced the Ranger captain. McDonald did not go down in history as a cop killer.

Questions also remain about those who inflicted McDonald's wounds. Sergeant Britton wrote central command that one of Matthews' companions shot the Ranger captain in one shoulder.[41] McDonald himself went so far as to declare in a letter attached to a monthly report that "some one else shot me twice beside Matthews."[42] Britton recorded that citizens who witnessed the shootout were "angry" that Captain Bill did not get a shotgun to end the dispute with the sheriff.[43] This scatter-gun became a favorite weapon of Old West lawmen in controlling armed parties at close range.

In the aftermath of the gunfight, Joseph Beckham, the former sheriff who figured so prominently in the troubles between McDonald and Matthews, joined a band of outlaws and desperadoes. Chasing Beckham and other bandits became an ongoing operation for the Rangers of Company B. At the end of 1893, McCauley, Sullivan, and other Rangers scouted mile after mile in their search for Beckham and his companions. Sheriff Moses of Motley County even wrote McDonald asking for assistance in tracking down Beckham and other outlaws. Sullivan did join the sheriff in a manhunt.[44] In the middle of the next year Sullivan also jailed Beckham at Seymour in Baylor County.[45] Yet the criminal activities of the renegade sheriff were not over.

Captain Bill knew that the Beckham gang had been "stealing cattle & robbing people on the highway" in Greer County and "robbing stores" in Wichita County. According to McDonald, the Rangers "have been attempting their capture ever since Beckham killed" Sheriff G. W. Cook of Motley County at Seymour in the spring of 1895. But the renegade lawman "invariably" snuck back into the Oklahoma Territory. Then the break in the case came at the end of 1895.[46]

The sheriffs of Wichita and Wilbarger counties together with five Rangers, including McCauley and Sullivan, and other lawmen followed the Beckham gang after one of their raids. The peace officers abandoned their pursuit at the Red River and then headed towards Greer County by a shortcut through the Oklahoma Territory. Attempting to find some food at a line camp in the Territory, they came upon the outlaws in a well-fortified dugout. In the ensuing gun battle Beckham was killed. Other desperadoes fled. The cold night forced the posse, except for Rangers McCauley and Harwell, who lost their horses, to seek shelter at a nearby ranch. The two Rangers eventually broke off the gun battle too, waded through the icy waters of the river, and walked to the safety of the ranch miles away. Later, the Rangers returned to the scene of the gunfight, where they met the sheriff of Greer County and recovered some of the stolen property of the Beckham gang. McDonald believed that, although the Rangers had orders not to enter the Oklahoma Territory, as he had previously informed federal deputy marshals in that area, the circumstances of the case justified their crossing the Texas border.[47]

The makers of American popular culture have turned the Matthews-McDonald gunfight into a Wild West shootout. At the same time Captain Bill gained a reputation as a gun-wielding man-hunter who had "many notches on his gun." In one story about his life, he carried an automatic weapon in one holster which "you cannot stop firing when you have once pulled the trigger, until you have thrown it into the river." In the gun battle with the Childress County sheriff McDonald "staggered" after his two companions, "tugging at the trigger of his pistol, but the cylinder would not work." Captain Bill "said afterward that if the cylinder of his gun had not caught he would have stretched out the two deputies along with Matthews." In reality, in the major criminal cases to follow, few, if any, Texas lawbreakers bit the dust from the blazing six-shooters of the hard-bitten Ranger captain.[48]

Chapter 5

PROCEED TO EL PASO: THE RANGERS AND PRIZEFIGHTING

There was trouble in Dallas.

A prize fight had been scheduled, and since there was a state law making ring encounters illegal, the town was divided against itself over whether the affair should come off as planned. Fearing serious disturbances on fight night, some of those among the citizenry had asked the governor to send Texas Rangers.

And so, on the day of the event Captain Bill McDonald, lanky, white-mustached state trooper, who spoke with a slow drawl in his voice, dropped off the train in Dallas. He was met by the mayor. His Honor was glad to see the Captain, but he appeared worried as he looked up and down the platform.

"Where," he asked, "are your Rangers?"

"Hell!" exclaimed Captain McDonald, "you've only got one prize fight, haven't you?"[1]

Unlike the legendary "one-Ranger-one-riot" story, Captain McDonald did not come alone to El Paso to stop a prizefight in February 1896. The Rangers came en masse. The chief executive of the state of Texas gave the order. In the midst of the dispute about holding the prizefight, Governor Culberson summed up his feelings of opposition to such an event in a succinct message to Adjutant General Mabry: "I will see it through."[2]

This unwavering attitude has been a characteristic of those individuals in America who have sought to make certain activities a crime against the health, welfare, morals, and safety of society. Through a mixture of religious, political, and economic beliefs, different people in this country have criticized play, games, and more organized sports as a misuse of time and have attempted to outlaw sporting ventures, from shuffleboard to bowling to prizefighting. By the turn of the twentieth century those who opposed such criminal acts could seek relief through a network of social control—from the populace to sympathetic state politicians to enforcement by the police.

The banning of pugilistic encounters by legislative action created a set of contradictions in American life since colonial days. From England to Puritan Massachusetts Bay to Texas and other states by the early 1900s, citizens had argued about the nature of sport—whether sinful or not—and about the time and place to carry out sporting activities. Thousands cheered or whispered in awe when the great John L. Sullivan threw a punch. For some, the manly art of boxing became a safety valve for aggression and surely built a martial spirit that the nation and the military could tap. For others, especially promoters and businessmen, two fighters in a ring brought additional benefits, all of which were acceptable to segments of the population in El Paso: attraction of tourists, economic gain, town-building, and favorable publicity from advertising and the news media.

Yet sport has raised moral and social questions that bedeviled earlier generations. Did not play and games interfere with one's work and family obligations? Was not bare-knuckle and glove prizefighting a brutal part of the combat sports that should be abolished along with the bloody entertainment involving animals like bullfighting and cockfighting? Should not the occasion for holding a sporting event be restricted: no recreation on Sundays and no boxing match that brought together undesirable, disorderly characters—gamblers, drunks, prostitutes, and pickpockets? From El Paso to points east and west such people were called "toughs" and a "rabble." Paradoxically, then, by 1900 pugilistic events were illegal in most places, scorned by upright citizens, trumpeted by promoters, tolerated by some authorities, and followed by all social classes.[3]

The outlawing of prizefights created problems of location and law enforcement jurisdictions. When Dan Stuart, the portly boxing promoter and head of the Florida Athletic Club, tried to match Heavyweight Champion James J. "Gentleman Jim" Corbett with challenger and Middleweight Champion Robert "Ruby Bob" Fitzsimmons, the fight had to be moved from Florida to Texas and Arkansas. As the prizefight came westward, a similar pattern of events took place: pugilistic encounters banned by legislative action; local citizens divided over the pros and cons of the sport; opposition parties led by ministers; state officials prepared to execute the laws; and police forces called upon to enforce the laws and make arrests. At the end of 1895 public officials in Arkansas attempted to prevent the prizefight from taking place in Hot Springs and arrest Corbett and Fitzsimmons, the former for even conspiring to commit assault and battery in the upcoming match. At one point a local sheriff in that state arrested both Fitzsimmons and another sheriff, probably for obstructing justice. Such events indicated that Texas had one advantage in the hue and cry about prizefights: a centralized state police force called the Texas Rangers.[4]

Before these happenings in Arkansas, Stuart tried to hold the match between Corbett and Fitzsimmons in Dallas, Texas. Dallas emerged in the late nineteenth century as an agricultural and commercial center, especially after the coming of the iron horse. With a population around 42,000 in 1900, the "Big D" had its share of controversy about athletic contests. Evangelical elements struggled with civic leaders in the city and the state at the turn of the century to eliminate the alcohol and gaming associated with cockfighting, horse racing, and prizefighting. At the same time Dallasites went from discouraging recreation in city parks in the 1890s (because of their beliefs in limited government and private gain) to building park facilities for sporting activities to improve the life of inner-city workers and their families in the decades to come. Into this arena of special interests, Stuart, treasurer of the Lone Star Athletic Club, tried to schedule the Corbett-Fitzsimmons contest for the end of

October 1895. Although not stopped by the Dallas city council, Stuart and his followers were no match for the governor and a legislature dominated by rural interests. State officials passed a new law prohibiting prizefights, which the residents of Dallas reluctantly obeyed. Fisticuffs had become another part of that rural-urban split in politics.[5]

The legal basis for the movement of the Rangers into El Paso in 1896 resulted from a mixture of legislative action and judicial decision. Texas had two laws controlling prizefighting: an 1889 statute that placed an occupation tax on different vocations, and a law of 1891 that prohibited pugilistic encounters. The former statute combined with other laws to set an amount of $500 for each performance of a "fight between man and man" or a contest involving animals, with a fine for not obtaining the appropriate license of not less than nor more than twice that sum of money. The 1891 law made participation by individuals in prizefights or animal entertainment a felony with a fine between $500 and $1000 and a jail sentence of sixty days to one year. Some judges ruled that this prohibition law did away with the portion of the statute levying an occupation tax.[6]

Within this complex legal picture several events in 1895 created more confusion. First, without the governor's signature a revised civil code with the occupation tax became law *after* a revised penal code with the prohibition statute. This raised a question whether there was any Texas law banning prizefights. Second, as an arena was being constructed to hold the upcoming championship bout in Dallas, the county attorney and the sheriff in that area raised questions about the validity and enforcement of the 1891 prohibition statute. Third, the attorney general of Texas then rendered his opinion that pugilistic encounters were still outlawed and that force could be used to stop an unlawful assembly of people at the Dallas fight.[7] Fourth, Judge J. M. Hurt of the Court of Criminal Appeals, in deciding a habeas corpus case of a person arrested for prizefighting, ruled that the new occupation tax law made the statute banning contests in a ring null and void.[8] And finally, most Texans had their own opinions about how to interpret such actions. One individual went so far as to conclude that the governor "won't send the rangers and he won't send the militia."[9]

One person not heard from in this affair was Governor Culberson. The charges that Culberson was a political opportunist or decided to make a grandstand play or had a personal dispute with Dan Stuart and some members of the Dallas sporting fraternity have been overplayed. Much more important in the governor's mind were his beliefs that prizefighting threatened "good order and public peace" and was an "affront to the moral sense and enlightened progress" in the state; that Judge Hurt's decision should not be taken as representative of the full court of last resort; that the will of the people as expressed in legislative acts was being subverted; and that the laws of Texas had to be faithfully executed.[10] Amidst actions and rumors about martial law, the use of court injunctions, and getting writs of mandamus to obtain licenses, Culberson did a sensible thing: he called a special session of the state legislature to clarify the statutes about prizefighting. On October 2, 1895, by a vote of 27 to 1 in the Senate and 107 to 5 in the House, the legislature passed a bill that prohibited pugilistic encounters, with or without gloves, between consenting persons or an encounter between a man and an animal (like a bull) for a purse, other items of value, any championship, or upon which admission fees were charged or money bet. A violation of this act, which repealed all laws in conflict with this emergency legislation, carried a felony penalty of two to five years in the penitentiary. The die had been cast.[11]

At this point the nature of the fight changed and the promoters had to find a new site. By the end of 1895 the contest became a match between Fitzsimmons and Peter Maher, an Irish slugger to whom Corbett bestowed his championship belt after he retired from the ring in order to concentrate upon his acting career.[12] In addition, Stuart moved farther west in his search for a new location. The unfavorable legal environment had forced the prizefight from

Florida to Dallas, from Dallas to Hot Springs, and now from Hot Springs to El Paso. Stuart seized the opportunity offered by the El Paso McGinty Club to hold a "fistic carnival" with championship bouts in several weight categories. The main entertainment—Fitzsimmons vs. Maher—would take place on Valentine's Day, February 14, 1896, for a purse of $10,000.[13]

The return of a major prizefight attraction to the soil of Texas would again face serious opposition. In retrospect Fitzsimmons' manager made a prophetic statement in January 1896: "Dan Stuart has the matter in hand and is not telling everybody where the fight is going to take place. He will keep quiet until the day of the fight."[14] No doubt the move to El Paso created new possibilities about where to hold the match: conduct the event in or around El Paso, step across the borders into Old Mexico or the New Mexico Territory, or make a run for the Arizona or Indian territories. Months before, though, federal officials took a negative view of holding the bout in the Indian Territory, even maintaining that marshals, troops, and the Indian police would be used to stop any prizefight in that area.[15] One by one the places to conduct the boxing contest had begun to be eliminated.

At the beginning of 1896 the chief executive of Texas and the sports promoter exchanged views about the upcoming carnival. Stuart wrote that printed materials that left the "impression" the contests would take place in El Paso were erroneous. More accurately, the fights will be staged "near El Paso." Stuart offered his "personal assurance" that training camps and the boxing ring would be set up in such ways as to avoid "any infraction of State or Federal laws." He ended by saying that his main office "has been established just across the river in the City of Juarez, where all business appertaining to the carnival will be conducted."[16]

In reply the Texas governor wrote that he had the responsibility to enforce the laws of Texas and was "not concerned officially with what may be done beyond its limits." In guarded fashion and with veiled threats Culberson warned Stuart:

> . . . The Boundary line between Texas and Mexico and New Mexico has been publicly defined, and in this case I shall respect and endeavor to give effect, if resisted, to the line recognized by the political authority of this State.
>
> It is an offense against the laws of this State to enter into an agreement or conspiracy here to commit a felony in another jurisdiction. I do not know positively whether prize-fighting is a felony in Mexico or New Mexico, but presume it is not. If this be so, it seems to me that the mere act of training in this State for a contest there does not violate our laws. It should be borne in mind, however, particularly in view of press reports during the past few days, that the statute which forbids pugilistic encounters between man and man to see which any admission fee is charged directly or indirectly or for any other of the purposes named, can not be violated under the guise of training.[17]

Governor Culberson made preparations to further restrict the possible sites for the match. With the authority from the newly enacted anti-prizefight law, the governor sent Adjutant General Mabry and the Texas Rangers into El Paso "to see that no such crime as was widely advertised to come off near El Paso should be perpetrated upon any isolated Texas soil, nor even on any so-called neutral strip between Texas and Mexico."[18] In time, Mabry, the four Ranger captains, and most of the rank and file of the Rangers in the state, between thirty to forty law enforcement officers in all, arrived in El Paso and kept watch over the participants, the railroad depot, and the cars loaded with ring equipment. This concentration of Ranger manpower did not happen too often in the annals of the Frontier Battalion.

In order to carry out their objective of stopping the fight from taking place on "Texas soil," the Rangers adopted a system of surveillance. Surveillance is an age-old investigative method in police work to prevent the commission of an offense or apprehend persons in the act of committing a crime. Strategies used in setting up a surveillance network range from shadowing a suspect to collecting information through sight and sound. The adjutant general described the system thus: "I had a close and constant espionage placed, not only on the principals, but also on the passenger depot and the cars loaded with paraphernalia of the ring, with instructions to follow the latter to wherever hauled."[19]

At the start of 1896 before the Rangers moved into El Paso in full force, Mabry contacted the four captains scattered throughout the state. When Captain Hughes of Company D, stationed near El Paso, asked for instructions about allowing the fighters to train in Texas, his superiors answered that training camps would be allowed in the state.[20] Later Hughes and his Rangers were asked by central headquarters to gather information about the prizefight and its exact location. The able and efficient captain responded, "I will be very careful while in El Paso and get all the information possible without letting any one know my business."[21]

At the same time the adjutant general sent a confidential message to Captain McDonald of Company B, stationed in the Texas Panhandle. In it Mabry gave instructions to McDonald, which he complied with, to send two Rangers, "incognito," to El Paso by rail and report to Captain Hughes until the adjutant general arrived. "You will select for this duty," Mabry wrote, "*discreet*, *cool*, & *determined* men, & able to act as detectives, & keep their own counsels. The object to be attained is to find out the location of [the] coming fight & prevent it from coming off on Texas soil."[22] In a similar vein four Rangers came to El Paso from the companies located in the southern portions of the state, two each from Company F headed by Captain Brooks and Company E commanded by Captain Rogers. By early February the surveillance network had begun to come together.[23]

The initial problem in the move of a large number of Rangers to El Paso was logistical in nature. The simplest maneuver was carried out by the men under Hughes' command who moved a few miles into the city from their base camp in El Paso County on

February 10, 1896.[24] Three days before, the other Ranger companies made preparations to head for West Texas. On February 9 the adjutant general arrived in El Paso with Brooks and three men of Company F and Rogers with his entire command of seven Rangers including three new recruits. These Rangers, who had traveled hundreds of miles, camped near the Texas and Pacific railroad station. The rest of the men in Brooks' company trickled into the town, with four more arriving after the captain got there.[25]

The complexities of communicating with and transporting an entire Ranger company were best illustrated by the movements of the rank and file under the command of McDonald. On February 6 the Ranger captain received a telegram from the adjutant general instructing him to enlist three "good men" and move his entire command to Fort Worth where orders would be waiting. On the same day McDonald sent two messages to Mabry informing him that the company was preparing to leave, but several Rangers were away on duty. Then McDonald got his sergeant who was a witness at a trial to board a train, enlisted four more Rangers, hired a person to look after the base camp and the horses, received orders at Fort Worth to buy railroad tickets at the "excursion rate" to El Paso, and arrived in that city on February 10. To augment this small force, McDonald also hired a man to chase down a detachment of four other Rangers and tell them to join him in El Paso. One thing was for sure: the Ranger organization was now in motion.[26]

The Texas Rangers came to El Paso with mixed feelings. With the arrival of the iron horse in the late 1800s this city at the historic "Pass of the North" grew in population to some 16,000 inhabitants by the turn of the century. At the same time the community went through periods of reform to get rid of saloons, gamblers, and prostitutes. In this atmosphere Rangers could be welcomed by some residents of the town in the mid-1890s.[27] Yet each Ranger had to balance his sworn duty to uphold the law with his feelings about liking the manly art of self-defense and desiring to be a spectator at a prizefight. Moreover, a Ranger like McDonald, with his law-and-order attitude and his showmanship qualities, would even request permission to go to El Paso on the day of the fight.[28] The local news media also pointed out that the Rangers were a "manly looking set of men," that Mabry, Hughes, McDonald, and other Rangers watched an exhibition by Fitzsimmons at his training camp in Juarez, Mexico, and that the Rangers stood around gambling tables at a bullfight in Old Mexico. Still, the infamous prizefight must not take place on "Texas soil."[29]

For two weeks a large part of the duties of the Rangers dealt with surveillance and cooperation with other peace officers in the area. This lengthy stay became necessary when an injury to Maher's eyes, real or not, brought about a postponement of the fight until February 21. During this time the adjutant general and the Rangers had to worry about the location of three possible sites for the upcoming match: on disputed lands between Texas and Old Mexico or New Mexico, in wooded areas near El Paso, or in the local opera house, where Maher, who trained in Las Cruces, New Mexico, and other boxers gave an exhibition on January 18 without arrests being made.[30] Shortly after his arrival, Mabry, in the presence of three Ranger captains and another person, told Stuart in "no *uncertain tones*" that he would prevent the fight from taking place in Texas or on "any ground where a doubt existed as to its ownership." "I have determined," Mabry wrote, "to prevent the fight on any ground where the line (boundary) is not clearly defined." Stuart replied that he would not stage the event in any area where the Rangers must act. When Stuart offered to take the adjutant general to the place he had selected, Mabry refused and told Stuart that he would be at the site when necessary without "such kindness on his part."[31]

At the same time the adjutant general exchanged information with United States Marshal Edward L. Hall of New Mexico (where public officials opposed the bout) and Governor Miguel Ahumada of the Mexican state of Chihuahua (who took a dim view of the match being brought into that area). Mabry agreed that he and Hall would board a train together at El Paso if needed and that both parties would act together on all "neutral ground" between Texas and New Mexico. The adjutant general even rode out himself to check the location of the "so-called islands" between Texas and Old Mexico. When Mabry heard that Ahumada would allow American officials to enter Mexico to prevent the prizefight, the adjutant general thought that without orders to the contrary he would not use "force" to stop the fight on "clearly and unmistakably" defined Mexican soil. Mabry concluded that he was working in "harmony" with Marshal Hall and that Texas officials were "masters of the situation."[32]

Pursuant to orders the Rangers carried out a constant surveillance, day and night, of the sporting fraternity and the railroad lines in El Paso. As early as February 6 Hughes wrote that he "trailed" Stuart's buggy tracks into New Mexico and Old Mexico. The Ranger captain was not sure if the boxing promoter had selected a place to hold the fight, but Hughes was sure that Stuart "did not leave the road at all in Texas."[33] In time the Rangers and federal deputy marshals watched the different railroad lines. At one point four Rangers got permission to board a freight train to the state line after Hughes detained the train under the belief that two cars were loaded with ring paraphernalia. In addition, McDonald drew the assignment of dogging the footsteps of Stuart and Brooks' Rangers "shadowed" Fitzsimmons.[34] One risk in the use of surveillance techniques—being given the slip—happened to the Rangers as the fight drew near. On February 20 Maher took a train from Las Cruces to El Paso and got off several miles from the city. "Rangers were posted," a news story read, "at every point from the railway station out to await him. A carriage was in waiting at the smelter, and into this Maher jumped, and the horses on a run reached this city. Hot after the carriage came two mounted rangers with their horses flecked with foam. Maher had evaded them."[35]

In El Paso surveillance work could lead to misunderstandings, complaints, and ill will between peace officers, the fight crowd, and local citizens. On the night of February 13, the eve of the fight as originally planned, Fitzsimmons attended a performance at Myar's opera house with his wife and mother-in-law. While seated ready to watch the "Wicklow Postman," they were approached by two Rangers who told "Ruby Bob" that he was under arrest. Then the adjutant general came forward and informed Fitzsimmons that the lawmen would keep him under surveillance while he was in the state. "This made Fitz feel uncomfortable," one newspaper reported, "as he had never violated any law of this country and did not know that he would have to pass through the state in bond. But the officers remained with Fitz until he recrossed into Mexico." At the same time two Rangers guarded the room of A. K. Albers where Maher was resting. When Albers protested this action to Sheriff W. J. Simmons, the Rangers withdrew. As a citizen and taxpayer Albers wrote a protest letter to the local newspaper about this harassment. In it he said among other things that the state officers "subjected me to the indignity of watching my . . . home as though it was the abode of a thief in the night."[36] Later Mabry noted that Albers' protest was an "outburst of virtuous . . . indignation," that Albers associated with disreputable characters, that a week later the Rangers would again watch Albers' room when Maher was present, and that state officials "usurped no authority, nor interfered with local officers in any duty they saw fit to perform."[37]

In the series of events on that fateful day, February 13, the local news media reported that Mabry threatened Martin Julian, Fitzsimmons' manager, and that the Rangers would be ordered to "shoot to kill" if the match took place on "Texas soil." Reactions to this meeting by El Pasoans ranged from disapproval to Mabry "running a bluff" to noting the ability of the Rangers to make arrests without bloodshed. In the exchange of telegrams and letters between the adjutant general and the governor, a telling point was made by Culberson on February 12: "I rely upon you to prevent [the] fight on any territory claimed by Texas regardless of [the] consequences."[38]

The longer the Rangers remained in El Paso the more likely city and county officials would criticize their stay. Intergovernmental relations between public servants, national, state, and local, have always involved both conflict and cooperation. Besides a perturbed local sheriff, City Alderman Edwin C. Roberts introduced a fault-finding resolution which passed the city council on a split vote on February 14. The gist of this statement stressed the ability of the city police and the sheriff's office to handle the criminal element, with the surveillance network carried out by the adjutant general and the Rangers being criticized for violating the rights of the freedom-loving people of Texas. At the end of the resolution state authorities were taken to task for trying to "gain cheap notoriety under the guise of enforcing the law."[39]

For a bright spot in the intergovernmental relationships a possible shootout between two lawmen failed to materialize. Sheriff Charles C. Perry of Chaves County, New Mexico, one of Marshal Hall's deputies, and Sergeant Sullivan of Company B had a falling out before the prizefight over the pursuit and capture of an outlaw. Perry's grudge almost reached flash point in El Paso when Sullivan tried to prevent some street violence from spilling over into a saloon. While Sullivan guarded the door, Perry moved behind him and pointed his revolver at the Ranger's back. But a warning from another Ranger and Sullivan's glance backwards made Perry put away his weapon. Later Sullivan recalled, "I could see the handle of his sixshooter, which he held in his hand behind him."[40] At one point a local newspaper reported that the city police thought the only disturbance in El Paso was "occasioned by outside people who are commissioned to carry guns; that all of the sensational gun plays have been made by visiting officials."[41]

During the ups and downs of the surveillance operations the Rangers protected property and made more arrests than usually recorded in popular histories. As early as February 3, Captain Hughes and two Rangers arrested and jailed three bunco men. Two weeks later, on February 18 to be exact, Captain Rogers with another Ranger and one more lawman arrested four robbers and put them in the calaboose. The records show that McDonald's company was especially active in collaring lawbreakers. His monthly report noted that a number of bunco men and pickpockets were taken into custody and turned over to city authorities. Then, on February 13 Sergeant Sullivan assisted a police and river guard in arresting twenty-seven burglars and pickpockets and handed them over to El Paso officials. Sullivan believed the area was crawling with "tough characters." One newspaper said, with some justification, that the Rangers made the "confidence gang keep on the move."[42]

Protecting property and making arrests in El Paso became more important to the Rangers than getting involved in acts of violence. At one point Mabry noted that distorted news dispatches about violent encounters and collusion between law officers and backers of the fight were prejudicial to himself and the Rangers. Important to note is the fact that except for the involvement of a Ranger in the shooting scrape which took place before Perry's attempt to kill Sullivan, the street violence with guns and knives in the city was handled by local police agencies.[43] As the time for the prizefight drew near state authorities made two attempts to guard property and prevent crimes. The adjutant general ordered the Rangers to guard the Western Union office in order to stop a reported extortion attempt; and Sullivan and twelve Rangers upon request protected the banks in the city on February 21, the day of the match. The time had come for the rest of the Rangers to leave El Paso.[44]

The Ranger force continued its surveillance operation until the evening of February 20, when a special Southern Pacific train with thirteen coaches pulled out of El Paso with the fight crowd. One newspaper declared, "During the long wait for the train the rangers seated themselves in a row along the station with their winchesters resting on their knees."[45] The day before, Sergeant Edwin D. Aten of Company D left for three days and traveled six hundred miles by rail to scout and investigate the arrangements made by the promoters of the prizefight. Aten trailed different trains with ring equipment and carpenters from El Paso to Langtry, Texas, and reported these movements to Captain Hughes. On the same day that Aten left, the adjutant general wired the governor that he believed the bout would take place in Old Mexico opposite Langtry, since this was the only area near a railroad on the Texas side that Mexican forces could not reach in time. Stuart had conspired with Judge Roy Bean to finally stage the celebrated match.[46]

On the trip to Langtry by the fight crowd and the Rangers and other lawmen, an ingredient in the mixture that leads to heroic images—the tall tale—wove itself again into Ranger lore. Not all the Rangers left El Paso—only the companies headed by Brooks and Rogers and other Rangers including Captain McDonald. Although McDonald's role in this affair was no more significant than the actions of the other Ranger captains, stories of glorification about him still arose. His name became linked with that of William Barclay "Bat" Masterson, frontier lawman, gunman, gambler, and boxing enthusiast. Masterson, whose name was mentioned as a referee for the match (which went to the rugged and honest George Siler), arrived in El Paso on February 5. Several contemporary accounts and later histories mentioned that stories circulated about Masterson and others being at the fight to protect visitors and to see that the match came off. Stuart did give Masterson security duties and Bat did tell the news media that he disliked the anti-prizefight sentiment. He also sent telegrams to his friends to come and see the bout. One newspaper report near the time of the fight noted that Masterson was "on hand and for the first time since he has been here has been active today."[47] No record, though, can be found of any violent confrontation between the ex-lawman and the Rangers before the fight crowd left El Paso.

The trip to Langtry was not much different. McDonald's official biographer went so far as to relate an account of a meeting between the Ranger captain and Masterson at a restaurant at a stopover by the train before reaching Langtry. When Masterson became irked with the service of a Chinese waiter and raised a table castor to teach the person a lesson, an encounter took place with McDonald. In those laconic phrases dear to the hearts of Wild West writers, the exchange went thus: Captain Bill grabbing Bat's arm spoke first: "Don't you hit that man!" Bat snapped back a sharp retort: "Maybe *you'd* like to take it up!" Captain Bill's quiet reply challenged Bat: "I done took it up!" But, instead of the gunfight for the "Law West of the Pecos," Masterson put down the table castor and McDonald walked away. When Masterson read an account of this story decades later, he wrote that it did not happen: no riders getting off the train along the route, no Chinese waiters working in an eating place, and no face-to-face encounter between himself and Captain Bill. Yet this tale has become part of the McDonald legend of the Texas Rangers.[48]

Although this gun battle failed to materialize, the prizefight itself in Ranger annals was still anticlimactic. After traveling several hundred miles to Langtry, the fighters, ring officials, and a few hundred spectators wended their way down from the cliffs to the Rio Grande, crossed that body of water to a sandy flat in Old Mexico about two miles from Langtry, and surrounded a makeshift ring. At this point the Rangers made sure that the two contestants and their audience crossed the state line into Mexico. Mexican soldiers were miles away. Despite all the time spent on the controversial events leading up to the match and the preparations to set up the site, Fitzsimmons, after some preliminary sparring, knocked out Maher with a right-handed punch in the first round on February 21. Although stories circulated that the Rangers crossed the river to see the prizefight, they actually stood on the cliffs and watched from afar. The infamous contest did not take place on "Texas soil."[49]

By the 1890s prizefighting had emerged from the corruption and decline that had characterized the sport in the decades after the Civil War. For years boxing matches had appealed to the laboring classes and ethnic groups. But other social classes, although drawn to the ring by its excitement and pageantry, could not easily accept the associations between pugilism, gambling, and the urban underworld. In Texas at the turn of the century prizefighting became a contest between different factions: evangelical groups and the rural folk versus the sporting fraternity and the urban masses. Until the fight game developed better integrated business structures and passed from the era of prohibition to the age of regulation in the twentieth century, Governor Culberson and his successors in Texas would not allow the anti-prizefight law to become a dead letter.[50]

The Texas Rangers came to El Paso with their command system and their manpower in order to prevent a law from being broken rather than pursuing those who broke the law. Once orders were sent through channels, the companies in the field made traveling preparations with a minimum of problems and moved with dispatch from their base camps to the city. From here the Rangers—not local law enforcement agencies—played the key role in preventing the prizefight from taking place on "Texas soil." This objective had been laid down by state officials and transmitted through a chain of command: governor to adjutant general to Ranger captains to the rank and file. By rail, on horseback, and on foot, noncommissioned officers and privates, like Sergeants Aten and Sullivan, carried out their assignments in a determined and vigilant way. Of the Ranger captains, Hughes gave efficient and able service and McDonald gained the most notoriety from this affair, even standing in showmanship form in one pose for the famous photograph of the Rangers taken near the courthouse before the fight crowd left El Paso.

The Rangers, though, brought ambivalent feelings to their duties in this case of victimless crime. They had to balance their sworn duty to uphold the laws of the state with their beliefs about liking the manly art of self-defense. Furthermore, the longer the Rangers stayed in El Paso the more their surveillance operations and their arrests of lawbreakers could be criticized for violating civil rights and interfering with the duties of local authorities. The Ranger organization also tarnished its image as a frontier force by staying in the city for weeks on end and having the news media raise questions about the cost to the taxpayer for keeping the services of the Frontier Battalion in El Paso. One can argue that state officials could have depended solely on Hughes' company to stop the prizefight. Bringing the other Ranger companies to the city was an overkill that should have been avoided. In part, this view has been predicated on the belief expressed by Hughes when he said to his superiors, "I have not tried to conceal the fact that I would prevent the fight from taking place in Texas but have always expressed myself that I did not think they would try it on Texas soil."[51] Yet Governor Culberson and Adjutant General Mabry brought the Rangers to El Paso not only to enforce the laws, but also to uphold the dignity of the state of Texas—to be "masters of the situation"—"regardless of [the] consequences."

Chapter 6

A BANK ROBBERY IN WICHITA FALLS

. . . I told the Judge I thought he was asking a good deal of me to let my small force go and stay there alone, all crippled up any way and nearly sick and tackle a mob of several hundred, probably have to kill some of them and get killed myself, and besides I had nothing to do with [the] prisoners after turning them over to the local authorities, which I had done, and was doubly assured they could hold them and did not need us.[1]

This self-analysis of his conduct shows that Captain Bill wrestled with his conscience in explaining his actions as a peace officer. McDonald's soul-searching experience occurred after a manhunt following a bank robbery in Wichita Falls at the start of 1896. This criminal act suited more the talents of the Ranger captain than his involvement in the controversial prizefight in El Paso. Yet his extraordinary effort as a manhunter was offset by his singular failure as a keeper of the jail. At the same time, though, other futile efforts to guard the prisoners and stop a lynch mob came from the sheriff's office, except for one deputy sheriff, and a citizen's guard of law-abiding residents.

The organization of Wichita County and the incorporation of the town of Wichita Falls occurred in the 1880s. Before that decade the area was basically Indian lands with a few white settlers, the most prominent ones being the Barwise family. The town became the county seat and a railroad transportation and supply center for the surrounding countryside. At the turn of the century the discovery of oil in Wichita County brought an economic boom. As settlers moved in, the population of Wichita Falls increased from 1,987 by 1890 to 8,200 by 1910. The town had come of age.[2]

In the late 1800s the reading public in Texas and the nation followed the adventures in the popular press of the notorious outlaw gangs led by the Daltons, the Youngers, Jesse and Frank James, and Sam Bass (the Texas Robin Hood). They robbed banks, trains, stagecoaches, and other enterprises. Sometimes they succeeded; sometimes they failed, as armed citizens and lawmen took action. In robbing banks in towns in Kansas, Minnesota, and Texas, these big-name bandits encountered stiff resistance. When the firing stopped, a number of them were headed for Boot Hill.

Notwithstanding these dramatic exploits, fewer bank robberies took place in the western lands in McDonald's day than occurred in the older states along the Atlantic seaboard. Until post-Civil War Texas, few chartered banks existed in the state. As more banks opened their doors for business, they still did not have a guaranty-fund system to secure deposits. By the 1890s banking institutions in the states and territories became more secure, with armed guards and better safes, vaults, and timing devices. Yet lawbreakers countered with daytime holdups and nighttime break-ins, even using nitroglycerin to blow the doors on those safes and vaults. At times these thieves cased the bank before trying to rob it. But they could not foresee all the things that could go wrong.

Like those who robbed trains, bank robbers stood at the apex of the pecking order of criminality in the Old West. Robbery can be defined as the use or threat of force to take property from another person. In western parlance the phrase, "cash in his six-shooter," meant an outlaw holding up a bank.[3] Motivated by greed and status needs, such desperadoes aroused deep-seated emotions of fear, revulsion, and outrage in law-abiding citizens. The residents of a town would especially take action when a robbery of a financial institution went awry. In the turmoil that followed, armed citizens pursued those who committed the crime of robbery murder. Hopefully, police officers and judges would enter the picture and arrest, jail, and try those who robbed banks, trains, and individual Texans.

In the formative stages of the development of Wichita Falls a bank robbery took place. Before the era of Captain Bill, three bandits tried to rob the private bank of John James in March 1884. One of the gang had informed on the others to the Rangers. Members of Company C under George Schmitt killed one outlaw and captured another. Those in the ranging company then pursued and overtook the third robber miles from the scene of the crime. They also arrested a fourth person, charged with being an accomplice of the bank robbers. All prisoners wound up in the jail of the sheriff of Wichita County. To his superiors Schmitt wrote, "all quiet now."[4]

On February 25, 1896, in the middle of the afternoon, two outlaws walked into the City National Bank in Wichita Falls. Inside the bank, housed in a three-story brick building, the robbers encountered four men: Frank Dorsey, cashier; O. J. Kendall, vice president and a director; P. P. Langford, bookkeeper; and John L. Nickles. Unlike the others, Nickles was not injured. One chronicler wrote, "Friends said he was so thin that he took refuge in an ink bottle."[5]

The particulars of this crime of robbery murder appeared in newspapers throughout the state. Between two and three o'clock in the afternoon, the two bandits without disguises entered the bank from different directions, one from the front entrance and the other through the rear door. The robber in the back of the bank, Elmer "Kid" Lewis, encountered Langford and said "Up! Up!." When Langford asked what was the meaning of this intrusion, he was struck across the head with a six-shooter. The next instant Lewis killed Dorsey when a bullet hit him in the shoulder and neck, as he reached for a gun under the cash drawer. The vice president of the bank narrowly missed being shot too. A bullet from Lewis' weapon struck a hypodermic case in Kendall's pocket and he went down. Langford managed to maneuver to the front of the bank in order to escape through that door, but he was fired upon and wounded in the hip by the desperado—Foster Crawford—entering the bank from that direction. The bookkeeper, however, still managed to give the alarm. The outlaws scooped up several hundred dollars and fled.[6]

Crawford and Lewis rushed out the back door of the bank to get their stolen horses in the alley. In their dash they "pushed aside unarmed J. D. Avis." Then Deputy Sheriff Frank Hardesty fired and hit one of the horses. In turn, Hardesty's life was saved when a bullet from Crawford's gun struck his watch in his vest pocket. The two desperadoes rode double out of town and headed towards the Oklahoma country. In their attempt to escape, they twice seized fresh mounts, once from farmer William Neal on his way to the town and the second time from another farmer working his land.[7]

The two bank robbers might have made their escape without the actions of the aroused townspeople. In the midst of gunfire and confusion, local residents took off after Crawford and Lewis. On horseback and on foot, scores of armed citizens, like City Marshal J. D. Davis and Will Skeen, a newspaperman, chased the outlaws through the countryside. Besides firing shots, these angry westerners accomplished two things. First, the pursuing parties harassed the two riders until they stopped and took refuge in a thicket before crossing the state line. Second, the armed men surrounded this hiding place and cut off escape routes for the bandits. Crawford and Lewis had two choices: either fight or surrender.[8]

At this moment the Texas Rangers entered the picture. Rumors about an impending bank robbery in Wichita Falls had existed for some time. In September 1895 Sergeant Sullivan and other Rangers guarded the banks in the town for several days at the request of the sheriff.[9] On February 23, 1896, McDonald and his men left El Paso after assisting in the stoppage of the infamous prizefight. On the way to their headquarters in the Panhandle by train, Sullivan and two other Rangers stopped off at Wichita Falls on the twenty-fourth, with two more members of Company B doing the same at Bowie. As the Rangers left these towns, word reached them and McDonald at Bellevue on the twenty-fifth that the City National

Bank in Wichita Falls had been robbed and several people killed and injured. Captain Bill and five Rangers, Harwell, McCauley, McClure, Queen, and Sullivan, rode the rails to the town, arriving about four o'clock in the afternoon. They mounted horses provided by the townspeople and the chase was on.[10]

In retrospect, the manhunt by the Rangers occurred in three stages. Initially McDonald and his men had to ride hard to catch up to the fleeing fugitives and their pursuing parties. Then the Rangers, after reaching the place where the bandits left their horses, had to move through rough country on foot at night to find the hiding place of Crawford and Lewis. Three Rangers went into the thicket and forced the outlaws to surrender without a shot being fired. Finally, the prisoners had to be brought back to Wichita Falls, placed in the jail, and guarded until the court trial. To the surprise of some, the final step became the most difficult to carry out.

During the manhunt the members of Company B traveled approximately sixteen miles. Around five o'clock the Rangers reached the place where the robbers quit their horses. Then they followed the trail afoot for three miles through brush and water up to their armpits. Although McDonald gave credit to the armed citizens for following and cornering the bandits, only McDonald, McCauley, and McClure went into the thicket in the darkness, covered Crawford and Lewis with their guns, and forced them to surrender. One news story had McDonald saying, "Throw up your hands, or I will bore a hole in you that will let the moon shine in." With the capture of the two outlaws around ten or ten-thirty in the evening, the Rangers also recovered the stolen money and horses. Captain Bill was "proud" of the way the Rangers carried out their duties.[11]

In communications with his superiors and interviews with newspapermen, McDonald filled in the details of the capture. At one point the Ranger captain said:

> ... you can imagine that it is a little more comfortable in other places I can name than in a dense thicket at night with now and

> then a stray moonbeam straggling through and the expectation that every moment two desperate men known as good shots would confront you. We were not long in finding our game sitting down across a small lake, about ten steps from us. Before we saw them up came the guns, but Crawford called me by name and said they would surrender if I would protect them. I can't shoot a man when his hands are up, so we waded the lake, keeping our game covered, secured their pistols and the sack of booty and were ready for the march to Wichita Falls. It is always the case that when danger is most imminent the amusing happens. The robbers were willing to do most anything but wade that lake, which myself and my two boys had just enjoyed, and it took muscle to get them in it, and as I may be churched I will not give you the mild language I used to urge them to take to the water.[12]

Sergeant Sullivan played an important-but-limited role in this affair. Deputy United States Marshal Chris Madsen of the Oklahoma Territory did request information from Sullivan about the robbery and the location of the outlaws so that appropriate action could be taken in conjunction with the Rangers and local peace officers.[13] But, as McDonald noted, "It was during the run that Sergt. Sullivan was thrown from his horse on account of a broken stirrup and had a rib broken."[14] In his memoirs Sullivan maintained that all the Rangers went into the thicket, McDonald and four men from one side and the sergeant from the other side. Together they forced the surrender of the robbers.[15] But that was not so. Sullivan had a deep-seated need to be recognized as a Ranger whose abilities matched those of his captain.

After their capture, Crawford and Lewis had to be transported to Wichita Falls and put in the jail. In the wee hours of October 26, the Rangers and the armed citizens brought their prisoners back to the town. The shackled robbers were placed in a wagon driven by John Hester with deputized Tony Thornberry beside the driver. Several Rangers also occupied seats in the wagon, while other members of Company B accompanied the conveyance. The journey ended around two o'clock a.m., when the wife of Deputy Sheriff Hardesty locked the cell door behind the desperadoes. With their incarceration the duties of the Ranger captain did not end. At one point he and others went looking for a third robber without success. At another time McDonald faced armed townspeople at the jail. He told them that the Rangers would protect the prisoners. Captain Bill ordered the crowd to disperse—which they did.[16]

From dawn to dusk on the twenty-sixth several events, good and bad, took place. For one thing, townspeople came to the jail and identified Crawford. Local residents knew him as a drinking-and-brawling cowboy who worked for ranchers in the area. Lewis turned out to be an eighteen-year-old-lad from Missouri. Both individuals broke the law in North Texas and elsewhere. For another thing, as McDonald and Hardesty ousted people from the jail and closed the doors, a rumor spread that the Rangers would remove the prisoners by rail to another town. Immediately, citizens with Winchesters appeared on the scene to stop such action. Then at five o'clock McDonald and his men left on the north-bound train.[17] Captain Bill knew that District Judge George Miller believed an attempt to lynch the captured robbers "might be made." But the Rangers of Company B, with limited manpower, needed to be at other hot spots and could not stay in Wichita Falls "indefinitely."[18]

Mob spirit prevailed on the day of the twenty-sixth. Locals and other Texans who came to the town gathered in small groups. They talked about the current robbery murder in terms of a crime wave in the region and vowed vengeance. The funeral of Dorsey in early evening further inflamed passions. One person described the thought-patterns of those who wanted to take the law into their own hands: "The gathering last night was not a mob, but a congregation of law-abiding citizens dealing out justice by a short cut."[19]

At one point a newspaper reported, "The storm was brewing." A number of townsmen had been selected to lead the actions of the mob in an orderly way. Between eight and nine in the evening of the twenty-sixth, the fire bell rang and shots were fired. With this signal, scores of armed men rushed the jail. Judge Miller and other leading citizens mounted the jail porch and tried to reason with the mob to allow the law to run its course to no avail. Miller finally said, "I have before God tried to do my full duty." At the same time Deputy Sheriff Hardesty prepared to defend the jail. He poked his rifle through the grating of one door. But those on the outside grabbed the barrel of the gun. Then more members of the mob battered down the other door and entered the jail. In the melee that ensued, they overpowered Hardesty and the other jail guards. Mob leaders even had to smash the lock on the cell door, as Hardesty refused to yield the keys.[20]

The mob finally had their hands on the two desperadoes. Crawford and Lewis were brought down the stairs from the second-story cell block. The lynchers marched their prisoners to a corner near the bank. In the light of a bonfire the killers were placed on the top of boxes and hanged from the telephone pole. Lewis went first, cursing and daring his attackers to pull the rope. "He had on high-heeled boots, black pants and a deep red flannel shirt," read a news release, "which added a grewsome [*sic*] brilliancy to the scene." As Crawford watched this happen, he became unnerved. With his "red face and short-clipped black mustache," he went to his death talking incoherently. The bodies of the hanged outlaws were not burned or riddled with bullets by those taking part in the lynching party. Several well-armed men, though, made sure that the bodies of Crawford and Lewis were not cut down until the wee hours of February 27.[21]

The ordeal of a lynching had ended. In analyzing the deaths of the two outlaws a newspaper reporter wrote, "The sight of a man hanged by the neck is a gruesome one. The features are contorted. The eyes seem about to leap from their sockets. The tongue protrudes, hideously. The neck seems much longer than in life and its length is to increase as the minutes pass."[22]

In this affair Sheriff C. M. Moses of Wichita County found himself in an untenable position. He had left town before the robbery murder looking for Crawford in the lands from Texas to Oklahoma. The sheriff returned to Wichita Falls a few hours after the two robbers had been hanged. Moses not only missed the manhunt and capture of the killers but also could not convince the townspeople to cut down the bodies of Crawford and Lewis from the pole.[23]

As acting governor in the absence of Culberson, Lieutenant Governor George T. Jester sent Sheriff Moses a telegram criticizing recent events. At one point Jester emphasized that the people in Wichita Falls who seized the prisoners from law officers "committed an act that is unjustifiable, indefensible and should be condemned by all law-abiding citizens, and casts a blot on the county and state."[24] In response the sheriff maintained, "I regret very much the actions the people took in lynching Crawford and Lewis. I was out after them at the time, 40 miles from home. When I heard it I came as soon as I could get here. My deputies did all they could. I was disarmed and taken away when I arrived, just as I was going in the jail."[25]

Years after the hangings a newsman pointed out a truism about the Rangers in the manhunt and its aftermath. "In the minds of many Wichitans," he wrote, "a question mark hung over the conduct of Bill McDonald that day. He must have known—no one could have failed to know—that the mob spirit was developing fast and that an attempt would be made to lynch the prisoners. In the face of that knowledge, he and his fellows left town, catching the afternoon train to Quanah, en route to the Territory."[26]

When Captain Bill heard about the hangings, he telegraphed his superiors that he would return to Wichita Falls on February 27. Upon his arrival, he viewed the bodies of Crawford and Lewis and questioned local residents. "The men are very dead," read McDonald's initial reaction to the lynchings, "but we feel that we have done our duty in full." Before the Ranger captain left town on the twenty-eighth, he also informed central command that he failed to "find anybody that knows anything about the hanging except that they were strangers or women [men?] in disguise."27

Why did Captain Bill and the men under his command leave the town to mob law? In his correspondence McDonald listed several reasons. For one thing, he noted that the members of Company B had been away from their headquarters for several weeks, as they took action against the prizefight in El Paso. He felt that other duties elsewhere needed to be taken care of by the rank and file of the company as soon as possible. McDonald also believed that the sheriff's office and a guard of twenty-five men would be able to handle the situation. Most important, the Ranger commander wrote that "everything was perfectly quiet when we left."[28]

Nevertheless, Captain Bill was stung by the criticism, as expressed to the governor by citizens of Wichita Falls, that blamed him and his men for not staying and holding off the mob. Judge Miller especially believed that McDonald should have stayed. In a rare moment of reflection, the Ranger captain notified his superiors that he told the judge two things. First, after "wading the river and getting wet and cold" in the manhunt, McDonald wanted to leave town on the twenty-sixth and return the next day. Judge Miller, though, "did not seem to think my men would do but wanted me to stay, that I could hold them down." Second, McDonald made a concise analysis of the outcome if he remained behind: " . . . I told the Judge I thought he was asking a good deal of me to let my small force go and stay there alone, all crippled up any way and nearly sick and tackle a mob of several hundred, probably have to kill some of them and get killed myself . . . ."[29]

In the mythical world Captain Bill kept coming on. In the real world conflicting thoughts crisscrossed his mind. In this case McDonald's ability to make a courageous stand can be questioned. And the decision he did make backfired on him. Then a Ranger must be able, in McDonald's own words, to "stand a reasonable amount of abuse [at long range]."[30]

In retrospect, McDonald's faith in the ability of local law officers to protect the prisoners was misplaced. Either all or some of the Rangers should have stayed or they should have tried to move the prisoners to another location for safekeeping. Captain Bill knew the outcome if he stayed there alone—being disarmed or gunned down by an angry mob. Still, in the southern code of honor, he needed to stay and save face.

In the aftermath of the bank robbery judicial officials carried out their duties. A justice of the peace held inquests into the deaths of Dorsey, Crawford, and Lewis at a funeral home and his office. In due time, members of a grand jury, at the insistence of Judge Miller, indicted five townspeople, one being a former sheriff, for taking part in the hangings. They were freed on bond. Then, with the transfer of the cases to other counties, and with dismissals of faulty indictments (one case being dismissed for lack of evidence), no convictions of the lynchers could be obtained.[31]

Some newspapers outside Wichita County both criticized and defended the actions of the lynch mob. The editorial page in a daily in Dallas condemned mob violence. Yet the editor noted that peace officers should have moved the prisoners to a safer place. The Dallas publishers also stated, "Justice has failed so often through petty technicalities that public confidence in the machinery of the law is at a low ebb."[32] In Fort Worth a newspaper openly declared war on outlawry. In the future border bandits could be "treated the same way."[33]

In the aftermath of the hangings, "Wichitans" had mixed feelings about the deaths of Crawford and Lewis. In the reaction to the critical statements made by the acting governor of Texas, Arch Anderson went so far in a letter to a newspaper to declare that the lynchings were "commendable and approved by the best citizens." "A more becoming sight I never witnessed," he continued, "than when I saw their bodies dangling in the breeze in front of the bank where they committed the foul murder." Yet a newsman, after talking with old-timers years later, had this to say:

One of those who expressed himself was I. Knight, who died early in 1951.

"I never held with mobs and lynching," he said; "I was kind of sorry things had to be that way."

He paused for a moment.

"You have to remember this," he said, presently, "Frank Dorsey was an awful good man."[34]

THE RANGERS, COMPANY B, AND CAPTAIN MCDONALD IN THE FIELD

A Pictorial Essay

Then mount and away! give the fleet steed the rein—
The Ranger's at home on the prairies again:
Spur! spur in the chase, dash on to the fight,
Cry Vengeance for Texas! and God speed the right.

—"War Song of the Texas Rangers," in Thomas Knowles, *They Rode for the Lone Star*)

Governor Culberson, from among the rest,
Chose four Rangers, whom he thought best.
He ordered us to San Saba to put down crime—
We met in Goldthwaite, all on time.
Two from the Panhandle, two from the Rio Grande,
Which made a jolly little Ranger band.

We stopped at a hotel to stay all night.
From what the people said, we expected a fight.
They puffed and blowed, and said we were in danger;
For a bushwhacker didn't like a Ranger.
We laughed at such talk, and considered it fun;
But wherever we went, we carried our gun.

—"Texas Rangers after the Mob," in W. J. L. Sullivan, *Twelve Years in the Saddle for Law and Order on the Frontiers of Texas*)

SOURCE: ALBERT BIGELOW PAINE, *CAPTAIN BILL MCDONALD, TEXAS RANGER: A STORY OF FRONTIER REFORM*, 1909, FRONTISPIECE.

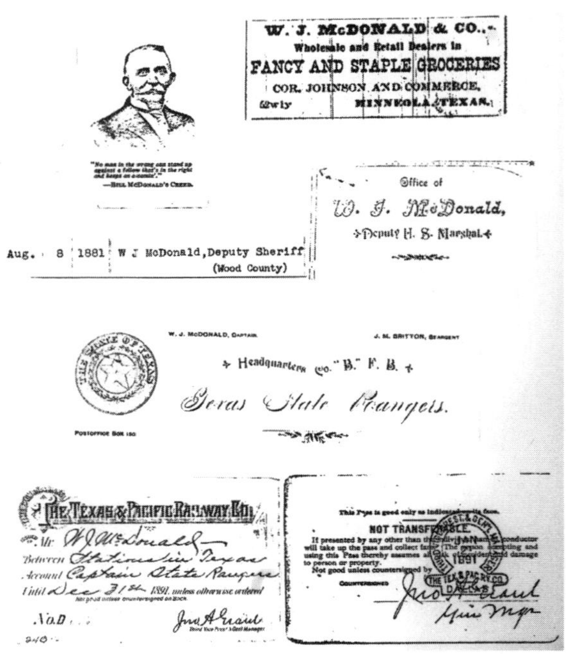

A collage of McDonald's careers outside and inside law enforcement. The advertisement for his grocery store came from the Dallas *Weekly Herald*, Feb. 28, 1874. The other items appeared in various archival records. Before his years as a Ranger captain, McDonald served as a deputy sheriff and a deputy US marshal. As an officer in the Frontier Battalion, he liked to use the phrase, "Texas State Rangers." During the era of the Frontier Battalion, railroads issued passes to the Rangers, either for the entire route or from station to station, in different ways: free trips or tickets issued at half-price or the full amount. At the end of his life McDonald's motto appeared on his letterhead paper. See AP 1114, PP. (COURTESY HAROLD J. WEISS, JR.)

Woodford H. Mabry (1856–1899) was a Texan by birth and adjutant general of Texas by appointment of the governor in 1891. In this role he replaced Wilburn H. King. Bill McDonald first served as a Ranger captain under the tutelage of the able and efficient Mabry. Mabry left the office of adjutant general in 1898 to serve in the Spanish-American War. (COURTESY TEXAS STATE LIBRARY AND ARCHIVES COMMISSION.)

The office of the adjutant general of the state of Texas at the turn of the twentieth century. The adjutant general and his staff, like E. M. Phelps pictured above, manned this command post for the Frontier Battalion (1874–1901) and the Ranger Force (1901–1935). Orders and reports passed between the adjutant general's office and Ranger Company B under the command of Bill McDonald. (COURTESY TEXAS STATE LIBRARY AND ARCHIVES COMMISSION.)

Standing from left: James A. Brooks, John H. Rogers, _____ Waite (or Thurlow A. Weed); seated from left: Lamartine P. "Lam" Sieker, John B. Armstrong, and William J. "Bill" McDonald. The classic photograph of the different types of Rangers by the late 1800s: the organizational Ranger, like Sieker; the intrepid Ranger in the citizen-soldier tradition, such as "Little McNelly" Armstrong; and the hard-bitten peace officers and dauntless crime fighters, including Brooks, McDonald, and Rogers.

Armstrong (1850–1913): Born in Tennessee, he came to Texas and joined the ranging company under the command of McNelly in the 1870s. He rose to the rank of lieutenant and became known as "McNelly's Bulldog." After his Ranger service, Armstrong served as a US marshal and owned a ranch.

Brooks (1855–1944): Born in Kentucky, he joined the Rangers in the early 1880s and rose through the ranks to be a celebrated captain until his retirement in the first decade of the twentieth century. In his later life Brooks became the faithful public servant by serving as a state legislator and as a county judge of Brooks County (named in his honor).

Rogers (1863–1930): Born in Texas, he joined the Ranger service in the early 1880s and rose through the ranks to become a captain in the next decade. Rogers belonged to the group called the "Christian Rangers," along with M. T. Gonzaullas, P. B. Hill, A. T. "Augie" Old, and Thalis Cook. In his later life Rogers also served as a United States marshal and chief of police in the city of Austin.

Sieker (1848–1914): Born in Maryland, he fought with distinction in the Confederate army in the American Civil War. By the early 1900s Sieker had joined the Rangers, rose through the ranks to become captain of Company D, and twice served as battalion quartermaster in the Frontier Battalion and the Ranger Force. In his administrative role Sieker stressed discipline and following rules and regulations. (Courtesy Chuck Parsons.)

Samuel A. McMurry (1847–1914): Born in Tennessee, he came to Texas in the aftermath of the Civil War. He first joined Lee Hall's Special Force of Rangers along the border in the late 1870s and then took command of Company B of the Frontier Battalion at the start of the next decade. In a quiet way Ranger Captain McMurry gave creditable service in frontier lands and in areas involved in labor-management strife. After McDonald succeeded him as head of Company B, McMurry entered the business world outside the state of Texas and is buried in Missouri. (COURTESY WESTERN HISTORY COLLECTIONS, UNIVERSITY OF OKLAHOMA LIBRARIES.)

Members of Company B at Thurber at the end of the 1880s. Unlike the change of commanders in other companies of the Frontier Battalion, the transition from McMurry to McDonald took place with a minimum of problems. Important in the changeover would be the coming and going of the sergeants pictured above (left to right): figure 4, Thomas Platt; figure 9, W. J. L. Sullivan; and figure 12, James M. "Grude" Britton. Britton replaced Platt as sergeant when McDonald assumed command of the company and Sullivan replaced Britton in 1894. Also notice figures 5 and 8, Sam Platt and his wife with her rifle. (COURTESY PRINTS AND PHOTOGRAPHS COLLECTION, CENTER FOR AMERICAN HISTORY, UNIVERSITY OF TEXAS AT AUSTIN.)

Texas rangers in camp near San Saba, Texas, 1897. Edgar Neal,(not present) was also a member (who was sheriff of San Saba county later.) From left to right: Ollie Perry, Jack Harrell, Dr. Donnelly, James Bell, Billie McCauley, Dudley Barker, Van Lane, Robert McClure and Captain Bill McDonald.

A mirror-like image of an encampment of Company B with dramatic overtones. On the one hand, Rangers in the field lived and worked together at semipermanent sites to fight crime and disorder. On the other hand, a closer look at McDonald's stance (far right) will show elements of the quintessential Texas Ranger: a badge of authority pinned on his chest; a revolver at his side and a rifle ready for mortal combat; and piercing eyes and a wiry body that made him a manhunter extraordinary. The captions for such photographs can contain numerous errors. In the one cited above the correct spellings of the names of two Rangers would be Jack Harwell and Ed Donelley. In addition, Edgar Neal was really a member of Company E who worked with McDonald's Rangers, and James Bell might not have been a member of Company B in that year. (COURTESY WESTERN HISTORY COLLECTIONS, UNIVERSITY OF OKLAHOMA LIBRARIES.)

The Panhandle Rangers: the "boys," as they were called, in time and space. Back row from left: Jack Harwell, John L. Sullivan, Bob Pease, Arthur Jones, Ed Connell, and Lee Queen. Front row from left: Billy McCauley, Bob McClure, Wesley Cates, and Ben Owens. (COURTESY TEXAS STATE LIBRARY AND ARCHIVES COMMISSION.)

The best-known photograph of the Frontier Battalion of Texas Rangers, as they gathered in El Paso to stop the prizefight. Bringing together the rank and file and their officers did not happen too often in Ranger annals. The first row shows the pyramid Ranger organization in the late 1800s (left to right): Adjutant General William H. Mabry (in a Napoleonic stance) and the "Four Great Captains," John Hughes (Co. D), James Brooks (Co. F), Bill McDonald (Co. B), and John Rogers (Co. E). To some McDonald's stance illustrates his showmanship qualities. A closer look at the photo, though, shows that other Rangers were also holding their rifles in unique positions. (COURTESY TEXAS STATE LIBRARY AND ARCHIVES COMMISSION.)

Another pose for the same picture. Here Bill McDonald blends in with the other Ranger captains. McDonald had the ability to subordinate himself in the organizational structure when he had to be less conspicuous. A number of the rank and file of Company B appear in the third row (left to right): first position, William McCauley (standing on the side of the steps with two rifles); second position, Lee Queen; fifth position, Ed Donelley; sixth position, Sgt. W. J. L. Sullivan (with the Moses beard); seventh position, Jack Harwell; and eighth position, Robert McClure. A few state Rangers from the various companies did not appear in the photograph. (COURTESY TEXAS STATE LIBRARY AND ARCHIVES COMMISSION.)

Hardeman County Jail: The plaque in front of the building reads as follows: "This native stone jail building was begun in 1890, when Quanah became Hardeman County seat, and completed in March 1891. The lower floor housed the sheriff's office and living quarters, while the second floor held prisoners' cells. Malon C. Owens served the longest term as county sheriff in this building, from 1936 to 1964. Jail facilities were relocated in 1973. This structure was renovated by community effort in 1976 for use as a museum." (COURTESY HAROLD J. WEISS, JR.)

Upon becoming a Texas Ranger captain: McDonald's well-dressed appearance at that moment. (COURTESY OF THE TEXAS RANGER HALL OF FAME AND MUSEUM, WACO, TEXAS.)

PART TWO

WANING DAYS OF THE FRONTIER BATTALION

His dogged persistence and stealthy tactics are the real secret of his success, not his feisty marksmanship or braggadocio. McDonald enjoys shooting at game from horseback. His proficiency at picking off prairie dogs and birds is notable.

—John Miller Morris, ed., *A Private in the Texas Rangers: A. T. Miller of Company B, Frontier Battalion.*

McDonald was an intrepid and resolute figure, of undoubted courage. There were, and are, those who doubt that he was the combination of Sir Galahad, David Crockett, Frank Merriwell and J. Edgar Hoover . . . .

—Column by John Gould in Wichita *Daily Times*, June 17, 1951.

"Well," said Captain Bill, sorrowfully, "I seem to be in a mighty bad fix. If I stay, I'll be filled with bullets, and if I go, I'll lose my wife. I s'pose I'll have to stay."

—Albert B. Paine, *Captain Bill McDonald, Texas Ranger: A Story of Frontier Reform.*

Capt. [McDonald] stood by me & the boys in all we had done [at San Saba].

—Sullivan to W. H. Owen, May 27, 1897, Quartermaster Returns, RR-AGR.

I dont know what Sullivan is going to do . . . .

—McDonald to Owen, June 24, 1897, Quartermaster Returns, RR-AGR.

Chapter 7

SAN SABA MOB: A MURDER SOCIETY

There are men still alive, however, who think the whole campaign against the Mob was unnecessary. "We didn't need the Rangers," they will tell you. "The Mob was made up of the best people and they were only trying to make the county fit for decent folks to live in. If they had let us alone we would have handled everything without outside help. We were doing all right."

Then they will caution you: "If you tell anybody I said this I'll say you are a liar."

So you don't tell anybody.[1]

As the decade of the 1890s came to a close, McDonald and Company B became involved in more complex criminal cases than in previous years. His attention was directed to the age-old phenomenon of feuding in Texas. He also strove to solve heinous murders by secretive mobs and unsuspecting parties who preyed upon their fellow Texans. Increasingly Captain Bill and the Panhandle Rangers were ordered to investigate acts of crime and violence in the central and eastern portions of the state. By the turn of the century, the need for the services of the Frontier Battalion had not diminished. Yet the use of a legal technicality in the courts brought a sudden end to that organization. In none of these celebrated cases did McDonald act as a sole Ranger.

The years in question overlapped several gubernatorial administrations in the state. No governor at the turn of the century equaled the deeds of Hogg as a champion of people's rights. Yet Governor Culberson (1895–1899) sympathized with Hogg's regulatory policies for big business. At the same time he supported tax relief for Texans caught in the depression years and tried to economize in governmental expenses. From 1898 to 1906, after the agitation of the Hogg years and the emotional events of the Spanish-American War, an era of political tranquility and governmental conservatism dominated Texan politics. Two genteel and principled governors presided over this age of harmony: Joseph D. Sayers and Samuel W. T. Lanham. In his two terms Sayers especially tried to attract new manufacturing concerns to Texas, and the discovery of the Spindletop oil field near Beaumont in 1901 brought an economic boom. In national politics new personalities in the United States Senate at the turn of the century, like, for example, Joseph W. Bailey, would come into contact with McDonald in the performance of his duties as a Texas Ranger.[2]

Through the centuries the farming and ranching lands of San Saba County in Central Texas attracted Indian tribes, Spanish grantees, and Anglo-American settlers. Well-watered by streams and rivers, the region became an agricultural frontier in early Texas. Economic activity centered around grazing cattle, goats, and sheep, as well as growing cotton, oats, and wheat. Organized in the middle of the 1850s, with the town of San Saba as the county seat, San Saba County increased in population until the years of Mob turmoil. Still, at the turn of the century 7,569 people lived in the area. By that time residents had fought for the Confederacy and helped to defend the frontier.[3]

Throughout history crowds of ordinary people can turn into a mob (some would say rabble) when their numbers increase, a sharing of information takes place, and a feeling of anonymity arises in their bosoms. From England to America mobs, either spontaneous or organized, have played many different roles. In the 1700s in London, England, mobs not only aided in apprehending criminals but also took to the streets to punish antisocial behavior and carry out political demonstrations. In the same century in colonial America, mobs opposed British rule. They especially carried out mob law by seizing those who remained loyal to the British crown. These

Loyalists were stripped of their clothes and then covered with tar and feathers. Mobs, in addition, rioted in Jacksonian America. Usually the leaders and the other members of this mobocracy were anti in nature: against, for example, abolitionists, Roman Catholics, and Irish immigrants. The struggle between the Irish newcomers and those who came before—the nativists—resulted in sacking and burning buildings and killing and wounding individuals. Both sides fired small arms and cannons at each other. By McDonald's day the fear of mob vengeance had not disappeared. Unruly Texans appeared before jails guarded by the Rangers. These disgruntled individuals were ready to disarm peace officers, break into cells, and take their prisoners to a necktie party.

In Texas there have been a great many different mobs over the years which have plotted in secret to scare, injure, run out, or do away with undesirable characters in their regions. One such mob arose in the 1880s and 1890s in San Saba County, particularly the northern parts of the county with the community at Locker at the center of mob activity. Active also in adjoining counties like Brown and Mills, the San Saba Mob arose in reaction to a gang of rustlers who ran off stock and used a group of witnesses to make up alibis and prevent the law from taking its course. Like all those involved in vigilante justice, the originators of this group found it difficult in time to control its activities, as inoffensive people and personal enemies became targets. By the late 1890s Texas Rangers had entered the area as state authorities in Austin became concerned about mob actions.[4]

In their investigations the Rangers substantiated the known facts about the San Saba Mob. First, preachers and pious men belonged to the secret society.[5] Second, the Mob, as it was referred to in McDonald's reports, was organized with "obligation instructions," "signs," and "pass words."[6] Captain Bill could not believe what he had run up against. He wrote the adjutant general that "this is the worst & biggest thing on earth made so by the prominence of many of their members. The Commanches [*sic*] were never so bad according to my notion nor nothing else I ever heard of."[7]

Dozens of killings have been attributed to the bloody work of the Mob. Four slayings over a span of seven years not only became the keys to the cases developed by the Rangers but also showed the nature of the Mob's vengeance. The trademark of these assassins was to put nine bullets into the head and body of each victim:

First murder: In the spring of 1889 J. R. Turner, an anti-Mob resident who ran the post office in Locker and kept a farm, received a warning from several men to leave town or face death. Three months later, members of the Mob caught Turner "in his field plowing cotton and riddled him with bullets." His wife and daughter, several hundred yards away—an important point in the subsequent murder trial—recognized the two killers. But fear made the women remain silent.

Second murder: In August 1893, James Brown, a young man whom the Mob thought was dishonest, went to a revival meeting near China Knob. As he rode away from the religious gathering, those in the Mob ambushed and killed him with a shotgun blast. Other shots wounded his wife.

Third murder: In June 1896, Mob members from their hiding place gunned down T. A. Henderson while he was cutting cord wood. His attackers wounded his brother who returned the fire. For years Henderson had tried to get those who had temporarily driven him out of the area tried and convicted. When this proved unsuccessful in the courtroom, Henderson himself was arrested on grounds of perjury and was out on bond when he was shot.

Fourth murder: A few days after the death of Henderson, members of the Mob shot and killed William James while he was getting water with a wagon from the Colorado River at Hannah Crossing. His corpse had the usual nine bullet holes in it. James had talked about the Henderson murder during a family gathering. His children repeated his remarks while playing and word spread that he had broken the silence.[8]

Public officials and concerned citizens in San Saba County and the surrounding areas informed state authorities about this homicidal violence by the Mob. In 1889 the district judge took pains to describe to the adjutant general the nature of the murders, the operation of grand juries, and the need to relocate and protect witnesses.[9] Another Texan wrote the adjutant general's office about the numerous murders, including that of James, in San Saba County. At one point he said, "The people in all counties around are afraid to speak of this mob—county is terrorized." He ended with a plea, "For Gods sake do something."[10]

The reaction of W. M. Allison, judge of the Thirty-Third Judicial District, to the violent acts of the Mob influenced state officials. At the end of 1895 he told the adjutant general that he would not contact Captain Brooks. The appearance of Sergeant Sullivan at a court session would suffice.[11] The murders of Henderson and James prompted Allison to contact Adjutant General Mabry in June 1896 about setting up a "permanent" Ranger camp in San Saba County. "Our people in the northern portion of this county," Allison's letter began, "are in need of such protection as can be afforded them by the Ranger force."[12] A few weeks later the judge noted to Mabry that he and the county sheriff would come to Austin to meet with the adjutant general and the governor.[13] When this meeting failed to materialize as expected, Allison sent a letter to the governor at the end of July. In it he stressed that Culberson knew the terrible "situation" in the county. The governor had to realize that the enforcement of the criminal laws in the region depended upon his "early action." Most important, the judge concluded that four or five Rangers, including Sullivan, who knew the people and the country, needed to be sent. Allison also wanted the state to offer rewards for the assassins of Henderson and James.[14]

Those in control of state government responded to the demands made by local authorities. On July 30, 1896, the adjutant general ordered McDonald to prepare to dispatch Sullivan and another Ranger to San Saba County to meet two members of the company commanded by Captain Rogers.[15] In communications to McDonald and Sheriff S. E. W. Hudson of San Saba County on August 6, Mabry filled in the particulars. He instructed the Ranger captain to send the two members of Company B to Goldthwaite, where they would meet the other Rangers and a wagon provided by the sheriff. The men needed to bring with them their saddles, blankets, and clothing. Horses would be provided by the sheriff. And tents would be sent from central headquarters. Sergeant Sullivan, as the officer in charge, and the other Rangers had the duty to assist the sheriff in "restoring order" and "making arrests" of those who violated the law.[16]

The Ranger organization was now in motion. Company B sent Sullivan and Dudley S. Barker on August 11. From southern Texas came Edgar T. Neal and Allen R. Maddox of Company E. These four Rangers arrived on August 13, pitched a tent camp at Hannah Crossing on the Colorado River, miles up the railroad tracks from the town of San Saba, and started to search for answers to the killings carried out by the Mob.[17] Sullivan later wrote that each Ranger "shook hands" and "made a solemn pledge that we would stay there and do our duty if we all had to die together."[18]

Five law officers became the key figures in the drama that followed: Judge Allison, Captain Bill, Sergeant Sullivan, the newly elected sheriff—A. J. Hawkins—and the incoming district attorney, W. C. Linden. Old-timers in Central Texas remembered the bearded Sullivan with "mixed feelings." His "strange combination of egotism and bravery" not only brought investigative results but also ended in conflict with McDonald, Captain Rogers, and the local sheriff.[19] Both Sullivan and McDonald believed that Hawkins was a pliant lawman in the hands of the Mob and that his predecessors had actually belonged to the murderous society.[20] Yet Hawkins and Linden praised Sullivan.[21] Linden wrote that the Ranger sergeant was the "man of all men to handle this matter," since his work was "intelligent, thorough and courageous."[22]

Like most Rangers, Sullivan had to handle a number of criminal cases at the same time. While looking into the Mob murders from the closing days of 1896 to the beginning months of 1897, the Ranger sergeant continued to carry out other duties. In September 1896 Sullivan went to Collingsworth County to help keep the peace.[23] Two months later he and his Ranger detachment went to Brown County and arrested three men for robbing a store. At the same time Neal went to New Mexico looking for a cattle thief wanted by the San Saba sheriff.[24] Then at the start of 1897 Sullivan and other Rangers in San Saba County and the surrounding areas took into custody lawbreakers for burglary, disturbing the peace, and theft of cattle and horses—and an overcoat. The Ranger sergeant even went to Vernon, guarded the jail, testified in assault and murder cases, and arrested a fleeing desperado.[25]

Initially, Sullivan informed his superiors that the Rangers had trouble gathering information about the Mob. Local residents were "afraid to talk."[26] Yet, through the efforts of Judge Allison and U. M. "Mitch" Sanderson, a local newspaper editor, some citizens admitted that the Mob was a dangerous element and started a crusade to ferret out its members. In response to the rising indignation, mass meetings took place in several communities. At one gathering resolutions were passed supporting the Rangers and condemning the "practice of secret assassination."[27]

Sergeant Sullivan and his detachment carried out investigative procedures that had become commonplace to the Rangers in their law enforcement work. Sullivan used his knowledge of the region, its inhabitants, and their court system to find people with knowledge of Mob members.[28] He and his men especially scouted in Brown, Mills, and San Saba counties.[29] At one point the Ranger sergeant made an effort to locate a brother of the murdered Henderson without success.[30] At another time, Barker, Neal, and Sullivan guarded a person who reported that the Mob would try to kill him.[31] In order to effectively carry out such actions, the Rangers needed patience and the ability to listen to people talk. District

Attorney Linden once wrote that county residents have "unlimited confidence" in Sullivan.[32]

Sergeant Sullivan, the other Rangers, and Linden began to collect information about several key killings, with emphasis on the Turner murder in 1889. Following established methods, Sullivan took the lead in collecting statements from witnesses, no matter who they were, in an attempt to get at the truth, offering protection to overcome the fear of the Mob, and handling threats of violence against the Rangers. A nighttime guard was kept around the Ranger camp.[33] Sullivan even suggested to the adjutant general that an undercover detective or two be planted within the ranks of the Mob.[34] As a result of these efforts, the cases against George W. Trowbridge and old, pious Matt Ford, who had been indicted by the grand jury in 1895 for the murder of Turner, was strengthened.[35] Sullivan wrote central headquarters on November 30, 1896: "We have got all the witnesses I think, & will do something if they will only try. We have got them bothered. I think they are scared pretty bad."[36]

At the end of 1896, Sullivan sustained injuries when his horse fell. This accident hampered the investigations by the Rangers. During a grand jury proceeding in another case Linden had a bailiff guard a perjured witness. When that law officer left him alone for a "few moments," the person fled. With his "usual promptness" Sullivan took off in pursuit and "while running over a very rough road his horse fell with him and broke one bone and dislocated the other of his right arm, and otherwise bruised him up considerably."[37] For a month or so, Sullivan stayed in town and did not return to the Ranger camp. The sergeant noted that his dislocated wrist had been "paining" him to "death." Sullivan returned to his duties when he could again use his guns.[38]

Judge Allison, the district attorney, and others thought about the best way to bring Ford and Trowbridge to trial for murder. The district judge informed the governor's office that he "found it necessary to change the venue" of these cases to Austin, where, presumably, Mob members had little or no influence. Allison also suggested that the state set aside funds to pay for knowledgeable San Saba lawyers to come to Austin to assist in the prosecution of the killers at the end of February 1897. The governor refused to endorse this additional legal assistance.[39] "As long as an officer dont bother that class of people," Sullivan said as the trials drew near, "he is all right with them. But just as soon as he begins to catch them & jail them, he is all rong [*sic*] in their estimation."[40]

The trials before Judge F. G. Morris of the Fifty-Third Judicial District became a drawn-out affair. At the end of February, Ford stood before the bar of justice, with District Attorney A. S. Burleson of Travis County, assisted by Linden, as prosecutors. About seventy witnesses traveled to Austin to give testimony. When no decision could be reached about murder with malice aforethought, a second trial for Ford, along with the first trial of Trowbridge, took place during the June term of the court. Witnesses who were attached in these two cases now totaled 278, with 139 testifying in the legal proceeding against Ford and seventy-two appearing at the trial of Trowbridge.[41] During the drama in the courtroom in June several Rangers appeared as witnesses: Barker, McClure, McDonald, Neal, Sullivan, and Eugene Bell of Company E.[42] The spectacle had begun.

The trials of Ford and Trowbridge during the first six months of 1897 resulted in a number of salient points. First, those who lived in San Saba County were divided into pro-Mob and anti-Mob factions. Second, Turner's wife, two daughters, and others in the know had remained silent or changed their stories out of fear of Mob reprisals. Third, a question arose whether the killers could be identified by members of the immediate family at a distance over 300 yards. Two local residents at the request of Sullivan tried to pick Trowbridge out of a group of people at that distance at the Turner place but failed. Yet McClure, Neal, and Sullivan, the latter at the request of Linden, took a similar test and recognized familiar persons at that distance. And lastly, relatives and friends provided alibis for Ford and Trowbridge in the murder of Turner. One of the more dramatic moments in the courtroom took place when a witness testified that Ford remarked he would kill Turner—that "d__d old s_n of b__h."[43]

The attempts to try and convict Ford and Trowbridge for murder ended the same way—in hung juries. Reportedly, after more than a week of deliberation, the members of the jury in the first trial of Ford were deadlocked, two for acquittal and ten for conviction (with eight for the death penalty and two for life imprisonment). The news media also reported that in the Trowbridge case the jury stood eight for conviction and four for acquittal.[44] The Ford-Trowbridge matter continued for years, finally being judicially dismissed in 1903 for insufficient evidence to bring a conviction.

Meanwhile Sullivan's troubles with Hawkins, McDonald, and Rogers increased. His overbearing manner irritated his superiors. Most important, Sullivan's deteriorating relations with the local sheriff began to affect the investigation of the Mob. Linden believed that the ill will between the Ranger sergeant and Hawkins was not personal in nature but resulted from the efforts of the Mob to get the sheriff involved in their plans to remove the Rangers from the region. In the spring of 1897 the friction between Sullivan and Hawkins reached its peak. A fugitive murderer who had been returned to San Saba County was given special visiting and meal privileges and put under lax supervision by the sheriff. Relatives of the murdered man asked Sullivan to investigate. The sergeant and other Rangers went to the jail, where, they felt, security was inadequate, the prisoner's gun even being in a place where he could get at it. Later, Sullivan publicly stated that he planned to make a complaint against the sheriff for negligence of his duties.

Then members of the Mob encouraged Hawkins to insist that this abuse and interference stop and to ask for the removal of Sullivan from the area. Linden advised Sullivan to adjust any differences with the sheriff in a peaceful way. When a meeting between the two took place in a hall outside a courtroom, Hawkins angrily replied to Sullivan's friendly advances that he was "not afraid" of the Ranger and wanted to have "nothing to do with him." Then the sheriff reached for his gun and said, "Dont you jump on me." Sullivan quietly responded by saying that nobody was going to "jump" on the sheriff and by warning Hawkins to leave his revolver alone. At the same time the Ranger "levelled" his six-shooter on the sheriff, while he was "fumbling" for his pistol. Neal stepped between Sullivan and Hawkins, and Linden informed Judge Allison of the row. Allison got Hawkins to go into the courtroom, and Sullivan and the other Rangers to move downstairs and outside into the square. Linden noted that the county assessor tried to get the sheriff to finish the fight and sought a weapon himself. Allison believed that he had more trouble handling Sullivan in this episode than Hawkins. The judge concluded, therefore, that the Ranger force in the county should be doubled and a commissioned officer, like McDonald or Rogers, should be sent in to investigate the Mob.[45]

Captain Bill now entered the San Saba affair. At the end of April 1897, the adjutant general ordered McDonald to go to the county, take charge of the Ranger force, and discuss the situation with judicial officials. The next month Mabry told McDonald to stay there until after the trials in June of Ford and Trowbridge. It was important to central command to let things return to their "normal condition." The adjutant general realized that Sullivan possessed valuable information about the activities of the Mob. He informed Linden that the Rangers, including Sullivan, would stand their ground in the fight for law and order.[46]

Captain Bill had not only to decide the status of his sergeant but also to look into the activities of the murderous society. Arriving in the county with McClure on May 4, McDonald attended court, scouted, and arrested a person for shooting up the town of San Saba. McDonald especially discovered that at first Hawkins said he would "not work" with Sullivan, although the captain warned him that in the Panhandle a sheriff who did not maintain the jail properly and failed to carry out his duties against the criminal element was ignored by the Rangers. Moreover, McDonald found that the opinion of leading citizens was divided on whether to have Sullivan return to the county or not. Since McDonald believed the Mob was trying to force the Rangers out of San Saba, Sullivan was brought back to work on the case. When Hawkins and Sullivan met, according to the Ranger captain, they "spoke as though nothing had happened."[47]

Sullivan's downfall as the investigative head in the county resulted not from his dispute with the sheriff but from his inability to get along with McDonald. His newly discovered friendship with Hawkins and elements of the Mob worried McDonald. This coupled with Sullivan's drinking sprees and, above all, his personal clash with McDonald, as he wanted more credit for the work of the Panhandle Rangers, led Captain Bill to ask for the resignation of his sergeant from the Ranger service. McDonald summed up the situation when he wrote to his superiors that he "had lost all confidence" in Sullivan.[48] Realizing that his options had run out, Sullivan resigned on July 3, 1897, and immediately sought and obtained a commission as a Special Ranger.[49] In later years he would serve in minor law enforcement roles in Texas. But the time spent in investigating the San Saba Mob proved to be the highlight of his career.[50]

Months after this chapter in Sullivan's life came to an end, Adjutant General Mabry outlined his position to several Texans on the removal of the sergeant from the Ranger service. He noted that Sullivan was an able officer who received promotions from McDonald and the central office. Sullivan's resignation did not come from a lack of bravery, but from his troublesome relations in the chain of command. After viewing the evidence, Mabry backed a Ranger captain and not a subordinate in the performance of their duties in the Frontier Battalion.[51]

Off and on throughout the rest of 1897 and 1898, Captain Bill and the other men in his command, including McCauley, the newly appointed sergeant, continued to investigate the murderous society. The San Saba detachment of Rangers now shifted the investigation to the killings of Brown and James. Although Linden and John

Seiders, county judge, gave verbal assistance, McDonald was worried about the machinations of Sheriff Hawkins and the lack of a "back bone" in Judge Allison, who seemed to treat members of the Mob with ambivalence. The Ranger captain also believed that the postmaster was reading his mail. Threats by the murderous society or their sympathizers to have the Rangers relocated or to harm McDonald and the San Saba detachment became commonplace. One warning told McDonald that they were "not a frade [*sic*]" of him or his Rangers. If Captain Bill did not leave the country, the note read, they would fill him "ful of led [*sic*]." After the Rangers left, the Mob warned, they would go after the anti-Mob residents and "kill the hole damd Shootin match [*sic*]."[52]

McDonald's strategy was simple but sound. He and the other San Saba Rangers rode around the countryside, sought out witnesses, interrogated them whenever possible, protected them at the Ranger camp if necessary to remove the fear that some people had of the Mob, and acted tough when members of the Mob appeared. If the Ranger captain could not immediately hang the members of the Mob by legal means, he could create a threatening environment for the murderous society.[53] McDonald and his men even scouted the San Saba area called the "buzzard water hole," the so-called "meeting place of the mob."[54] Patiently enough, evidence was gathered to bring a number of indictments by the grand jury at the end of 1897: A. K. Bailey, W. J. Burnett, and William Ogle, accused of doing away with Brown; and Jim Ford, John Haas, William Kimmons, and Nelson Smith, charged with the murder of James. In December McDonald wrote the adjutant general that he was a "little surprised" that more indictments were not handed down, but he figured the grand jury wanted to handle the matter by "degrees." He noted that the Rangers "furnished the evidence and rode all over different counties for the witnesses" without any help from the public officials in San Saba County, especially the sheriff.[55]

In response to a report from the field in the fall of 1897, the adjutant general informed Captain Bill that he was "pleased" with his "work." Mabry cautioned McDonald, however, to try to "conciliate" Sheriff Hawkins as "much as possible." Central command realized the Ranger captain's predicament when a "large portion of the citizens may be in sympathy with a mob element." "But if you are attacked," the adjutant general concluded, "I would move a greater force to your assistance."[56]

While investigating the Mob, McDonald and the Rangers under his command arrested a number of Texans for various crimes in Central Texas. These criminal actions included the usual wrongdoings: carrying a pistol, disturbing the peace, fighting, stealing horses and a saddle, and assisting in murderous activities.[57] In a span of five months in 1898 Rangers Barker and McCauley took part in corralling twenty-eight lawbreakers in San Saba and the surrounding counties. Their misdeeds ranged from burglary, drunkenness, and theft of hogs to being a fugitive from justice.[58] In October of that year the adjutant general even ordered the San Saba detachment to Junction in Kimble County to "assist in holding court."[59]

Bringing William A. "Bill" Ogle to justice, for using a shotgun to kill Brown, became a special cause for McDonald. Two who knew Ogle, Miles "Jeff" McCarty and William "Josh" McCormick, gave the Ranger captain valuable information about Mob operations. A detachment of Rangers—Barker, McCauley, McClure, Neal, and Van Lane—arrested Ogle for murder on August 26, 1897, and put him in the jail at San Saba the next day. By the end of the month the examining trial occurred. Held without bail, the prisoner was then taken by McCauley and another Ranger to the jail at Llano for "safe keeping."[60]

The arrest of Ogle resulted in a flurry of activity. Rangers sought witnesses for the prosecution and the Mob threatened the state officers. According to his official biographer, McDonald made Ogle tremble with fear and fall to the ground, when he accused him of the murder of Brown.[61] In addition, Judge Allison advised McDonald to let Ogle leave the country and show by this act that he was guilty.[62] McDonald also learned that most of the witnesses who testified for Ogle at the preliminary hearing acted out of fear for their own safety.[63] "Ogle's rearrest [since the first one did not result in a trial] and denial of bail created quite a sensation among the faction to which he belonged," a newspaper reported, "and while the lawless element has made some strong talk, still nothing further has been attempted and Capt. McDonald feels that with his Ranger force and backed by the law abiding people of the county, he is able to cope with the lawless element and suppress further mob law and kuklux proceedings."[64]

As a man and a Texan, Bill Ogle did not stand out in a crowd. Around six feet tall, with dark hair, brown eyes, and numerous scars on his body, the thirty-six-year-old accused murderer resided in Goldthwaite in Mills County (a hotbed of nefarious activities at the turn of the century).[65] Although able to read and write, Ogle had little formal education and worked as a laborer.[66]

The essential facts in the legal proceedings against Ogle can be summarized as follows: His trial occurred during the May term in 1899 of the district court, Llano County, presided over by Judge M. D. Slator. Ogle was convicted of first-degree murder and sentenced to life in prison. He appealed his conviction on procedural grounds. In June 1900, the Court of Criminal Appeals, in the words of Judge J. Brooks, affirmed the decision of the lower court. In October of that year the same court refused a motion to rehear the case. Ogle served his sentence in the state prison at Huntsville.[67]

Bill Ogle penned a letter to McDonald in 1908 from his cell in Huntsville. In it he noted that he had heard about McDonald's opposition to his release from prison out of fear for his own life. The convicted murderer took time to assure Captain Bill that he harbored "no feeling of bitterness" against him. On June 4, 1908, McDonald wrote Ogle that he did not fear for his own life and would always speak the truth about the murderous society. He also urged Ogle to give a full confession about the Mob. Although the Ranger captain knew that Ogle's prison record was excellent, he stressed to the pardoning board that not only was Ogle guilty of murder but other signers of a petition before the board should be in jail too.[68]

At the end of 1909 Governor Thomas M. Campbell pardoned Ogle and restored his citizenship and suffrage. In his proclamation the governor noted that the trial judge, the prosecuting attorney, ten members of the jury, and numerous other citizens supported executive clemency.[69] Although some believed that Ogle was the central figure in the activities of the Mob, Linden viewed Ogle as a weak character, a pawn in the hands of the murderous society.[70] A better case can be made that Matt Ford was the leader of the Mob in San Saba and the surrounding counties.

Bill Ogle was the only person connected with the San Saba Mob who was sentenced to prison. The other defendants in the Brown case and those accused of the murder of James, with some of their cases being moved to other counties, were never convicted. Yet the courage and audacity of District Attorney Linden at the close of the 1890s brought an end to the violent era in San Saba County. At one point a newspaper commented that "great credit is due District Attorney Linden for his untiring zeal in securing the conviction of Ogle."[71] At another time, over the wishes of Judge Allison, Linden accused some people in the courtroom of being members of the Mob and attacked others for being too weak and cowardly to do anything about it. Then, in an armed showdown in the street, Linden forced the Fords, Jim and Matt, and others to back down. Under pressure from the district attorney, some of the adherents of the Mob members facing trial began to leave the county. The factional hatred that had divided San Saba began to subside.[72]

Only one serous shooting incident between the Rangers and the citizens of San Saba County took place. It occurred when the presence of the Rangers in the county had become less important. On November 3, 1898, Jones Boren while drunk was bothering a black Texan in a store. Ranger Barker and others escorted Boren to a hotel where he could sleep off his intoxication. But Boren, too drunk and mad at the interference by the Ranger, went to a relative's house for a rifle. When he returned and found Barker, he leveled his weapon. But the Ranger fired first—"five times in rapid succession"—and killed Boren. The grand jury refused to hand down an indictment against Barker; it was justifiable homicide in self-defense.[73]

The Texas Rangers remained in San Saba County for some time. This happened despite the calls for their removal from Judge Allison, former sheriff Hawkins, and other citizens at the start of 1899. Several residents of the county expressed a heartfelt belief: " . . . our best people are of the opinion that the Rangers have served their purpose fully & the desire now is to relieve us of the stigma of having this branch of our police force quartered on us, reminds us of the old Martial law of the days of Davis [the governor during Reconstruction in the early 1870s]."[74]

Correspondence about the Mob between Sergeant McCauley, now the key Ranger in the county, McDonald, and state officials in Austin continued well into 1899. At that time McCauley realized that conditions at San Saba seemed "quiet" on the "surface," but ill-feelings against those who had been "instrumental" in getting indictments against Mob members still existed. Especially important would be the actions of the Rangers during the month of May. Here the state law officers made further arrests and McDonald, at the urging of Linden, attended the court proceedings against Ogle. At the same time Captain Bill and his men had to deal with issues of law and order in Panhandle towns, like Claude, Memphis, and Wellington, and worried about the impact of Mob doings on Borden, Mills, and Scurry counties.[75]

On July 24, 1899, the adjutant general ordered Captain McDonald to send the San Saba Rangers, with their equipment, horses, and supplies, to San Angelo by rail.[76] By then the role of the Rangers in the suppression of Mob activities was mainly psychological: to keep fear at a minimum.

In the San Saba affair the members of two companies of the Frontier Battalion came together to enforce law and order. In doing so, two Rangers from Company B—McDonald and Sullivan—

stood out. Both officers were action-oriented individuals who had grandiose thoughts. Yet in their actions and writings about the murderous society the two lawmen did differ. Sullivan gave a chameleon-like performance, from carrying out investigations with skill to engaging in personality clashes that would be his undoing. Furthermore, Sullivan's brief and inept statements in his memoirs about his days at San Saba did not explain the ups and downs of his role in the affair (although one historical writer believed that his "account of the San Saba Mob is the best ever written by a ranger participant of that strife-torn county").[77]

The audacity and untiring efforts of McDonald, as well as District Attorney Linden, brought about a more orderly state of affairs in San Saba and surrounding counties. A Ranger historian went so far as to say, "Captain Bill proved no more temperamentally suited than Sullivan to handle the delicate relationships in San Saba County."[78] McDonald's official biographer also misread the role of the Ranger captain by giving too much emphasis to the Buzzards-Water-Hole story and by overplaying the role of Ogle in the murderous society.[79] Although distrusting several county leaders for not doing their jobs, McDonald nevertheless carried out his duties with a steadfast disposition. His bludgeon-like actions did help in putting members of the Mob on the defensive. At one point Captain Bill said that the "sight of rangers" will make those engaged in Mob activities "sick with something." The "boys" of Company B called this "ranger fever."[80]

The San Saba Mob, or the Assembly, as it was called, kept its secrets. A local authority wrote that the Mob was a "bizarre mix of military structure, ritualism and religion that kept the organization together."[81] The words to a romantic song revealed the emotional ups and downs of shedding blood and hiding trails. The first and last stanzas went thus:

The Mob had a meeting last night, Love
Down on Cottonwood Pond.

It was a terrible sight, Love
The most terrible sight above ground.

Some day this Mob rule will be over
With the help of the Father above.
I'll return to my home and family
And claim you for my own true love.[82]

Chapter 8

REESE–TOWNSEND FEUD AT COLUMBUS

> *During the month of March, 1899, Capt. McDonald, with two men, were ordered to Columbus, Colorado county, for the purpose of preventing trouble there between the Townsend and Reece [*sic*] factions. Capt. McDonald went alone, his men not being able to reach him in time, and his courage and cool behavior prevented a conflict between the two factions. The district judge and district attorney both informed him that it was impossible to handle the situation, but he told them that he could make the effort, and he gave the members of each faction a limited time in which to get rid of their weapons, stating that he would put those in jail who refused to comply. His order had the desired effect.*[1]

This report by the adjutant general added to McDonald's growing reputation as a two-gun crusading knight. Yet Captain Bill was only one of a number of Rangers who became involved in the affair over a period of time.

Columbus is situated in the south central part of the state in Colorado County. Settled by pioneers from Stephen Austin's colony in the 1820s, the town began as a ferry site, took part in the Texas Revolution, became the county seat, and prospered through growing cotton, raising cattle, and exploiting sand and gravel deposits. Due to the coming of the railroads and economic activity, the population of the county increased to about 22,000 residents by 1900, as Germans and other nationalities moved into the area. The locale had come of age.[2]

For years two of the more prominent families in Colorado County were the Townsends and the Staffords. The former traced their lineage back to the Texas Revolution, made a fortune in the cattle business, and entered law and police work through the sheriff's office. In time, members of the Townsend clan married into families named Burford, Clements, Hope, Lessing, and Reese. The Staffords, on the other hand, entered Texas from Georgia on the eve of the Civil War. Less educated than the Townsends, the enterprising Stafford brothers got rich in the cattle industry and became well schooled in practical affairs within the county. One writer said that the Townsends of note—Mark and Sheriff John Light—"were tall, handsome, blond men with strong wills and much personal force."[3] They would come up against the equally tough-minded and headstrong Staffords.

The relations between the Townsends and the Staffords were changeable, lively, and unpredictable. Among the factors that provoked a violent clash was the fatal shooting by a posse of a fleeing A. Stapleton Townsend for stealing horses in 1867. In the various trials of posse members four years later, the testimony of Robert Stafford angered the Townsends. The first bloodshed occurred in December 1871 in a shootout in Columbus. When the smoke cleared, Bob Stafford still held his ground unscathed. Sumner Townsend received wounds in the arm and shoulder. And Ben Stafford had a painful ankle injury, probably due to Sumner's aim being deflected. Although the environment remained hostile after the numerous rounds fired in this altercation and the time spent in the subsequent investigation by the State Police, the two families spoke and coexisted for nearly two decades. The friendly encounters included seeking legal advice from the Townsends, attending a funeral together, and even marrying each other after the turn of the 1900s.[4]

In the summer of 1890, Larkin and Marion Hope, deputies of their uncle Sheriff Townsend, arrested and handcuffed Warren Stafford, son of Bob Stafford, for intoxication. Early that evening Stafford's enraged father held a heated talk with the Hope brothers outside a saloon in Columbus. A remark about his friendliness with blacks led Larkin Hope to shoot and kill Bob and John Stafford in cold blood.

Although the Hope brothers were never convicted of the shootings, the sheriff's office became a focal point of criticism. Some people in the county had always been dissatisfied with the way Sheriff Townsend carried out his duties and held office through the manipulation of the black vote. When the sheriff died in November 1894, Samuel H. "Sam" Reese, husband of Keron (or "Keetie") Townsend, took over his duties. With the appointment of Reese the stage had been set for a major conflict.[5]

Two viewpoints have arisen about whether this spur-of-the-moment violence between the two families led to the Reese-Townsend feud. One expert on Texas feuding declared, "The Stafford-Townsend feud had now been replaced by the Reese-Townsend feud."[6] Ever since, this point of view has been accepted by many historical writers. Certainly similar names appeared in the chronicles of local violence during these decades and the continuing saga of Larkin Hope in the 1890s became a disruptive force. Yet a student of the bloodletting at Columbus maintained that "there was no continuing pattern of violence between the Staffords and the Townsends." This discerning historian also wrote about the gunning down of Bob Stafford by Larkin Hope: "It was simply the unfortunate result of a lengthy, heated, very public argument between a rich and powerful man with a reputation for violence and a small, poor, man with a pistol in his pocket." Gunplay on two occasions over nineteen years would be a "very long time to hold a grudge."[7]

The focal point of the upcoming feud would be the character and actions of Sam Reese. The good-looking and capable Reese was a popular choice to replace Sheriff Townsend, as he had served as a marshal, a constable, and a deputy sheriff in the Columbus area. The new sheriff won another term (1896–1898) at the polls, defeating Charley Shropshire by over a 600-vote margin, with the help of the political machine headed by Mark Townsend. At this time a charge arose that Reese mishandled a criminal case, but the sheriff denied the accusations.[8]

The Reese-Townsend feud, in the words of one writer, "began as a squabble for control of the sheriff's office."[9] With the support of Townsend's political machine, Larkin Hope decided to oppose Reese in the election for sheriff in 1898. During the heated campaign, Hope was murdered in an ambush. Hit by a shotgun blast, he still fired three times before collapsing and dying soon after. The killer ran down an alley, mounted a horse, and disappeared in the night. In time, Jim Coleman, related to the Townsend and Reese families, was taken into custody for the crime but was later acquitted. Talk spread, meanwhile, that Sam Reese had a hand in the murder. Then, Will Burford, who had replaced Hope on the ticket, polled more votes than Reese and Shropshire in the election for the sheriff's office.[10]

The showdown between the antagonists came in Columbus on March 16, 1899, between five and six o'clock in the evening. Sam Reese had returned to town from his farm and stopped his horse in front of a saloon. He overheard an argument nearby between Deputy Sheriff Will Clements and an unarmed Ed Scott who had just been let out of jail. Reese heard Scott say that he would end the heated talk if he only had a gun. The former sheriff, no friend of Clements, offered Scott his weapon. Clements then challenged Reese and the two began firing at the same time. Others joined in and when the smoke cleared, Reese was mortally wounded, stray bullets hit and killed a farmer, and a small boy was seriously injured by a shot in the hip. A local doctor reported that the bullet which ended Reese's life "traversed" his "windpipe," "severed" an "artery," and "deluged his lungs with blood." Clements, Marion Hope, and Mark Townsend were arrested for manslaughter but were not prosecuted for the shootings.[11]

After the shootout, supporters of each faction came to town from far and near. "The people of Columbus," a judge explained, "became much alarmed at the presence of these two armed bodies of infuriated and dangerous men."[12] At such times any slight, real or imaginary, can be turned into a bloody vendetta. The feudists in

Colorado County now had their first fallen hero—Sam Reese. His son gave the word:

Reese was a sheriff bold,
For four years or more;
He always did his duty—
People could ask no more.
The people in Sam Reese
Much confidence they had;
Enemies to law and order,
When he was killed were glad.[13]

In this volatile situation District Judge M. Kennon sent for the Texas Rangers. His telegram of March 20 even asked Governor Sayers to dispatch "fifteen or twenty rangers." In addition, George McCormack, a former judge, requested that the adjutant general be sent. On the same day the governor informed Kennon and McCormack that orders had been issued to transport a Ranger officer and his men to the town.[14]

The Ranger service had to handle another time-consuming case. The request by the judge resulted in a series of communications between state officials. On March 20, Governor Sayers told Adjutant General Scurry to send three Rangers and an officer to Columbus and have them report to Judge Kennon. On the same day the adjutant general responded to the governor from Laredo, where violent disturbances had taken place. He noted that only McDonald's company (with Rangers stationed in Borden, Hall, and San Saba counties) would be available for duty at Columbus. In turn, Sayers directed Scurry to dispatch as quickly as possible McDonald and four Rangers to Colorado County. The adjutant general complied with his orders on March 21. State authorities had decided upon their initial response to the Reese-Townsend feud.[15]

On March 22, McDonald and two members of Captain Hughes' company arrived in Columbus. Soon after two Rangers from Company B, located at San Saba, followed their captain. Although some people in Colorado County thought more Rangers were needed, McDonald felt that his force was sufficient. In fact, the next day he wired headquarters that if Hughes' men were needed elsewhere, the feud could still be controlled.[16]

During his stay in the town Captain Bill used two well-established procedures in handling feudists, lynchers, or rioters: namely, (1) consult with local officials to plan strategy and see whether they had maintained a neutral stand; and (2) take action to see that the warring parties do not gang up on each other. These undertakings, in McDonald's words, meant assisting in court proceedings, helping the "sheriff daily," guarding prisoners, and preventing "trouble between factions." At one point McDonald arrested a person for carrying a pistol and McClure of Company B took into custody J. Perry (alias Ed Scott) for burglary. Scott had been part of the row that ended in the death of Sam Reese.[17]

To keep the peace of the community Captain Bill immediately consulted with the district judge and the district attorney. The three agreed on a course of action. McDonald demanded that the "warring factions" surrender their weapons and "proposed to disarm them if they did not do so & file complaints against them." This resulted in the disarming of the feuding parties and the dismissal of the sheriff's special deputies.[18] The Ranger captain received another communication from central command on March 25. Scurry told McDonald that after the court hearing for Jim Coleman, Hughes' men should return to their station. If more Rangers are still needed, the adjutant general pointed out, "wire me at once, and help will be sent you from another Company."[19] But the crisis in the town had passed. The only disturbance was an attempt to shoot Will Clements.[20] McDonald and the men under his command left Columbus on March 30.

The course of action by the Ranger captain in defusing the volatile situation in Colorado County has been praised by those inside and outside the state ever since. McDonald's official biographer especially stressed his singular piece of heroism in making the feudists give ground.[21] But Captain Bill was no "Lone Ranger." He and his small force worked together to achieve their goals. Less exaggerated statements came from the pens of local officers. County Judge J. J. Mansfield wrote that McDonald "immediately took the necessary steps to avert further blood shed."[22] A few prominent officials, which included Kennon, Mansfield, and District Attorney S. L. Green, put their signatures on a letter to the governor which summed up the role of the Rangers in the affair and paid tribute to McDonald:

> . . . we desire to attest the efficiency of Capt. McDonald and the rangers under his command, who in our opinion have by their conservatism and general efficiency, prevented further bloodshed. We wish especially to commend, Captain McDonald, without detracting from others of the command, who in our opinion, is an officer, particularly efficient in such emergencies as we have recently experienced here, and who, we beleive [*sic*], can always be depended upon to do his whole duty. The crisis has passed and we anticipate no further trouble in which the gallant rangers could assist us.[23]

But peace between the feuding parties was temporary. In reality, the Reese-Townsend feud went through five more stages: two killings in May 1899; more dead and wounded in January 1900; another shooting in July 1900; a deadly gun battle in June 1906; and the climactic struggle in May 1907. These bloody events brought to an end the conflict between the Burford, Hope, Reese, and Townsend families of Colorado County. In a number of the violent encounters the Texas Rangers intervened to try to uphold law and order.

During the evening of May 17, 1899, Dick Reese, Sam's brother, and a black man were shot and killed on their way into Columbus by two deputy sheriffs, James G. Townsend and Step Yates. These lawmen had orders to prevent people carrying weapons from entering the town. In the encounter Reese stood up in a buggy, drew his gun, but did not fire. A newspaper reported that he "was shot twice from the front with a shotgun and once with a pistol, the shots taking effect in the head, face and upper part of the chest and neck."[24] For the second time in a few months members of the sheriff's office took part in a violent episode in the feud.

This time County Judge Mansfield telegraphed the governor to send "eight or ten" Rangers. The judge stressed, in his message of May 18, that the "situation" was "entirely beyond the control of local authorities." On the same day Governor Sayers ordered several Rangers to go to Columbus and report to the judge. This intervention in the feud by the state law officers would be more prolonged than their previous stay in the town.[25]

Adjutant General Scurry dispatched Battalion Quartermaster Sieker to Columbus, for the purpose of "enforcing the law, and quelling any reported disturbances." "You will act," Scurry told Sieker, "with the local civil authorities of that County, but be careful not to take sides in any existing fueds [*sic*]." At the same time the adjutant general ordered three Rangers from Company E, commanded by Captain Rogers, to proceed to Colorado County.[26]

Captain Sieker arrived on the morning of May 19. On that same day he telephoned the adjutant general and reported that a "large number of both factions had arrived in town and an open street fight was expected." Initially, Sieker "persuaded" the feudists to "disperse." Then, after the arrival of the Rangers from Company E on May 20, the battalion quartermaster "proceeded to disarm all men not entitled to carry arms under the law." He also tried to "persuade those of each faction, who did not live in the town of Columbus to return to their homes." Yet feudists still "lingered" in the town, although they were not "seen on the streets so often, nor in such large groups."[27]

With the possibility of an escalation of the feud, Adjutant General Scurry decided to go to Columbus. He arrived on the morning of May 23. At the same time Scurry ordered McDonald and one of his men to proceed to the town. They arrived the next day with instructions to work with Captain Sieker. Central command had now dispatched to Colorado County a considerable number of state law officers.[28]

In the midst of charges and countercharges by the feuding parties, state officials realized that three factors stood out: (1) the operation of the sheriff's office; (2) the attitude and actions of Will Clements; and (3) the intransigence of Mrs. Sam Reese. As the adjutant general began to look into these aspects of the feud, he telegraphed the governor: "Everything seems perfectly quiet today will write."[29]

Scurry knew that the sheriff's office had not remained neutral in the outbreak of the feud. In the appointment of his deputies, Sheriff Burford "allowed himself to be managed" by the Townsends. Since the sheriff refused to resign, the adjutant general consulted with the district judge about having Burford removed from office. But "sufficient charges could not be made and sustained to have him removed." Scurry then proposed that if the sheriff dismissed all of his deputies except two, he "would allow the rangers to do the work of deputies as long as they were stationed at Columbus." Especially important would be the discharge of Deputy Sheriff Clements.[30]

On May 25 Adjutant General Scurry left Columbus for Austin, leaving McDonald in charge of the investigation. By the end of the month the Ranger captain notified his superiors that Clements still carried a gun.[31] When the adjutant general returned to Columbus on June 12, he again talked with the sheriff. But Burford "declined to discharge this deputy" (although he did send him out of town for several days). Scurry had two reasons for wanting Clements removed as a deputy sheriff. First, Clements, young and antagonistic, "acknowledged" he killed Sam Reese and, along with Mark Townsend, would be considered by the members of the Reese family as "their most obnoxious enemies." Second, the adjutant general reasoned that Clements walking the street with a weapon "emboldens or encourages the others on his side to say and do things of a character aggrivating [*sic*] to the opposing side, and his presence armed is like 'waving the red flag' to the Reeses."[32]

Adjutant General Scurry tried to get the members of the Reese clan to stay away from Columbus. But Mrs. Sam Reese "would do all in her power to inflame them and prevail on them to stay." The adjutant general wrote that she took one Ranger to "her room and showed him the picture of her husband and told of his courage and many virtues. She then took a sheet off of two chairs, on which was spread out the bloody clothes of her husband and of Dick Reese, and she said nothing would satisfy her but the heart of Mark Townsend."[33] At another time Mrs. Reese reclaimed a shotgun which contained two shells, state officials noted, with markings to be used against Sheriff Burford and Mark Townsend.[34]

Captain Bill stayed for about two weeks in Colorado County during his second tour of duty in combating the feud. He handled the usual assignments: working with local officials, keeping track of feudists, making arrests, and staying in touch with his superiors. During his sojourn in Columbus, the Ranger captain kept receiving messages from central headquarters. Scurry reminded McDonald that the Rangers under his command must remain impartial in their dealings with the feuding parties. The adjutant general also inquired about the agreement with Burford about the role of Deputy Sheriff Clements and the whereabouts of Mark Townsend. At one point McDonald noted that in discussions with the sheriff about Clements, he did not believe Burford was "sincere." On June 5, 1899, the adjutant general ordered McDonald to go by train to Athens to investigate a lynching. Within a few months the Ranger captain had to shift his thought patterns from one major case to another in the counties of San Saba, Colorado, and Henderson.[35]

After the shooting of Dick Reese, the Rangers of Company E played a key role in the investigation. On May 18, Captain Rogers reported that he had received orders to dispatch four men to Columbus, i.e., Sergeant E. M. Dubose and Privates W. A.

Old, T. C. Taylor, and W. L. "Will" Wright (a future captain of note).[36] During the early summer months Taylor and Wright kept track of the feudists, particularly the coming and going of the Reeses. In their rounds they sometimes did not sleep at night. At one point Wright noted that the sheriff "relied" upon the two Rangers, instead of his deputies, "to do all his work." Wright also said that he and Taylor were "searching" every man on "both sides" of the street and "will not allow more than 2 to come together." Such aggressive patrols became a hallmark of the old-time Ranger service.[37]

One incident in early summer showed just how much Columbus had become a tinderbox. During the evening of June 7, Ranger Taylor and Deputy Sheriff Robert W. Westmoreland, on their way to have dinner, heard a shot in a saloon. When they arrived the two lawmen found several members of the Reese family inside the barroom and some Townsend backers outside the door. The latter individuals turned out to be Deputy Sheriff Will Clements, with his gun drawn, an angry Jim Clements, and Marion Hope. The Reeses explained that a boy had accidently discharged a weapon and put a hole in the floor. With difficulty Taylor and Westmoreland tried to get the feudists to go their separate ways. At one point Taylor escorted the Reeses across a street, while Westmoreland watched the Townsend men in a store. Then someone yelled at the Reeses that there goes the "assassinating S____ o__ B______s." After the members of the Reese family ran back to the saloon, the process of getting each side to go home began again. Taylor even had to disarm Step Yates who entered the scene. Finally both factions dispersed. The Ranger private ended the story by writing, "Westmoreland & I then went to supper."[38]

At this stage of the feud the Rangers of Companies B and E used their arrest powers to intimidate and remove feudists and their sympathizers from the streets—at least temporarily. At the end of May Private Barker of McDonald's company took Yates into custody for carrying a pistol.[39] More important, during an eleven-day period at the end of the same month, the four Rangers of Company E arrested and jailed seven residents of Colorado County. The charges against these lawbreakers ranged from assault to murder and fighting to carrying a pistol and stealing property under fifty dollars. The Rangers had taken a stand against crime and violence in the area.[40]

The aggressive patrols and arrests increased during the summer months. In June McDonald apprehended a member of the Reese family for carrying a gun.[41] Then both factions felt the heavy hand of Ranger Wright during the same month. At one point he took Walter Reese into custody for using abusive language. Soon after, Wright collared five men of the opposite side for carrying weapons: Jim Clements, Marion Hope, Mark and Jim Townsend, and Steph Yates. In addition, Wright arrested four robbers (three for stealing cattle) in Colorado County and recovered several head of livestock.[42]

In the months to follow the Rangers of Company E continued to use their arrest powers in the struggle against crime and violence. During July and September of 1899, Taylor and Wright kept on traversing the county. In the former month they arrested and jailed in Columbus seven lawbreakers, mostly for fighting and disturbing the peace.[43] In the latter month they took into custody nine local residents for breaking the law. Their crimes ranged from the less serious, like carrying a pistol, to the more serious, as, for example, the act of murder.[44]

In August and September of 1899, a new Ranger force entered the scene. Members of Company F under the command of Captain Brooks moved into the county. During these months two Rangers of this company made four arrests for assault and cattle theft.[45] More important, Brooks and his detachment came to the area to attend a court session in September and keep the peace by "disarming all parties."[46] McDonald even recorded that he sent a Ranger to Columbus to report to Brooks for duty.[47] Slowly but surely the

Ranger companies commanded by the "Four Great Captains" were being drawn to the locale of the Reese-Townsend feud.

During the last half of 1899, the Rangers "quieted" Colorado County so "effectively" that the feud did not enter the "headlines" again until the next year.[48] In January 1900, Jim Townsend went on trial for the murder of Dick Reese in Bastrop, Texas. Several hundred people took the train to be present in the courtroom as witnesses or spectators. The legal proceedings were brief. A motion for the continuance of the case was accepted.

As people left the courthouse and walked the streets, another violent clash between the feuding parties took place. In late afternoon of January 15, 1900, some of the Reese faction returned to a saloon where they had left their weapons. Here a chance encounter occurred with the detested Will Clements; Arthur Burford, the sheriff's son and a lawyer; and Howard Townsend, an attorney who had not been involved in any hostilities. As this unarmed trio approached the saloon on the sidewalk, the Reeses opened fire. The burst of gunshots seriously wounded Clements and killed Burford instantly by putting a hole in his head. Townsend fled the scene without injury. A newspaper reported, "Everything is quiet now, but anxiety is intense and further trouble is feared."[49]

In this violent outbreak in the feud the Rangers intervened in its various stages: in the events leading to the court session, in the investigation of the shootings, and in the subsequent judicial proceedings against the killers. Captain Brooks and three Rangers arrived in Bastrop on January 12, with orders to "assist the sheriff in preventing trouble" between the feuding parties. The Ranger captain and the sheriff of Bastrop County, according to Brooks, met the feudists and their friends at the "depot and accompanied them to their boarding houses, notifying them that all interested parties on both sides must dispense with all arms, to which all agreed; continual searching on the street and at the court house was kept up. Everything appeared reasonably quiet until the shooting occurred."[50]

After the violent showdown in the town, Rangers and local lawmen rushed to the scene. Within twenty minutes they quickly arrested and jailed numerous members of the Reese faction and seized weapons from bystanders, while one Ranger stood guard at the courthouse door to stop the Townsend crowd. Records of the Ranger service showed that a dozen or more lawbreakers were taken into custody for carrying a pistol or committing murder on that fateful day. The men of the Frontier Battalion involved in the arrests included Brooks, Sergeant W. B. Bates, and Private J. T. Armstrong of Company F and the indomitable Taylor and Wright of Company E.[51] "Though many of the arrests were made solely to prevent further trouble," one local chronicler noted, "four men, Walter Reese, Jim Coleman, Tom Daniels, and Les Reese, were charged with the murder of Burford."[52]

Governor Sayers, in the words of the adjutant general, gave "positive directions that further trouble must be prevented at all cost."[53] This attitude made Scurry go to Bastrop himself. At the same time he called for more Rangers. On January 15, Sergeant McCauley of Company B received orders to take his detachment of five men to Columbus and obey any orders given by Captain Brooks at Bastrop. Two days later the adjutant general advised McCauley to report to his superiors "any probability of trouble in the near future" between the feuding parties.[54] Then McDonald went to Bastrop on January 22 and stayed for several days. He "assisted in holding court" and "preventing a clash" between the feudists. Captain Bill, along with Brooks and Bates, also arrested and jailed two more individuals implicated in Burford's murder.[55]

With the indictments by a grand jury of Coleman, Daniels, and the two Reeses for the murder of Burford and the assault on Clements with intent to kill, the Rangers tried to cover in their patrols the lands from Bastrop to Columbus in order to prevent trouble at the upcoming court hearing. Adjutant General Scurry explained that Ranger squads went to La Grange and West Point to "disarm everybody on trains bound for Bastrop."[56] Equally important, the adjutant general found it "necessary to direct the rangers to prevent any suspicious packages being shipped to either faction by express, baggage or otherwise, and through the co-operation of local authorities a great number of arms were stopped in this way. One trunk of arms had been shipped to the Townsend faction, and several packages of arms had been shipped by express to the members of the other faction."[57] Within the town of Bastrop the Rangers had orders to disarm and arrest anyone found with weapons. Scurry then directed that "any person making any demonstration, such as drawing a pistol for the purpose of shooting, shall be riddled with bullets."[58] Twenty Rangers, more or less, took part in this dragnet operation.

The people in Bastrop dreaded that the "stillness may prove only a 'calm between storms.' "[59] But the "storm" never came. In the legal proceedings against Burford's murderers the judge approved a motion for continuance. Eventually, the cases against Coleman, Daniels, and the two Reeses, as well as the one against Jim Townsend, were dismissed.[60]

The location of the feud now shifted to another town. Walter Reese moved to Rosenberg, Texas, in Fort Bend County, where he opened an ice cream parlor. On July 31, 1900, at around six o'clock in the evening, a train pulled into the local station with several noteworthy passengers: Frank Burford, a law student, Will and Jim Clements, Mark Townsend, and a fifth companion. With prior knowledge of the coming of these antagonists from talking with a kinsman, Jim Coleman and Walter Reese, heavily armed, especially with rifles, stood on the platform. As the train began to move again, a gun battle erupted. Who fired the first shot can not be determined. But Reese and Coleman fired into the coach carrying the Townsend party without hitting anyone. The return shots from the train wounded the two feudists. Reese had a hole in his thigh. The seriously wounded Coleman had bullets in both arms and his chest. Later Reese explained that he went to the depot to get his brother's luggage. Coleman came along because of the fear of the Townsend faction.

Members of the Houston Police Department met the train in another town on the line and arrested and jailed Burford and Will Clements. A constable from Fort Bend County then took the prisoners back to Richmond. Criminal cases against all five of the Townsend faction were developed and they posted bond. In the end, though, all those involved in this violent act escaped prosecution.[61]

For several years the feuding parties failed to come together and shed more blood. This happened for a number of reasons. For one thing, residents of Columbus became tired of the violence. For another thing, feudists were disarmed and arrested by local peace officers in other towns, once in San Antonio at the end of 1904, and then in Houston in the spring of 1905.[62] Noteworthy, too, would be the fact that the Rangers continued their interest in affairs in Colorado County. In November and December of 1900, for example, McDonald stayed in Columbus for weeks in search of "evidence in a murder case."[63]

The next chapter in this unfortunate affair took place in Columbus on June 30, 1906. In the late morning hours Marion Hope and Herbert Reese engaged in a fistfight at a skating rink. After losing, an enraged Reese went to get weapons and his brother, Walter, who had moved back to the town. The two Reeses, carrying a rifle and a shotgun, hurried back looking for their enemies. When they stopped in front of a saloon, Hope fired a shotgun from a drug store. In the shooting melee that ensued, Dr. Joseph Lessing gunned down Hiram Clements. Wild shots also hit a mule, store windows, and awning posts. Several bullets even struck a door and wall of a law office. Although Sheriff W. E. Bridge of Colorado County jailed Lessing and both Reeses (who had minor wounds), proof of their guilt was lacking.[64]

At this juncture in the Reese-Townsend feud the Rangers of Company D entered the scene. On July 17, Captain Hughes and four men traveled to Columbus and arrived the following day. For the next week or so the Ranger officer and subordinates, like Sergeant Tom Ross, moved in and out of the town.[65] Immediately, Hughes met with several local officials, including the county judge and the sheriff. He reported to his superiors that most of the townspeople seemed to be "glad to see the Rangers." The members of Company D watched the feuding parties come and go. At the same time a few feudists stayed around and spied on the Rangers.[66]

Judge Kennon made sure that this stalemate continued during the upcoming term of the district court. Near the end of August he asked the governor to send two Rangers to keep the peace in the courtroom. In addition, the judge recommended that a Ranger be "stationed" in Columbus after the court adjourns. Kennon concluded that the "condition of affairs" in the town created a "great danger" for the "shedding of blood, which danger will, in all, probability, be averted by no other means."[67] State officials responded by sending Rangers H. A. Carnes and Milam H. Wright of Company D to Colorado County in September to assist in keeping order during a session of the district court.[68]

The stationing of a Ranger at Columbus until local authorities deemed otherwise resulted from a unique event. In the month of July in 1906, townspeople came together to discuss ways to handle the factional violence in the community. A number of resolutions were passed, which ranged from calling for strict enforcement of the laws about carrying pistols to the need for bringing back the office of city marshal and the necessity of stationing a Ranger in the town. J. W. Towell, chairman of the mass-meeting of citizens, forwarded these resolutions, which carried over a hundred signatures, to the governor's office. By a close vote the city council turned down the request to reestablish the office of city marshal. Angry citizens then petitioned County Judge Mansfield to order an election to abolish city government. In early August residents voted by a three to one margin to disincorporate the town and place the administration of Columbus under county commissioners. At the same time state officials responded to the requests by the townspeople and Judge Kennon to place a Ranger within their midst by sending J. C. White of Company D to Columbus. He stayed in the city for two months, returning to his other duties in the middle of October.[69]

Every feud must have a final chapter. This came on May 17, 1907, in the age-old Texan settlement of San Antonio. During the evening on this fateful day Jim Coleman encountered Marion Hope in a saloon. Hope opened fire and Coleman went down with several bullet holes in his body. Although Hope and others were arrested in the confused aftermath, no convictions ever resulted from the actions of the local police. The feud, which gave Columbus and Colorado County a bad name, finally ended.[70]

The Reese-Townsend feud left its imprint on Columbus and Colorado County. The disincorporation of the town lasted for twenty years. Economic activity declined in the aftermath of the violent outbursts. A deep gloom settled over people's lives. In the years to follow other participants in the feud ended their existence in tragic deaths from shootouts and horse and car accidents, The names on their tombstones read like a Who's Who of the families in Colorado County who became bitter enemies—Will Clements, Marion Hope, Jim Townsend, and the two Reeses, Herbert and Walter.[71]

The Reese-Townsend feud holds a unique place in the histories of the Texas Rangers. Members of all four companies in the Frontier Battalion at the turn of the twentieth century played a role in the feud at different times and places. This did not happen too often in Ranger annals. Battalion Quartermaster Sieker, the "Four Great Captains," and the rank and file of the ranging companies, like Taylor and Will Wright, faithfully carried out their orders. In addition, two deputy sheriffs of Colorado County, Westmoreland and A. B. "Gunger" Wooldridge, worked with the Rangers and did a creditable job. Much more violence by the warring factions could have been committed had not the Rangers continually searched for and confiscated firearms and arrested feudists whenever necessary. Keeping the feuding parties apart became a singular goal of the state peace officers. As a newspaper reported at one point, "The Rangers are 'camping on all the trails.' "[72] Although several Rangers could be commended for their work in maintaining a semblance of order during the feud, Captain Bill gained the most notoriety for "twice disarming members of the opposing factions in the Reese-Townsend feud."[73]

Chapter 9

HUMPHRIES CASE: AN EAST TEXAS LYNCHING

You will remember that at the request of the sheriff, county attorney and other local authorities of that county, Capt. McDonald and Private Old were sent there to assist them and myself in the investigation of that horrible murder which was then enshrouded in a mystery that it seemed almost impossible to uncover. Before the rangers reached us the people in the neighborhood of the murder seemed afraid to talk. They said they would be murdered, too, if they took any hand in working up the case. About the first thing Capt. McDonald did was to assure the people that he and his associates had come there to stay until every murderer was arrested and convicted, and that he would see that all those who assisted him would be protected. They believed him, and in consequence thereof they soon began to talk and feel that the law would be vindicated, and I am glad to say that it was. The work of the rangers in this one case is worth more to the State, in my opinion, than your department will cost during your administration. In fact, such service cannot be valued in dollars and cents.[1]

While the Reese-Townsend feud went through its violent stages, a tragedy occurred in May 1899 in East Texas. Here, in a timbered bottom between two bodies of water known as the Trans-Cedar country in Henderson County, a lynching took place. This murder case became noteworthy for three reasons: (l) the unprecedented gathering of a large number of local and state law officers; (2) the involvement of the Rangers and other police agencies in an investigation based upon the interrogation of witnesses and the collection and analysis of physical evidence; and (3) court trials in which several lawbreakers turned state's evidence and helped to send eight lynchers to prison.

At various times in American history the residents of a community, even the more prominent ones, have believed that they had the right to take the law into their own hands. These extralegal actions in social control have taken many forms. Unorganized mobs have gathered to handle threats to their existence. Vigilance committees, called Regulators or Moderators or some other apt designation, have formed in order to carry out mock trials and punish offenders. An early example of a vigilante movement against crime and disorder occurred in the backcountry of South Carolina in the 1760s. A decade or so later lawlessness in Virginia resulted in mock-court proceedings led by Colonel Charles Lynch (from whom "Lynch law" supposedly gained its name). Punishments varied from whipping to hanging by the thumbs to being killed.

These two forms of extralegal justice—vigilantism and lynch law—came with the settlers across the Appalachian Mountains and the Mississippi River. In the 1800s Texas had fifty-two vigilante movements and many more lynch mobs who executed both whites and blacks. Vigilantes justified their actions by stressing self-preservation and the need of the common folk to rule themselves. In McDonald's day in the counties of central Texas, vigilantes especially gained the upper hand by forming law-and-order leagues. Those who visited this area, with some exaggeration, would be able to see bodies hanging from the trees. In carrying out this rough justice vigilance committees had one dilemma. They had no limits on the use of their power. At times vigilant Regulators went so far in intimidations and executions that vigilant Moderators arose to oppose the actions of the Regulators. Just as important, vigilantes existed in Texas and elsewhere until lawmen and judicial officers decided to take a stand opposing this extralegal form of righteous indignation.[2]

In the years that followed the admission of Texas to the American Union, Henderson County was formed and reduced to its current size. Athens became the county seat. Residents formed self-sufficient farms with the growing of crops, like corn and sweet potatoes, the raising of livestock, especially cattle and hogs, and the hunting of wild game. The coming of the railroads at the end of the 1800s "brought new life, as citizens moved to start new communities and rename old ones." By 1890 the population of the county increased to 12,285.[3]

The lynchings took place in the lands between Cedar Creek and the Trinity River in the western part of Henderson County. In this Trans-Cedar area Texans spent their time farming, fishing, and hunting. No big towns dotted the landscape. As one newspaper stated, "Until the snaky tempter in the hideous form of mob law, the Trans-Cedar was an earthly paradise."[4]

The coming together of the lynching party was not a spontaneous occurrence. On May 23, 1899, in the evening hours, those involved in this planned event, armed with pistols and shotguns, gathered, talked, and rode to the home of James Humphries (also spelled Humphreys) and his family. In the early morning hours of May 24, some of the lynchers with slouched hats entered his small farm house and, posing as peace officers, asked about the whereabouts of a man suspected of being involved in the recent killing of a constable. Then they took Humphries outside and proceeded to the nearby homes of his two sons, John and George. At this point the three men were taken to a tree not too far away and hanged alongside each other on the bending trunk. They were also buried in the same grave.[5]

The exact nature of the triple lynching can not be ascertained with certainty. Testimony from a relative of the hanged men who happened to find their bodies showed the positions of the father and the two sons on the leaning hickory tree: George, next to the main stem; John, next to him; and James, placed at the outermost part of the stooping trunk. The feet of James and John, but not George, were pulled backwards and tied to their bodies.[6] According to a news report, this happened in order to "keep their feet from touching the ground."[7] Yet two well-known sketches of the hangings differed with the particulars of this story. One drawing, based upon a news analysis, showed all the bodies dangling from the bending tree with their legs drawn up.[8] The other dramatic depiction, which appeared in an account by one of the lynchers, had the middle person on the leaning tree with his legs extended and off the ground.[9] Such visual representations might not fit the facts.

The causative factors for the lynching of the Humphries can not be explained in simple terms. The least satisfactory answer for the hangings was the accidental approach. "The death of old man Humphreys is believed to have been unintentional," a newspaper reported, "his neck being broken when he was pulled up to choke him into telling where the constable's slayer was . . . ." At that point the two sons went to their deaths "in order to prevent them from giving testimony against members of the mob who they doubtless knew."[10]

A key figure in the planning and execution of the slayings was Joseph L. Wilkinson. Standing about five-feet-eight-inches tall, he had a slim figure and an angular face, with a goatee at the time of the trials. His missing left eye, moreover, gave him a sinister appearance. A resident of Henderson County for many years, Wilkinson worked the land and served as a local law officer. Although he learned to read and write, he had little formal education. Yet Wilkinson put together a memoir about the crime and his incarceration which revealed his bitter feelings about the course of events.[11]

Joe Wilkinson believed that he and his followers upheld law and order against thieves and murderers led by the Humphries clan.[12] At a court hearing one lyncher said that Wilkinson told him the "Humphries were ruining the country and stealing everything and harboring men to kill others."[13] At the same time sworn testimony indicated that during the night of the lynchings Polk Weeks "climbed the tree" and tied the ropes. Then "Joe Wilkinson drove the horses out from under them."[14] Three members of the Humphries family went to their deaths. To uphold the law Wilkinson turned to mob law (with the lynchers taking an oath of secrecy).

A belief existed in the minds of the lynchers that Jim Humphries and his sons harbored the person who killed a constable. Time after time those who carried out the hangings, cursing and smelling of liquor, asked the Humphries the same question: Where is the murderer, James Patterson (or Jim Patison in the press)? The mob-law gang even tried to enlist local peace officers in their endeavors. At one of the houses the lynchers searched downstairs and upstairs for Patterson, looking under the "beds and everywhere." But Patterson had left the state. He read about the hangings in the newspaper. When he returned to Henderson County, he was arrested and put in jail, charged with the murder of Constable John Rhodes. The peace officer had been killed during the investigation of a theft case involving Patterson and the Humphries clan.[15]

An underlying cause for the lynchings was the theft of hogs that belonged to Joe Wilkinson. A grand jury indicted George and John Humphries and Jim Patterson for this crime. The two Humphries posted bond, but Patterson fled. Numerous Texans testified in court during the trials of the lynchers that the stealing of the hogs angered Wilkinson. At one point a farmer in the area said that Wilkinson stressed about the Humphries, " . . . I am going to make their d__n necks look up a limb."[16] In his memoir Wilkinson explained in detail the stealing of forty hogs from his farm and the subsequent butchering by the Humphries. To Wilkinson the "leniency" of the judge in this case only made criminals more bold in breaking the rules of society.[17]

Another reason for the lynchings surfaced in the press. A newspaper quoted a prominent resident of Henderson County as follows:

> I am satisfied that hog and cattle stealing or the killing of Constable Rhodes had nothing whatever to do with the lynching. It is a matter-of no-little notoriety that "moonshining" has been going on in Henderson county for quite a while, and you will see later on that it was this that led to the hanging. Old man Humphreys and

> his two boys knew too much about the moonshiners and their operations to suit the crowd engaged in the business and their knowledge proved to be their death warrant.[18]

Such talk has made writers speculate about the motivation of the lynchers. McDonald's official biographer noted that the Humphries knew about an "illicit still" run by two of the lynchers, Polk Weeks and W. A. Johns. He also wrote that the stolen hogs had really been sold by Wilkinson.[19] Another author claimed that the hogs were sold "to someone in Corsicana while they were still obligated as collateral on a loan held by a bank in Athens that Wilkinson had not paid off."[20] A third researcher stated a truism—after all is said and done, "questions about why the mob lynched the Humphries is still shrouded partially in mystery."[21] For whatever reason the lynch mob stopped talking and acted.

In this affair Justice of the Peace Elihu H. Garrett of Aley (a small settlement in the Trans-Cedar) was one of the first law officers on the scene. A resident of Henderson County for years, he had an elegant appearance, with a prominent nose and a mustache. Garrett not only cut the ropes of two of the hanged men but also conducted an inquest into their deaths. For weeks he took sworn statements, either verbatim or in summarized form, from those who would talk. In the press state officials praised him and his constable for their "tireless and efficient service" in this case to the "neglect of their crops and other interests."[22]

The office of sheriff played a key role in the investigative process and the resultant arrests and trials of the lynchers. Initially, Sheriff K. Richardson of Henderson County and his deputies went to the Trans-Cedar region to search for the killers. Within a few days they took into custody John Greenhaw and Joe Wilkinson and his son, Walter, for their part in the triple murders.[23] The heavyset Richardson with his hawk nose and goatee declared that he was doing all in his "power" to capture those responsible. But the sheriff noted that he could find little or no evidence. "There were no placards found on the dead bodies," Richardson said, "and all residents of the neighborhood professed absolute ignorance of the manner of the death of the Humphreys."[24]

In time, state and local officials brought into this homicidal case the sheriffs of the surrounding counties. Requests for assistance went to the law enforcement officers of the counties of Dallas, Ellis, Hill, Kaufman, Navarro, Rusk, and Van Zandt.[25] "These officers were not put in the field because Sheriff Richardson was inefficient," a state official reported, "but because the job was simply too big for any one sheriff and his deputies."[26] At one point during a preliminary hearing for the lynchers, the sheriffs of Dallas, Hill, and Rusk counties divided the courtroom into three sections in order to keep order in a more efficient way. Sheriff Tom Bell of Hill County "mounted the platform" and told the crowd: "You fellows caused a whole lot of disturbance yesterday. Don't do it to-day. If you do you will be yanked up here and fined. Now, you red-faced fat man over there, I'm talking to you just as much as anybody else, and I want you to understand it. Climb out of them windows over there now and let's have some fresh air."[27] After this the spectators kept their eyes on the three sheriffs.

Within a week or two after the hangings state authorities intervened in the criminal investigation. The chief executive of Texas offered a $200 reward for the capture and conviction of each person involved in the lynchings.[28] On May 31, 1899, Governor Sayers then ordered Assistant Attorney General N. B. Morris to give his "earnest and undivided attention" to working with local officials in solving the crime.[29] At the same time the governor informed County Attorney Stephen Faulk that Morris would come to Athens to assist him in the investigation and prosecution of those who took part in this horrifying act.[30] Sayers took the final step in putting together a legal team when he requested on June 3 that District Attorney J. M. Crook of the Third Judicial District of Texas be dispatched to Henderson County to cooperate with Faulk and Morris in their endeavors. The governor stressed to Crook, whose expenses would be paid for by the state, that he give the lynching cases the "very best effort of which you are capable."[31]

The final piece in the coming together of local and state law officers in Henderson County occurred on June 5. McDonald received orders from the adjutant general to go from Columbus to Athens by train and work with Morris and the county attorney. The next day the Ranger captain wired back that he would "obey orders promptly."[32] This meant that Captain Bill went from battling feudists to chasing lynchers. At the same time Private W. A. Old of Company E (who would be transferred to Company B on August 1) traveled to Henderson County to take part in the investigative process.[33] An old-timer reminisced about the coming of McDonald and Old to the area:

> The Rangers came to town in the finest buggy I'd ever seen. It was pulled by two black stallions that would make the front of the buggy jump up in the air when they started off. They had a big lap rug to keep them warm pulled up over their legs, and it had the face of a lion on the front of it. There were two rangers, but only one of them did the talkin'. The other one sat there with a razor strop tied to his arm. While the other one asked the questions, the man with the razor strop sharpened a dirk. He ran it along the razor strop so loud that it came off with a "ting." If any man hesitated in his answerin', the first ranger, the one with the dirk would whip it up with a "ting," and say, "Answer the questions as asked you, sir," in a firm, loud voice. He always got an answer.[34]

The investigation of this criminal case by Captain Bill followed timeworn procedures: collect evidence, question residents, make arrests, and guard prisoners inside and outside the courtroom. McDonald's presence, according to Morris, quieted the fears of those who wanted to talk, as the Ranger captain promised protection to witnesses and stressed that he and Old would stay in the locale until the murderers were caught.[35] Especially important to McDonald and others in the search for the killers was the analysis of physical evidence, from identifying faces and voices to looking at the ropes used in the hangings. Utilizing such methods could solve a mystery.

By the end of June 1899, the investigation of the lynchings led to dramatic results. Eight men were taken into custody and incarcerated: W. B. Brooks, Ed Cain, John Gaddis, Sam Hall, W. A. Johns, Bob Stevens, and Joseph and Walter Wilkinson (also spelled Wilkerson in some records). The evidential cases that led to their arrests and legal proceedings were put together by law officers in several ways. Three of the lynchers, John and Arthur Greenhaw and Polk Weeks, confessed and turned state's evidence. In addition, family members of the hanged men recognized the unmasked faces and voices of some of those who took part in the lynching party. The courtroom drama also included discussions of physical evidence like ropes and the tracks left by horses. Local and state officers had cooperated to put together a formidable case for the prosecution of those who had employed lynch law.[36]

In the midst of the investigations, arrests, and trials of the lynchers stood Bill McDonald. He arrived at Athens on June 7, 1899, and immediately went to the Trans-Cedar.[37] He also scouted in Kaufman and Navarro counties. On June 9 McDonald and Old arrested Ed Cain. On the twenty-second the two Rangers pursued and captured Sam Hall and Polk Weeks. Two days later McDonald and Old followed Arthur Greenhaw from Aley to Navarro County and took him into custody. Slowly the jail at Athens began to fill up with prisoners charged with murder.[38]

Captain Bill kept his superiors informed about his actions.[39] In these messages the reasons for the arrest of Cain showed that McDonald was observant. Initially, the Ranger officer made a "complaint" against Cain based upon the identification of his voice by one of the widows.[40] A newspaper reported that, in the presence of McDonald, Mrs. John Humphries recognized the voice of Cain (although she could not be positive).[41] Then McDonald learned from Cain that he "was not there [at the hangings]," but he did know who "got up the mob."[42] In the end, Cain was charged with being an accessory to murder.

McDonald, Morris, and Crook expressed their opinions to officials in Austin about the state of affairs in Henderson County. At one point the Ranger captain told the adjutant general that the mob was a "big thing" with some "prominent men" involved.[43] At another time McDonald said, "We have certainly got the lynchers in a bad fix. Of course they are an ignorant class to go into anything of that kind."[44] At the same time Morris informed the governor that the law officers had been working in a "quiet orderly manner."[45] In an extensive report about the lynchings and their aftermath, the assistant attorney general even pointed out to Sayers that he preferred to work with the Rangers and other peace officers rather than with "detectives" whose "interest in the case would, of course, be measured by dollars and cents."[46] District Attorney Crook agreed with these assessments. The work in the Trans-Cedar, he wrote the governor, "was arduous and full of hardship but those representing the State were sturdy and persistent achieving the result as quickly as it possibly could be done."[47]

Off and on for more than a year law officers returned to Henderson County and the surrounding areas to take part in the judicial proceedings. The courtroom drama began with a preliminary hearing at Athens during the last week of June 1899. Then in the same town in the middle of August a habeas corpus hearing took place. This was followed in December of the same year by the trial of Ed Cain, charged with being an accomplice in the crime. Of medium height and weight, Cain, on a change of venue, stood before Judge A. D. Lipscomb of the District Court of Anderson County located at Palestine. The same judge conducted the murder trial of Bob Stevens, a well-dressed Texan with a receding hairline and thin lips, from the end of 1899 into the following year. During the summer of 1900 two more lynchers appeared before Judge Lipscomb on a charge of murder in the first degree: W. B. Brooks and Walter Wilkinson. Like Cain and Stevens, the well-groomed

Brooks, with his sad-looking eyes, and the youthful Wilkinson were found guilty and sentenced to life in prison.[48]

In these trials the testimony of the lynchers who had turned state's evidence had to be corroborated by other facts. Besides the statements by the widows of the hanged men about recognizing faces and voices of those who took part in the lynching party, the prosecuting team, Crook, Morris, and Guy Green, also introduced physical evidence in order to clinch their cases against the lynchers. At one of the trials, testimony showed that one rope used in the hangings was an "old wellrope," while the other two turned out to be a "stakerope" and a "plowline." In questioning about the owners of such ropes, a witness implicated Joe Wilkinson.[49] McDonald's official biographer went even further. During his investigation Captain Bill proved that the cut in one of the hanging ropes matched the part of a well-rope found on Wilkinson's property.[50]

During the judicial proceedings those who took the witness stand talked about the tracks left by horses before and after the hangings. The hoofprints of a dozen horses or so could be seen at the site of the crime. These tracks then went in the direction of Aley. Several people testified that one horse had only its front legs shod, while another animal had no horseshoes. The unshod horse, in the words of those who examined the tracks, belonged to John Gaddis. The other animal, with only its front legs shod, was linked to Joe Wilkinson (although Bob Stevens had a horse with new shoes on its hind legs).[51] McDonald's official biographer went so far as to write that Captain Bill followed the tracks of five horses to the "houses of Joe Wilkinson and his tenant, and to the homes of John and Arthur Greenhaw."[52] A newspaper correctly stated that "enough was learned of the lynchers" from these trackers to give peace officers a "clew [*sic*] which finally led to arrests."[53]

During these legal proceedings McDonald and Old assisted local peace officers in maintaining order. They guarded the jail in Athens, escorted prisoners to the courtroom, and summoned witnesses.[54] At one point the Ranger captain rushed from the courtroom when a black woman who had been clubbed by her husband gave a "wild agonized cry."[55] At another time the judge ordered McDonald to bring the defense lawyers and their clients back to the courtroom. As a newspaper noted, "The ranger chief executed his orders expeditiously."[56]

McDonald and Old especially took part in crowd control. During the preliminary hearing the two Rangers and several sheriffs had to remove prisoners from a train. As people surged forward, McDonald and Old, with "words more forceful than elegant," made a lane through the crowd for the sheriffs to escort the prisoners to a safe place. One person refused to do as told. Then Captain Bill "stepped in front of the man and placed one hand on the intruder's chest and the other backward on his own belt." The fellow "turned around and walked slowly away," accompanied for a "short distance" by Old.[57]

During the trials McDonald kept looking for gun-toters. While the preliminary hearing took place, a newspaper story appeared under the heading, "RANGER CAPTAIN FOOLED." As he stood on the courthouse square in the afternoon in Athens, McDonald saw a Texan with a "large bump in the back of the coat near the region of the right hip pocket." Captain Bill's eyes "stuck out like knots on a log at the sight." When the Ranger officer called out and started in pursuit, the man ran into a store. The rest of the story then appeared in McDonald's words:

> I quickened my pace, he said, and followed in right behind him. As I entered the front door the man with the deformed pocket disappeared out the back door. I went through that building on a dog trot, and overhauled him as he was crossing the back yard.
>
> "Hey there!" I says to him again, and he stopped. "What's your name?" I says, kind of savage like, for I was out of breath. "Give me that gun you've got."
>
> "I ain't got any gun," he says, as he turned a little paler. "Don't lie to me," I says. "Hand it over and be mighty quick about it."

> And, sir, I just reached around behind him and made a grab. Well, what do you think I got? I'll be blamed if it wasn't the biggest bottle of red-eye liquor I ever saw in my life. Then I got pale myself.
>
> "Have a drink," he says. "No, thank you," I says. And I handed him his bottle and walked off.
>
> "That's a remarkable story," dryly remarked Assistant Attorney General Morris.[58]

In the midst of the tribulations in investigating and prosecuting those involved in the lynchings, McDonald and Old, and at different times, Rangers Eugene Bell, John Blanton, N. B. Jones, and Otto Race, encountered other lawbreakers in Henderson County and the surrounding areas. They made numerous arrests, mainly on charges of carrying a pistol, fighting, being drunk and disorderly, and disturbing the peace. Another crime occurred that also angered westerners. A thief was taken into custody for stealing a mule.[59]

Near the end of August 1900, the trials of the lynchers at Palestine came to an abrupt end. In accordance with an agreement between the state and the defendants, the remaining lynchers, Gaddis, Hall, Johns, and Joe Wilkinson, entered the courtroom. In rapid succession a trial took place from beginning to end. A jury was impaneled. Pleas of not guilty were recorded. Polk Weeks took the stand and testimony from the previous trials was introduced. Then the judge instructed the jury to bring in a verdict of guilty, with life imprisonment. At the same time motions to dismiss the cases against the three lynchers who had turned state's evidence were filed. In this sequence of events the defense lawyers did not object to the process, although Attorney J. J. Faulk said to the jury, "This is the saddest day of my life." But the prosecuting team of Crook and Morris saw the convictions of the lynchers as a "vindication of the law."[60]

On August 22, 1900, the Rangers performed their final act in the lynching drama. Captain Bill and Privates Blanton and Race escorted eight prisoners—Brooks, Cain, Gaddis, Hall, Johns,

Stephens, and the two Wilkinsons, Joe and Walter—to Rusk Penitentiary.[61] Before the doors of the prison opened and closed, McDonald informed his superiors that the "sentiment generally is against the mob now."[62]

Before the court proceedings against the lynchers had come to a close, the Court of Criminal Appeals handed down three decisions. On November 29, 1899, the court agreed with the district judge that John Greenhaw, who had turned state's evidence, could not be released on bail until the final disposition of the lynching cases. Then, on June 27, 1900, the appeals court upheld the convictions of Cain and Stevens. In an extensive analysis of the two cases the judges looked at the definition of malice aforethought, the use of alibis, and the meaning of conspiracy in legal parlance. At one point an appellate judge wrote that Stevens and others formed a "conspiracy" and "took the Humphries to a tree near their homes, fastened ropes around their necks, and hanged them until dead, in the cruelest and rudest manner."[63]

During the first decade of the new century those involved in the administration of justice talked about the release of the convicted felons. Such discussions especially involved Cain and Walter Wilkinson. At the end of 1902 Morris told Governor Sayers that he was still bothered by the conviction of Cain as an accomplice to the crime. The prosecutor mentioned that, in the presence of himself, District Attorney Crook, Captain McDonald, and the defense lawyers, Joe Wilkinson not only confessed "his own guilt" but also said his meeting with Cain did not deal with the "proposed lynching." Morris suggested that the governor should either "pardon" Cain "outright or commute his punishment to a term not to exceed five years."[64] Several weeks later two prominent residents of the Trans-Cedar country sent the governor a moving letter in support of a pardon for Cain. They even gathered evidence to show that his "conduct in the pen is without a blot."[65]

During 1907 an exchange of letters took place between a lawyer in East Texas and Governor Thomas Campbell. The attorney talked about letting Walter Wilkinson out of prison. He wrote that at the time of the lynchings Wilkinson was an "ordinary country boy" of "17 years" who had "little education or cultivation" and had "merely followed the leadership of his father and his neighbors." In reply the governor explained that the application for a pardon for Wilkinson was still "pending" before the Board of Pardon Advisors. When necessary, Campbell added, he would give the matter his "faithful consideration."[66]

With the recommendations urging clemency by judges, lawyers, prison officials, the advisory board on pardons, and respected citizens, Governor Campbell pardoned the eight convicted lynchers. The first one to receive a remission of penalty was Cain at the end of 1908. The next year Stevens and Walter Wilkinson left prison with their pardons. Then in September 1910, the governor signed the legal documents which allowed Brooks, Gaddis, Hall, and Johns to return to their families and friends. The last prisoner to be pardoned was the ringleader of the lynching party—Joe Wilkinson. Among the factors that brought about the release of the one-armed ex-Confederate soldier in 1911 were his "age" and his "ill health."[67]

In his memoirs Joe Wilkinson lashed out at John Greenhaw, Weeks, and McDonald for their actions in the lynching affair. For turning against his fellow lynchers in the courtroom, Greenhaw became a traitor—the "vilest of vile."[68] In the same vein Weeks was "too sorry for the dogs to bark at."[69] In Wilkinson's mind McDonald deserved "immeasurable condemnation" for his methods of collecting evidence.[70] Captain Bill, old Joe wrote, "showed himself as devoid of moral courage as a jelly fish is of backbone."[71]

Those who carried out the investigation and prosecution of the lynchers did not agree with the opinions of Joe Wilkinson. District Attorney Crook informed the governor that the "result" reached in the courtroom was in a "great measure" due to the "efforts" of state officers, Morris, Green, and McDonald. The selection of Morris by the governor, in Crook's words, was a "most happy one."[7]

Chapter 10

FINALE OF THE FRONTIER BATTALION

On the killing of T. L. Fuller of Company B in the line of duty: shot "without warning."[1]

The troubles at Orange, Texas, where Fuller went down, led to the demise of the Frontier Battalion at the turn of the twentieth century.

During the last half of the 1890s, the lifestyles of the members of the Frontier Battalion remained similar to the existence of those who served in the early Rangers. They still wore nondescript clothes, rode horses, carried revolvers, rifles, and shotguns, and lived under harsh conditions imposed by nature and distances traveled. In addition, the men in the four companies in the field continued under the command of Brooks, Hughes, McDonald, and Rogers. These captains tried to maximize the use of their time and energies in combating crime and maintaining order.

At the start of the twentieth century, the Lone Star State faced a growing population and an increasing number of farms, ranches, towns, and larger urban centers. For some time the Rangers of Texas tried to change their operations to meet these new conditions. Although the headquarters of their companies remained in the less populated western and southern areas, they also established subcompanies in the towns and became more involved in combating crime and disorder in East Texas. Yet the Ranger service had to face these additional responsibilities with limited resources and manpower.

Financial exigencies forced state officials to reduce the number of Rangers to a mere handful. In order to cover vast distances, this small band of peace officers increasingly traveled by rail and communicated by telegraph. Most important, the Rangers, like their counterparts elsewhere in the country, improved their investigative skills. The Rangers as detectives had gained acceptance in many quarters.

For nearly two decades the central headquarters of the Ranger service remained stable under Adjutant Generals King and Mabry. This steadily directed command system came to an end with the resignation of Mabry in 1898 in order to serve in the Spanish-American War. He was replaced as adjutant general by Alfred P. Wozencraft, who served in the position for a short period of time. In 1899 Thomas Scurry then took Wozencraft's place and held the office for several years. John A. Hulen became the fourth adjutant general in a decade, as he replaced Scurry and carried out his duties from 1903 to 1907. These adjutant generals ably headed both the military and police forces of the state.

As these changes took place, turnover also occurred in the personnel of the office of battalion quartermaster at central headquarters in Austin. The long-standing career of Sieker in this role came to an end in 1893. During the rest of the 1890s, this key position in maintaining the Ranger companies in the field was filled by G. A. Wheatley (1893–1895), W. H. Owen (1895–1899), and E. M. Phelps (1899). At the turn of the century Sieker came back to direct the "Four Great Captains" as battalion quartermaster for six more years.

Captain McDonald continued his dual roles in the Ranger service: running a company and investigating crime and disorder. By the opening of the 1900s, McDonald still had to manage the company, write reports, and deal with organizational problems. Cartridges for the revolvers and rifles had to be purchased, mostly .45 caliber handguns and 30/30 Winchesters. Then came the need for handcuffs and leg irons, feed for horses and mules (hay, corn, and oats), and rations for the men (in one monthly report more bacon than beef, more potatoes than beans, and a lot of flour). McDonald agreed with his superiors, in addition, that each Ranger company should be furnished with a two-horse hack. He felt that at times wagon travel was too slow. Most important, Private Eugene Bell got drunk and was put in jail. The Ranger captain took his commission away from him. At one point his superiors in the central office sent McDonald blank forms to be used in recording his actions in running Company B: forms for muster and payrolls, monthly reports, ration returns, vouchers, and discharge certificates.[2]

While McDonald and some of his Rangers went after feudists, lynchers, and mobs in high-profile cases from San Saba to Columbus and Athens, other members of Company B continued to go after lawbreakers elsewhere in the state. The extent of their actions can be seen in the statistical record published by the adjutant general every two years:

1. From December 1896 to December 1898, McDonald's company, now headquartered at Memphis in Hall County in the Panhandle with a detachment at San Saba, traveled 45,523 miles (more than any other company), carried out 331 scouts, arrested 206 persons—with the majority being for assault and murder, robbery and burglary, horse, cattle and other thefts, and minor offenses—failed to arrest on twenty-five occasions, guarded jails thirteen times, gave seventy-eight assists to courts and judges (nearly three times the number for the next nearest company), and aided civil authorities on 207 different occasions. During this time period no Rangers were killed in the line of duty and only one suspect went to his death at the hands of the members of Company B.[3]
2. From December 1898 to November 1900, Company B, in time stationed again at Amarillo, traveled 48,262 miles, carried out 405 scouts (more than the other companies), conducted twenty-four escorts (the only company to do so), made 370 arrests—with seventy-three for assault and murder, fifty-three for carrying con-

> cealed weapons, twenty-six for horse, cattle and other thefts, and twenty for swindling, embezzlement, and forgery—guarded jails three times, and assisted civil authorities and judges on eighty different occasions (more than any other company). McDonald's Rangers, in addition, still handled six cases of fence cutting. Because of legal questions about the law establishing the Frontier Battalion, a number of the rank and file were promoted to lieutenant in 1900. Sergeant McCauley, for example, was raised to that rank and given command of Company C, stationed at Colorado City in Mitchell County. In reality, McDonald directed the operations of McCauley's small company, although its activities were listed separately in the statistical record.[4]

Month after month during 1896, Captain Bill and the rank and file of Company B moved around the state and carried out varied operations. From arresting a person for "whipping his wife" to going after those who committed murder, McDonald and his men gave Texas badmen no rest (although their old nemesis—George Knighten—still could not be found). In particular, the Rangers attempted to locate and arrest cattle and horse thieves. Here the counties, like Childress, Deaf Smith, Parmer, and Wichita, along the New Mexico and Oklahoma borders were troublesome. The Panhandle Rangers were forced to cooperate with local sheriffs and federal marshals to maximize results of investigations and manhunts. McDonald and Sheriff Coffer at one point, for example, ran down two cattle thieves and jailed them in Quanah. In addition, the Ranger captain considered conflicting requests for Rangers from townspeople and the sheriff at Texline in Dallam County. McDonald acknowledged that the sheriff and the local citizens were a "little cross ways." By the end of 1896 McDonald refused a request to station Rangers in Collingsworth County but kept a detachment in Mills County in Central Texas.[5]

For the next several years the political leaders of Texas had to wrestle with three issues. In the first place, the outbreak of the

Spanish-American War in 1898 made Texans rush to join the military effort and forced state officials to send more Rangers to the southern border. Equally pressing, crime, disorder, and natural disasters made governmental authorities send the Rangers into more counties and towns. The members of Company B, for example, had to move in several directions, east, south, and west, from their old base in northern Texas. And lastly, the troubles at Orange at the turn of the twentieth century resulted in violent acts, legal and judicial disputes, and the resultant demise of the Frontier Battalion.

TEXANS AND THE WAR WITH SPAIN

A pivotal event in American history occurred in the spring of 1898. An expansionist mood in some parts of the country coupled with the destruction of the *Maine* in Cuban waters led to a war between the United States and Spain. Texans served in the 1st U. S. Volunteer Cavalry Regiment, better known as the Rough Riders, with Theodore Roosevelt as a colorful second in command. The regiment trained near San Antonio, used a large herd of Texas horses, and fought in Cuba (mainly on foot, although Roosevelt rode his horse called Texas).[6]

During the war those in charge of the government in Austin faced a particular problem: securing the southern border of Texas. Governor Culberson did not believe that the military conflict would strain relations with Mexico. But he did see that the lawless elements on both sides of the border would take advantage of the need for troops elsewhere.[7] Some Texans wrote letters to the governor asking for permission to raise volunteer companies to go to the frontier lands. A few petitioners were even former Texas Rangers. However, the manager of the King Ranch and James B. Wells, Jr., a regional kingpin, argued against allowing "Home Guards" to roam the area of South Texas. Wells added that in Cameron County the Ranger company commanded by Captain Brooks "would do far more good than ten times any other force that could be sent there."[8]

At the start of the war, state officials ordered Captain McDonald and his men to move to the border in order to augment the Rangers already there. On April 22, 1898, the members of Company B, with their horses, mules, and supplies, traveled to Spofford Junction, which placed them in between the companies commanded by Captains Hughes and Rogers. At this time McDonald enlisted several new recruits and his muster rolls showed the names of dozens of Special Rangers. The arrival of these state peace officers meant that the four Ranger companies covered the borderlands from Brownsville to El Paso.[9]

For two months the rank and file of Company B patrolled the boundary with Mexico. They chased train robbers to the Rio Grande. They guarded a bridge that an "armed band in Mexico" threatened to blow up. And they arrested an Hispanic for murder and jailed him at Eagle Pass. On the seventeenth of June, McDonald's Rangers left their camp at Spofford Junction and arrived in northern Texas ten days later. At the same time the Ranger captain received orders to discharge five men because of the lack of funds to sustain their positions.[10]

During McDonald's sojourn in southern Texas, Governor Culberson and Mexican President Porfirio Diaz communicated with each other. In the spirit of friendship Diaz proposed that the forces of Texas and Mexico along the borderline should cooperate with each other whenever needed. "To this effect," Diaz said, "I have given orders to the chiefs of Detachments who are on the right bank of the Bravo, that whenever the settlers on the left bank are seen to be injured by robbers to offer and render their services to the american authorities without reserve, always when said authorities accept them or solicit them, I authorizing them to ask the same help from the armed forces of the left bank, in identical cases."[11]

Several days later Culberson informed the four Ranger captains about the proposal made by Diaz to maintain law and order. He instructed them to "act in accordance therewith."[12] McDonald responded by reporting that these instructions will be "strictly complied with." "It is a move in the right direction," he continued, "& with the assistance from officials in Mexico we can certainly hold the scoundrels down altho our force is small to cover so much teritory [*sic*]."[13]

LAW AND ORDER IN EAST TEXAS

At the end of the 1890s a newspaper reporter aptly noted that the Rangers were "scattered all over the state."[14] Before and after the Spanish-American War the members of Company B moved deep into East Texas. The pressing need for law and order made state officials send McDonald's Rangers into Longview, into Galveston, into San Augustine, and into Orange. At the turn of the century the personnel of Company B had changed dramatically. Gone were a number of the Panhandle Rangers from the early years, such as Britton, Harwell, McClure, Queen, and Sullivan. New names added to the muster rolls of the company included John Blanton, T. L. Fuller, J. W. Keeton, Carl Ryan, and A. L. Saxon. The principal officers in the company, though, continued to be the captain and the sergeant: McDonald and McCauley.[15]

Two of the less colorful roles of the Rangers were guarding jails and transporting prisoners. At the end of 1897, Captain Bill, Sergeant McCauley, and Private Barker traveled to Longview in Gregg County to assist the sheriff in guarding the jail. The prisoner turned out to be Jim Nite, killer, convicted cattle thief, and supposed member of the Dalton gang that robbed a bank in Longview in 1894. The Rangers escorted the prisoner between the jail and the district court. The judge changed the venue of the trial of Nite, charged with murder and bank robbery, to Smith County. To carry out a judicial order, McDonald and his men took Nite to the penitentiary at Rusk for "safe keeping." The Ranger captain pointed out to his superiors that he and the sheriff, at different times, had taken saws away from Nite. But the Rangers had "no trouble" in bringing the prisoner to the state pen.[16]

For the next year or two Captain Bill and other Rangers journeyed off and on to the port of Galveston. Here they carried out their orders to stop prizefights banned by law during the administrations of Governors Culberson and Sayers. In August 1898 McDonald received instructions from his superiors to assist the district attorney in bringing an end to a prizefight in the city. The Ranger captain learned that an attempt would be made to circumvent the law by not charging any "gate fees." But the fight did not come off, since the promoters and the pugilists, as McDonald put it, "decided it would not be healthy for them."[17] Before this happened, McDonald informed the governor that he did not "know" if he would need "any more assistance." He understood that some officials were going to protect the fighters during the bout. But the Ranger captain stressed that he would not let anyone "override the law."[18]

For the rest of 1898 the governor and public authorities in Galveston carried on a war of words. Culberson, District Attorney J. K. P. Gillaspie, and Sheriff Henry Thomas of Galveston County exchanged letters on a course of action. The governor and district attorney ruled out prizefights in the city; the sheriff and county attorney believed they were within the law. Attorney General M. M. Crane informed Culberson that there would be "very little difference in principle" between an "assessment" of members for the "purpose of securing such attractions and an admission fee to be charged at the door." By the end of the year, the governor, after reading in the news media about several bouts taking place, demanded to know whether the sheriff would "prevent the exhibitions so-called before the Galveston Athletic Club."[19]

This subterfuge came to an end at the start of 1899. In the middle of January the promoters tried again to stage a prizefight with the same contestants—Joe Choynski and Jim Hall—in a rented opera house. This time Sheriff Thomas and his deputies joined McDonald and several Rangers in telling those who ran the Galveston Athletic Club that the boxing match could not be held. At one point the Ranger captain wired central headquarters, "Couldn't conceal my identity as they expected me." In the end the organizers presented a disappointing program: the two pugilists took turns punching a bag, with black singers and dancers before and a few local black fighters hitting the bag as a finale. The audience was dissatisfied. And Sheriff Thomas thought he could have enforced the ban on the fistic contest—without the help of McDonald and his Rangers.[20]

At the turn of the twentieth century the members of three Ranger companies were drawn deeper into the Piney Woods of East Texas—to Nacogdoches and San Augustine. The latter town had faced feuding parties in its early history. This time the violent acts occurred between two factions that coalesced around those named Broocks and Walls. In the maneuvering that took place, the sheriff's office did not remain neutral, but joined one side in the conflict. A citizen wired the governor in June 1900: "Riot at San-Augustine three killed for gods sake send rangers." Into the area came Adjutant General Scurry and the military and police forces of the state. From Nacogdoches the Stone Fort Rifles marched and rode in vehicles through mud and water to reach the town. From other directions Captains Brooks and Rogers and their Rangers entered the region. The state peace officers took control of the sheriff's office, kept order, made arrests, and guarded and transported prisoners. In these endeavors Lieutenant W. B. Bates carried out his duties with verve and skill. Bates had been assigned to McDonald's Rangers from Company F. In the fall of 1900, Captain Rogers and Private J. Armstrong of Company B also assisted the sheriff at Nacogdoches in protecting a prisoner from a lynch mob.[21]

While the rank and file of Company B went after lawbreakers in the eastern and southern parts of the state, Captain McDonald still had to allocate resources for the protection of those who inhabited northern and western Texas. At the end of the 1890s, McDonald's Rangers chased cattle and horse thieves, fence cutters, murderers, and bank and train robbers from the Panhandle region to Borden, Scurry, and Tom Green counties in West Texas. The Ranger captain noted that travel by wagon in the Panhandle was difficult over washed-out roads. At one point McDonald arrested two men for attempting to stop a train near Fort Worth by "pulling the bell cord & using the break [*sic*]." They were fined and released. At another time McDonald went to El Paso and took into custody a person charged with disposing mortgaged property. Other duties that occupied the time and energies of the members of Company B ranged from assisting local officers at Amarillo in enforcing the quarantine law against smallpox to keeping order at a county fair. The adjutant general directed McDonald to "manage" the police force run by the Hardeman County Fair Association at their fairground in September 1900. "Of course," Scurry concluded, "you will be relieved from Quanah in the event any emergency arises requiring your presence elsewhere."[22]

In these undertakings a complex process taxed the ability of the Rangers to pursue those who broke the law. The extradition of fugitives between the states and with foreign countries became a time-consuming procedure for the Ranger command system. In the return of a fugitive from Mexico, for example, more than one method could be used. One basic way called for Texas officials to forward the requisition papers to federal authorities in Washington who would then contact Mexican office holders.[23]

This scenario happened in the case of William F. Brice, charged with forgery in Hardeman County, who fled to Mexico in the mid-1890s. Initially, the appropriate requisition forms were filed with the U. S. government and Captain McDonald proceeded to Mexico in early 1895. But he failed to get Brice, who had been arrested by Mexican officers, because the papers were not "properly arranged at Washington." A few months later the governor even asked McDonald to take blank requisition forms and have them properly filled out and documented. In such confusion the forger remained at large for several years. Then in 1898 Texan officials filed requisition papers for the return of Brice with a federal court in the Indian Territory. But the judge refused to honor the request, since Brice was now in the hands of a United

States marshal for committing a federal crime (which took preference over state law and the Rangers). In law and in fact, Brice finally got extradited from Mexico.[24]

TRAILS AND TRIBULATIONS AT ORANGE

At the start of the 1900s, the governor and the adjutant general praised the "excellent work" of the Ranger service. To Captain Bill and the members of Company B, they said, "The unhesitating manner in which yourself and men have performed your duty, acting with firmness and courage under the most trying circumstances, in the face of great danger and without rowdyism, is most commendable."[25] Yet the involvement of McDonald and his Rangers in the troubles in Orange County, which was underway, led to two consequences: first, a member of the company lost his life in the line of duty; and second, legal entanglements made state officials disband the Frontier Battalion—in law if not in fact.

Orange, Texas, intersected by waterways and railroads near the border of Louisiana, had a population of several thousand people and a thriving lumber industry by the end of the 1800s. The town became the county seat and a gateway to Texas and the West. Pioneers of all creeds and colors moved into the area. As the town prospered, so did Orange County. By the opening of the 1900s, the county had over 5,900 inhabitants engaged in farming and commercial enterprises.[26]

In the middle of August 1899, Governor Sayers received a request from public officials in the town of Orange for aid in maintaining law and order. Through intimidation and violence (one black dead and two wounded), a local group called "Whitecaps" had attempted to stop blacks from working in the lumber mills and drive them out of the region. The county sheriff and city marshal even wrote that the town was "virtually in the hands of the mob." State authorities responded by sending in troops and ordering Captain Rogers and several Rangers to the area. After making some arrests,

Rogers, who was suffering from an old wound, removed himself from the case. To relieve him McDonald and his men moved in.[27]

In time, Adjutant General Scurry went to Orange to investigate the conditions in the town. In his report to the governor he recorded that the proprietors of the Lutcher-Moore Lumber Company, other mill owners, and their hired hands believed the need to import black laborers from Louisiana during the summer months resulted from four factors: extreme heat, sickness, absenteeism, and contractual deadlines. They also saw blacks and whites working together without trouble. Other residents, though, felt that those in charge of the lumber mills were trying to "lower wages and oppress labor" by getting rid of white workers. In the opinion of the adjutant general there was "no organized plan on the part of the white laborers to run the negroes out of Orange." About "25 or 30 men" banded together and committed the recent crimes.[28]

The adjutant general, in addition, found the townspeople divided into two factions over the presence of the Rangers. One side, consisting of numerous mill men, professionals, merchants, and blacks, stressed that the Rangers were "necessary to preserve the peace and protect property." The other side, including a number of town and county officials, professionals, merchants, and white workers, believed that the "call for rangers was unnecessary and ought not to have been made." They saw the actions of the Rangers in two ways: as preventing efforts to resist bringing in outside laborers; and as hurting the "good name" of the town. Over 300 individuals formed a "Citizens Law and Order Club of Orange" to assist in combating lawlessness. Although some claimed that the deadly shots were really fired into a black gambling den and that the bullying of the blacks was nothing more than a "frolic" by the "boys," Adjutant General Scurry concluded that the "rough treatment" of prisoners by the Rangers was "necessary with the class of men dealt with."[29]

In the middle of September of 1899, state officials pondered the role of the Rangers at Orange. Conflicting views of residents had reached the governor. Sheriff P. F. Eastin and County Judge George F. Poole called for the removal of the Rangers, as, in their eyes, the trouble has "blown over and matters are again quiet."[30] Instead of following this advice, the adjutant general asked McDonald on September 20 if he could go to the town and relieve Captain Rogers.[31] Two days later McDonald with Privates N. B. Jones and W. A. Old reached the troubled area. By the end of the month, from Ranger personnel stationed in one place or another, Privates Fuller and A. Y. Old made their way to Orange. In their usual workmanlike manner, McDonald's Rangers quickly arrested and jailed three residents for murder, two for arson, and five for fighting.[32]

The next month Captain Bill and his men, now consisting of Sergeant McCauley (who arrived on the tenth) and Privates Eugene Bell, Fuller, Jones, and W. A. Old, went after lawbreakers in Orange County with a vengeance. They took into custody and jailed twenty-five individuals. Sixteen of these arrests were for murder and conspiracy to commit murder; the rest were charged with adultery, aggravated assault, arson, disturbing the peace, and robbery. In carrying out these endeavors, the Rangers cooperated with Sheriff Eastin and his deputies and testified before a grand jury. In addition, McDonald and Old went to nearby Beaumont to arrest a murderer and traveled to Louisiana to search for fugitives and gather information for use in criminal cases.[33]

Captain Bill had become concerned about working relations between those who broke the law and public officials of Orange County. The Ranger officer saw County Judge Poole as the "legal advisor of the mob." The judge influenced the actions of the sheriff and county attorney and protected his "boys" who were involved in the recent troubles.[34] At one point Poole left two accused murderers go free upon judicial use of writs of habeas corpus. One person released fled to another state; the other individual McDonald placed in the jail at Beaumont.[35] A statement made by a committee representing mill men contained these words: "The County Judge has during all the trouble sided with the rough element, opposed the Rangers and every legitimate effort to bring to justice the guilty parties."[36]

In a letter to the news media Judge Poole reiterated his beliefs about the troubles in Orange. In his mind the recruitment of black laborers from Louisiana by the owner of a lumber company made white workers worry about undesirable changes in their employment. Then two events of importance took place. A "gang of so-called whitecaps" found blacks in an "outhouse gaming" and shot and killed the black recruiter who went to Louisiana. A few days later a notice, with "skull and cross bones," was "posted on a saloon door, telling negroes to get out of town by a certain time." Few people took these words seriously, as it was "thought to be the work of some devilish boys with no evil intentions whatever, or expectations of trying to make the negroes leave." The town, in the eyes of the judge, "is not, and has not, been in the hands of a mob." Since local officers had the ability to handle any disturbance, the military and police forces of the state were not needed to "restore order."[37]

In the waning months of 1899, the small detachment of Rangers remained at Orange until after the holiday season. This force now included Sergeant McCauley (in charge when McDonald had to be elsewhere) and Privates Bell, Fuller, Jones, and Saxon (and for a time, W. A. Old). The arrests made by this band of state peace officers—twenty-three in November and twenty in December for crimes ranging from murder to the theft of a watch—worried the local gang, although some did not remain in jail very long. By the end of November McDonald realized that the Rangers were merely policing the streets and preventing any further intimidation of citizens.[38]

THE DEATH OF FULLER AND THE DEMISE OF THE FRONTIER BATTALION

For the next two years the members of Company B went back to Orange off and on. Their main crime-fighting operations, however, were still centered in the northern and western parts of the state.

Here they scouted, made arrests, guarded jails, and attended courts. As McDonald and his Rangers moved around the Texan landscape, a few key events stood out: the actions of Private Saxon, first in Orange County, then in Hall County in the Panhandle, which led to a judicial charge of making unlawful arrests; the death of Oscar Poole at the hands of Ranger Fuller; a written opinion made by the state's attorney general which led to a legal change in the status of the Ranger service; and the gunning down of Fuller by Thomas Poole. Such acts impacted the workings of Company B and the Frontier Battalion.[39]

Captain Bill's concern about the machinations of the Poole family was justified. The violent encounters between Fuller and Judge Poole's two sons resulted in tragic deaths. The adjutant general characterized Fuller as a "young man of temperate habits, quiet in his manner and a fearless ranger." He joined the Rangers in June 1899 after gaining experience as a local lawman. At the same time he was trying to save enough money to finish his collegiate education. Literate and capable, Fuller had a promising career in the Frontier Battalion.[40]

Around five o'clock on December 21, 1899, Oscar Poole, in an attempt to free a prisoner, was shot and killed by Fuller in the discharge of his duty. Poole never regained consciousness; he was struck in the forehead while standing in the door of a saloon. Sergeant McCauley quickly placed the Ranger private under arrest and took him to a hotel "under guard not deeming the county jail a safe place." The next day the sergeant and the sheriff removed Fuller, charged with murder, to Beaumont to be incarcerated. For several days the Rangers guarded the jail off and on and talked with judicial officers. In the middle of January of 1900, McDonald assisted in returning Fuller to Orange for a court hearing. The governor and the adjutant general believed that they could not legally allocate funds to defend officers prosecuted by the state. They asked the members of Company B to seek private funds for Fuller's defense. This approach infuriated Sergeant McCauley. In time, Fuller survived the judicial labyrinth and returned to his Ranger duties.[41]

In the spring of 1900, Captain Bill worried about the reaction of the toughs at Orange to the return of Fuller and Saxon. He told his superiors that the local "rascals" have "no love for me" and might start a "row" with the two Ranger privates. Months earlier Adjutant General Scurry wrote McDonald that Fuller and Saxon were "excellent rangers" who would not fail to do their "duty." At the same time the two privates could "very likely rub the rough element the wrong way." Yet Scurry had no "fear" that Fuller and Saxon would be killed by the "mob element at Orange."[42]

On October 14, 1900, the three Rangers—McDonald, Fuller, and Saxon—traveled to Orange to attend a court session. The next day Fuller (now a lieutenant) and Saxon went to a barbershop. Fuller stood in the middle of the room at a basin washing his face, while Saxon sat in the chair having a shave. Around 5:30 a bullet from a Winchester struck Fuller in the "temple" and he "fell to the floor and expired in a few minutes." Then Thomas Poole with a rifle ran into a butcher shop close by and was taken into custody by a local police officer. Later Poole was removed to Beaumont and jailed.[43]

During McDonald's captaincy only one Ranger lost his life in the line of duty: T. L. Fuller. He would also be the last Ranger in the Frontier Battalion to die a violent death. In his report Captain Bill viewed his murder in "cold blood" as a "conspiracy," with other killers "near by."[44] McDonald, who rushed to the scene of the crime when he heard the shot, always regretted not being able to gun down Fuller's murderer. In counties with corrupt public officers the Rangers called the killing of a badman "getting a conviction."[45]

The death of Fuller was one more episode in the deadly violence that plagued residents of East Texas at the turn of the twentieth century. From Athens to Columbus to San Augustine and Orange, Rangers took to the streets and made their stand. "The Orange County feud of 1899–1900," wrote a noted penman, "featured a lethal array of ingredients: lynchings, assassinations, efforts to purge the county of blacks, arson, anonymous death threats, a corrupt county judge, and, not least, the mercurial Captain Bill himself. In the line of duty, a Ranger shot and killed the son of the county judge, only to be shot down himself, from behind."[46]

Although McDonald thought that District Attorney W. L. Douglas at Orange wanted legal assistance from the attorney general's office at Austin in the prosecution of Thomas Poole for Fuller's murder, that was not the case. But Douglas was concerned that the district judge did not have the "backbone" to grant a change of venue. If this did not happen, in the words of Douglas, the "trial of the case in Orange County will be a farce and will result in an acquittal of Poole." With the "tough and hoodlum element" in the ascendancy in the county, the good citizens will not speak out, for "fear of being assassinated or having their property destroyed."[47]

A grand jury indicted Poole for murder in the first degree. In early May of 1901, a jury trial took place in the district court at Orange. Poole pled not guilty. After hearing the evidence and the charge from the judge, the members of the jury gave their verdict: not guilty of the felonious crime.[48]

The story of the push by the Rangers to enforce law and order in Orange County would not be complete without recording the legal browbeating of Private Saxon. He had enlisted in Company B in November 1899. Although one of "McDonald's most efficient men," he quickly became a scapegoat in a judicial system gone astray.[49]

The end of the Frontier Battalion of Texas Rangers in 1901 did not come about in a fiery gun battle, nor from a lack of work as the frontier era came to a close in the Lone Star State. It resulted from a legal stand about the powers to make arrests. Could all members of the state constabulary make arrests—or only those Rangers who carried special writs of authority?

In November 1899, during the troubles in Orange County, Privates Bell, Fuller, Jones, and Saxon took into custody and jailed five men for disturbing the peace. One of them "resisted arrest and had to be knocked down."[50] Saxon struck the individual "across the head with a pistol." In his trial Judge Poole charged the jury that Rangers, in McDonald's words, "were *not* peace officers and had no right to make an arrest." The result for the moment was a hung jury.[51] Months later a jury fined Saxon $25. A seething McDonald thought this was an "outrageous verdict."[52] When Judge Poole requested Austin headquarters to provide the arrest record of another Ranger, Captain Bill advised his superiors not to let the judge "belittle the ranger service."[53]

Use of the legal principle of false imprisonment against the Rangers spread. In a case dealing with the arrest of three men for cutting miles of wire fence belonging to a rancher in Hall County, Saxon was again charged with putting one of the suspects, who had been released at an examining trial, in jail illegally. During the investigation this person was taken into custody because his tracks matched those found at the scene of the crime. In late May of 1900, Saxon was found guilty of false imprisonment and given thirty days in jail and fined $50. County Judge W. M. Pardue, soft on the prosecution of criminals, according to McDonald, charged that a Ranger "had no more right to arrest than a private citizen." McDonald noted the "whole thing was cut & dried." Later Saxon was also arrested on a charge of perjury stemming from the same wire cutting affair in Hall County. But the judges, in time, dismissed this case. By then Saxon had petitioned the governor for a pardon and requested a ruling by the attorney general on the right of a Ranger to make an arrest.[54]

In order to better understand the state of affairs in Hall County, the governor asked J. B. Daniel to make a report. In a scathing attack he outlined the skullduggery and criminal conduct of Judge Pardue and other officials elected to office on the Populist ticket. These public servants tried hard to stop the drive by the Rangers to protect lives and property. In the Saxon case the judge and sheriff wanted to immediately jail the Ranger. But McDonald stopped these actions by filing an appeal and making bond. To Daniel the county needed martial law and more Rangers.[55]

On June 8, 1900, Governor Sayers granted Saxon a pardon for his jail sentence and fine for the offense of false imprisonment in Hall County. The governor declared that Saxon acted "within the scope of his official authority and in accordance with the uniform and unquestioned practice of State Rangers for many years."[56] Within a year, to the surprise of no one, Saxon resigned from the Ranger service.[57]

At the beginning of 1901, the presiding judge of the Court of Criminal Appeals notified Governor Sayers that an appeal of the Saxon case was still before the court. "As long as the appeal is pending," the judge wrote, "there is no conviction." Thus, the pardon was null and void. The judge went on to say that the "proper disposition" of the case would be to "temporarily" withdraw the pardon and then remove the appeal and "extend" the pardon. McDonald was so informed. But the records do not indicate that state officials took such actions.[58]

On May 24, 1900, Attorney General T. S. Smith, responding to a communication from Adjutant General Scurry, sent a lengthy memorandum to Governor Sayers outlining his thoughts on the subject of Rangers making arrests and executing criminal processes. Reviewing state laws back to 1874 and the creation of the Frontier Battalion, Smith concluded that only commissioned Ranger officers and not noncommissioned officers or privates could make arrests and carry out the criminal process. "The commissioned officers have all the power of peace officers," the attorney general went on to say, "which they can exercise anywhere throughout the state."[59]

The ruling by the attorney general was foreshadowed by events in the early 1880s. Defense attorneys for Rangers involved in a shooting raised the question whether privates in the Frontier Battalion could legally make arrests.[60] In one of his reports in 1882, Adjutant General King recommended that the legislature revise the law creating the Frontier Battalion. He thought that all Rangers should have the powers of peace officers, including making arrests (like the law had given to McNelly's armed force).[61] Although this failed to materialize, the adjutant general did inform a company commander a year later that the men under his command had the power of peace officers—if they acted under orders or had legal papers in a given case or saw the crime committed.[62]

Upon learning of the opinion of the attorney general, McDonald stated in an interview that Saxon's "chances" of being promoted to the rank of lieutenant were "good."[63] In fact, the Ranger captain and his superiors did forward contracts to some men of Company B, like Fuller, McCauley, and Saxon, to make them lieutenants in the Frontier Battalion.[64]

The move to reassign Rangers happened for one simple reason. On May 25, 1900, the attorney general informed Adjutant General Scurry that the governor had the legal authority to reorganize the Frontier Battalion.[65] The next day Scurry issued General Order No. 24. The four current companies hereafter would consist of one captain, one first lieutenant, one second lieutenant, and three privates. Two new companies were created to be manned by a first lieutenant, one second lieutenant, and two privates. The six first lieutenants would be compensated at the rate of $50 per month (first sergeant's pay) and the six second lieutenants agreed to serve for $30 a month (private's pay). Only a commissioned officer had the power to "make the arrest and execute criminal process." Privates would assist their officers in this endeavor and "perform such other duties as rangers which do not involve the exercise of authority as peace officers." Finally, Special Rangers were honorably discharged, as they had no legal authority to act as peace officers under the new interpretation of the law.[66]

On July 3, 1900, Adjutant General Scurry issued Special Order No. 67 to temporarily reassign personnel in the Ranger service. First Lieutenant McCauley (promoted from sergeant) left Company B and took command of one of the new companies, lettered C. This diminutive company, however, continued to receive "instructions" from Captain McDonald. The adjutant general wanted to disrupt as little as possible the current Ranger organization.[67]

For a year orders, men, and reports passed between Companies B (McDonald) and C (McCauley). Other officers in these companies at different times included Lieutenants Bates, Blanton, Fuller, and Keeton. The murder of Fuller was even recorded in the monthly returns of both companies, although he rode with McCauley's Rangers. The few members of Company C, stationed at Colorado and San Angelo, went after the usual lawbreakers: burglars, counterfeiters, murderers, robbers, thieves, and those drinking and fighting.[68] At one point McCauley arrested two Texans for having "pistols" and "playing Co 'B' Rangers."[69] In addition, as his career in the Frontier Battalion came to an end, McCauley took part in a shooting scrape and had to violently subdue a drunken prisoner.[70]

In his two-year report at the turn of the century Adjutant General Scurry recommended that the Ranger regulations be changed to read that commissioned and noncommissioned officers and privates be clothed with all the powers necessary to make arrests and execute criminal processes. This new force would not exceed four companies of twenty men each and the pay of privates would be increased in order to insure better recruits for longer periods of time. "The Texas Volunteer Guard and the rangers," the adjutant general wrote, "have each been a most efficient and reliable force in their respective spheres."[71]

Months went by as the details of new legislation were worked out in the state capital. On July 8, 1901, the Frontier Battalion of Texas Rangers was quietly disbanded and its members were mustered out of the service of the state. A new Ranger force was organized in its stead. An era in Texas history had come to an end.[72]

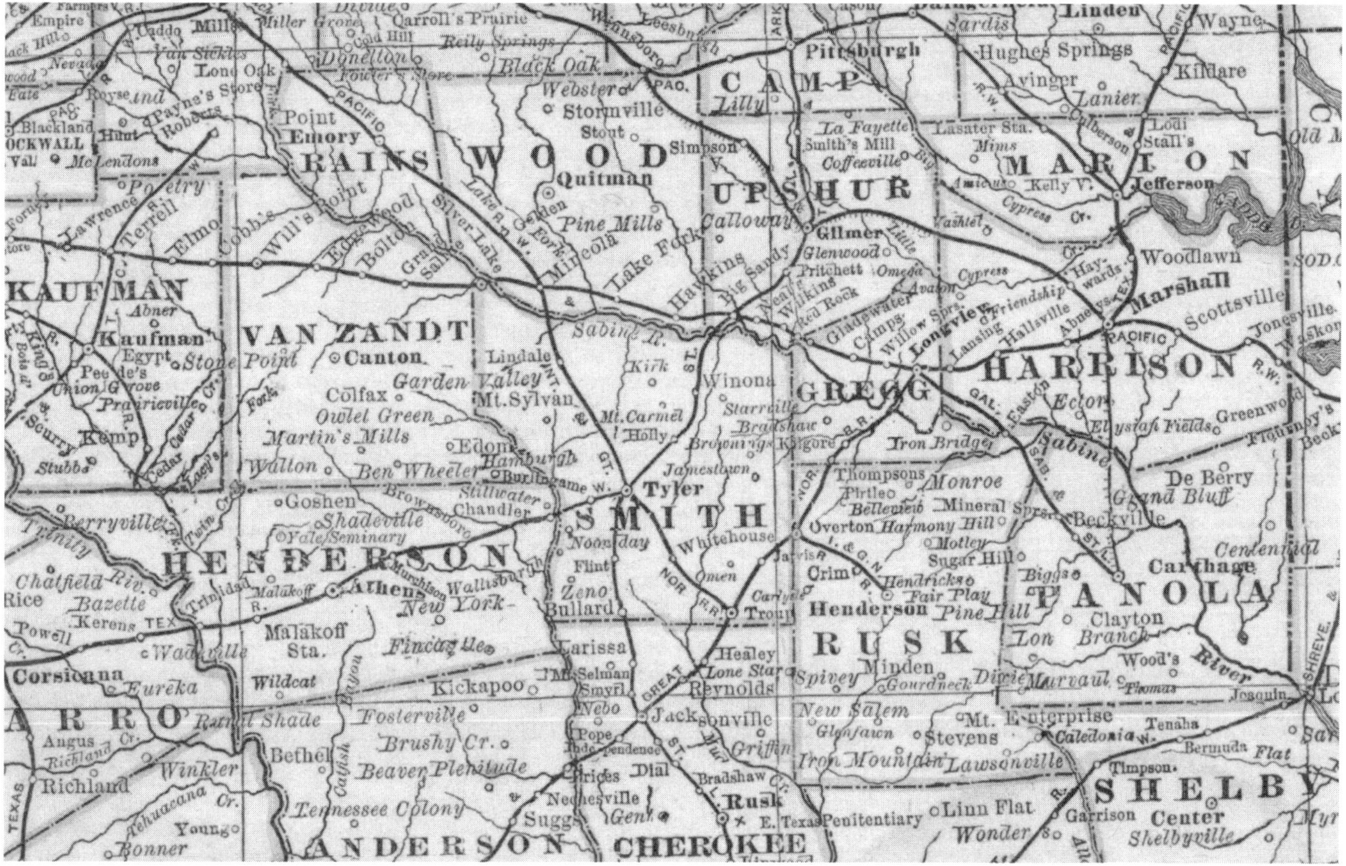

F. B. Chilton—1888: East Texas: Map No. 1031, Texas State Library and Archives Commission, Austin, Texas.

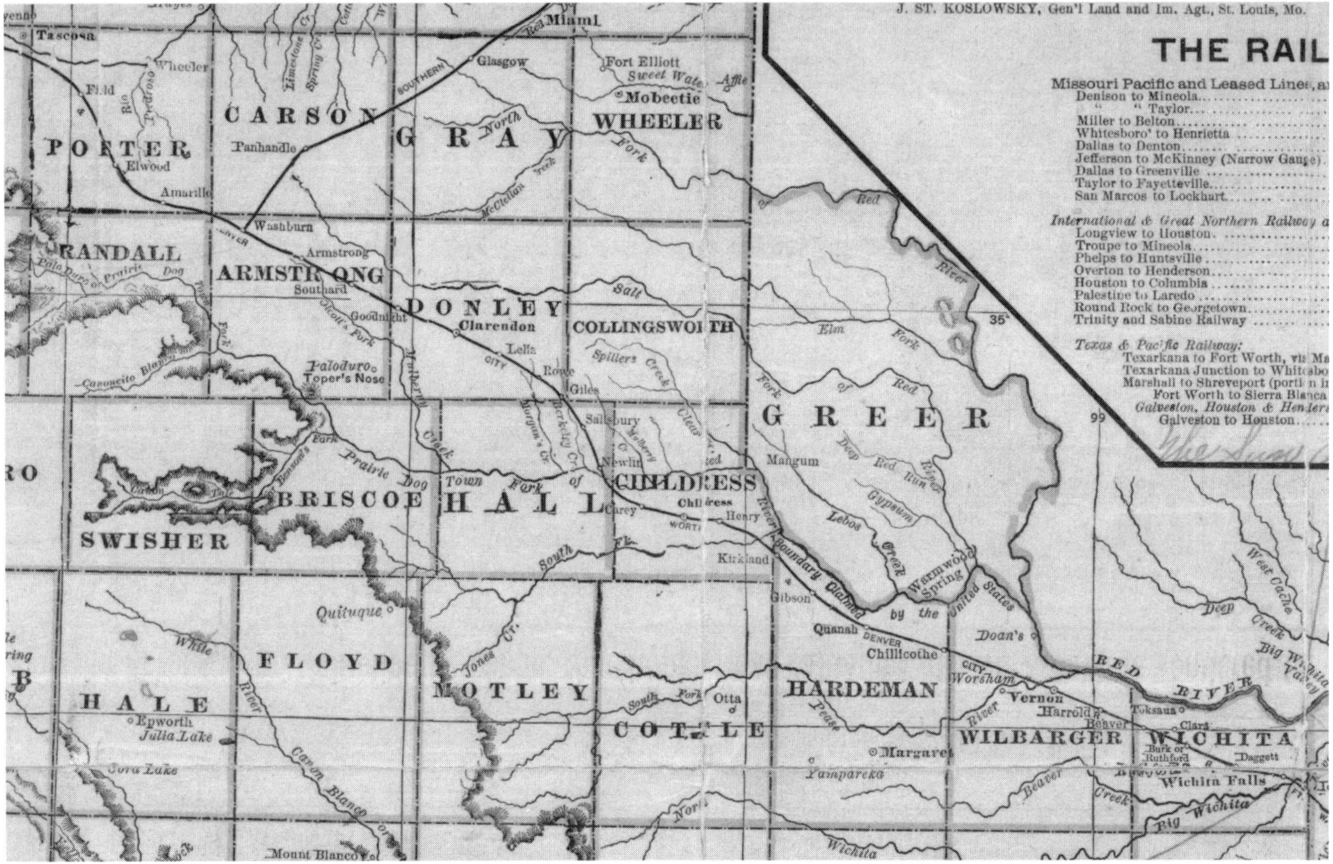

F. B. Chilton—1888: Gateway to the Panhandle: Map No. Texas State Library and Archives Commission, Austin, Texas.

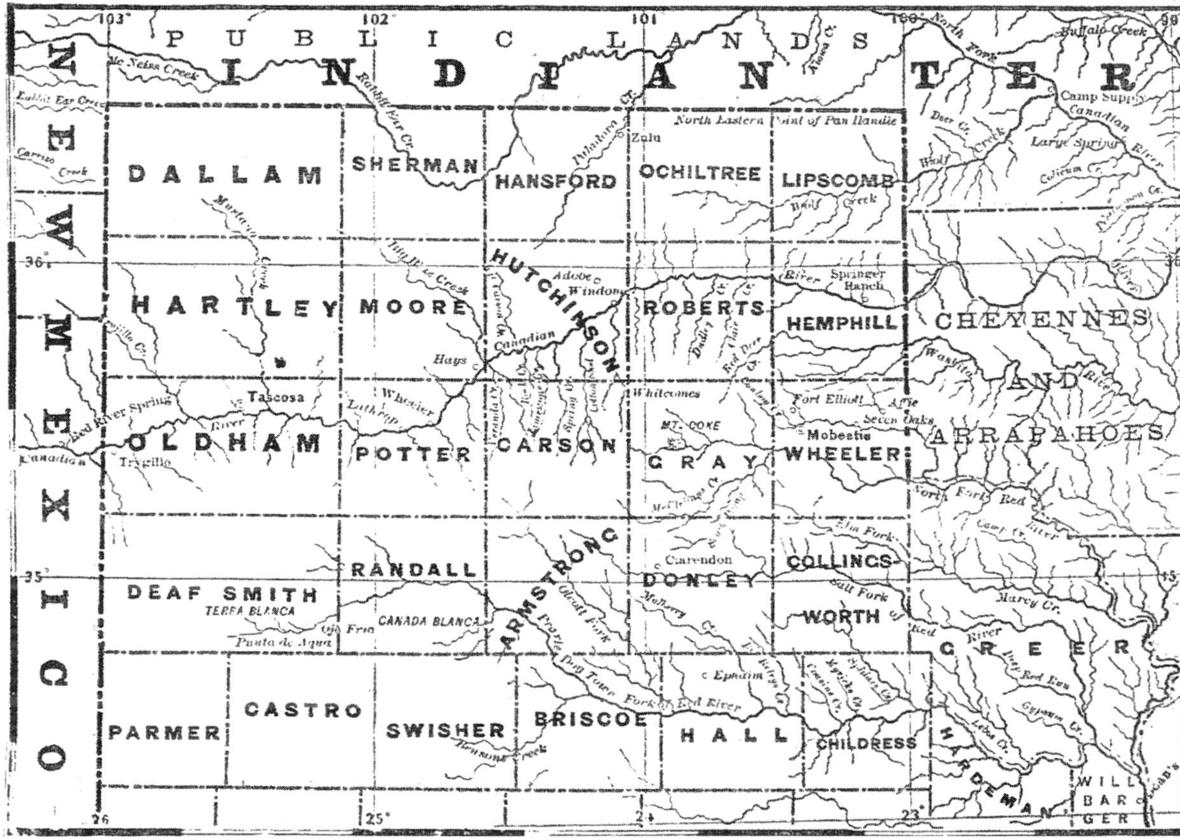

Alexander A. Grant, *Railroad and County Map of Texas* (New York, np, 1885): The Twenty-six Counties of the Panhandle (Courtesy Harold J. Weiss, Jr.).

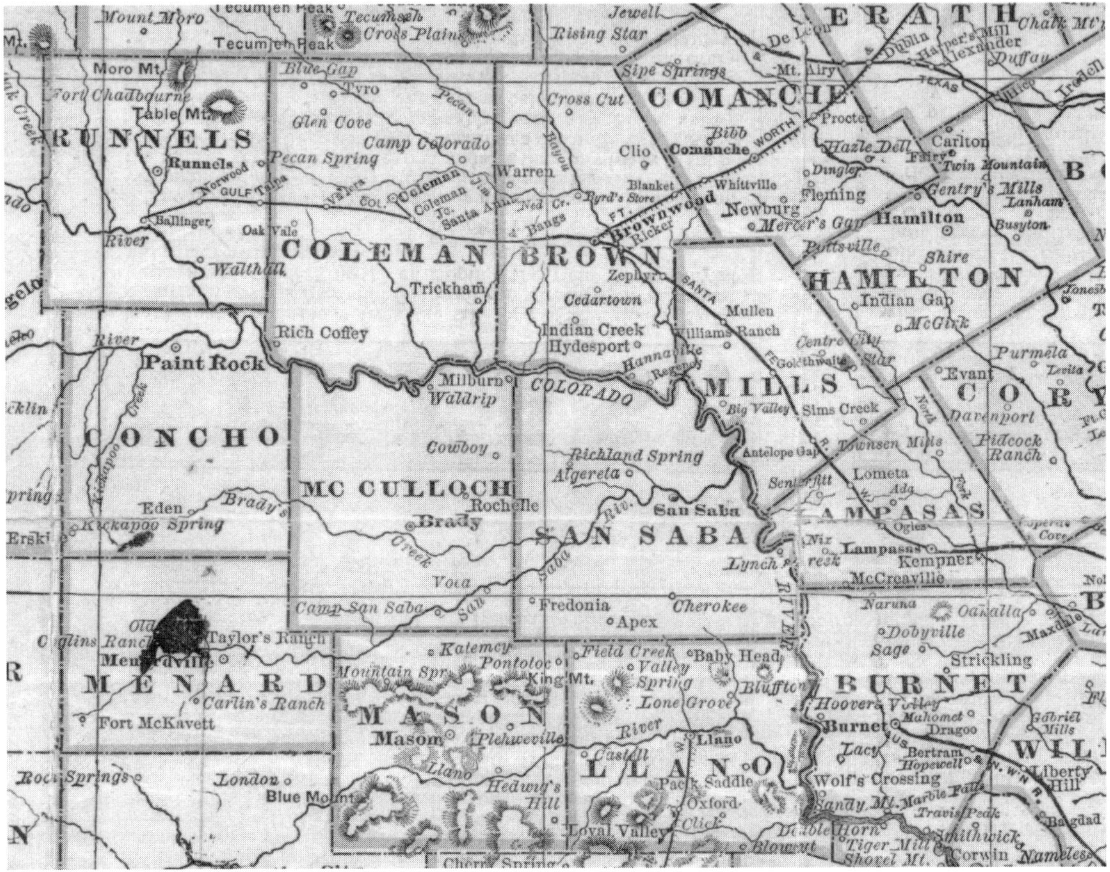

F. B. Chilton—1888: Central Texas: Map No. 1031, Texas State Library and Archives Commission, Austin, Texas.

F. B. Chilton—1888: Southeast Texas: Map No. 1031, Texas State Library and Archives Commission, Austin, Texas.

F. B. Chilton—1888: Far East Texas: Map No. 1031, TEXAS STATE LIBRARY AND ARCHIVES COMMISSION, AUSTIN, TEXAS.

F. B. Chilton—1888: Texas Border: Map No. 1031, TEXAS STATE LIBRARY AND ARCHIVES COMMISSION, AUSTIN, TEXAS.

PART THREE

AN AGING LAWMAN: HIGHS AND LOWS

In the process of sorting it out, Bill Jess McDonald became a Texas Sherlock Holmes—eccentric, deductive, fearless, psychological, eager to examine arcane physical evidence, and ready to disguise or dissimulate to get his man.

—John Miller Morris, ed., *A Private in the Texas Rangers: A. T. Miller of Company B, Frontier Battalion.*

The major charged forward, furious. "Captain McDonald! You can't stop the United States army from moving its troops! Are you mad? Start the train, engineer!"

—Tyler Mason, "Hell in Boots," Part 5.

Although McDonald was a man of few words, newsmen were soon printing stories about his marvelous feats of marksmanship. In one it was alleged that he could hit a mosquito's eye at fifty paces. When asked if this was true, McDonald is supposed to have growled, "Which eye?"

—John W. Davidson, ed., *A Crossroads of Freedom: The 1912 Campaign Speeches of Woodrow Wilson.*

MCDONALD, BILL:

Eyes: gray-blue.

Height: tall.

Face: prominent nose, brown mustache.

Demeanor: always alert and direct.

General: angular, quick quiet movements, catlike; Texas Ranger captain.

—George D. Hendricks, *The Bad Man of the West.*

Chapter 11

FORMING A NEW RANGER FORCE

. . . I ought to get off & go to see my wife for a day or so, for she is liable to sue a good old man for a divorce, as I hav'nt seen her for several months.[1]

In many respects the new Ranger service that emerged in 1901 was similar to the organization, manpower, and duties of the Frontier Battalion. The "Four Great Captains" continued to lead the small companies in the field. McDonald, in addition to his investigative work, still managed Company B, wrote reports, informed his superiors about company personnel, and was away from his wife and friends for long periods of time. The Frontier Battalion was gone, but the Texas Rangers marched on.

At the end of March of 1901, the state legislature (with just three dissenting votes in the Senate) passed a law creating the "Ranger Force." This new body of state peace officers was organized to protect "frontier" lands and suppress "lawlessness and crime" throughout the state. The legislative act repealed all previous laws in conflict with this statute. It also would take effect in ninety days after adjournment.[2]

On July 3, 1901, five days before the end of the Frontier Battalion, Adjutant General Scurry issued General Order No. 62. The first sections reiterated the provisions of the legislative act. Four Ranger companies were set up, each with one captain, one sergeant, and not more than twenty privates. The company commanders and the quartermaster in central command served at the pleasure of the governor. The pay for officers and men ranged from $100 per month for captains to $50 per month for sergeants and $40 a month for privates. Each Ranger provided his own clothing, horse, and riding equipment, with the proviso that if the horse was killed in action the state would reimburse the Ranger at a fair market value. The state furnished supplies for men and horses, ammunition, and camp equipment. Furthermore, the state gave each Ranger a rifle and a revolver, the cost of which would be deducted from the first month's salary. To show continuity with previous Rangers, the quartermaster, paid $100 a month, would still carry out the duties of commissary and paymaster.[3]

By legislative act *all* Rangers had the power to make arrests and execute the criminal process throughout the state. When arrests were made, the Rangers had to take the prisoner to the county where the crime was committed and turn the person over to the proper authorities. Adjutant General Scurry stressed in his order that only men who were "courageous, discreet, honest, of temperate habits and respectable families" would be appointed as Rangers. The adjutant general also emphasized that Rangers would not aid or abet the election of a political candidate and that the new force would not supplant other peace officers in the state, since its operations would be "confined to arrests of persons charged with the commission of felonies and the carrying of concealed weapons, and to the prevention of breaches of the peace."[4]

The new Ranger Force was distributed much like the Frontier Battalion. Of the four companies in the service, Company A was under the command of Captain Brooks with its headquarters at Alice; McDonald still had control of Company B at Amarillo; Captain Rogers took charge of Company C at Laredo; and Company D, headquartered at Fort Hancock, came under the supervision of Captain Hughes. In addition, Sieker was commissioned as captain and quartermaster of the Ranger Force. The company commanders would make out and transmit reports and discharge Rangers for abusing citizens. The adjutant general noted that the appropriation of $30,000 per year would keep in the field a small group of thirty-two officers and men. These Rangers stood ready, especially in the less populated areas of southern and western Texas, to maintain law and order.[5]

The personnel of the newly organized Company B consisted of experienced veterans and fresh recruits. These included Captain McDonald, Sergeant McCauley, and Privates Armstrong, Blanton, Frank Johnson (soon replaced by N. B. Jones), A. D. Jordan, Keeton, L. P. Moore, Ryan, and H. B. Smith. Within a year or two the number of privates would be reduced for financial reasons and new names, like J. D. Dunaway and M. G. "Blaze" Delling, would appear in the muster rolls. These Rangers completed the work on criminal cases held over from the days of the Frontier Battalion and opened up new avenues of investigation.[6]

By the end of the first decade of the twentieth century, Texas had nearly four million inhabitants (with about twenty-four percent living in cities). Farming and cattle raising, therefore, still remained the dominant forms of economic activity. But a major event took place in 1901 at Spindletop near Beaumont—oil gushed from a well and took its place in myth and economics. An oil boom spread across the eastern and northern portions of the state and became a basis for future industrial growth. Within this framework Texans of all creeds and colors tried to eke out a living and improve their existence. Important reform laws, in banking, insurance, taxation of property, and prison work, occurred during the administrations of Governor Thomas M. Campbell. Texas had become part of the Progressive Movement, which gained national prominence during the eras of Presidents Theodore Roosevelt and Woodrow Wilson.[7]

RANGER FORCE—1901–1902

From the organization of the new Ranger Force in July 1901 to the end of December 1902, the typical pattern of Ranger activities emerged. Captain McDonald and the rank and file of Company B scouted miles of territory, chased and captured cattle and horse thieves, and took into custody burglars, murderers, and robbers. At the same time Captain Bill and the men under his command escorted prisoners, guarded jails, testified at trials, maintained order at court sessions, got involved in labor problems, and became embroiled in the control of alcoholic beverages. In the performance of these duties the Rangers tried to cooperate with sheriffs and other local officials, although the lack of jails in some localities hindered the work of the state peace officers. Most important, McDonald had to deal with minority groups—blacks and Hispanics—inside and outside the law.[8]

One of the first duties that Company B performed as part of the Ranger Force was to proceed to Nacogdoches and keep the peace. At the end of July of 1901, County Judge V. E. Middlebrook wired the governor that local lawmen were "trying to kill each other." "It is dangerous," said the judge, "to be on [the] streets."[9] Former Adjutant General Wozencraft, Captain McDonald, and two of his men went to the town to investigate. They found that the trouble centered around the sheriff and a constable, both of whom came close to a shootout on a sidewalk. Part of the ill will between them dealt with politics, with the former being a Populist and the latter a Democrat. After a series of meetings for about a week, state officials realized that bloodshed could be averted, as residents welcomed the intervention of the governor. At one point Wozencraft told his superior that McDonald and his Rangers had the "situation well in hand."[10]

During the operations in the field to the end of 1902, the members of Company B carried out some unusual assignments. In March 1902, Private Delling arrested an individual in Mitchell County for exposing his "private person" in public.[11] Then in August of the same year McDonald, Blanton, and Ryan kept order at the fair in Quanah. They performed this duty, in McDonald's words, "to the letter."[12] In September 1902, Sergeant McCauley and Delling "escorted a party of surveyors, who had been run out of pastures with Winchesters, and protected them from violence" in Midland County.[13] The next month McCauley assisted a sheriff in taking a "crazy man" to the asylum in Austin.[14] Such duties taxed the resources of the Ranger service.

Two controversial moves by the Rangers of Company B occurred in the spring and summer of 1902. First came their intervention in the labor troubles at Port Arthur. At the end of February, Adjutant General Scurry ordered McDonald to take four Rangers and proceed to the town. Here they would protect Texas-Mexican laborers employed at oil refineries from intimidation and violence. Scurry ended by saying, "The Governor desires you to act with the utmost caution but you will be expected to protect such men as may go to work."[15]

The basic problem was that Hispanic laborers agreed to take lower wages than union members. The representatives of the labor unions, in the words of the adjutant general who investigated, would not "stand" for different pay scales. They would "kill" the Tejanos and "make the streets run with blood." Nothing like that took place, as the Rangers and the sheriff's office kept the peace.[16] McDonald and his detachment arrested only one person for "intimidating workmen." They took the prisoner to Beaumont to be jailed. Then McDonald and Keeton left the area on March 6 to attend a court session elsewhere. Three Ranger privates stayed in the town until the sixteenth.[17] In noting the charged atmosphere at Port Arthur, the official record of the state simply concluded: "The rangers succeeded in preventing trouble."[18]

McDonald faced another serious issue when complaints reached central headquarters about the conduct of Private Keeton at Amarillo. The Ranger captain traveled to the town by train to investigate. He found that Keeton was an active member of Company B. The Ranger private had worked on a number of cases, such as stopping and questioning two residents after shots were fired in an alley (which led to a charge of false imprisonment and further altercations). He also had a fistfight with a "big fellow" who wanted to beat up a Ranger. Most important, Keeton had assisted local officers in stopping violations of the liquor laws in the summer of 1902. This action led to name-calling and fighting, as, in McDonald's words, the "saloon element has it strictly in for Keeton."[19] The Ranger captain did instruct Keeton "not to fool with misdemeanor cases" like liquor violations. McDonald wondered, in addition, if Keeton "should be discharged for indiscretion." Within a month Keeton's name did not appear on company rolls.[20]

In the exchange of messages about the Ranger private, Adjutant General Scurry informed McDonald that he might have to find another location for the base camp of Company B. The Ranger captain responded by saying he would follow any instructions given by his superiors. He suggested that Hereford in Deaf Smith County in the western Panhandle would be a "suitable place." However, McDonald added that Amarillo had better railroad connections than Hereford.[21]

Two events at the turn of the century had an impact on both Anglo-Hispanic relations and the stationing of Ranger companies at various geographical locations. One dealt with the saga of Gregorio Cortez. The other involved the conduct of the members of Company A commanded by Captain Brooks, particularly the shootings by Anderson Yancey Baker.

Too often Texas Mexicans have been seen as a monolithic group in thought and deed. In reality, borderland Tejanos differed from Hispanics in the rest of the state. Spanish-speaking residents on the American side of the Rio Grande kept customs from Mexico more than their counterparts in and around urban centers like Dallas and Houston.[22] In borderland culture, therefore, differences between Anglos and Tejanos became magnified and led to violent headstrong actions. A novelist depicted the conflict like this:

> But it's like a holy war along the Rio Grande. Been that way since the battle of the Alamo and doesn't show any sign it's fixin' to

> change. You're automatically somebody's enemy on sight. It just depends on how light or dark your face is.[23]

The contested modes of living by those residing on the border appeared in the accounts of the uproar about Gregorio Cortez. The facts in the criminal case are clear. In June of 1901, Cortez and his brother had an encounter with a local lawman who was looking for horse thieves. In the charged atmosphere that resulted from a misunderstanding in the translation of Spanish words by an interpreter, shots were fired. A sheriff wounded the brother (who later died) and, in turn, Gregorio killed the sheriff, with the fatal bullet entering his body as he lay on the ground. Then Cortez fled the scene by foot and horseback. Posses pursued the fleeing fugitive for days, as he stole horse after horse. In the manhunt Gregorio gunned down another sheriff and a number of people of Mexican descent were killed and wounded in retaliatory violence. An Hispanic informer who sought the reward money brought the chase for the fugitive to an end. Captain Rogers and a federal customs inspector captured Cortez near the Mexican border without firing a shot.[24]

Texas newspapers gave extensive coverage to the killings, manhunt, and court trials. White readers saw Cortez as a horse thief, a murderer, and a fugitive from the law. Those of Spanish ancestry viewed Gregorio as a poor farmer who fought persecution and became a folk hero in border ballads. One *corrido* included these lines:

> Then said Gregorio Cortez,
> With his pistol in his hand,
> "Ah, how many mounted rangers
> Against one lone Mexican!"[25]

The emphasis on the Rangers in Hispanic storytelling was misleading. "Although the reproach fell chiefly on the Texas Rangers," a Ranger historian pointed out, "in the hunt for Gregorio Cortez *rinches* were sheriffs and posses, not Rangers. One of Rogers's men accompanied a posse, and Rogers himself made a routine arrest."[26] In addition, state peace officers assisted local authorities in protecting Cortez from mobs in his court trials at various locations. In September of 1901, for example, Captain McDonald and four Rangers from Companies B and C went to Columbus to assist a sheriff in escorting Cortez to Karnes County. Here McDonald and others protected the prisoner from "mob violence." By order of the district judge, the Rangers then took Cortez back to the jail in Columbus for "safe keeping."[27] Members of the Ranger Force became the villains in the folk tales with their dramatic overtones. But in the real-life scenarios of this overdrawn affair, they quietly carried out their duties.

In Ranger operations at the turn of the century the doings of Cortez had less impact than the conduct of the rank and file of Company A under Captain Brooks. Against Anglo and Tejano residents of Brownsville and the surrounding areas, several members of this company allegedly committed numerous acts of verbal and physical abuse.[28] Most striking was the violence that involved Sergeant A. Y. Baker in 1902. While riding the line of the King ranch and looking for cattle thieves, Baker encountered Ramón Cerda using a branding iron. Both men fired, with the Ranger's horse being killed and Cerda falling dead with a bullet in his head. Then the sergeant and others were ambushed by unknown parties. The shots fired wounded Baker and killed another Ranger. The gunplay came to an end when Sergeant Baker acted first and shot and killed Alfredo Cerda, one of the suspected ambushers. The Cerda brothers never gained the renown of Gregorio Cortez in border ballads. But their deaths showed that the Anglo-Tejano clash in economics, politics, and law enforcement would not go unnoticed by state leaders in Austin.[29]

The governor ordered Adjutant General Scurry to investigate. At the end of October, Governor Sayers told Scurry to make sure that no Ranger interfered with those who wanted to vote in the upcoming election, either through "persuasion or intimidation." A violation of this order meant dismissal from the Ranger service. Furthermore, the adjutant general had to decide whether to keep Captain Brooks and his men at Brownsville in order to assist Captain Hughes and his Rangers, who had been ordered to the town, in "acquainting themselves with existing conditions" in the region.[30]

Adjutant General Scurry proceeded to Brownsville, investigated, and submitted a detailed report. In it he pointed out that the charges and threats made against Brooks' Rangers made them "apprehensive." Their resentment about being called murderers who should be eliminated, one way or another, made them take harsh actions in going after criminals and maintaining order. The adjutant general believed that "extenuating circumstances" should "excuse" the behavior of the Rangers under the command of Brooks. Scurry did agree with the governor, however, that Company A should be relocated for the good of the service.[31]

NEW HEADQUARTERS FOR COMPANY B

The die had been cast. On November 12, 1902, a day after his report on the conditions at Brownsville, Adjutant General Scurry informed the governor about the new geographical locations of the Ranger companies. The "Four Great Captains" switched places with each other. Brooks and his men were now headquartered at Laredo. Company D under the command of Captain Hughes went to Alice, with a detachment at Brownsville. McDonald and the members of Company B did not remain in the Panhandle country, as their base camp shifted from Amarillo to Fort Hancock along the Rio Grande in West Texas. To replace McDonald in northern Texas, Captain Rogers and Company C moved their headquarters to Colorado City, with a detachment at Amarillo.

Adjutant General Scurry dismissed the objections to such changes in a few paragraphs. He believed that transportation costs would be minimized by the use of the rail system. He also noted that Rangers would become acquainted with the new lands through their scouting expeditions. Central command did not even consider a third objection: that the "change of climate may be bad for the health of men and horses." Rangers had to "serve anywhere in the State."[32]

Captain Bill had qualms about accepting his new assignment. He confided to a friend that the governor and the adjutant general knew about his objections to the move. McDonald believed he would be less effective in the new role, since he did not speak Spanish and had little knowledge of the land and its people. He also realized newcomers to law enforcement in northern Texas would face a similar situation, not being Panhandle Rangers like Company B. This would encourage the lawless element. At least the governor stressed that McDonald's transfer was not being done because of complaints about his conduct. In the end, Captain Bill obeyed orders. He still wanted to be a Ranger.[33]

In his correspondence Governor Sayers said that he had been thinking about relocating the Ranger companies for "more than a year." "As a rule, which applies as well to the regular as to the volunteer force," the governor emphasized, "troops should not be permitted to remain at any one place more than two years for the reason that they become too strongly identified with the citizens, and, for that reason, lose their efficiency."[34]

On Dec. 17, 1902, Captain McDonald and four privates of Company B left for Fort Hancock. Another Ranger rode with the railroad car carrying the livestock. The next day McCauley and Delling followed.[35] The adjutant general advised McDonald and his men to travel by both land and rail, with camping equipment being left at Amarillo and Colorado City, if possible, for the use of the Ranger company transferred to that region.[36] After their arrival, McDonald and two Rangers met with Captain Hughes and traveled to El Paso and Marathon.

Throughout 1903 the Rangers turned their attention to crimes committed by Anglos and Hispanics along the border. Scouting expeditions were carried out over dusty trials and along the banks of the river. All types of criminals surfaced: burglars, forgers, murderers, thieves, rapists, and those trying to rob a railroad caboose and shooting up a town. At one point McCauley and a fellow Ranger took into custody two men for the "theft of wood" and another person for stealing a horse. At another time Dunaway and McCauley assisted in the enforcement of "quarantine regulations" against cattle coming across the Rio Grande.[37]

MAYHEM AND MURDER IN EAST TEXAS

State authorities still turned to Captain Bill, because of his background and experience, to investigate crime in East Texas. In Walker and Trinity counties in that region, McDonald and the members of Company B went after violent criminals from the end of 1903 through 1904. Of this locale McDonald reminisced:

> If a whole community has no use for law and order it's not worth while to try to enforce such things. You've got to stand over a place like that with a gun to make it behave, and when you catch a man, no matter what the evidence is against him, they'll turn him loose. In Groveton [Trinity County], for instance, when I was there they had only two law-respecting officers—the district clerk and the county attorney, and the county attorney they killed. Good citizens were so completely in the minority that they were helpless. Kittrell's Cut-off was probably one of the most lawless places you could find anywhere, though it was named after a judge. It's a strip cut off of Houston and Trinity counties and added to Walker, and its name is the only thing about it that ever had anything to do with the law. Many murders have been committed there and no one ever convicted for them, so far as I know.[38]

The "rascality" in some places, as McDonald called the propensity for criminal actions by people in Trinity, Walker, and other counties, infuriated him. Especially distressing to the Rangers were the suspected connections, personal and otherwise, between criminal elements and local public officials. In Trinity County, for example, Captain Bill realized that only two officers—a deputy sheriff and the county attorney—had the backbone to stand with the Rangers in keeping law and order.[39]

In the middle of December 1903, McDonald, in time assisted by Delling, went to Walker County to aid the sheriff in investigating a murder committed in Kittrell's Cut-Off. On the fourth day of that month farmer Bob James was gunned down while riding in a horse-drawn vehicle on the road to his house. The local sheriff arrived at the scene and used bloodhounds to track the killers. The trail, however, had been wiped out by hunters. Through rounding up witnesses, counteracting intimidation methods, and breaking down alibis, the Ranger captain and the sheriff began to apprehend those who waylaid the farmer. Among those arrested was Buck Shaw, the "king bee," according to McDonald. At different times the prisoners were then taken to the penitentiary at Huntsville which was close by for "safe keeping." The cases against Shaw and the others, with some of them held without bail, some not, continued in the judicial system for several years. They ended without convictions. Although someone said the Rangers held a "kangaroo court," McDonald was pleased with his work in the case—so pleased that he wrote, in a rare moment, that "there has been so many complimentary remarks I am beginning to be a little stuck up."[40] The chief clerk in the adjutant general's office told Captain Bill that "in your field you have no superior."[41]

A more sensational crime in East Texas came to the attention of Captain McDonald and his superiors in early 1904. At Groveton in Trinity County Mary Jane Touchstone had been murdered. One night a group of relatives, seeking a hoard of money that Touchstone, an elderly woman, had supposedly hidden away, went to her house, seized the old lady, and tried to make her disclose the location of the secret hiding place. Failing in this, they struck her with a stick, slit her throat, and left her body in a doorway where the hogs could mangle it. A search of the body and the premises by the murderers uncovered less than a dollar. After attempting to make the killing look like an accident, they scattered with the understanding that two of them would return to take care of the hogs and the body. Before this happened, however, the crime was discovered.[42] McDonald viewed this murder as the "worst thing" he ever encountered.[43]

By the time the Rangers of Company B entered the case, the trail was getting cold. An investigation led by McDonald, assisted by Delling, however, collected facts and uncovered some physical evidence, half-burnt matches under the house that were used in the fruitless search for hidden cash. This led to the arrest of Albert "Ab" Angle and several others as his accomplices. McDonald himself even pursued one culprit into the state of Louisiana. An official report stated that the Ranger captain also caught one murderer over the line in Arkansas.[44]

Through the efforts of Captain McDonald, District Attorney A. M. Campbell, H. L. Robb, county attorney of Trinity County, and N. B. Morris, hired by the state to assist in the prosecution (for the sum of $600), one person taken into custody—Ab Angle—did go to prison. In his mid-twenties, of medium height, with a freckled face and a dark complexion, Angle had a limited education and worked as a laborer.[45] At first he confessed to the murder, implicating several relatives and friends (including his brother). Angle did this after being told by McDonald and the lawyers, among other things, that if he testified to the true facts at the trials he would be granted immunity from punishment.[46] At a hearing, though, the confessed murderer "contradicated" himself so much in the cross-examination that his testimony became nearly worthless.[47] Then, through the efforts of his kin folk, Angle "repudiated" his confession at a session of the grand jury. At this point McDonald and the attorneys were able to obtain an indictment of Angle for "false swearing." To this charge he pled guilty and was sentenced to three years in prison (being released in June of 1907).[48]

For his efforts in fighting crime in East Texas, Captain Bill and his Rangers were both criticized and praised by those in the legal profession. Morris pointed out that in Trinity and Walker counties the "work" of McDonald and the rank and file of Company B "has been of a clean, decent, high order."[49] Robb chimed in and said McDonald performed "valuable services."[50] The county judge of Walker County even wrote that the Ranger captain realized the "accused has some rights."[51] Another lawyer supported such sentiments, but also added that an attorney or two differed—characterizing the "rangers as E. J. Davis' police force [during Reconstruction] and the Captain individually as the Czar of Russia."[52]

During the rest of 1904 Company B carried out the usual pattern of Ranger activities. McDonald's reports for the year made the hard work of law enforcement sound humdrum. One difficulty, though, existed: the distances that separated the Rangers in the company. They had to move between West Texas and the eastern portions of the state. "I want to go out on the border soon," McDonald wrote central command from Walker County, "& renew my acquaintance with those people on the border & see about our camp."[53]

Central headquarters kept shifting the personnel of Company B from one area to another by rail in 1904. At one point Privates Dunaway, Smith, and T. C. Taylor left West Texas to be with McDonald in East Texas. Sometimes these Rangers faced similar criminal acts at both ends of the state, from murder and burglary to carrying a pistol. Surprisingly, McDonald and his men in East Texas, rather than those located in the western lands, chased and arrested train robbers and the gunmen who tried to shoot at the cars. Other regional differences appeared in official records—like rustling and the theft of sheep out west, and wire cutting and the stealing of hogs back east. Most important, as seen in these pages, the Rangers of Company B faced troubling black crime in East Texas and controversial Hispanic crime in West Texas. From their base camp at Fort Hancock, Sergeant McCauley and his small force scouted and arrested Texas Mexicans who stole cattle, horses, and saddles. The Ranger sergeant, in addition, took action to stop armed parties from crossing the Rio Grande in a murder case.[54]

In these field operations Captain Bill worried about several things. He was concerned about the violent settings the Rangers of Company B were placed in. He decried the inexperience and the lack of support from local public officials. Bad men with shotguns once told a justice of the peace to stop aiding the Rangers—or he would be killed.[55] Especially troublesome to McDonald were places where those taken into custody could not be moved to a safer jail if they did not like the move. "I like to treat prisoners nicely," the Ranger captain wrote his superiors, "but dont like for them to select a place to stay . . . ."[56] Mob rule also bothered him. In an East Texas case involving a rapist, which stirred the feelings of some for a lynching, members of Company B guarded the jail "continually." When asked what could a few Rangers do against hundreds of people bent on extralegal justice, McDonald at least would answer that "we can do our duty & that we will do so with our lives." But, he also called for Rangers to replace those who had to leave to work on cases elsewhere. There were too few Rangers left to stand off such a crowd.[57]

RANGERS AND BLACK LAWBREAKERS

Away from the Texas Panhandle, Company B became more involved with black crime. In East Texas the Rangers had to deal with black burglars, rapists, robbers, and shooters. In January 1904, for example, McDonald and a deputy sheriff pursued a "bad negro," an escaped convict, wanted by a sheriff. After taking him into custody at his home, the Ranger captain allowed the man to go into his house to get some clothing. Breaking away from McDonald at the doorway, the culprit seized a shotgun. In an instant his wife blocked the view and he ran out the back of the house as McDonald fired.

In the shooting that followed outside, McDonald "emptied" his six-shooter. Although the man escaped, the Ranger captain later wrote that he "wounded him in the side." In time, the injured man turned himself in and was taken to a convict farm. It was an unpleasant episode, and McDonald initially hoped that the two lawmen did not hit the fleeing fugitive.[58]

In criminal cases involving blacks, violence, and rape, Captain Bill displayed a belief in severe punishment and a sensitivity to openly discuss sexual matters. At one point McDonald assisted a sheriff in "hanging a negro charged with rape."[59] In March 1904 Dunaway and another Ranger arrested a man who, with others, broke into the residence of several black females. They forced one of the screaming naked women outside and raped her. In an attempt to sum up this event tactfully, McDonald reported that, under the threat of being killed, the black woman had "connection" with one of her attackers before help arrived from a nearby white resident.[60]

Captain Bill knew that sometimes, in a case against a black, episodes would be magnified in order to harass others—even Rangers—by local toughs and peace officers to satisfy their white constituents.[61] McDonald could give a verbal lashing to those people who would try to stir up racial hostility in order to get "sufficient prejudice to get a mob and hang them."[62] As a law enforcement officer McDonald could both castigate and protect black offenders.

ADVENTURE WITH THEODORE ROOSEVELT

A pleasant interlude in McDonald's life occurred in 1905 when President Theodore Roosevelt visited Texas in early April. An important part of his trip was to attend a reunion of the Rough Riders from the Spanish-American War in San Antonio. His itinerary took him by train to Dallas, where he arrived April 5; Austin, where he spoke before the state legislature; and San Antonio. A tumultuous reception occurred as throngs of people surrounded the train at each stop in the small towns along the way.[63]

After the festivities were over in San Antonio, Roosevelt traveled to Fort Worth to meet those, including Captain Bill, who would accompany him on a hunting trip into the Oklahoma Territory. He arrived in that town on April 8. Because of accommodations on the train northward, McDonald was ordered by the adjutant general to meet the president's train in Fort Worth on that date rather than in San Antonio the day before. Also included in the hunting party among others were several high-ranking military officers and John R. "Jack" Abernathy, well-known wolf hunter. By train and overland vehicles the group moved through Texas, stopping briefly in various towns, to a camp on the Red River, not far from Frederick, Oklahoma, on land leased from the Indians by two ranchmen, Burk Burnett and Tom Waggoner. During the trip McDonald acted as a bodyguard to Roosevelt, doing effective work in crowd control among Texans who tried to get a glimpse of the president at the train stops.[64]

Reluctant to accompany a Republican officeholder, because of his affiliation with the Democratic party, Captain Bill came to admire Roosevelt the more he was with him as a guide during the week of the hunt. On horseback Roosevelt, McDonald, and others rode for miles, cutting across ravines, while Burnett and a military officer followed in a buggy. Seventeen wolves were caught, some by Abernathy with his bare hands, and a number of raccoons and rattlesnakes were seized. Roosevelt even killed a snake with his riding whip. One member of the party said that the president "had the time of his life."[65] Later, as Roosevelt left Texas for Colorado, McDonald wrote: "We had a big time on the wolf hunt. Think the President a great fellow. & he certainly appreciates his reception in Texas."[66] Years later Roosevelt wrote the Ranger captain, "I shall always look back with pleasure to our wolf hunt in Oklahoma."[67]

Before and after the wolf hunt, McDonald's poor health hampered his law enforcement work with Company B. His skin turned yellowish. He found it necessary to spend more time at Mineral Wells, recuperating from kidney troubles and malaria. When McDonald regained his health, he and the other Rangers made scouting expeditions, attended court sessions, rounded up witnesses, aided sheriffs, and investigated all types of crimes—murder, thievery, horse and cattle rustling, smuggling, stealing pigs—as well as keeping armed groups apart in political elections. The Ranger captain was even asked to assist an investigator of the Cattle Raisers Association of Texas in crimes committed in West Texas. In these endeavors the members of Company B encountered Anglos, blacks, and Spanish-Americans. Most newsworthy, Private Dunaway killed a Tejano in a border skirmish. At one point McDonald reported that he "prevented trouble" by taking "guns from several parties" and removing the shells from shotguns—"that had special loaded shells to kill the rangers."[68]

A NEW BASE CAMP FOR COMPANY B

By the summer of 1905, Company B had moved its headquarters to Alice in Jim Wells County. "The country looks good down here," McDonald added as a postscript in a message, "& I think I will like it better than I thought I would."[69] The company now consisted of McDonald, as captain, Sergeant McCauley, and Privates Delling, Dunaway, L. E. Flach, Sam McKenzie, W. A. Millican, Ryan, and Collie Taylor.[70] McDonald thought McKenzie was a "fine ranger," but he did not think too highly of Flach. He noted that his replacement should understand the "mexican lingo."[71] But the state legislature reduced the Ranger appropriation (from $28,000 to $25,000) for the fiscal year starting September 1905. This action prompted central headquarters to notify the Ranger captain that no vacancy in the company would be filled unless the number dropped below "seven enlisted men."[72]

For the aging McDonald, 1906 was a year of triumph and tragedy. The Rangers of Company B continued to go after lawbreakers who committed felonious crimes and misdemeanors. They aided sheriffs. They responded to requests for assistance from judges. They carried out their sworn duty to protect the state.[73] Most important, McDonald became involved in three controversial events that taxed his abilities as a Ranger captain. He had to deal with the ups and downs of the Conditt murder case, his most intriguing investigative effort (Chapter 12). Happenings in the aftermath of the raid on Brownsville made him take a stand that infuriated local officials and US army officers (Chapter 13). Then the doings of the political factions with their violent-prone agendas in Rio Grande City resulted in McDonald's final gun battle (Chapter 14). To some, this conflict was Captain Bill's Armageddon.

JIM HOGG AND RHODA MCDONALD PASS AWAY

In the midst of these trying actions, McDonald had to face the loss of those who supported him in the past. The death of his old friend, former Governor Hogg, saddened the Ranger captain. Early in March of 1906, Hogg died after a prolonged illness, and McDonald, assigned to a court session in Houston, deeply regretted that he could not attend his funeral. In a newspaper interview after the burial, Captain Bill expressed his grief and talked about his lifelong friendship with Hogg. He noted the companionship between the two in their early years as well as the quarrel between them when they supported different candidates in a congressional race. He also spoke about their reunion after Hogg, as a district attorney in East Texas, supported McDonald's actions, as a deputy sheriff, against a band of outlaws in a county where he had no authority. McDonald's grief was real; their friendship had continued after Hogg's appointment of McDonald as a Ranger captain over the protests of some people.[74]

A saddened McDonald faced even more grief. The passing away of his wife—May 21, 1906—was a genuine blow. When the headquarters of Company B was moved to southern Texas, Rhoda

McDonald, though in poor health, accompanied her husband and moved from the ranch in the Panhandle to Alice to set up housekeeping. When McDonald became more involved in the investigation of the Conditt murders in the spring of 1906, Rhoda went to San Antonio to be under a doctor's care. The need for an operation made McDonald rush to her side. After the operation and recovery, Rhoda, a loyal and self-sacrificing wife, insisted that her husband resume his work on the Conditt case—which he did. For awhile her condition continued to improve. But then she took a turn for the worse and died before McDonald could return. In her last note to her husband, Rhoda disclosed much about the character and dourness of their relationship when she wrote, "I am sorry for every cross word or look that I ever gave you, but feel sure you will not hold them against me. With lots of love—Good-by." McDonald took her to Greenville for interment. An era in his life had come to an end.[75]

Chapter 12

CONDITT MURDER CASE: A STUDY IN DETECTION

One of the rangers of shrewdness, ability and wide experience in handling such cases was quoted by a county official as saying that if the people would only exercise patience the "whole thing would come out sooner or later."[1]

Near the end of his sixteen-year career as a Ranger captain, McDonald faced a multiple murder case that would test his investigative skills. A white man, Joseph Fagan Conditt, his wife, Lora, and their five children, rented a farm in a mixed neighborhood of whites and blacks near Edna in Jackson County. In the morning hours on September 28, 1905, while the father was working land a few miles away, the mother and four of her children were brutally murdered. Inside the house lay the bodies of Lora, whoso skull was crushed with an adz, and her oldest daughter, Mildred, who had been raped and had her throat slashed. Outside in the yard the bodies of three sons were found. One boy's head had almost been decapitated, while the other two sons had their skulls caved in with a metal bar. Only a small baby boy with a head injury survived the horrible crime.[2]

Monk Gibson, a young black laborer working on the Conditt farm, left the land and told neighbors nearby that unknown individuals had been chasing Mrs. Conditt and her children. Blood found on Gibson's clothes and body, though, landed him in jail instead. Here he was roughly treated, even whipped, in order to get a confession. Fearing a lynch mob, Sheriff Albert Egg attempted to remove the prisoner to the lockup in Hallettsville for "safekeeping." A few miles from Edna, Gibson broke away from two deputy sheriffs. At one point in the chase that followed, Monk's horse failed to clear a fence, as did the horse of one of the deputies. In the darkness the other lawman followed a riderless horse. The next day peace officers and angry citizens with bloodhounds scoured the countryside.[3]

At this point state officials intervened after a call from local officials. The governor ordered Adjutant General Hulen to accompany two infantry companies and two troops of cavalry to the inflamed community. The official records noted that the state military went to Edna "for the purpose of protecting the lives of certain persons there threatened with lynching and burning, which grew out of the murder of the Conditt family."[4] On October 3, 1905, the soldiers arrived by train and camped near the jail. Inside the brick building some of Gibson's relatives had been incarcerated. Whenever they could friends and relatives kept telling Monk to remain silent.

At the same time the adjutant general ordered Captains Hughes, McDonald, and other Rangers from Companies B and D to proceed to the beleaguered town. On October 4 McDonald wired Hulen at Edna from his base camp at Alice: "I will come with dogs in [the] morning."[5] The Ranger captain also ordered three members of Company B in south Texas to follow: Sergeant McCauley and Privates McKenzie and Ryan. At this point McDonald and his three Rangers represented about one-half of the manpower of Company B. In the days to come other rank-and-file Rangers of Company B would also come to Jackson County. They planned to help guard the jail and investigate the murders.

Formed by settlers, especially from Alabama, in the early days of the Republic of Texas, Jackson County became an important agricultural region at the turn of the twentieth century. Crops, like cotton and sugar cane, and the raising of livestock, especially cattle, brought prosperity to local residents. The coming of the railroads in the late nineteenth century also aided economic growth. Created in the early 1880s as a railroad center, Edna soon became the county seat and the largest community in that area, with a population of about 1,000 citizens at the time of the Conditt killings.[6]

To the surprise of some, the inquiry into the deaths of the Conditt family would take years to bring to a conclusion. In retrospect, this would not have happened if Gibson had been killed during the manhunt. Later one person noted that the recapture of Monk after the militia arrived to guard the jail was a "lucky" thing for the prisoner and local officials.[7] Yet the belief that local authorities conspired with state officers to keep the fugitive in hiding remains a conjecture. No evidence surfaced to support the proposition that the sheriff and others allowed Gibson to roam free for a long period of time. But the arrival of the military and the Rangers did stop lynch talk from turning into a bloody incident.

Monk Gibson remained at large until October 9, 1905. The manhunt for the escaped prisoner went on for days. Searching the countryside and running down rumors about his whereabouts took up the time and energies of local lawmen, Rangers, and armed citizens. McDonald especially kept watch over Gibson's place of residence. One newspaper said that the soldiers "are holding the jail while Gibson holds the brush."[8] The break in the case came when a black individual spotted Gibson. He had been hiding in a barn close to his house and stayed alive by eating raw corn—which was later proved by using a stomach pump and checking his teeth. When the alarm was sounded, Adjutant General Hulen, Captain McDonald, other Rangers, and the sheriff and his deputies rode out and brought Monk back to jail.[9]

Captain Bill continued to play an active role in the Conditt affair. He correctly reasoned from the condition of some of the bodies that the murders took place after breakfast and not at dinner time. He also took seriously his sworn duty to uphold the law, protect the prisoner, and stop lynchers from storming the jail. On October 10, McDonald arrested two individuals, one for carrying a weapon and the other for disturbing the peace while drunk, and turned them over to the local sheriff. In addition, the Ranger captain took a stand against the use of torture to extract a confession from Gibson, and he held to his belief, which few supported in the beginning, that others were involved in the crime. On October 13 McDonald even arrested Felix Powell, a black male in his thirties, for being implicated in the murder, but this prisoner would soon be released by local authorities. Yet it was an indication of things to come.[10]

The Texas Rangers had one more duty to perform. A few days after the recapture of Monk Gibson, the state troops, who disliked the mistreatment of Gibson and had ably protected the jail, removed themselves from the quiet town. That left only the Rangers and local law officers to carry on. After Gibson was indicted for murder by a grand jury, Judge James C. Wilson granted a change of venue in the case to San Antonio. On October 18 Sheriff Egg, Captains Hughes and McDonald, and Rangers from Companies B and D, eleven privates and sergeants in all, were detailed to escort Monk to a train station and accompany him over the rails to San Antonio. A few of the Rangers made the long trip, with the prisoner being chained to the wrist of one of them. These peace officers turned Gibson over to the sheriff of Bexar County.[11]

Captain McDonald and the members of Company B now went on to other duties in the state. As Gibson's trial date approached, McDonald, while in Austin to see his superiors, told a newspaper reporter that the upcoming court proceedings would likely take "several days" because of the "large number of witnesses who have been summoned from Edna and that vicinity." He also noted that he had visited Monk in his cell and that the prisoner appeared in "good spirits." The interest of Captain Bill in this case was such that he went back to San Antonio from December 10 through the sixteenth to watch Gibson have his day in court.[12]

The trial of Monk Gibson took place in San Antonio at the end of 1905. It opened in mid-December in the courtroom of Judge Edward Dwyer of the Thirty-Seventh District Court of Texas. Prosecuting attorneys were District Attorney Charles Baker and W. W. McCrory, county attorney of Jackson County. The defense team consisted of C. A. Davies and V. M. Clark. Since no eyewitnesses to the murders had surfaced and the judge excluded from the trial a confession made by the defendant in the Edna jail during a third-degree interrogation, the case against Gibson was circumstantial. Questions about motive and the presentation of conflicting evidence in the trial—about Monk's bloody clothes and the boy's age, size, and strength—resulted in a hung jury. The members of the jury were about evenly divided between conviction and acquittal.[13] Although a majority of the jurors, according to a newspaper report, thought that Gibson had "guilty knowledge of the crime," no one on the jury believed that he was the "principal" criminal in the case.[14]

During 1906 the investigation into the Conditt murders took on new dimensions. This was partly due to the work of a number of citizens of Jackson County and two lawyers who had been retained by prosecuting officials, H. S. Crawford of San Antonio and J. V. Vandenberge of Victoria. They noted in various messages to the governor and the adjutant general's office the importance of keeping Captain McDonald working on the Conditt murder case. Crawford wrote that he had concluded that others besides Gibson had been involved in the killings. He also said that McDonald should go back to Edna and investigate. At one point Crawford wrote the governor, "Cap't McDonald has shown wonderful ability in ferreting out this crime, and with all respect for the other members of your Ranger Force, I do not believe any one else could do as well on this case as he can."[15] Vandenberge and local residents and officials, like L. Ward and Sheriff Egg, concurred in this assessment.[16] By the end of April 1906 central headquarters had ordered Captain Bill and at least one other Ranger to return to Edna to continue the investigation of the murder case.[17]

Bill McDonald's interest in looking into the Conditt killings never waned. One problem with detective work in McDonald's day was that securing a crime scene and storing and protecting physical evidence did not meet the standards in today's world. During the lengthy investigation into the Conditt murders, for example, blood stains on one weapon used in the crime got smeared and another weapon with clotted blood turned up missing. In addition, bloody prints in the house got erased and a bloodstained shirt disappeared. McDonald realized this fact when he wrote his superiors in early 1906 that one piece of evidence found at the crime scene had been "handled" so much it could no longer be useful in solving the case. Yet Captain Bill also began to figure out that a bloody handprint found on a board in Conditt's house, which was sawed out months ago by a military officer at the scene, might match the hands of Monk Gibson or Felix Powell. This piece of detection would help to break the case.[18]

From May 1906 to the end of the year, Captain McDonald and his Rangers with orders from their superiors went to Edna and Victoria time after time. In conducting his investigation McDonald kept central headquarters informed about his actions in the field. In May he wrote that the case was in "much better shape," as he talked with local whites and blacks. He also said he would take an "imprint" of the fingers of Powell to "compare" with the handprint on the board. A few days later McDonald noted that an "impression" of Powell's hand and the hand stain found at the crime scene were a "fit."[19] At the end of June the Ranger officer obtained arrest warrants for Felix Powell, charged with murder and rape, and for Augusta Diggs, a black neighbor of the Conditt family, for being an accessory to the crime. They were put in the jail at Edna. Early the next month McDonald assisted by Sergeant McCauley took into custody four more black individuals: Amy Howard, for aiding and abetting the crime; Irene Powell and Bethel Reed, accused of the same offense; and Henry Howard, charged with murder. These black prisoners were housed in the jail at Edna. The case had begun to unfold.[20]

The imprisonment of these individuals raised several questions: What were their motives? Did a conspiracy exist in the black community to do in the Conditt family? Joseph Conditt leased property in which blacks had recently lived. He fixed fences and cut off the pathway to the water supply on his land that blacks had taken (although Henry Howard was told his stock could take the long way around to the water). Such actions increased tensions between the white household and their black neighbors. They saw these recently arrived whites living within their midst as " 'poor white trash' and felt that they could take many liberties with the members of the family."[21] Revenge can be a powerful motive for violent actions.

Two other possible motivations for the killings stand out: robbery and assault. The robbery theory is based upon the fact that clothing, food, quilts, sheets, and possibly money disappeared from the premises after the crime. In addition, Felix Powell had an opportunity to purchase the land he lived on and needed cash for a down payment. Reportedly Powell also made indecent remarks to Mildred Conditt. The rape of the daughter and possibly the mother were powerful motives for those involved. In this line of reasoning in the assault theory, then, the boys died because they could identify the killers who were known to family members.[22]

Events now shifted to the town of Victoria, the largest community and county seat of Victoria County. Established in the 1820s, Victoria became an historic site, as residents witnessed the clash of arms between Texans and Mexicans in frontier days. By the opening of the twentieth century, stock raising, railroad construction, and business enterprises made the municipality a commercial focus of surrounding counties. Victoria County itself was formed during the Republic of Texas and remained primarily an agrarian region at the time of the Conditt killings.[23]

Captain Bill and his Rangers continued their actions in the murder case. In July 1906, McDonald got a ruling from the attorney general's office that a special term of a district court could be called to try parties for murder.[24] By the end of that year,

McDonald obtained a bench warrant and returned Monk Gibson to Edna from San Antonio; law officers went before a grand jury and got indictments against those involved; and Sheriff Egg and Ranger Ryan brought the prisoners to Victoria for trial in the district court.[25] At this time Captain Bill especially wrote his superiors about forty-six-year-old Henry Howard. At one point McDonald said that Howard was "badly scared up & he cant rest at all."[26] At another time McDonald explained that Howard told what he knew about the crime to the Ranger captain, Privates McKenzie and Ryan, and Sheriff Egg. Howard stated that "Mrs Conditt was knocked in the head with the adz by Felix that Monk cut the girls throat with a case knife & Felix the boys throat with a pocket knife & Monk killed the biggest boy that his first hit didnt get him & he ran him about twenty steps & Felix killed the other one with an iron rod . . . ." McDonald continued that although Howard said Powell told him these things, he believed Howard "couldnt have explained it like he did if he had not been present."[27]

The dramatic trial of Felix Powell took place in Victoria in December 1906 in the courtroom of Judge James C. Wilson of the Twenty-Fourth District Court of Texas. The prosecution team consisted of R. L. Daniel, county attorney of Victoria County, W. W. McCrory, county attorney of Jackson County, District Attorney G. E. Pope, and ex-District Attorney J. V. Vandenberge. Two prominent lawyers, Ben W. Fly and A. B. Petticolas, defended Powell. Deputy sheriffs, Captain McDonald, and Rangers McCauley and Ryan guarded the prisoner in the courtroom. Although Powell took the stand in the trial, which began on December 5, and coolly declared his innocence, damaging testimony came from other witnesses. A number of Powell's friends turned on him, saying they were no longer afraid of the defendant. Augusta Diggs testified that Felix confessed that he, Monk Gibson, and Henry Howard committed the murders. Howard denied on the stand he was involved and said he told McDonald that Felix related to him that he and Gibson did the killings. Irene Powell, wife of one of the defendant's brothers, testified that Felix stated he would get even with Mr. Conditt for being mean and that she noticed blood-like stains on the pants of the defendant. And Bethel Reed declared that she washed the bloody clothes of Powell on the night of the murders. Since such witnesses were under arrest for aiding and abetting the crime, supporting evidence needed to be presented in the trial to clinch the case for the prosecuting attorneys.[28]

A piece of physical evidence became crucial to the prosecution's case. Imprints of a hand found at the scene of the crime had an unusual characteristic. Sergeant McCauley testified, according to a news story, that he saw an impression of "three finger prints and a dot below" in Conditt's house.[29] This peculiar mark would be shown in the trial to have come from the defendant's deformed little finger on his right hand (which was stiff from a bone felon that enlarged a knuckle). Captain L. H. Younger, in command of some of the troops sent to Edna in 1905, came to the stand and stated he sawed a board with a bloody handprint from Conditt's home and turned it over to the adjutant general.[30] The board plus a photograph were introduced as evidence to support the state's case against Powell. Captain Bill then related that he took this board and tried to match Monk Gibson's hand with the bloody imprint without success. In time, McDonald took impressions on smoked paper of Powell's hand, opened and closed, with his consent. One newspaper account of this procedure between the Ranger officer and the defendant read thus: "When I made the imprint of his hand I put a knife in it and made it with the fist closed. This imprint fitted the photograph of the bloody imprint exactly."[31] The jury had a chance to look at the bloody handprint and Powell's right hand, opened and closed, with the abnormal little finger.

On December 12, 1906, a unanimous jury found Felix Powell guilty of murder in the first degree and sentenced him to death. The verdict was appealed. At the end of January 1907, the Court of Criminal Appeals of Texas affirmed the decision of the lower court. The appellate judges ruled on several points of law, upholding, for example, the decision to allow Captain McDonald to act as both a guard and a witness in the trial. The appeals court also noted that the evidence about Powell's right hand obtained by McDonald with his consent could be introduced into the court proceedings. About the facts of this issue the judges said, "It appears that appellant's little finger on his right hand was abnormal, was shorter than ordinary, and was stiff and in doubling and in grasping an object the little finger made a peculiar mark, different from an ordinary hand, or in clinching the fist, the knuckles made an impression on an object, different from an ordinary hand." The decision of the appeals court ended with the words that the record in this case "points to the guilt of this defendant with the unerring finger of fate."[32]

Early in March, Powell, handcuffed and chained, was brought to a special session of the district court and sentenced to be hanged the following month. Powell, visibly shaken by the ordeal, returned to his cell in Victoria to await the execution of the law.[33] In the middle of the day on April 2, 1907, a calm-yet-nervous Powell, dressed in new clothes, walked up the steps of the gallows, said a few prayerful words, had his feet and arms bound and the noose adjusted around his neck, and, with McDonald and Sheriff Egg on the scaffold, dropped through the trap door to his death. Then the orderly crowd, which came from Jackson County and elsewhere and numbered in the hundreds, dispersed.[34]

In due course the legal machinery of the state also took the life of Monk Gibson. Since one of the charges against Gibson was that he was an accessory to the crime, his retrial had to wait until Powell's appeal and sentence had run its course.[35] At the end of June 1907, Gibson was tried again for the Conditt murders in DeWitt County in the courtroom of Judge James C. Wilson of the Twenty-Fourth District Court of Texas. The defendant, older and heavier since the crime had been committed, had been brought to DeWitt County from Victoria in early June and turned over to the local sheriff. The prosecution team in the trial included Vandenberge, and W. L. Atkinson and Horace Wimberly served as defense attorneys. The usual witnesses, including McDonald and McCauley, took the stand and explained under oath what they knew about the crime. The blood found on Gibson's clothes and body, his presence in the Conditt house, the conflicting statements made by the defendant in the course of the investigation, and the previous testimony of those involved in the criminal act in the trial of Felix Powell—all combined to result in a guilty verdict. Gibson was convicted of first-degree murder and given the death penalty.[36]

The verdict was appealed. Near the end of April 1908, the Court of Criminal Appeals of Texas, ruling on complicated points of law like the change of venue and the relationships between this case and the trial of Felix Powell, affirmed the decision of the lower court. The appellate judges even accepted the conclusion that Monk Gibson was seventeen years old at the time of the murders, which was a necessary condition to inflict capital punishment. The court concluded with the statement, "While the testimony is circumstantial, and while having regard for the fallibility of human reason, the appellant may be innocent, we have not thought so, but have been led to the conclusion by proof that compels acceptance, that his guilt is incontestably established by such testimony as admits of no escape."[37]

Housed in the jail in Cuero, a calm Gibson appeared in court the next month to hear the date set for carrying out the sentence. Following orders law officers executed Monk during the afternoon on June 27, 1908. Spectators cane from Edna and elsewhere. Upon the scaffold Gibson maintained his innocence to the end. Yet, during the morning hours on that fateful day, he talked with McDonald without clarifying his role in the crime (although in confinement he did implicate Augusta Diggs, Henry Howard, and Felix Powell in the killings). One newspaper reported the carrying out of the sentence thus: "When the black cap was adjusted and everything was in readiness some officer said, 'Good-by, Monk,' and he replied, 'Good-by.' "[38]

Of those arrested off and on for taking part in the Conditt murders who were still alive, the cases of Augusta Diggs, Henry Howard, and Bethel Reed continued in the courts. In March 1909, with the agreement of the attorneys for the prosecution and the defense, Judge Wilson transferred the case of Howard to the district court in Guadalupe County and ordered that Henry be turned over to the sheriff of that county. McDonald always kept his interest in bringing this defendant before the bar of justice. But on December 13, 1909, an attorney for the state of Texas filed a motion to dismiss the criminal action against Howard. The reason given in the court's minutes was that the evidence was "not sufficient to warrant a conviction." The judge agreed. Seven days later the district attorney made a motion to dismiss the charges against Diggs and Reed which was accepted by the judge in Victoria. So ended the criminal investigations carried out by the Texas Rangers and local lawyers and peace officers.[39]

In three ways in this murder case the relatives of Felix Powell took actions that raised questions about their solidarity with family members, friends, and the community at large. First, Warren Powell, Felix's brother, was the black person who told authorities where Monk Gibson was hiding after his escape from deputy sheriffs in 1905. Three years later he even had his lawyer seek the $300 reward offered by the governor for the arrest and conviction of those responsible for the killings.[40] Second, as previously stated, Irene Powell, Felix's sister-in-law, testified against her relative at his trial. For some time her actions in this matter angered Felix. And lastly, a member of the Powell family took part in one more tragic event before the book closed on the Conditt murders.

Vowing vengeance after his brother's execution, Arthur Powell, armed with a gun, went to Edna at the end of April 1907 looking for Sheriff Egg in order to shoot him on sight. He went from place to place in the town trying to find the local lawman. In the meantime, warned about the coming attack by both white and black friends, Egg went in search of Powell. While sitting on a barrel in a store, Arthur saw the sheriff and reached for his weapon. But Egg fired and Arthur Powell followed his brother to the grave. The sheriff was then charged with murder but a jury acquitted him of the killing by reason of self-defense and justifiable homicide.[41]

Descendants of the Powell family in today's world still believe that J. F. Conditt committed the murders after he learned about a liaison between his wife and Felix. There was also the belief in the black community that the father confessed to the killings on his deathbed. Later one Texan wrote that this dying scene was "branded as 'nigger talk.' "[42] However, no confession has surfaced and no witnesses have confirmed a deathbed admission of guilt. In addition, at the time of the killings the father was miles away from his house. And two things ran counter to his wife having an affair with Felix Powell: she was sickly and she feared blacks.[43]

The role of Sheriff Albert Egg in the Conditt murder case has been underplayed. Although young and inexperienced as a lawman, he did decide to remove Monk Gibson from the Edna jail to stop lynch talk in 1905. When the prisoner escaped from his deputies in the process, Egg showed courage by talking back to citizens who blamed him for Monk's escape. With a "drawn revolver" the sheriff even "asked anyone present to step into the street and settle the matter personally with him."[44] In addition, the local lawman sought the assistance of state officials, believed that more than one person committed the crime, guarded and transported prisoners with care, and placed himself at the command of McDonald. Egg and the Ranger captain especially worked together in deciphering the bloody handprint. Interestingly, the sheriff even opposed the death penalty in order to keep searching for answers to questions about the crime from those arrested and convicted. Egg served as a lawman for years to come and became a prominent citizen in Edna and Jackson County.

The dismissal of the cases against Henry Howard and the other defendants in 1909 was the last chapter in the Conditt killings. For more than four years this homicide mystery involved—yet transcended—the issue of race relations in American culture. Although black individuals tried to cover up the gruesome murders and white people talked about holding a lynching party, the actions of attorneys, judges, and police officers, especially McDonald and the Rangers, resulted in a more orderly atmosphere in the community. McDonald's stand against mob rule and the third-degree treatment of a prisoner especially aided those interested in maintaining law and order. At one point two men came to Edna to push for mob action. They left town on a train after the Ranger captain told them that if they persisted he would chain them to Felix Powell in his cell.[45] At another time Captain Bill even wrote that he did not want local citizens to go "crazy again" like they did in Gibson's case.[46] Although McDonald should have gathered and protected physical evidence in a more systematic way, his investigative work in this act of homicide deserved special recognition. He doggedly sought answers to questions from those inside and outside prison cells, and he showed skill in handling and analyzing the board with the bloody handprint. As a local newspaper said, "He deserves the gratitude of the entire public for his wonderful detective work."[47] By the time Felix Powell and Monk Gibson went to their graves, however, Bill McDonald had moved on to investigate other criminal cases—particularly the raid on Brownsville and the troubles at Rio Grande City. Then he left the Ranger service to become state revenue agent of Texas.

Chapter 13

BROWNSVILLE AFFAIR: A MUDDLED INCIDENT

Gallant Ranger Would Have Stood Off Any Number of Soldiers While He Had the Authority.[1]

This newspaper headline summarized the trouble between Bill McDonald and the United States Army, during the aftermath of the raid on Brownsville, Texas, by "unknown parties" in the middle of the night on August 13, 1906.[2]

In the "Brownsville Affray," so-called in official documents, the raiders within a few minutes riddled buildings with bullets, killed one individual, and wounded two others. Soon after the raid McDonald and several other Rangers were ordered to Brownsville to assist state and local officials on the scene in maintaining order and discovering the identities of the attackers, allegedly black soldiers of the Twenty-Fifth Infantry stationed at Fort Brown. Captain Bill's investigation took place in an environment of confusion, fear, suspicion, hostility, and—more significant for the operation of the American federal system—jurisdictional disputes about the authority of the national government and the powers of a state. At one point in this charged atmosphere, Major Augustus P. Blocksom, an army investigator on the scene, reported to his superiors, "It is said here he [McDonald] is so brave he would not hesitate to 'charge hell with one bucket of water.' "[3]

The origins of Fort Brown and the settlement at Brownsville in the southeastern corner of the state can be traced back to the coming of Spanish-Mexican pioneers and the impact on the area of the U. S.-Mexican War. By the 1850s Cameron County had been formed, with Brownsville as the county seat. Between 6,000 and 8,000 people lived in the town at the turn of the twentieth century. Nearly two-thirds of the population were Hispanic Texans, with only a few hundred black residents. At the same time the coming of the railroads and the development of truck farming and citrus growing brought more economic prosperity. By the early 1900s the lifestyles of the citizens of Brownsville not only had the imprint of southern and western beliefs but also had the outlook of a Mexican border town.[4]

With a sudden and inexplicable thrust raiders carried out a small-scale attack on Brownsville. The often-told story was that around midnight on August 13, 1906, a group of black soldiers, numbering about a score, opened fire on the townspeople for several, ghastly minutes. This band of troops began shooting from inside Fort Brown, one of the American military posts along the Mexican border. Leaving the confines of the fort, which was situated on the outskirts of Brownsville, by vaulting a low wall, the raiders assaulted the areas of the town within several hundred yards of the military post. More than a hundred bullets from the rifles of the black soldiers riddled buildings, killed one individual, and wounded two others. Then the invaders returned to the garrison without being captured by either the residents or policemen in Brownsville or the army personnel who were on duty at Fort Brown.[5]

The aftermath of the raid went through various stages for several years. The first steps included reactions by local, state, and national leaders; investigations and reports by army officers, especially Major Blocksom and General Ernest A. Garlington; the arrest of thirteen former and current black soldiers by Ranger Captain

McDonald; and the discharge "without honor" of the black troops at the fort by President Theodore Roosevelt. Instead of bringing closure to the affair, however, such actions ignited a fire storm of criticism from people throughout the country. Into the fray came black national leaders, those involved with the Constitution League, members of the Committee on Military Affairs of the United States Senate, and army generals sitting as a Court of Inquiry. In the days after the raid the Brownsville newspaper complained about slow-moving events. The first stanza of a poem went thus:

> Of governor who's slow to act
> When minutes mean to die or live;
> Of people's servants loath to move,
> And of a chief executive
> Who asks for full particulars
> Of "that" and "this," the "how" and "why,"
> Say, have we time for all of this
> When hours may mean to live or die?[6]

The volumes of testimony, which were compiled by these investigative bodies about the reasons for and the details of this bloody affair, contained insufficient evidence to indict any black member of the troops in the vicinity of the town for the violations of human and property rights during the raid. In fact, the more the witnesses testified, the more baffling the case became. The endless rounds of questions and answers resulted in uncovering pertinent information—and in clouding the issues with repetitive and muddled statements.

The basic reason for the contradictory evidence was the initial response of Major Charles W. Penrose, the commanding officer at Fort Brown, and his staff to the firing of weapons in Brownsville. Believing that the post was under attack, the white officers ordered the black rank and file to defend the fort. Reports about the confusion that ensued make it impossible to ascertain to everyone's satisfaction whether any soldiers were shooting at buildings and people in the town. The records also pointed out to some observers the probability of the error of the military judgment about the gunfire. Although a number of the black soldiers and other participants testified that firing had come from the direction of Brownsville, no physical evidence was found to indicate that the post had been attacked. In addition, Major Penrose ordered Captain Samuel P. Lyon to take some troops and march into town to locate Captain Edgar A. Macklin, the officer of the day. Although Macklin was bedded down for the night (and noted to be a sound sleeper), Penrose thought that he had heard the shots, left the fort, and come to some harm as he attempted to capture the raiders. Lyon, at the head of a black contingent, further confused the issue, when, upon encountering a body of armed men in Brownsville, he failed to find out whether any of the weapons carried by these townspeople had recently been fired.[7]

After the Civil War and Reconstruction, black Americans continued to look for ways to improve their second-class citizenship. They migrated to urban centers; they became better skilled workers; they tried to join the labor movement; they withstood violent racial attacks over and over; and they fought for social and political rights in and out of the courts. The raid on the town in southern Texas took place, said Mr. Dooley, "when the negroes had been fully deprived of the homely privileges of dependence in exchange for the dubious gift of civil rights—unshackled in Virginia so's he [*sic*] could be lynched in Ohio."[8]

The underlying cause of the violence in Brownsville was the racial climate in the American Southwest at the turn of the twentieth century. The rising expectations of black servicemen who fought with distinction in the Spanish-American War collided with a rising tide of segregation abetted by local Anglo and Hispanic police in the border towns of Texas. At the start of 1899, at a rest stop in Texarkana, soldiers of the black US Tenth Cavalry left their train, angered a prostitute, and had a bloodless confrontation with local police and citizens. When this train passed Harlem, Texas, unknown parties fired at the cars and the troopers shot back. Then two more incidents occurred at the end of 1899: in October black members of Company D, US Twenty-Fifth Infantry, stationed at Fort McIntosh, had violent confrontations with Anglo and Hispanic police officers in Laredo—the result being one soldier was assaulted, one lawman was attacked, and the enlisted men remained silent; in November a showdown took place between Troop D, US Ninth Cavalry, at Fort Ringgold, and the residents of Rio Grande City, with the townspeople firing on the fort and the black troopers shooting back, even with a Gatling gun. In another episode in February 1900, black members of Company A, US Twenty-Fifth Infantry, stormed a jail in El Paso to free a comrade arrested for drunkenness. In the melee that resulted, one lawman lost his life and one soldier was killed. By the late 1800s black soldiers had reached the point of fighting back against their tormentors. Such turmoil showed that a complex set of equations governed the relations between Texans and the black military in federal service: town versus fort, police versus soldiers, and Anglos plus Hispanics versus blacks.[9]

To know this scenario is to understand the course of events in Brownsville. Racial ill-feelings produced tension between the townspeople, white and Mexican American, and over 180 black members of Companies B, C, and D, First Battalion, US Twenty-Fifth Infantry, who were stationed at Fort Brown. At their previous post in Nebraska the battalion faced less of a color line than they would encounter in southern Texas. Shortly before these troops arrived at the Rio Grande in late July 1906, word reached them in Nebraska that white Texan militiamen in Austin did not want to participate in the current maneuvers with the "colored" soldiers of the Twenty-Fifth Infantry. The timetable for the movement of the black troops was altered to by-pass these training exercises; the maneuvers, to the relief of some white Texans and army officials, did not turn into a real war between the races. "Texas, I fear," wrote the black regimental chaplain, "means a quasi battle ground for the Twenty-fifth Infantry."[10]

During the few weeks between the arrival of the black troops at Fort Brown and the raid on the town, tension between the whites and the blacks was exacerbated by the alleged black abuse of Caucasian women and the consumption of alcohol. Both contributed to most of the racial problems. At the turn of the century Brownsville had eleven saloons, with four owned by Anglos and six run by Tejanos. Usually the black soldiers did not visit segregated saloons with a white clientele. If they did, they encountered a mixture of baffling responses: acceptance, hostility, a refusal to serve, and separate bars. Often, black men at arms frequented establishments owned by Mexican Americans or a saloon and gambling den operated by a member of Company B and a black Texan former soldier. Evidence showed that in these places the black personnel of the Twenty-Fifth Infantry received better treatment than in segregated drinking places.[11]

There were two alleged incidents involving Caucasian women. In one case two black soldiers were accused—they denied the charges—of "jostling" several white women on a sidewalk. The husband of one of the ladies used a handgun during the incident to strike and knock down one of the blacks. The white man denied that he had used insulting language during the act. In another case a white woman reported that, while in her backyard, she was seized from the rear by a "colored" individual in khaki clothes and thrown to the ground. When she cried out, her assailant escaped. When Major Penrose learned of this incident—possibly in a threatening manner from two townspeople—he ordered the troops restricted to the post after eight o'clock on the evening of August 13—the night of the raid.[12] Thus, racial hostility, rumored incidents, and confusion marred the relationship between a number of the black soldiers at the fort and some of the residents of Brownsville during the days prior to the attack.

The events of the raid itself are just as perplexing as the background of the fracas, because they leave unresolved the principal question: who was responsible? Evidence indicated that three key answers could be given. First, at least in contemporary accounts if not in fact, vindictive black soldiers of the Twenty-Fifth Infantry committed the outrages. Second, and a likely scenario, Anglo Americans attacked the town and then blamed the black infantrymen whom they detested. Third, and still a viable answer, residents of Brownsville of Spanish ancestry vented their frustrations about social injustice in southern Texas against the black troops who represented the authority of the American government. For decades, Mexican Americans also did not like "colored" soldiers looking for female companionship in their communities. In time, some public officials in Texas and elsewhere would agree with Major Penrose when he said, "I would give my right arm to find out the guilty parties."[13]

Other scenarios, some unlikely, some raising questions for future researchers, have been constructed to explain the outbreak of violence in Brownsville. Mainly, these points of view deal with outside raiders striking the town. A noted biographer mentioned that the "midnight attack" might have "been made by a gang of Mexicans from across the river."[14] At one point Private William R. Jones of Company D said, "When I first wakened, I thought, the first thing jumped in my mind, I thought it was Mexican soldiers firing across the river on the post."[15] At another time Lieutenant Harry G. Leckie testified that he went into Mexico to check on the rifles used by the Mexican army. But he could not recall who sent him or what he found or reported.[16] Did Mexican nationals really cross the border, as happened in other eras, and fire on the townspeople to get even with the Yankees for past wrongs? After all is said and done, the answer is still—no.

The conduct of the Texas Rangers on and off the battlefields has stirred the imagination of westerners—and a black soldier. Sergeant George Jackson of Company B replied to a question about those who assaulted the town by saying, "I thought probably it was cowboys, or the rangers, as they call them, the rangers. I thought probably it was them that were out on a brawl, or something of the kind." To the sergeant a "brawl" by the Rangers meant that they "had been out on a drunk and were shooting up the town."[17] Yet the Texas Rangers of Company B, stationed at Alice and commanded by Captain McDonald, would not arrive in Brownsville until after the raid.

Another causative factor might have been the beliefs, duties, and operations of officials of the US Customs Service. Customs officers, black soldiers, and smugglers along the southern border became entangled in events that could lead to violent actions. A well-known story before the raid concerned A. Y. Baker, a mounted inspector of customs, who "pushed" an intoxicated black soldier—Private Oscar W. Reid—into "mud and water about knee-deep" at the Mexican border.[18] Then two US senators, one being Joseph B. Foraker, theorized that the firing into the house owned by Fred Starck was not done because the attackers thought it belonged to his next-door neighbor, Fred Tate. In the days prior to the raid, Tate, a customs officer, had knocked down Private James W. Newton for bothering white women on a sidewalk. More likely, in the eyes of the senators, smugglers went after Starck and his family. As a customs officer Starck had arrested hundreds of smugglers, with a recent one, who had a grudge against Starck and knew the layout of his home, jumping bail and becoming a fugitive.[19] Did black men at arms hide their retaliatory acts against customs inspectors by shooting at other buildings and people? Not likely. Did smugglers seek revenge on those who worked for or supported the US Customs Service? Perhaps. Perhaps not.

The main players in the drama at Brownsville, Anglos, blacks, and Hispanics, stood as silent sentinels to the violent act. The changing thought patterns of contemporaries and historical writers ever since was best illustrated by the testimony of First Sergeant Mingo Sanders, an able veteran of the Twenty-Fifth Infantry. He said that "my opinion was at one time that the soldiers done it, another time the civilians done it." When pressed about how the men, women, and children of the town, like the black soldiers, "could keep the secret so long," Sanders declared, "I did not say all the women and children of Brownsville did it; I said I believed the rough element of Brownsville did it."[20]

Many citizens of Brownsville testified that they heard and saw some black members of the Twenty-Fifth Infantry attack the town. No specific black soldier was identified, but the shapes, voices, uniforms, and weapons of the raiders—particularly the clothing and the shells and clips left behind—all belonged to the black troops at Fort Brown. The markings on several shells that matched specific weapons of the soldiers especially became a controversial point.[21] Such evidence, however, is suspect because of contradictory statements, because nighttime vision proved to be faulty, because attempts to plant incriminating physical evidence came to light, and because small-town nonentities tried to use the "nigger raid" to become celebrities.[22] Yet some confusion, especially within Company C, did occur inside the garrison during the attack on the town. Two black sergeants of this company testified that, during the excitement of the raid, a gun rack was broken open under orders before it could be unlocked. In addition, because of poor lighting and a desire to defend the fort, roll call was stopped and a count of individuals was taken. The tally was accurate, one sergeant acknowledged, if he was "not mistaken."[23] These hurried actions, although natural in a state of emergency, only heightened suspicions that black soldiers raided the town and then slipped back into Fort Brown unnoticed.

The most extensive analysis of the evidence against the black troops at the fort, a treatise of more than 150 pages, came from the pen of Captain Charles R. Howland, who served as the recorder for the Court of Inquiry of the US Army. The report in 1910 covered the testimony of civilians and soldiers on the usual topics: the background of the affair, the arms and ammunition used in the attack, the geographical locations of the shootings, and the workings of the three companies of the First Battalion. But Howland also included other pertinent information, from the views about the time of the raid to the talk about the firing being done in military-style volleys. He even covered the riding of horses or not by the raiders and the doings of the black dog of Company B seen in the town during the attack. In the end, after viewing about 13,000 pages of evidence, the black soldiers were still found guilty as charged.[24]

Most of the evidence incriminating the black troops can be interpreted to show that other attackers of the town could have carried out the violence in order to implicate the black soldiers. Inflamed by the alleged attacks upon white women by "colored" men at arms, angry citizens of Brownsville did gather and denounce the troops at Fort Brown. They met in the town's saloons. As events are reconstructed by those who blame the townspeople, there was a good deal of anti-black hostility by white saloonkeepers with segregated bars and the owners of Hispanic beer joints because of the recent opening of a saloon run by two black soldiers themselves. These disgruntled saloonkeepers helped to incite the populace, who, realizing that the discipline among the troops at Fort Brown would prevent the blacks from firing first, armed themselves with revolvers and rifles, approached the fort, and shot over the buildings to attract the attention and draw the fire of the soldiers. Then, in the darkness the raiders retreated through the town to arouse the citizenry, shooting at the lights burning in the houses to prevent detection as they went. As this happened, Frank Natus, a barkeeper who surprised some of the raiders, was accidentally shot and killed and a police officer was wounded in order to settle an old score. The final outcome was a classic case of putting the blame on someone else. Even the khaki-like clothing of the raiders, which the town's Mexican constabulary also wore, resembled the uniforms of the soldiers stationed at Fort Brown.[25]

In retrospect, the record will not reveal the identities of the attackers. But the raid on Brownsville was more than a clash between whites and nonwhites that could have happened in a southern town or a western frontier outpost. The violent act in the town must also be examined within the outlook of a Mexican border settlement. In this perspective a complex equation arises: black soldiers versus Anglos plus Hispanics. In southern Texas elite whites and Tejanos had a way of cooperating and getting the lower social classes to do their bidding. Either the Anglo-Hispanic populace struck first or the black troops beat them to the punch.[26]

Because of the suddenness of the assault, local policemen on duty in Brownsville that night, eight patrolmen and an officer (possibly twelve in all), failed to identify any of the raiders or capture a single participant. At one point in the attack, however, three police officers ran into a few of the armed invaders—and with unfortunate effect. M. Ygnacio Dominguez, the lieutenant of police, had his horse killed and his right arm from the elbow to the hand shattered—it was later amputated—before he could return the fire. He thought that he had to stay alive and rouse the townspeople. Macedonio Ramirez and Genaro Padron, the two policemen who met the lieutenant, separated and withdrew—to put it mildly—from the scene of action. Ramirez's hat was shot off. Padron twice returned the fire as he ran in an attempt to find a safe place. Although two members of the town police sought refuge in a hotel for a time, other policemen began to assemble on one of the streets. In the midst of this confusion Sheriff Celedonio Garza of Cameron County came to Brownsville and proceeded to protect the jail, keep the peace, and investigate the shootings.[27]

After the raid on Brownsville the initial response of the local governmental authorities to the attack was to formulate plans to protect the fort and town, discover the identities of the culprits, and seek the assistance of state and national officials. The townspeople prepared to defend themselves and search for the guilty parties. Several hundred citizens purchased arms. A number of police officers and scores of other individuals patrolled Brownsville day and night, particularly the area next to Fort Brown. In addition, a mass meeting led to the appointment of a Citizens' Committee to find out what happened during the raid. Chaired by William Kelly, the committee consisted of prominent Anglo and Tejano residents, including County Judge John Bartlett, Chief of Police George Connor, and Sheriff Garza. Major Penrose attempted to cooperate with this group and Mayor Frederick J. Combe of Brownsville. Penrose also restricted all troops to the military post, arranged for a twenty-four-hour guard, permitted no person to enter the garrison without proper authorization, and began an investigation of the affair.[28]

Still, uneasiness prevailed. The military personnel worried about an assault on the fort by the townspeople. The residents of Brownsville, in turn, feared that another attack by the black soldiers at the garrison was imminent. Women and children feared to leave their homes. Many of the people living near Fort Brown moved. Politicians, judges, lawyers, law enforcement officers, and leading citizens of Cameron County telegraphed the governor, the adjutant general, the two United States senators from Texas, the president of the United States, and the high-ranking army authorities. In these messages the residents, who had been "stirred to the very soul," explained the terrible situation in Brownsville. They demanded that the black soldiers at Fort Brown be replaced by white troops.[29]

At first the officials in Washington replied that no removal would be forthcoming until an investigation was completed. Within a week after the raid, however, President Roosevelt and the army chiefs decided not to send an additional company of black soldiers of the Twenty-Fifth Infantry to Fort Brown, and to relocate the First Battalion of the Twenty-Fifth Infantry before the completion of the investigations. The fort would be "temporarily abandoned." Initially, the new site for the First Battalion, which was chosen by the executive branch of the federal government, was Fort Ringgold, a deserted outpost in southern Texas. To make the preparations for the abandonment of Fort Brown—and only for this purpose—a company of white soldiers, over fifty men, received orders to proceed to Brownsville. But then the plans were revised. Because of the cost of preparing Fort Ringgold for occupation, and the racial tension in southern Texas, the black troops would be sent to Fort Reno in Oklahoma.[30]

Meanwhile, Governor Lanham and Adjutant General Hulen considered requests from the residents of Cameron County for state troops to relieve the tense situation in Brownsville. Those townspeople who opposed the abandonment of Fort Brown thought that white soldiers would restore the community's morale and guard the black prisoners when they were arrested. But the state authorities procrastinated. The citizens of Brownsville, upset over the lack of communication from the governmental leaders in Austin and Washington, demanded action. One newspaper editorialized, "The state of Texas ignores the situation at Brownsville, apparently regarding our people as a lot of silly, hysterical, timid creatures." Yet a "state of war" has existed between the black soldiers and a "heavy armed force of citizens."[31]

Adjutant General Hulen hesitated for several reasons. Two days after the raid Major Penrose told him that new disturbances were unlikely. State authorities also feared that the dispatch of white Texan soldiers to the area, many of whom wanted to go to Fort Brown, would aggravate the situation. Furthermore, the desire in Austin to wait for federal action contributed to the decision by state officials not to send state military forces to Brownsville immediately after the raid. The only solace for the townspeople was the dispatch by state authorities of several Texas Rangers, only a handful intended to assist in maintaining law and order for hundreds of men, women, and children.[32]

The raid on Brownsville brought a state law enforcement agency into the investigation of a local episode with national overtones. Decades after the crisis, Judge Harbert Davenport wrote: "It so happened, of course, that the Rangers' part in this affair was wholly in the newspapers. The 'riot' occurred between midnight and daybreak; and when the dawn came, it was all over. There was nothing for the Rangers or anyone else to do but to allay the uneasiness of

Brownsville's inhabitants. . . . What remained to be done was for the army and not the police—either state or local."[33] Notwithstanding Davenport's analysis, the Rangers did more than keep the peace. They carried out an investigation which ultimately brought them into conflict with local leaders and the military personnel at Fort Brown.

At the request of the sheriff on August 14, Privates Delling and McKenzie came to Brownsville before McDonald and the rest of Company B arrived. The two Rangers helped restore calm and assisted in the protection of property and human life. In addition, Delling provided some hearsay testimony—of a trivial nature which reflected adversely on the Ranger service—to the Citizens' Committee:

> I am a State ranger. I have come into the possession of some information this morning, which I got from this soda-water man, who sells soda water. He told me that this soda-water man had been told by a saloon man who keeps a saloon in the edge of town that some shooting had been done last night, and that Company C could have taken the whole town if they had wanted to, and that they could take the whole damn State.[34]

This inauspicious beginning by two members of Company B was followed by the arrival of Captain Bill. In the evening of August 21, McDonald, accompanied by Sergeant McCauley and Private Ryan, stepped off a train at Brownsville. At the same time Stanley Welch, judge of the Twenty-Eighth Judicial District of Texas, and the white soldiers of Company H of the Twenty-Sixth Infantry, who had been committed to make the preparations for the abandonment of Fort Brown, also arrived in the town. Captain McDonald, unlike some of his superiors in Austin, believed that the conditions in Brownsville—despite the involvement of federal troops—called for the immediate intervention of Texan military and police forces.[35]

McDonald and his entire command had now arrived in Brownsville. In the events that followed in that town, two factors stand out: personal decisions by Captain Bill, and the command system of the Ranger organization, from the field station of Company B to the Austin headquarters. In the charged atmosphere and the rush of events in the affair for a few days, the actions by McDonald have been both praised and criticized. One writer castigated the Ranger captain by quoting a local resident who said that the "guns he [McDonald] carried were almost half his size" and that these weapons "helped him, proportionately, to the publicity he craved."[36] On the other hand, Captain Bill can be likened in this incident to a "frontier marshal who knew no other way to face a dangerous situation but head-on . . . ."[37]

On August 20, the day before McDonald arrived in Brownsville, Major Penrose wrote William Kelly, chairman of the Citizens' Committee, that in order to remove the suspicions of the residents about the "sincerity" of the inquiry, which was being made at Fort Brown about the raid, he should appoint three townspeople to accompany him, as the head of the new committee, to the garrison to investigate the whole matter. Penrose said that the committee could examine the evidence already collected by the army officers and question any soldier at the military post. The next day this group of local and state leaders, which included a banker, a district attorney, and two judges, began their deliberations at the fort. This committee, however, virtually "delegated" its power, according to one army officer, to Captain McDonald.[38]

Kelly and Mayor Combe informed McDonald that Penrose was doing all he could to ferret out the guilty parties. McDonald also talked to the sheriff who told him how Lyons' company of black soldiers had approached the jail and marched through Brownsville right after the raid. In addition, McDonald spoke with Mack Hamilton, former soldier, who was jailed after the raid, when Sheriff Garza learned that he knew something about the affair. The Ranger captain concluded that Hamilton was among the raiders and was "evidently" engaged in "showing the negroes where parties lived that they wanted to kill." Although Hamilton incriminated

Corporal Willie H. Miller, McDonald believed that he was "evidently lying to shield himself."[39]

On the morning of August 22, McDonald learned that he had been added to the citizens' subcommittee of Kelly, County Judge Bartlett, District Attorney John J. Kleiber, and Judge Welch. Kleiber, Welch, and others told the Ranger captain that the "law authorized arresting criminals, U.S. soldiers or any one else, anywhere . . . ." This conformity to the rule of law in the volatile situation in Brownsville, to the surprise of no one, could result in a clash between the powers of a state and the authority of the nation. What really mattered to McDonald, though, was less complex. He wanted to be able to go after the criminal element or "rascality," as he called it, at the military post.[40]

In order to carry out their duties, McDonald and McCauley, armed with a shotgun and a rifle respectively, walked slowly towards Fort Brown. Shrugging off the warnings by townspeople about not coming back alive, McDonald bellowed, when he encountered the guard of black soldiers, "I'm Captain McDonald, of the State Rangers, and I'm down here to investigate a foul murder you scoundrels have committed. I'll show you niggers something you've never been use' to. *Put up them guns*!"[41] The black soldiers allowed him to pass (although standing there in a likely state of suppressed rage). This encounter, which came from the pen of McDonald's official biographer, has become part of the legend of Captain Bill. It can be seen in several ways: either as the outburst of an arrogant Ranger or the expression of a bigoted officer—or just the command of a riveting personality common in stories about the commander of Company B. Since the incident can not be found in official reports, it could also be apocryphal.

Once inside the fort, McDonald was unimpressed with Penrose, Macklin, and others who could not learn the identity of the raiders. Penrose's talk about "skeleton keys" and insistence that noncommissioned officers would not reveal what they knew only increased McDonald's suspicions. In the presence of Blocksom,

Kleiber, McCauley, and Penrose, Captain Bill then questioned Miller. The black corporal, on pass, visited places on both sides of the Rio Grande the night of the raid and was in a saloon in Brownsville when the first shots were fired. McDonald realized that Miller's return to the fort after roll call contradicted the statements of the white officers. The Ranger captain also interrogated Private C. W. Askew. A cap with the initials C. W. A. was found in the street after the raid. Askew, insisting that he was asleep during the attack, produced a new hat with his initials, which matched the writing in the cap found at the scene. Months later, Askew explained that a box of old hats shipped to the fort was opened and some of the contents stolen by Mexican-American residents of the town. McDonald noted in his report that "there seemed to be no doubt in the minds of those present from his manner and this circumstance [the cap and initials] of his being one of the guilty parties." Before McDonald ended his inquiry, Macklin testified that he had slept through the raid. Captain Bill wrote: " . . . I couldn't help thinking Macklin must have been out with the coons who were committing murder and trying to kill ladies and their children . . . ."[42]

From the evidence McDonald concluded that Companies B and C were involved in a cover up of the guilty parties. The "managers" of the raid, he theorized, were Hamilton and Ernest Allison, the former soldier who operated a black saloon with Private John Hollomon. Joining them among others were Askew and Miller. To avenge past wrongs, they fired at certain houses McDonald thought, but "some mistakes were made by shooting into the wrong houses." To McDonald's dismay, his line of reasoning led him to conclude that Captain Macklin had accompanied the raiders. And he also said in his report that his "impression is that Capt. Lyon and his companies [*sic*] part was to go and finish up the job and to find Capt. Macklin and other missing men who had not shown up." Yet no confessions from any suspects were recorded in order for the Rangers to clinch their case.[43]

More than any other investigator, McDonald implicated both the black enlisted men and the white officers at Fort Brown in the raid. The fundamental mistake in his analysis was more than racial; he could not distinguish between soldiers, whether black or white, and the residents of the town. Although the sheriff mentioned to McDonald that the members of one company from the military post believed citizens had fired on the fort, the idea that the townspeople could have been responsible for the raid never became an integral part of his investigation. His dislike for the white officers at Fort Brown, even Penrose and Blocksom, reinforced his one-sided reasoning. In his report Captain Bill wrote that he told these two officers: “I thought more of the murderers themselves than I did of those who were attempting to cover it up after catching them doing so.”[44]

On August 23 Judge Welch at McDonald’s urging issued a warrant for the arrest of thirteen alleged raiders. The list included Allison and black members of all three companies. Men named in alphabetical order were: Private Askew of Company C; Sergeant Darby W. O. Brawner, in charge of the quarters of Company C and the racks of rifles; Private James C. Gill of Company D, in an encounter with a customs inspector and present inside the fort and part of the force that went looking for Captain Macklin; Private Hollomon of Company B, asleep and awakened by the gunfire; Private Joseph H, Howard of Company D, on guard duty in the area of the enlisted men’s barracks; Sergeant George Jackson, in charge of the quarters of Company B and the racks of rifles; Corporal Charles H. Madison of Company C, on pass and seen in front of the company barracks before the firing ceased; Corporal Miller of Company C; Private James W. Newton of Company C, involved in an altercation with white women prior to the raid and on guard duty asleep in the guardhouse; Corporal David Powell, in charge of the quarters of Company D and the gun racks; Sergeant James R. Reid of Company B, sergeant of the guard; and Private Oscar W. Reid of Company C, involved in an affair with a customs inspector previous to the attack and listed as present at roll call. The black soldiers were charged with "conspiracy to commit murder."[45]

Unlike other investigators, McDonald's short-lived inquiry led to the issuance of a judicial writ to bring into a court those who had carried out the raid. Conspicuously absent from the list of warrants, however, were Hamilton, the Ranger captain's initial suspect, and the white officers at Fort Brown. Judge Welch and District Attorney Kleiber probably refused to arrest Penrose, Macklin, Lyon, and the other white soldiers at the military post. Months later McDonald wrote about Penrose and Macklin, "I wanted to make complaint against them for being accesory [*sic*] to the murder but was persuaded out of it."[46]

Upon receiving the bench warrants, McDonald and McCauley immediately proceeded to Fort Brown to see Major Penrose. The commander of the post agreed to lock up the men in the garrison's guardhouse until their trial. At the same time McDonald telegraphed his superiors: "Have just turned warrants of arrest over to Major Penrose for Twelve soldiers and one ex-soldier for being connected with murder of civilian."[47] Later a high-ranking army officer wrote, with some justification, that the method of collecting evidence which led to Judge Welch's decision to issue warrants was either "guesswork" or a "dragnet proceeding."[48]

Such viewpoints did not deter Captain Bill. He felt he had to move quickly to end the crisis in the town—before a possible confrontation took place between the harried soldiers and the armed citizens. In doing so, his criminal case against the black infantrymen was based not only on evidence but also on his intuitive mind. One historian, who viewed McDonald's investigative evidence as either "highly circumstantial or nonexistent," said it best:

> McDonald leveled charges against three men because of their absence from the fort on the night of the assault, one because of the discovery of his hat near one of the scenes of the shooting, two because of their involvement in altercations with local citizens, and

> the rest because of their service as sentinels and noncommissioned officers in charge of the quarters and guns. Operating on the assumption that black soldiers had committed the outrage, the Ranger captain concluded that these guards and noncommissioned officers must be aware of who had left the fort to participate in the raid.[49]

The new developments in Brownsville placed army authorities in a quandary. The members of the Twenty-Fifth Infantry at Fort Brown had already been ordered to Fort Reno in Oklahoma. And a company of white soldiers had already arrived at the military outpost to prepare for its abandonment. How should the prisoners be held? Should they accompany their comrades to Fort Reno? Should the departure of the three companies of the Twenty-Fifth Infantry be delayed? Could one company of white troops hold the prisoners or prevent their escape? Should these white soldiers take the accused men to another prison? Could civil officials adequately protect the black soldiers under arrest if they were left behind? Could a fair trial be obtained in southern Texas? Should an attempt be made to change the location of the trial?

In the morning hours of August 24, Major Penrose received orders from the War Department, some in confidential terms, to delay his departure, to keep custody of the prisoners, and to forward any notice from civilian officials for the return of the accused soldiers to the military authorities in Washington before compliance.[50] On the same day President Roosevelt and his military advisors sent secret orders to Major Penrose to leave the garrison with his command for Fort Reno as soon as possible. The black soldiers under arrest would accompany the rest of the battalion as far as San Antonio, Texas. They would then be imprisoned in Fort Sam Houston, until their safe surrender to civil officials. The confidential message to the commander at Fort Brown stressed one point:

> This movement of accused men should not be announced in advance, and should be made so as to avoid attracting attention or bringing on conflict with civil authorities. There is no intention of

> taking these men beyond jurisdiction of State of Texas or of withholding them from civil authorities a moment beyond time when they can be turned over safely. It is not believed safe to leave them at Fort Brown, as the one company to be left there is insufficient to do work of shipping property and supplies and at same time guard prisoners so as to prevent their escape or protect them if need be. You can make this explanation if it becomes necessary.[51]

In a series of meetings and confrontations, the events of the climactic day of August 24 came to an end. McDonald learned "privately," from James B. Wells, Jr., prominent lawyer, who got it from an operator in the telegraph office, that the battalion would take the prisoners with them when they left Fort Brown.[52] In order to check the validity of this intelligence, McDonald went to see Judge Welch. In a meeting with Blocksom, Kleiber, and Welch, the judge and the major assured the Ranger captain that the prisoners would be held at the fort. Blocksom also tried unsuccessfully to relieve McDonald's fear that the black soldiers under arrest were not in the guardhouse. When McDonald refused to tell Kleiber where he got his information about the removal of the prisoners, "insulting" remarks passed between them.[53]

While the Rangers watched the entrance to the military post, McDonald had an important meeting with Welch, Penrose, and Captain John F. Preston of the Twenty-Six Infantry. Violating his orders, Penrose informed Welch about his secret instructions to remove the prisoners from the fort. He believed that this was necessary because of his previous assurances to Welch and others that the prisoners would be left behind and that the judge would be notified of any change in their status. When McDonald asked to see the telegram, Penrose refused. Captain Bill stressed that he represented the state of Texas; the major noted his orders came from the War Department and the president of the United States.[54]

McDonald had already taken a significant step to seize the prisoners. The confidential orders to Penrose to remove the battalion and the accused soldiers arrived in Brownsville shortly after five o'clock in the afternoon of August 24. Within an hour McDonald sent a message, by way of Captain Preston, to the commander of the military post. In it he demanded the return of the prisoners and the delivery to him of other soldiers who were connected with or had knowledge of the raid. The Ranger captain ended by saying, "An immediate reply will greatly oblige."[55]

Major Penrose sent back the arrest warrants with a stinging reply. In his note of refusal to comply with the demand, he declared, " . . . I have the honor to inform you that I am directed by higher authorities to assure their safety, but they will be cared for subject to the jurisdiction of the civil authorities and will be delivered to the said civil authorities for trial when their safety is assured." "After a most careful investigation," Penrose concluded, "I am unable to find anyone, or party, in anyway connected with the crime of which you speak."[56]

In turn, Captain Bill stood his ground. He returned the warrants to Penrose for the black soldiers under arrest and made a second demand for the return of the prisoners. McDonald noted that Judge Welch had agreed to protect the accused soldiers and guarantee a fair trial. "I now notify you," McDonald ended his second demand, "that I have wired my superior officers of what is being done and call for assistance to hold my prisoners, and I ask you to await said instructions from them." The die had been cast.[57]

Meanwhile, McDonald wired the governor expressing his fear that the battalion would be moved to Fort Reno, Oklahoma, beyond the power of state officials. The governor immediately telegraphed several state and national leaders. He was assured, within twenty-four hours, that the accused soldiers would remain in the state for return to civil authorities in the near future.[58] "Referring to your telegram this morning," General William S. McCaskey, commander of the Department of Texas of the United States Army, wrote Governor Lanham on August 25, "negro soldiers held on civil warrants at Fort Brown, to be transferred to Fort Sam Houston by order of the president of the United States. The president further directs that these soldiers shall not be removed from jurisdiction of the state of Texas."[59]

This information did not help Captain Bill the night of August 24. No doubt a certain amount of conflict between the Rangers and the army had to result from the discovery of the secret orders to remove the prisoners from Fort Brown, despite the previous assurances by Major Penrose to Judge Welch and others to the contrary. For the "shrewd" and "vindictive" McDonald, according to Blocksom, did not like or trust the army officers at the military post.[60] "It is possible McDonald might have fought the entire battalion with his four or five rangers," wrote Blocksom, "were their obedience as blind as his obstinacy."[61]

The different positions of Captain McDonald and Major Penrose had become irreconcilable. McDonald's point of view was well-illustrated in his last-minute message to the governor and the adjutant general on that fateful day of August 24:

> The military authorities are trying to take our prisoners away from here for the purpose of thwarting justice and will attempt to do so at once over my protest. Please send plenty of assistance to prevent this outrage. The officers are trying to cover up this diabolicle [*sic*] crime that I am about to uncover and it will be a shame to allow this to be done. I turned warrants over to them in due form with the promise that they would hold them in the guard house and turn them over to me when called for. Everything is quiet but I propose to do my duty.[62]

Major Penrose realized that his confidential orders to remove the prisoners took preference over other agreements. Even prior to the secret instructions, however, Penrose disagreed with McDonald over the understanding between them. The major believed that he, Kleiber, and McDonald had agreed at the time of the confinement of the accused soldiers not to remove the prisoners from the guardhouse except when ordered by Judge Welch. Penrose concluded, "I would consent to nothing else."[63]

Until new instructions were received from their superiors, Captain Bill and his small band of Rangers prepared to prevent at all costs the removal of the prisoners by the army. McDonald notified railroad officials to hold the train with the battalion until he was sure the accused black soldiers were not aboard the cars. Later in an interview McDonald said that "railroad officials had agreed to listen to my orders . . . ." A number of armed townspeople were ready to back whatever action the Rangers took. One newspaper, playing up the confrontation, concluded that, if the troops had tried to leave Brownsville around midnight on August 24, "there would doubtless have been serious consequences."[64]

Judge Welch and the state authorities in Austin prevented a possible bloody clash between McDonald's Rangers, backed up by armed townspeople, and the soldiers of the Twenty-Fifth Infantry. McDonald sensed a change in the atmosphere in Brownsville. As the days went by without another outbreak of violence, he was accorded less and less authority by local officials. He could not believe that leading townspeople were afraid the battalion would not march out of the fort and leave their friends in the guardhouse without a fight.[65]

The changing attitude of community leaders was best illustrated by the viewpoint of James Wells. The boss of the local Democratic party summed up the current feeling thus: "McDonald, I am a friend of yours, but you are only a Ranger captain, and if you keep along the way you are doing, you are going to precipitate us into trouble. You are zealous, you are a good officer, and you think you are doing right, but if you attempt to interfere with those soldiers down there, this matter will break out anew, and we will lose a great many lives. You must remember our wives and children."[66] In the beginning the residents of Brownsville sought aid against the vengeful black soldiers after the raid. At the end public officials sent the battalion north to save them from the ire of the townspeople and the Rangers.[67]

During the night of August 24, Judge Welch withdrew the warrants for the arrest of the thirteen blacks. "This is to direct you to immediately return to me," the judge stated in his message to McDonald, "without any further attempt at execution the three certain warrants of arrest placed in your hands by myself yesterday . . . ."[68] In emotional scenes with the judge and others, including District Attorney Kleiber and Sheriff Garza, McDonald refused to comply, even when threatened with arrest for contempt of court, without instructions from his superiors in Austin. He honestly believed the governor would sustain his position in the end.[69]

In these heated encounters McDonald and McCauley were determined and ready. "The Ranger Captain and his sergeant stood together," McDonald's official biographer recorded, "their automatic guns, as usual, in position for quick and easy service. They made a picturesque pair, with their typical Texas hats, and arms, and dress, and their determined faces."[70] As words flew back and forth between the participants, McDonald finally received a brief telegram that Governor Lanham had sent when he had contacted General McCaskey. The last sentence read: "Consult District Judge and Sheriff and act under and through them."[71] The confrontation with Welch was over.

McDonald agreed to the revocation of the warrants. Some townspeople wanted him to make a complaint against the accused murderers before a justice of the peace, but the Ranger captain knew the governor's instructions ruled out this procedure. Judge Welch, in turn, ordered the sheriff to escort the soldiers to the train.[72]

More than once, Captain Bill expressed his indignation over his treatment by Judge Welch and other public officers in those final hours. At one point McDonald told his superiors that Welch "took my warrants away from me in a very haughty and insulting manner and said mean hateful things to me . . . ."[73] The Ranger captain and local leaders did not part in an amicable way.

In the early morning hours of August 25, the entire battalion of the Twenty-Fifth Infantry left Brownsville by train for Forts Sam Houston and Reno. Daylight, Mayor Combe thought, was a better time to stop an act of violence by townspeople than darkness. Along the route taken by the soldiers Combe placed armed guards, and he and the sheriff and others, including the town police, escorted the three companies, as a church bell tolled, to the railroad cars. With such precautions no trouble with local residents or the Rangers occurred.[74]

Shortly after nine in the evening of the same day, after the battalion arrived in San Antonio, Penrose reported, "Journey made without the slightest trouble or demonstration of any kind."[75] The twelve black soldiers accused of the raid on Brownsville—the former soldier had been left behind—were turned over to a military guard at the railroad station. They were then placed in "military custody" in Fort Sam Houston, which had been reinforced with white troops for such purpose. Recognition of a new warrant for their arrest by state authorities would be "deferred."[76] The rest of the battalion immediately left for Fort Reno, Oklahoma, where, on August 27, they made an uneventful arrival.[77]

In September 1906 a grand jury in Cameron County failed to indict any of the accused black soldiers held at Fort Sam Houston. The Rangers of Company B, who left Brownsville the same day as the soldiers, presented evidence before this body. McCauley turned over Askew's cap to the grand jury. Although affidavits from McDonald were placed in evidence, the captain failed to personally appear. He was suffering from bronchitis, aggravated by old lung wounds, and was on leave recuperating at Mineral Wells, Texas. To a newsman McDonald "intimated" that if he had the "cooperation of the local authorities at Brownsville," the result of the grand jury proceedings "would probably have been different."[78]

Unable to discover the identities of the culprits, although military charges were placed against the prisoners at Fort Sam Houston, President Roosevelt accepted the recommendation of the Inspector General of the Army and dismissed without honor in November 1906 all black members of the Twenty-Fifth Infantry who were present at Fort Brown during the raid on Brownsville. A total of 167 members of Companies B, C, and D, some of whom had served in the Spanish-American War, were discharged from the military service. Eleven of the black soldiers in Brownsville during the raid, however, had already left the armed forces, either honorably or dishonorably, before the presidential order. The editors of a newspaper in the state capital of Texas "commended" Roosevelt and his military advisors for their action in this matter.[79]

The discharge of the black men at arms did not end the controversy about the violence in Brownsville. For several years Roosevelt was severely criticized by Senator Joseph B. Foraker of Ohio and other individuals, particularly the leaders of the black community, over the course of action taken by the executive branch. Foraker, motivated by political ambitions and a belief in the innocence of the black soldiers, challenged the president's authority to take such measures. He wanted, as other people did, a more just decision. Eventually Congress recommended that a military tribunal appointed by Roosevelt should reexamine the cases of the black members of the Twenty-Fifth Infantry who were discharged without honor. This body, in time, allowed a few of the black discharged soldiers to reenlist in the service. The other discharged men were barred from serving in the army and denied any retirement pay. They could, however, be housed in a soldier's home and be buried in a national cemetery. In 1972 the secretary of the army converted the discharges without honor to honorable discharges, thereby exonerating the black soldiers of their guilt in the affair.[80]

Captain McDonald and his adversaries in the episode in Brownsville carried on a war of words for some time. During a recess in the court-martial trial of Major Penrose in 1907, the former commander of Fort Brown called McDonald a "contemptible coward" in the presence of other people. A "wrathy" McDonald stressed again that Penrose tried to shield the guilty parties.[81] In a speech before the US Senate, Foraker also "referred" to the Ranger captain in a "contemptuous manner." McDonald responded, "I'll go forty miles out of my way to give Senator Foraker an opportunity to cross-question me."[82] Captain Bill had an appellation for Foraker—"Senator Firecracker."[83]

In retrospect, the commander of Company B did not change his position on the attack on Brownsville as the story unfolded. In 1910 the Court of Inquiry of the United States Army brought to an end the hearings into the raid on the town. McDonald believed that the findings of this body—that black soldiers did indeed shoot up the town—"fully vindicates," in his words, "the position I had taken of the matter."[84] Before this happened, the Ranger captain in an interview would not entertain the idea that the "citizens of Brownsville murdered one of her own citizens and shot into houses where women and children were sleeping when there is not a single disinterested person who ever intimated such a thing."[85] McDonald's investigative skills had their limitations.

The "Brownsville Affray" left a heritage of both conflict and cooperation for national, state, and local leaders. The battle between Roosevelt and Foraker was symptomatic of the flawed processes and overbearing personalities in the affair from the beginning. Intercommunications between the three levels of government were hampered by secret instructions formulated within one layer of governmental machinery and by the inability of political and military leaders at all levels to quickly make decisions and answer inquiries. At times the antagonistic positions between the authority and personalities of the Texas Rangers and the power and personnel of the United States Army dominated the course of events. The raid and its aftermath can be reduced to a series of personal clashes: a white red-neck versus a black soldier, McDonald versus Penrose, Welch versus McDonald, and Roosevelt versus Foraker. Yet the commander at Fort Brown also attempted to cooperate with local officials and the Rangers in investigating the events of the raid and maintaining law and order. In addition, Captain Bill acquiesced at the end to the authority and decisions of the governor and Judge Welch.

The reactions by contemporaries to McDonald's role in the "Brownsville Affray" were mixed. Some Texans in the state capital and elsewhere praised the Ranger captain for his struggle with the army to keep the black soldiers under arrest in Brownsville.[86] Residents in the lands around Alice and Falfurrias in southern Texas especially expressed their feelings about McDonald's "good service as an officer and his dauntless bravery" at Brownsville and other localities.[87] The Democrats of Atascosa County in a convention passed several motions dealing with the troubles at Brownsville. One read: "Resolved, That we heartily approve the action of that gallant Ranger, Captain McDonald, for his valiant stand in defense of the civil authorities."[88]

Other Texans had less kind words to say about McDonald's performance. Some newspapers reported that the Ranger captain was bitter about the army taking the prisoners away and was critical of the lack of support from leading residents of Brownsville.[89] Certainly Kleiber and Welch had harsh words to say about McDonald's actions.[90] Kelly answered in the negative when queried about McDonald's role in helping the Citizens' Committee "ferret out any criminals." Combe thought that McDonald's experiences in East Texas made him think he could handle the situation with the blacks better than the townspeople.[91] The editors of the newspaper in Brownsville even denounced the Ranger captain's "rantings" after the raid—after he left the town in a "huff."[92]

To balance these views one must remember that McDonald tried to come to grips with some of the complexities of this case. For decades he experienced criminals escaping justice through the influence of friends or the protection of public officials. This disturbed him, even more so as his age and health brought his career to an end. The Ranger captain was a man of action. Yet his investigation of the attack on the town was no more or no less imperfect than other investigators'. His findings, which led to the arrests of the black soldiers that no one else would make, may have been flawed, but so were other statements about what happened that fateful night. The dichotomous positions in this case—black versus white, soldier versus civilian, Washington versus Austin—were beyond McDonald's ability to unravel. One Texas historian went so far as to say that McDonald was an "inveterate grandstander and race baiter" and that his conduct in this affair was a "flagrant abuse of his authority to make arrests."[93] Still, the "Brownsville Affray" was not Captain Bill's Armageddon (although he was as "popular as a rattlesnake").[94]

Chapter 14

RIO GRANDE CITY: THE LAST STAND

WE WANT RANGERS AND MORE OF THEM, LIKE CAPT MC DONALD.[1]

Such sentiments, coming from people in southern Texas in the aftermath of the raid on Brownsville, revived McDonald's spirits. "The mere presence of a Ranger in a vicinity," one person noted in his message to the adjutant general, "causes quiet among the law breakers."[2]

Rio Grande City, county seat of Starr County, became an important center in the 1800s for shipping, the marketing of cattle, and the servicing of US troops stationed at nearby Fort Ringgold. This old settlement in South Texas increased its population between 1896 and 1914 from 1,800 inhabitants to 2,100 residents. At the same time Starr County, first settled by Indians and Spanish-speaking colonists engaged in cattle and sheep ranching, had a population of 11,469 in 1900. By then the interplay between Anglos, Tejanos, and black soldiers turned violent. It would happen again.[3]

The events that resulted in the shootings in Rio Grande City and the surrounding areas at the end of 1906 can not be traced back to the raid on Brownsville. The violent affair in Starr County dealt with political rivalry, skullduggery, and the willingness, in the words of one author, "to resort to almost any tactics."[4] Both political parties used colored ballots to guide illiterate Spanish-speaking voters in using forms written in English. The Democrats called themselves the "Reds" and the Republicans became known as the "Blues" (although the colors would be reversed in other counties). Both parties tried to gain the upper hand in elections in several ways: by paying the poll taxes of those who voted, by giving tipsy voters colored ballots after a night of eating and drinking, and by bringing Mexicans across the border to vote after they declared their intentions of becoming citizens.[5]

These techniques of controlling the masses were used by political bosses in South Texas at the turn of the twentieth century. At the apex of this concentration of power in the hands of Anglo and Hispanic leaders stood James Wells, who did not see eye to eye with McDonald in the raid on Brownsville. Wells oversaw those in control of the Democratic machines in the counties of Cameron, Duval, Hidalgo, and Webb. He also brought together a triumvirate of Democratic leaders in Starr County: County Commissioner Manuel Guerra, banker, merchant, and rancher; County Judge John R. Monroe; and Sheriff Washington "Wash" Shely, former Texas Ranger and stagecoach driver. The political control of these individuals lasted until 1906 when Shely came down with a debilitating nervous disorder. Then Deputy Sheriff Gregorio Duffy led breakaway Democratic dissenters, while Edward "Ed" Lasater, powerful land owner and rancher, took charge of the Republican onslaught.[6]

Partisan politics and not party principles dominated the contested election in November 1906 in Starr County. The two major parties organized paramilitary bodies of armed men to intimidate voters. A bitter contest for sheriff took place between Deodoro Guerra, the Democratic candidate who replaced Shely as sheriff, and the embittered Duffy, whose name appeared on the Republican ticket. A clash between party stalwarts was imminent.

At a Democratic gathering on the night of October 25 at a ranch miles from Rio Grande City, an armed body of Republican partisans, including customs inspectors, rode up and intruded upon the meeting. Sheriff Guerra and others ordered the armed men to disperse or a posse would be summoned. After an exchange of words, the intruders withdrew. The next day Guerra told District Judge Stanley Welch that he and his nine deputies would be unable to handle any serious trouble at the upcoming election. The sheriff requested that the court appoint special officers. Welch granted this request, selecting twenty-four special constables for stationing in the various election precincts in the county. In time, Welch authorized the naming of twenty more men. These special peace officers of the Democratic party were opposed by thirty Republicans, appointed by a county commissioner, to stand guard at the courthouse. One historian described the situation like this:

> The combination of these special appointees and a sheriff's force of nine deputies provided the Democrats with a legally sanctioned army of over fifty men, while the Republican ranks, which included the seven customs officials for the county, totaled almost forty. The two political clubs also hired additional undeputized gunmen. Although the Red forces held a numerical advantage for the whole county, the Republicans concentrated their armed recruits in Rio Grande City, the scene of the election-day showdown.[7]

Welch and District Attorney John Kleiber decided to remain in Rio Grande City and keep open the term of the district court until after the election in order to insure that the legal processes would not be interfered with. On the night of November 5, according to Kleiber, he and Welch retired to adjoining rooms on the ground floor in a small house. By an hour or two past midnight both men were asleep. The next morning, after calling several times and receiving no answer, Kleiber entered Welch's room and found the judge dead on the bed.

Welch had been shot with a bullet from a .45 caliber handgun. Kleiber's account of the ins and outs of the shooting, given to the news media, did not square with the facts. The district attorney said that the judge, while lying on his side, was shot in the back, with the bullet passing through his heart. But a medical examination showed that, while lying on his back, Welch died from a shot fired downward through his heart, with the bullet exiting through his back. Kleiber also believed that the killer fired through a window with the "sash" raised and the "shudders closed." But a newsman, writing about this generally accepted theory, pointed out, "There are no powder marks on the window shutters and no marks to positively indicate the bullet was fired through the window." One thing was certain: in this confusing picture the assassin had gotten away.[8]

The upcoming election had become chaotic, violent, and unpredictable. The murder of Judge Welch, in the words of one observer, "proved to be but one more incitement in an uncommon contest, one that ultimately became more bizarre, even by Lower Rio Grande frontier standards."[9]

As the news of Welch's death spread on the morning of election day, the Democrats became demoralized. Intimidation and violence took place at the polling booths. In a lengthy report to the adjutant general from Rio Grande City, T. B. Skidmore, presiding official in Precinct No. 1 during the election, explained that he met with Francis W. Seabury and Rentfro B. Creager, who spoke for the Democratic and Republican clubs respectively. They agreed to appoint election clerks and peace officers at the courthouse from both political parties. They also came to an understanding that people would enter and vote in pairs—one Democrat and one Republican. But this arrangement only lasted for a short time. Armed Republicans took possession of the "staircase and lower door and would only let such Democrats in as forced their way by them at peril of their lives." When asked if four "desperate characters with Winchesters" stationed at the "lower entrance" to the courthouse were voters, Duffy replied, "No, they are only some posts driven in the ground there for a rear-guard to keep out the Democrats." Scores of those who belonged to the Democratic party did not mark their ballots.[10]

The turmoil during the election and its aftermath forced local authorities to call for state intervention. Three Democrats—

Seabury, Wells, and Sheriff Guerra—wired officials in Austin for Rangers and soldiers to prevent further "bloodshed." Both Seabury and Wells pointed out in their messages that Captains Brooks or Hughes would be better able to handle the situation than McDonald because of "party feeling."[11] Governor Lanham and Adjutant General Hulen responded by dispatching troops and Rangers to the area at different times. Eventually, Captains Brooks, Hughes, and McDonald arrived in the troubled town. But the indomitable McDonald came first.[12]

After the raid on Brownsville, the rank and file of Company B traveled the border in search of lawbreakers. In October of 1906, Rangers went to Del Rio and Eagle Pass looking for outlaws. At the latter place McDonald, McCauley, and two privates assisted Mexican officials in the extradition of fugitives from south of the border. To McDonald a "few bold bad men" did the killing and robbing under the "pretext of a revolution." A similar situation existed in Del Rio. By the end of the month the members of Company B returned to Alice and nearby communities.[13]

In a telephone conversation with McDonald in early November, Governor Lanham inquired whether the ill will between the Ranger captain and Judge Welch from the "Brownsville Affray" would affect his actions in this case. An indignant McDonald answered, as he thought any Ranger should, in the negative. Then the governor told McDonald to take whatever Rangers from his command that were available and proceed to Rio Grande City. Remembering the Brownsville affair, the governor added as an afterthought that McDonald should be "conservative" in his actions in looking for Welch's killer and keeping the peace. Captain Bill answered that he would be as "conservative as the circumstances will permit."[14]

The trip to Rio Grande City took McDonald and his men two days. On November 7 (or a day earlier) the Ranger captain, Sergeant McCauley, and Crosby Marsden, a new recruit, left Alice by train for Harlingen. On the way McDonald picked up McKenzie and

Delling, who had been in and out of the Ranger service for several months. In the morning hours of November 8 these five troubleshooters left Harlingen by train for Sam Fordyce, a railroad terminus miles from Rio Grande City. Here they obtained a driver and a wagon and proceeded overland to their destination as night fell.[15]

The road along which McDonald and the Rangers traveled the night of November 8 had been built to connect Forts Brown and Ringgold in the lower Rio Grande valley. It followed the river for the most part. Dense vegetation of chaparral, dotted here and there with Mexican-American settlements, lined the road. Travelers at night went armed. In the darkness Captain Bill and the rank and file of Company B had their last shootout.[16]

While McDonald and the other Rangers were riding in the hack toward the town, another vehicle approached them from the opposite direction in the pitch-dark night. Few words, according to McKenzie, were spoken by either side, although the Mexican Americans said something and McDonald yelled out "Rangers," which McKenzie repeated in Spanish. The conversation did not last long. The Rangers found themselves in an ambush near a ranch. Five Hispanics in a wheeled vehicle and two hiding on the ground opened fire. Some of the attackers and Rangers at one point or another jumped from the horse-drawn conveyances to the ground. In the ensuing gun battle both sides fired at close range. "From where I stood in the hack, I could see the whites of their eyes," McDonald recalled, "and I felt as if I could pick the buttons off their coats. I let go as fast as I knew how, and at a different Mexican every time."[17] Rounds of ammunition were spent. As the smoke cleared, four Tejanos were dead, one wounded, and two captured and put in jail. No Rangers were hurt, although one shot went through the shirt of their driver. McDonald worried that the governor would think their actions were not "conservative enough."[18] One state official, though, called the "battle of Capt. McDonald" a "complete victory."[19]

Within a day or two after the gun battle, a coroner's inquest ruled that the Rangers acted in "self-defense."[20] Those killed in the gunplay were C. C. Farias, Gaspar Osuna, Juan Garcia Perez, and Jose Venecio.[21] The news media took pains to report that the wounded man—Manuel Osuna—and those living in and around the town "fully" confirmed the account of the shootings by the Rangers.[22]

Ever since the shootout, questions have been raised about the motivation of those who fought McDonald and his Rangers. A generally accepted theory would be that the Hispanics, as a newspaper stated, were "merely drunk and murderously inclined toward all officers and law-abiding citizens."[23] A chronicler of events in South Texas went so far as to declare that "authorities concluded that the assault had resulted from a drunken spree."[24] In a more likely scenario, another account merely pointed out that the Mexican Americans "copiously" fortified "themselves with mescal."[25]

Another favorite explanation for the gun battle would be that inebriated Tejanos carried out a planned attack. The plot, as weaved by storytellers, went like this: Word had reached Rio Grande City that two Rangers, McDonald and McCauley, were on the way with reinforcements to follow. This information about the coming of the Ranger captain and his sergeant spread through the surrounding areas by the "cactus telegraph."[26] It encouraged those residents who disliked the Rangers and wanted disorder during the election process to attack so few state peace officers. Tejanos met, talked, drank, and decided to wipe out the Rangers. As the hacks approached each other, the bad blood between Hispanics and the Rangers made the Mexican Americans curse, yell, and shoot. But, in the words of one who valued the Ranger service, "The hated *Rinches* did not play fair."[27] They understood Spanish; they had more firepower than expected; and they "invoked the old Ranger rule of shooting first and talking later."[28]

Elements of the truth are contained in the planned-attack approach. An important factor, though, is underplayed: the crazy-quilt pattern of politics in Rio Grande City in 1906. Three of the Mexican Americans gunned down—Osuna, Perez, and Venecio—had been part of the armed group who threatened peace officers and intimidated Democratic voters during the election in the town.[29] Republican partisans realized that Democratic votes cast in other areas in the county, like La Grulla and Roma, would be brought to Rio Grande City to ensure a victory celebration for the Democrats. This had to be stopped. The Blues decided to continue their quest for political ascendancy through the use of force. They sent armed men to the village of La Grulla to overawe officials. On the way, the rough-and-ready Republicans made a fatal mistake. Instead of running into the Reds who were bringing election returns to the county seat, they accidently encountered McDonald and his Rangers on the road. In the confusion and darkness both sides fired pointblank.[30] The Blues not only lost the gun battle but also failed to win the election. When votes were counted, with Rangers guarding the door to the room, only a few Republican candidates defeated their opponents in the towns and countryside. Duffy even lost the sheriff's race to Guerra.[31]

The shootout along the Rio Grande was one of a series of clashes between the Rangers and Spanish-speaking inhabitants dating back to the 1870s. This particular gunfighting finale for McDonald, furthermore, had several repercussions. For one thing the governor had criticized the lengthy and costly telegraphic report to him from McDonald about the "Brownsville Affray." Now the telegrams by the Ranger captain to central headquarters about the gunplay near Rio Grande City were terse and less expensive.[32] More important the news about the one-sided gun battle enhanced the ability of the Rangers to maintain law and order in the area. McDonald and his men quickly put an end to the threat of violence in the town. In one message the Ranger captain said, "We have the situation well in hand. Have ordered both factions to lay off their arms or abivide [*sic*] the consequences."[33] In another telegram to the governor, he ended with the words, "Everybody disarmed; everything quiet."[34]

Such actions by Company B made it less urgent for other Rangers and soldiers to arrive in Rio Grande City. Still, they came.

On November 9 Captain Brooks joined McDonald and his men, as he traveled overland to the town from the railroad terminus at Sam Fordyce. On the trip he learned that peace prevailed in the beleaguered town.[35] Then came a show of force by the state that would overcome any opposition. On November 10 Adjutant General Hulen, a troop of cavalry (with horses provided at the railroad terminal by the King Ranch), and Captain Hughes and his Rangers arrived in Rio Grande City. They came to stop "mob violence."[36] By then, as a newspaper reported, "The town is quiet. No armed men have been seen since the arrival of the Rangers. Gangs in surrounding ranches have been broken up and some have taken refuge in Mexico."[37]

The troubles at Rio Grande City and the resultant gun battle reinforced McDonald's public image, in the twilight of his Ranger career, as a two-gun Sir Galahad. Throughout the state people compared the Ranger captain to the Texan and national heroes of the past. A newspaper in Forth Worth lauded him by saying, "Perry [*War of 1812*] and McDonald are made of the same stuff. If McDonald had been in Perry's place he would have been equal to the emergency. If Perry had been in McDonald's place he couldn't have done better."[38]

It is ironic, though, to contemplate that Captain Bill might not have shot anybody in the gun battle. At the time, according to a knowledgeable Ranger, he was carrying a newly developed semiautomatic Winchester rifle. The other four Rangers with him still cherished the Winchester carbine shooting the 30-40 Krag-Jorgensen cartridges, which had replaced the 44-40 weapon. McDonald, no doubt, was trying to set an example in the procurement of better weapons for the Ranger service. The border Rangers, however, were slow to accept the new automatics, calling them "systematics." They feared the guns would fail to work when needed. That is exactly what happened to McDonald the night of the gunfight along the Rio Grande. As the mules lunged with the noise of the shots, the Ranger captain's automatic Winchester jammed after the first shot. The other Rangers, using the slower but more reliable Krags, killed the ambushers. When asked later how many attackers his new weapon hit, McDonald drawled, "Oh, well, hell (very reluctantly), I don't guess I *missed* any of 'em!" This evasive answer had the ring of truth. One does not miss when one cannot shoot.[39]

Few violations of the law occurred while the Rangers and soldiers remained in Rio Grande City. At one point Private McKenzie and another Ranger jailed a person for theft and two other people for disturbing the peace.[40] In addition, one night three Rangers, two being Marsden and McKenzie, went looking for medicine for use in their camp. They had to draw their weapons when surrounded by seven Hispanics. But bloodshed was averted, as the men decided to scatter and fight another day.[41]

In his messages to central command McDonald talked about running down the murderers of Judge Welch.[42] But he left the town on November 14 for duties elsewhere in the state, too soon to unravel the mystery of the judge's death. The next day the soldiers were ordered home too.[43] For the rest of 1906, Captain Hughes and his men kept the peace and tried to find Welch's killer.[44] In time, Alberto Cabrera, a member of the Blue Club, who was arrested and extradited from Mexico through the efforts of the sheriff's office, stood before a judge in DeWitt County for the crime of murder. He was convicted for shooting Judge Welch and sentenced to life imprisonment in 1908 (although he escaped and fled to Mexico four years later). By the end of the first decade of the new century, bitterness still lingered between Democrats and Republicans in Starr County, with such feelings being exacerbated by another killing: the gunning down of Gregorio Duffy.[45]

Captain Bill summed up in one telegram the basic preventive measures that stopped further disorder in Rio Grande City in 1906: no one carried firearms except county officers and no "drunks" were "allowed."[46]

Chapter 15

THE END COMES: STATE REVENUE AGENT AND OTHER ROLES

"Cap, you have eyes in the back of your head and can smell a criminal in the dark," was once said to him, and perhaps this statement was not so wide of the mark.[1]

Age, ill-health, weariness, and grief induced Captain Bill to leave the Ranger service early in 1907 and accept another position in state government. He became an energetic and controversial state revenue agent. In time, his desire to be a lawman would again be fulfilled, when he served as a bodyguard to Woodrow Wilson in the presidential election of 1912 and as a federal marshal in the Southwest for a few years before his death. As McDonald's life drew to a close, his official biographer wrote, "He could *wear* out, and he might some day stop a conclusive bullet, but he declined to *rust* out."[2]

As McDonald's career in the Texas Rangers came to an end, the old group began to dissolve. In a letter to central command, Captain Brooks resigned, effective November 15, 1906. In it he stressed that "private business" matters demanded his "personal attention." Two days later the adjutant general's office accepted his note giving up his post.[3] Then, at the start of 1907 Hulen left his position as adjutant general. Sergeant McCauley also moved over to Company A. He had been a key member of McDonald's company for many years. Of the "Four Great Captains," only Hughes and Rogers remained in the Ranger service.[4]

STATE REVENUE AGENT: FIRST TERM (1907–1908)

On January 15, 1907, Thomas M. Campbell, the newly elected governor, appointed McDonald state revenue agent. The announcement of this action took McDonald and knowledgeable people in the capital by surprise. The general belief existed that the new administration would take care of the Ranger captain, but the appointment as state revenue agent was unexpected. McDonald read about his new role in government service in a newspaper. As soon as he could, he set out for Austin to meet with the governor.[5]

Doubts about whether to accept the new position filled McDonald's mind. Although in poorer physical condition than in earlier years, he still preferred the freewheeling life of a Ranger to a desk job in the capital. Furthermore, he disliked the belief that the new position was a reward for past deeds, with good pay but little or no work. In the meeting with Captain Bill, Governor Campbell stressed the remuneration—$2,000 a year—and the safety factor. He did not want McDonald to be gunned down or die from "going about in all kinds of weather." The Ranger captain appreciated these thoughts. Then McDonald realized that a basic need in his life could still be fulfilled in the new position—to enforce the law.[6] One newspaper concluded that, if McDonald is as fearless in carrying out his duties in his new office as he was as a Ranger, "his friends predict that he will get after the tax dodgers in great shape."[7]

As state revenue agent, McDonald had a small budget and staff. This initially consisted of $1,000 per year for an office assistant and clerk; another $1,000 for travel and other expenses incurred by McDonald; and $175 for stationery, stamps, and telegrams.[8] This small office had to see that the tax laws dealing with people, property, and businesses were faithfully carried out.

For four years during the two administrations of Governor Campbell—he was reelected in 1908—McDonald enforced the law in a number of different ways. He caused an uproar when he attempted to carry out the provisions of the newly enacted Full Rendition law, which assessed property at its true value and not at a fraction thereof. In addition, he enforced certain provisions of the Baskin-McGregor liquor law, especially in obtaining licenses, and the occupation tax against lawyers and other people. McDonald went after tax delinquents, influential or not, from those running business firms to peddlers of patent medicines. Most colorful and newsworthy were his attempts to make the circuses traveling through the state pay the maximum taxes allowable by law. In these endeavors as state revenue agent, the former Ranger captain needed the support of the governor and the cooperation of the state comptroller and the attorney general's office.

The Full Rendition law was not effectively enforced. Texans were supposed to swear under oath to the value of their real estate, monies, stocks, and other property. The county assessors could then change these sums to correspond to the real value of the property as they saw it at the time of the assessments, not using, though, the criterion of value of what such property could bring at a forced sale. Following this, a commissioners' court, acting as a board of equalization, would consider the figures before they were used to fix the tax rate throughout the state. Traditional methods, apathy, and political power struggles, however, made the operation of assessing property less than ideal.[9]

McDonald, as well as Governor Campbell, recognized the basic problem in full valuation of property in the state. Some people undervalued their property. Poorer counties, of necessity, had a more difficult time in handling taxation rates, local and state, than their more affluent neighbors. But the inequalities in the assessment of property, allowing rich counties to avoid their fair share of taxes, bothered the new state revenue agent.[10]

To rectify this situation McDonald sent a general letter to the county assessors on March 15, 1907. In it he pointed out the "fact that both real and personal property is assessed at only a certain per cent of its value, instead of 'at its value,' as required by the Constitution and laws of the State." Furthermore, McDonald stressed that he would visit such counties as "practicable" to examine the "'mode of rendition and assessment." After stating the appropriate laws and judicial decisions about oaths and penalties under consideration, the state revenue agent added near the end of this letter that in carrying out his legal duties in investigating these matters, the law must be followed. If so, no "embarrassment" would come to the county assessors.[11]

The immediate result of this action was a storm of protest. County assessors were furious. The public became indignant. McDonald, vilified for holding up the Texan citizen at the point of a revolver and bringing more money into the state treasury to become prey for all types of schemers, sat quietly in Austin responding to questions. He and the governor stood their ground. Some support came when the association of county judges proclaimed their support of the letter and spirit of the Full Rendition law.[12]

McDonald decided to meet with the county assessors. At the end of March 1907, the County Tax Assessors Association of Texas met in Austin. Various assessors in attendance recognized that some farmers, corporate interests, banks, and other parties having investments in stocks, bonds, and other notes, were underreporting their holdings and avoiding their fair share of taxation. In an address to the conference McDonald again stressed that assessment of property was to be made on its real value and not a fraction thereof. Not only should assessors render property at its true value, but they should also seek out property hitherto unassessed and place it on the tax rolls. Such actions would reduce the tax rate. In their efforts to accomplish these goals, McDonald stood behind the county assessors. But he warned those gathered in the assembly that he would bring impeachment charges against those negligent in their duties.

When questioned about what to do with assessment rolls already completed for 1907, the state revenue agent responded by telling the county assessors to go back to their offices and redo the lists in order to give a true picture of the value of property in their counties.

The convention then acted favorably upon a number of resolutions. These supported redoing the rolls for 1907 and complying with the letter of the law thereafter. They took favorable note of McDonald's instructions in this matter, recommended changes to the legislature to improve their work, and authorized the notification of assessors not present of these actions and urging cooperation. At the end of the meeting the members passed a resolution requesting that the news media publish the following notice to tax assessors by McDonald, dated March 29, 1907: "You are directed to give notice to taxpayers in your respective counties to call and correct their assessments and give in any money and notes or other property not heretofore given in, and place the full value on all property. Instruct them that if they do this, you will ask the commissioners court to place the proper valuation on same."[13]

Favorable comments about McDonald's role in the debate over assessments and his actions at the convention appeared in print. One newspaper noted that he had the law and right on his side. A New York paper commented that although the county assessors came to Austin with a "feeling of animosity" towards McDonald, the state revenue agent "brought them all into line."[14]

In the months to follow McDonald answered questions and tried to resolve problems that arose in replacing custom with the letter of the law in the assessment of property in the state. He obtained opinions from the attorney general's office that showed the illegal nature of the procedure by which commissioners' courts advised county assessors on the value of property before the property lists were turned over to the courts. County assessors had a duty under penalty of fines to obtain the real value of property from its owners through an oath administered by the assessors. McDonald insisted that those responsible for assessing property should prosecute people for "false swearing" to the true value of their assets.[15] The state revenue agent also sought a judicial opinion that held that county assessors had the power to revise assessment rolls already completed in order to reassess them at their true value.[16] Although some county assessors and members of commissioners' courts tried to circumvent McDonald's edicts, others adhered to his rulings.[17]

The state revenue agent had made his point. There was no need for Captain Bill to follow through on one of his positions: "In some sections they are so indignant," he opined, "that it may be necessary to increase the ranger force . . . ."[18] Yet, as McDonald's official biographer noted, "It was rumored that, though a civil officer, he still wore a 'forty-five' in a holster and carried an 'automatic' in his hip-pocket."[19]

Within a year the state revenue agent toured North Texas to see if county assessors were obeying the provisions of the law to assess property at full market value. He found that assessed valuations of property had indeed increased.[20] McDonald's official report for his first two years in office showed that the increase in assessments in the state in 1908 over 1906 amounted to nearly one billion dollars, with the tax rate declining by approximately two-thirds (to six and one/fourth cents on $100). Yet McDonald believed that large amounts of paper money and notes had escaped taxation.[21] At one point a newspaper reported that the increase in taxable valuations of property in the state can be attributed to two reasons: "the first being the natural increase in the valuation of property, and the other is the efforts of State Revenue Agent McDonald in requiring assessors to assess property at its market value."[22]

During his first term as state revenue agent (1907–1908), McDonald faced two more burning issues: handling the complexities of enforcing the liquor laws and dealing with the shenanigans of the circuses traveling in the state. With the former the state revenue agent had to look at the need for licenses in the selling of alcoholic beverages. With the latter McDonald "had much trouble in trying to have circuses and other shows pay the taxes required by law."[23]

The state revenue agent went after saloonkeepers who failed to take out their licenses under the Baskin-McGregor liquor law. In his biennial report McDonald gave a detailed account, county by county, of monies collected or not in the issuance of liquor licenses.[24] The state revenue agent paid special attention to country clubs and other social organizations, like the Eagles and the Elks, who had federal liquor licenses but no retail permits to sell alcoholic beverages in the state of Texas.[25] In addition, McDonald obtained a legal opinion that separate licenses must be obtained for each bar in a saloon.[26] And he personally went to San Antonio to handle violations of the law in that town. Here he collected thousands of dollars from those who ran drinking establishments.[27] Later McDonald discredited a news story in San Antonio that said he had entered a "billard hall" and "unscrewed the sides of the tables."[28]

MCDONALD, CIRCUSES, AND "BUFFALO BILL" CODY'S WILD WEST SHOW

For several years McDonald had to deal with the questionable conduct of the owners of the circuses. They tried to evade occupation taxes in two ways: by disputing the tax on each performance, claiming day and night shows as one continuance performance; and by getting around a sliding scale of taxation based on the price of admission. Those who ran the circuses paid less tax by charging customers one cent less than one dollar or a penny less than seventy-five cents or a similar reduction on a fifty-cent ticket.[29] In his report for the years 1907 and 1908, the state revenue agent listed collections from circuses and carnivals that totaled more than $5,000. Yet McDonald realized that traveling shows, like Barnum and Bailey, Buffalo Bill's Wild West show, Ringling Brothers, and Sells Floto, owed the state of Texas several thousand dollars.[30]

These deceptive practices by the circuses and other shows moving from town to town in the state angered McDonald. He sought rulings from the attorney general's office. He personally left his desk and went to the places where the circus entertainers performed. In the fall of 1908, McDonald and the state comptroller (after an inquiry by a local official) sought the advice of the attorney general about the application of the taxation laws to the circuses and other shows. The chief legal officer of Texas replied that if a circus gave one continuous performance, running from the afternoon into the evening without "any intermission" and allowing people to stay as "long as they desire," then the owners would be liable for the tax on a single admission ticket. Otherwise, the proprietors of the circuses that charged an admission fee for each show must pay a tax on each performance.[31] At the same time the state revenue agent had followed circuses in the state and made them pay a separate tax on each performance. As a result rumors spread in Texas that the circuses would not return for a new season.[32]

A special problem in the circus debate was the role of William F. "Buffalo Bill" Cody's Wild West show. On request from McDonald and a local official, the attorney general's office held that Cody's Wild West show was a circus and had to pay the state tax on each performance. Buffalo Bill maintained that his show was an exhibition—one that portrayed frontier scenes of the American West. The state through its "intrepid ranger agent" sought to convince Cody to pay the occupation tax on circus performances rather than the smaller amount of money for an amusement license. Cody's refusal brought a civil suit by the state of Texas and Travis County to recover several hundred dollars for two shows given in the city of Austin.[33]

The trial at the end of 1908, which captured the imagination of the populace, took place in the courtroom of Judge George Calhoun of the Fifty-Third Judicial District of Texas. The prosecution of the case was handled by John W. Brady, county attorney of Travis County. The defense team consisted of James H. Robertson and John L. Peeler. State and local officials, including McDonald, testified for the plaintiff. In defense of Cody, employees, friends, law officers, even an old Texas Ranger, took the stand and made their case. The testimony of those for and those against showed that the Wild West show fitted the either-or category of circuses. As one Texan concluded, "I will say that in some ways it is a circus and some it is not."[34]

Captain Bill grasped the complexities of staging the Wild West show. He knew that in "some ways" it looked like a circus. Putting up a tent, opening the ceremonies with a grand parade, having acts with trained horses and riders, letting performers do somersaults and make pyramids—all these happenings McDonald had seen at circuses. Yet the state revenue agent recognized that in other ways Cody's exhibition was not a circus—no clowns, no trapeze artists, and no wild animals. Furthermore, acts that showed life in the Old West in Cody's view would not usually be found in a circus. McDonald took time to see Buffalo Bill and his followers try to depict emigrant wagons crossing the plains, soldiers and Indians engaging in battle (with Tall Bull going down), Pony Express riders taking off, and trains being robbed. Captain Bill concluded, "As to there being very little in this exhibition which would come under the head of a circus,—I thought it was a circus."[35]

In the give-and-take during the trial McDonald commented on the life and times of Buffalo Bill. While attending a Wild West show, McDonald enjoyed watching Cody riding and shooting at glass balls thrown in the air. Captain Bill reflected, "As to whether I could do that myself,—I will say that I could shoot at glass balls, but I don't know whether I could hit them. I was formerly a very good shot, but I am not so good now."[36] Some numbers in the program in Cody's exhibition dealt with a "Zouave drill" (Civil War soldiers in colorful dress) and Cossacks doing their "wild riding acts."[37] McDonald testified that he saw Indians in his early days in the Panhandle. But he "never saw any Cossacks in the wild west of Texas."[38] Nor had he seen a "circus that carried with it a company of Zouaves, who drilled."[39] During the redirect examination, Captain Bill commented further: "In connection with this being termed a Wild West Exhibition, I will say that I have never seen a company of Zouaves drilling in the West, nor have I seen the Princess of Wales riding in a stage coach."[40]

After all was said and done in the trial, the district judge sustained Cody's position, and the state appealed the decision to a higher court. At the end of April 1909, Buffalo Bill again won. The chief justice of the Court of Civil Appeals not only ruled that the Wild West show was not a circus, but also declared that the law which taxed a "circus and other exhibitions" did not apply in this case. "It is a circus and other exhibitions," the judge wrote, "to which this statute relates and not merely an exhibititon [*sic*] disconnected and separate from a circus."[41] The appellate justice, in addition, gave a colorful statement about why the Wild West show was not a circus:

> There was an absence of the lady with a paucity of garments, the gentleman in spike-tail coat with whip in hand, the clown that tries to be funny and often fails, the trick pig or hog, but both doubtless to be found in the audience[,] the trained animals, bareback riders, high and lofty tumblers, the trapeze performers, rope walkers, chariot races and many others, and last but not least, the genial artist that delights my soul in obligingly taking the photographs of my country cousins as they appear upon the scene[.][42]

One newspaper concluded, "Colonel Cody wins, and therefore Captain McDonald loses."[43]

During his initial term as state revenue agent, McDonald carried out other duties. At the end of 1907, he brought to the attention of county attorneys the failure of numerous lawyers to pay their occupation tax. He asked these local legal officers to institute court proceedings against such delinquents.[44] In his official report the state revenue agent noted that the state legislature had reduced the occupation tax on various professions, to be effective at the start of 1908. Yet McDonald believed that loan agents, peddlers of patent medicines, and those who brought merchandise into Texas for reshipment owed the state government thousands of dollars. Captain Bill wrote that the tax laws "should be promptly and vigorously enforced."[45]

STATE REVENUE AGENT: SECOND TERM (1909–1910)

As his first two years in office came to an end, the former Ranger officer said in an interview, "I have not tendered my resignation to the governor nor am I going to resign, unless I am fired."[46] To the disappointment of those who had evaded the tax laws, McDonald did not leave his post. Governor Campbell reappointed him as state revenue agent for another two-year term. The chief executive of Texas wanted to keep McDonald within his official family.[47]

In 1909 and 1910, Captain Bill continued to hold to his dramatic law-abiding stance against tax dodgers. During that time, the assessed value of property increased more than one hundred and eighty million dollars, with a drop in the tax rate to four cents on $100.[48] The state revenue agent also noticed that liquor dealers were less likely to violate the Baskin-McGregor law and the Robertson-Fitzhugh law.[49] Yet McDonald continued to raise questions with the attorney general about wholesale liquor dealers organizing their physical plant and business practices in order to make retail sales without the appropriate license. The state revenue agent, in addition, went after druggists who "admitted selling alcohol and medicated bitters capable of producing intoxication." The owners of these drug stores had federal licenses because "they were afraid of Uncle Sam." McDonald tried to make them fear his office too.[50]

In the enforcement of the tax laws the state revenue agent made no distinction between the big fellows and the little guys. He kept after corporations, like those involved with gas and oil, to pay the tax on their gross receipts, and he began to collect the small fee required to start a new business.[51] At one point McDonald instituted court proceedings against an oil company and its receivership in North Texas for nonpayment of the gross receipts tax. He won the case.[52] The state revenue agent even went after those businesses that published, distributed, and sold textbooks to schools in Texas. He learned that some firms owed the gross receipts tax; other book merchants did not.[53] In his final report McDonald was proud of the fact that his office had collected more than $63,000 in a two-year period from enterprises that owed taxes on their gross receipts.[54]

Captain Bill relished the pursuit of those who dodged the payment of state fees. His office became instrumental in collecting the occupation tax from those who ran bowling alleys, pool halls, and theaters. He tried to apply the same tax, with some success, to pawnbrokers, photographers, and dealers in lightning rods, pianos, and sewing machines.[55] At one point McDonald obtained an opinion from the attorney general that an occupation tax was imposed upon those selling "cannon crackers or other combustible packages of a similar nature," and not upon "Roman candles," "sky rockets," or other "fireworks."[56] Revenue Agent McDonald made sure that money kept flowing into state coffers.

Captain Bill continued his "relentless pursuit" of circuses in his last two years in office. Ringling Brothers became the new target. Questions still existed about the number of performances given and the price of admission collected by the circuses. An official of Ringling Brothers met with McDonald to resolve these issues. When this failed, the state revenue agent followed this circus. He collected taxes, instituted court proceedings to obtain back taxes, and impounded horses under the law. In this struggle both sides tried to influence public opinion—either by pointing out the virtues of having circuses or by stressing the need to maintain law and order.[57]

McDonald did not give up his crusade to enforce the circus tax. His efforts led to an agreement in the fall of 1910. The state accepted an out-of-court settlement, due to the lack of sufficient testimony, of ten suits against Ringling Brothers (who also ran Barnum and Bailey and Forepaugh and Sells) for back taxes. The circus combine paid the state $12,000, less than one-half of the amount owed.[58] At the same time a lawyer for Forepaugh and Sells sent a letter to Texan officials. He wrote that one continuous performance, day and night, at a charge of ninety-nine cents, would be given in the upcoming circus season. He also offered to join the state in any legal action necessary to test this decision. To McDonald this proposal was "brazen effrontery."[59]

Flushed with success and indignation, Captain Bill followed the circuses around the state during the new season. He even thought of using an airplane.[60] Finally circus owners obtained a temporary court injunction to stop the state revenue agent from collecting taxes for more than one performance in the small towns.[61] "I have been enjoined against doing anything, except to breathe," McDonald said, "and I can not breathe aloud." But he could see and collect "data to be used at a later date against these shows."[62] In his final report the state revenue agent noted that when a circus tried to carry out a continuous performance, "confusion and pandemonium prevailed" among the performers between the day and night shows. The practice came to an end in the small towns in 1910. By then McDonald had collected $26,500 in taxes from the owners of the circuses.[63]

Captain Bill ended his last year as state revenue agent in whirlwind fashion. With the cooperation of the governor and the attorney general, McDonald claimed that he had brought several hundred thousand dollars into the state treasury during his administration that would otherwise have been lost. Undoubtedly, he was right.

MCDONALD, HOUSE, AND PAINE: PUBLICIZING A RANGER CAPTAIN

While McDonald served as a state official under Governor Campbell, he became better known to Americans outside Texas. In 1908 McDonald took some time off from his duties as state revenue agent to visit the East. He traveled to New York City. While the former Ranger captain was in that town, he met with Albert

Bigelow Paine, who was writing his official biography. Paine's services had been obtained through the efforts of Edward M. House (who had been McDonald's confidant for many years). Through Paine, Captain Bill had a dinner with Mark Twain and played pool with him, rather poorly, though, as McDonald hit the ball off the table several times. At another time McDonald went out with House and Paine for dinner without a collar—which amused everybody at the Players' Club. House described McDonald's first meeting with Paine at the New Amsterdam Hotel thus: "It was a cold, wet night, and Bill came in with his 'slicker' and big Stetson hat. We went upstairs with him. He took off his coat, pulled from one side his .45 and from the other his automatic. He did this just as an ordinary man takes out his keys and knife. I explained to Paine that Bill had to carry his artillery in this way in order to be thoroughly ballasted—that he would have difficulty in walking without it."[64] Early the next year McDonald received a prospectus of his official biography written by Paine. In the news media this work was known as the Ranger captain's "memoirs."[65]

From New York City McDonald traveled to the nation's capital, where he had the "time of his life hobnobbing with President Roosevelt." At the White House Roosevelt gave Captain Bill a warm reception. They talked about old times when they hunted together in Oklahoma. Roosevelt introduced McDonald to members of a baseball team from Cleveland, Ohio, and persuaded the former Ranger captain to extend his stay in Washington. While in the East, McDonald wore a hat and coat more suited to the fashions of that region. Because of the "strenuous" nature of his trip, McDonald was "anxious" to return to Texas in June of 1908.[66]

Paine not only authored a study of the life and times of Bill McDonald in book form (published in 1909), but also wrote articles about the adventures of the Ranger captain for *Pearson's Magazine*. The stories for the popular monthly periodical covered events from his days in the Panhandle (like the killing of Matthews) to his final actions at Brownsville and Rio Grande City.[67]

These writings about the famed Ranger officer resulted in an exchange of letters among House, Paine, and McDonald. The three collaborators had to deal with several things: putting the yarns down on paper, satisfying publishers, and carrying out advertising campaigns. Some discussion took place about the Conditt murder case and the Brownsville affair. With the agreement of House and McDonald, Paine played down the torture of Monk Gibson to get a confession during the investigation of the Conditt killings. House also believed that McDonald's harsh words for the actions of state and local officials in the aftermath of the raid on Brownsville should be toned down. House and Paine agreed that the Ranger captain did not understand the ins and outs of the publishing business. At times House quieted McDonald. In the end, the biographer, his subject, and the publishers made money. And House just enjoyed the days spent with Paine and Captain Bill.[68]

McDonald lived long enough to witness vast changes in American culture. A dramatic statement about the old and new ways and their impact on a person's life came from the pen of McDonald's official biographer. While on his trip to New York City, the Ranger captain "said anxiously to a companion who was steering him through the mess of traffic at one of the Twenty-third Street crossings: 'Look here, you'll get me killed, yet, in a place like this. I don't know the game.' " Then Paine wrote:

> The muzzle of a Colt 45, or of a Winchester, had no terrors for him, but a phalanx of automobiles and traction-cars, mingled with a medley of other vehicles, bearing down from four different directions—a perfect tangle of impending death—proved disturbing to one accustomed to simpler, even if more malignant, dangers.[69]

In 1911 the newly elected governor of Texas, Oscar B. Colquitt, selected E. B. House of San Saba County to replace McDonald as state revenue agent.[70] Months before a newspaper report indicated that McDonald was considering a return to the Ranger service. The state peace officers were undergoing reorganization, and Captain

Bill was mentioned as the new head.[71] But he did not secure the appointment, and he served instead as a sergeant at arms to a state Senate committee investigating the election process in Texas. Here he got involved in a controversy between the two houses of the legislature when the Senate committee sought testimony from members of the other house. McDonald's role was to inform members of the House of Representatives of this action and to take their responses back to the Senate committee. However, he was charged with making arrests of some members of the assembly—which he did not—and testified himself about this matter before a committee of the lower house.[72]

PRESIDENTIAL BODYGUARD IN THE ELECTION OF 1912

In the presidential campaign of 1912, an attempt was made to assassinate Theodore Roosevelt, the Bull Moose candidate for the White House. Although wounded, Roosevelt continued in the contest. The attack on the former president temporarily halted the speaking engagements of Woodrow Wilson, the Democratic nominee. A threat on Wilson's life worried his advisors. Although the Democratic candidate opposed obtaining a personal bodyguard, Wilson allowed Edward M. House, one of his campaign leaders, to telegraph McDonald on October 15: "Come immediately. Important. Bring your artillery." The next day from Quanah, Captain Bill tersely wired back, "Coming."[73]

This event, more than his friendship with Theodore Roosevelt, propelled McDonald onto the national stage. The mixture of fact and fiction in the life of the Ranger captain had given him a regional reputation in Texas and the Southwest. Now, from this day forward, McDonald's words and actions will be covered by the national press. In retrospect, this point—becoming a national icon—set apart the lawman from Quanah from his fellow Ranger captains.

Thinking that House was in "trouble," McDonald "borrowed a shirt" and some money and took a train to New York City. His arrival, about two days later, with a "big white Stetson," a "four days' growth of beard," and his guns, created a "sensation" at Democratic headquarters.[74] Initially, Wilson's wife was more pleased than Wilson himself to see the former Ranger captain. Soon after McDonald's arrival in New York, however, House wrote, "I arose at seven and went over to see Governor Wilson and Captain Bill at the Hotel Collingwood. They were just leaving for the train, but we had a few minutes' conversation. Bill said the Governor was the finest fellow in the world, and the Governor seemed equally pleased with Bill and said he was taking good care of him."[75]

In the weeks that followed, McDonald, dubbed "Silent Bill" by newspaper reporters, stayed with Wilson, day and night. He dogged the footsteps of the Democratic candidate, took part in controlling crowds, and kept his mouth shut. On October 19 in New York City, for example, Wilson spoke at two different places. At the Brooklyn Academy of Music, McDonald cleared a path through the crowd at the entrance of the auditorium for Wilson's party. Later, at Carnegie Hall, McDonald and others tried to protect Wilson from the buffeting of his overenthusiastic admirers after his speech was completed.[76] While in New York City, McDonald obtained a permit to carry a weapon. He said that he just did not "feel natural" (only "half dressed") without his revolver.[77] In carrying out these security duties, the former Ranger captain spoke very little. "I told him when he came not to say a word to anybody," House wrote, "and he is carrying it out literally. I heard a reporter ask him who I was, and that is the only time I have heard him speak. He told the fellow that he was a stranger in New York and did not know."[78]

A few days before the election, Wilson and McDonald were returning to Princeton, New Jersey, by a chauffer-driven limousine after a speaking engagement close by. The automobile, moving at a speed of about fifteen miles per hour, hit a mound of earth in the road. The jolt threw Wilson and McDonald against the roof of the car. Although McDonald was just "shaken up and bruised," the Democratic candidate received a head wound which had to be treated by a physician. This was Wilson's only injury during the campaign.[79]

On the day of the election, Wilson and McDonald went for a walk in the town of Princeton after breakfast. Then, as election bulletins showed the Democratic candidate winning, McDonald exclaimed, "I wonder if I'd get arrested if I just shot off my guns. If it keeps up this way, I'll have to just turn 'em loose."[80]

Captain Bill did not immediately leave the East after the election. On November 6 the newly elected President accompanied by McDonald took a brisk walk in Princeton. Wilson saw a snake and pointed it out to McDonald, who, borrowing Wilson's cane, killed the snake, although he also broke the cane.[81] On November 8, just before he departed, McDonald looked over the Secret Service agents assigned to guard Wilson. The only things the Ranger did not like were their .38 caliber weapons. He thought that this gun would kill a person—"if you give him a week to die in."[82] As McDonald left for Texas, a saddened Wilson said, "I formed an affectionate regard for him. He has a combination of shrewd sense and simplicity of character that is very rare these days."[83]

Although Captain Bill was glad to return to Texas—"I get awful tired of walking on these rocks [city pavements]," he once complained to House[84] — his influence on President Wilson's advisors lingered on. Wilson asked McDonald questions about the abilities and background of Colonel House.[85] In later years, McDonald became a defender of Wilson's policies and reputation. When queried about the opposition to the president in the events leading to America's entrance into World War I, McDonald responded, "I would give [Robert] La Follette a swift, hard kick where it would do most good and take his tobacco away from him."[86] When rumors linked Wilson's name to several women after the death of his wife, a physician wrote that he felt "like sending for Captain Bill and shooting."[87] Then, when House left for Europe on a diplomatic mission early in 1915, McDonald sent him a message:

. . . If I could have seen you before you left for Europe, I would have tried my utmost to persuade you not to take this trip on account of the waters being mined as well as other dangerous conditions in that Country. Don't suppose it would have done any good, though, after you decided to go, as you and I are very much alike when we make up our minds to go against anything. I am not certain of your mission there, but am sure you will make a success as you generally do when you take hold.[88]

The coming together of Wilson and McDonald in the presidential election of 1912 was beneficial to both men. It enhanced McDonald's reputation as a loyal member of the Democratic party. It made Wilson want to continue the role of Captain Bill in federal law enforcement. And, in the words of one biographer, McDonald's "presence beside Governor Wilson was a great comfort to the candidate and his family. He added a bit of color, which was not unhelpful to the Governor's personality."[89]

UNITED STATES MARSHAL (1913–1918) AND REMARRIAGE (1914)

As the life of Bill McDonald came to an end, two years—1913 and 1914—were crucial to his personal and professional well-being. In the spring of 1913, President Wilson rewarded McDonald by appointing him United States Marshal of the Northern District of Texas at a salary of $4,000 a year.[90] On April 2, the newly appointed marshal took the oath of office to "support and defend the Constitution of the United States" before District Judge Edward R. Meek.[91] Wilson's personal desires in this matter, reinforced by advice from political leaders, ruled the day. Both senators from the state of Texas supported the nomination of McDonald as a U. S. marshal.[92] On March 24 House recorded in his diary:

I went to the White House this morning at about half past nien [nine] o'clock. The door-keeper said the President was then trying

> to reach me over the telephone. When I went into his office he had the Commission of Captain [John H.] Rogers for U. S. Marshal of the Western District of Texas, on the desk before him. He did not know who Rogers was, and asked me if he was all right, and whether that was not Captain Bill's place. I explained that Bill lived in the Northern District and that I had already spoken to McReynolds about him.[93]

Working out of Dallas, Marshal McDonald carried out a variety of duties related to the federal courts. He usually had a staff of seven people (salaries budgeted for years at $7,320 per year) to assist him in these endeavors, including a chief deputy and several deputies assigned to the various divisions in his district: Abilene, Amarillo, Dallas, Fort Worth, and San Angelo.[94] Together these federal lawmen summoned members of grand and petit juries, brought prisoners into court for trial, conveyed convicted persons to penitentiaries, disbursed court funds—for which McDonald was bonded—and adjourned court in the absence of the judge.[95] To carry out these duties McDonald's office had a travel and subsistence expense budget of several thousand dollars.[96]

Marshal McDonald usually worked on cases different from those investigated by Ranger McDonald. The federal marshal dealt with violators of the liquor laws, the national banking laws, and the White Slave Traffic Act (i.e., transporting women between states for immoral purposes). McDonald also brought into court those who possessed interstate stolen property and tried to smuggle narcotics into the country. In addition, Marshal McDonald and his deputies appeared in court with counterfeiters and lawbreakers who used the mail service to defraud citizens. In McDonald's day, the marshalcy kept a national presence in the states and localities.[97]

In the midst of carrying out his duties as a federal marshal, Bill McDonald remarried. On Dec. 27, 1914, McDonald and Pearl Wilkirson (also spelled in other ways) entered into a state of matrimony in Hardeman County in a house ceremony carried out by the Reverend J. W. Bruner of the Baptist church.[98] Bill first met Pearl when he paid a bill at her father's place of business in Quanah in 1911. Their courtship progressed slowly: from horseback riding together to trips in a buggy to McDonald's ranch. They corresponded with each other as McDonald carried out his duties as a presidential bodyguard and a federal marshal. Bill was worried that Pearl, much younger than he was, would be more interested in men of her own age. But Pearl wrote that " . . . his [McDonald's] deep steel blue eyes and slightly wavy hair, just turning grey were so attractive; his rather low voice with his slow southern drawl was so pleasing that I admired him immensely." After the marriage they took a trip across northern Texas to New Orleans on their honeymoon.[99]

Pearl McDonald assisted her husband in his work as a federal marshal in several ways. For one thing, she became a stenographer (with a yearly salary of $100) in McDonald's office.[100] For another thing, McDonald bought a horseless carriage, with the "understanding" that Pearl "would do the driving." When asked if he drove the car, Bill would answer no—"my head ain't shaped right."[101]

REALITY AND MYTH IN DEATH

McDonald's marriage and marshalcy lasted only a few years. His death came suddenly and prematurely on January 15, 1918. For days he struggled in a characteristic way to overcome an attack of pneumonia before he succumbed. Having a lung damaged from a gunshot wound did not help his recovery. Funeral services were held at Wichita Falls where his sister, Mary McCauley, resided. A delegation of relatives and friends accompanied the body to Quanah for interment. Messages of sympathy came from numerous people in Texas and the nation, including President Wilson who took McDonald's death as a "personal loss."[102]

In death as in life McDonald was surrounded by a mixture of reality and myth. One newspaper circulated a story that he was known to Secret Service agents as a Ranger who had been shot in "so many encounters that he dared not go in swimming for fear that the lead bullets lodged in his body would sink him."[103] Years after his demise, Tyler Mason (pseud. of Madeline Mason Manheim McKesson), with the cooperation of Edward M. House, put together a book on the wild-and-woolly adventures of the Ranger captain.[104] At the same time Mason, a literary figure of note, published several articles in *Liberty*, a popular weekly magazine, about the "Saga of Bill McDonald, the Greatest Man-Hunter of Them All."[105] In death he still captured the public's imagination.

Throughout his life Captain Bill encouraged such fanciful thoughts. As his second wife said, "He refused to claim any rabbit that was not shot through the left eye."[106] When someone asked how old he was as his life came to an end, McDonald would reply—"103."[107] He did not reach that age. In the afterlife the Texas lawman with the salty wit might still be smiling.

By the time Bill McDonald passed away, his service as a Texas Ranger was fading into the past. For more than a decade he held the positions of state revenue agent, presidential bodyguard, and U. S. marshal. The first role gave McDonald the opportunity to not only do desk work but also go into the field and chase tax dodgers. He did this with glee and enjoyed the hoopla in the press about his actions. When called to protect a future president of the United States, Captain Bill carried out his duties with fervor and skill. Woodrow Wilson came to admire this Texan with his guns. Too much emphasis, though, should not be placed upon McDonald's final post—that of U. S. marshal. It was a political appointment. It gave him status, a pay check, and the time to be with his new wife more often. But the marshal's work did not allow him to be a man-hunter extraordinary or a hard-boiled detective as in the days when he rode with the Texas Rangers.

The outpouring of sympathy from people in Texas and the nation after McDonald's death showed that he was the best-known Texas peace officer in two capital cities: Austin and Washington, D. C. His critics—who saw Captain Bill as an armed troublemaker, a swaggering braggart, and a curmudgeon—could not believe that the masses were so gullible as to idolize this show off. With governors and presidents, the action-oriented McDonald made his mark.[108]

THE RANGERS, COMPANY B, AND CAPTAIN BILL: MAJOR FIGURES AND CASES

A Pictorial Essay

McDonald: First View:
McDonald, a sergeant, a teamster, and the twelve privates in Company B proved very effective at closing illicit corridors and curbing lawlessness [in the Panhandle]. With each new exploit and devious outsmarting of outlaws, his [McDonald's] reputation also grew.

—John Miller Morris, ed., *A Private in the Texas Rangers: A. T. Miller of Company B, Frontier Battalion.*

McDonald: Second View:
Given his two-fisted, chin-out nature, his utter fearlessness, his disregard of odds, and his amazing ability at gun slinging, if he had been thrust outside the law by the savage, stupid barbarities of the Bloody Shirt forces during Reconstruction, it seems to me that [Bill] Longley and [John Wesley] Hardin would not have surpassed Bill McDonald in reputation for grim gunplay.

—Eugene Cunningham, *Triggernometry: A Gallery of Gunfighters.*

McDonald: Third View:
But I have never found a Border man who had the slightest respect for Bill McDonald. He was, to them, a trouble maker, an advertiser, a dealer in false tales of which he was usually the hero, inclined to act—and act violently—on false information, vain and selfish.

—Harbert Davenport to Walter Prescott Webb, Dec. 26, 1934, WP.

McDonald: Fourth View:
Direct, straightforward, with a quaint flair for phrasemaking and an unusual ability to seek—and find—the limelight, Bill McDonald chose the right profession for his talents in late nineteenth-century Texas.

—Ben Procter, *Just One Riot.*

George B. Black (left) enlisted in Company B as a private in September 1891. On the right, James M. "Grude" Britton (1863–1910) was a carry over from the days of Captain McMurry and became McDonald's first sergeant of note. Capable and dependable, Sergeant Britton helped the captain run the company and took part in numerous criminal investigations (as covered in Chapters 2 and 3). Before entering the Ranger service, Britton served as a local peace officer. After leaving the Frontier Battalion in early 1894, he operated saloons in Amarillo and Forth Worth. At the start of 1910, Britton had acrimonious encounters with a police officer in Fort Worth. The city cop gunned down Britton in a senseless killing. The former Ranger sergeant was buried in Weatherford. (Courtesy of the Texas Ranger Hall of Fame and Museum, Waco, Texas.)

The most prominent sergeant of Company B. Born in Winston County, Mississippi, William John L. Sullivan (1851–1911) served in Company B under Captain McMurry. Tall, bearded and chameleon-like in nature, Sullivan became McDonald's sergeant in 1894 after Britton left the service. A sure-footed Ranger with a commanding presence, Sullivan was a nemesis to Texas badmen. He is best remembered for his investigative work in the murders committed by the San Saba Mob (Chapter 7). Sullivan left the Rangers in 1897, as McDonald lost faith in his ability to take orders and carry out his duties. In time, the former sergeant served as a Special Ranger and wrote a rambling memoir full of stories. He also worked as a stockman and ended his life as a doorkeeper for the Texas House of Representatives. Sullivan's burial site will be found in Round Rock. (Courtesy Texas State Library and Archives Commission.)

McDonald's faithful companion as sergeant of Company B. William J. "Billy" McCauley rose through the ranks and replaced Sullivan as sergeant in 1897. For a time he even served as lieutenant in charge of Company C. Born in Gregg County, Billy was the son of McDonald's sister. This nepotism, however, did not affect his performance. Although diminutive in stature, McCauley carried out his duties with a fearless desire to corral lawbreakers and gunmen (as found on pages scattered throughout the text). Like Britton and Sullivan, McCauley stayed in the Rangers for years and rode with more than one captain. He died at Marlin in 1910 from natural causes while still serving in his beloved Rangers. His body was taken to Wichita Falls for burial. (COURTESY TEXAS STATE LIBRARY AND ARCHIVES COMMISSION.)

A realistic sketch of the gunfight between Texas Ranger Captain Bill McDonald and Sheriff John Matthews of Childress County (as described in Chapter 4). Notice, however, that the illustrator made the figure of McDonald loom over the drawing. At the same time the opponents of McDonald look sinister. The captain and the sheriff had one thing in common: they were both strong-willed individuals who refused to back down. (ALBERT BIGELOW PAINE, *CAPTAIN BILL MCDONALD, TEXAS RANGER: A STORY OF FRONTIER REFORM*, 173.)

Members Company "B," Texas Rangers, camped on San Saba River, Sept. 1896. Left to right: Edgar T. Neal; Allen R. Maddox; Tom Johnson,(cook);Dudley S. Barker; John L. Sullivan.

In reality, Barker and Sullivan were members of Company B under the command of Captain Bill McDonald. Neal and Maddox, on the other hand, belonged to Company E led by Captain John Rogers. U. T. "Buck" Chamberlain (not shown), noted local lawman, served as a teamster for the detachment in San Saba County. These Rangers came together to assist local officials in the investigation of the murders committed by the San Saba Mob. In the late 1800s Ranger companies established semipermanent camps, sometimes with tents, sometimes with more substantial structures, in order to patrol and ferret out those who broke the law. The above photo, though, was really of a subcompany station with Sergeant Sullivan in charge. In their investigations these Rangers and others that followed acted tough when members of the Mob appeared; sought out and protected witnesses to criminal acts; made arrests; and took part in the judicial proceedings that followed (Chapter 7). (Courtesy Western History Collections, University of Oklahoma Libraries.)

The Reese-Townsend feud in Colorado County (Chapter 8). Sheriff Samuel H. "Sam" Reese (right) and his deputy, Bob Kollmann, on the left, after returning from hunting a fugitive. The murder of Reese in 1899 led to several years of bloody events. At times Sam's wife inflamed the passions of the populace and the Reese faction published the *Flaming Feuds of Colorado County*. In this violent encounter the Rangers, in cooperation with local authorities, tried to confiscate firearms, patrol the roads, make arrests, and keep the warring parties apart. In the end, the four Ranger captains—Brooks, Hughes, McDonald, and Rogers—and other members of their companies took part in this affair. Yet Captain Bill gained the most notoriety. (Courtesy Nesbitt Memorial Library, Columbus, Texas.)

Beasley and Conditt families at the turn of the twentieth century (Chapter 12): top row, from left, adult fourth position, Joseph Fagan Conditt; fifth position, his wife, Lora Lee Beasley Conditt; bottom row, the Conditt children, middle position, Joseph; and in a semicircle around him on the second step, from left to right, Jessie, Mildred (the oldest), and Hercial. Lora and the four children were brutally murdered. Born in 1867 in Arkansas, the father went to school in Campbell in Hunt County, Texas. In time, he farmed and worked as a skilled tradesman, like machinist and carpenter, in various places in the Lone Star State. The mother, a devout Methodist who was born in Tennessee in 1873, met her future husband in the school in Campbell. They married in December 1892 in Hunt County. During the course of the murder investigation, J. F. Conditt and his wife's father, Samuel H. Beasley (middle row, from left, adult third position seated), gave inflammatory speeches that stirred mob action against the black suspects. Conditt and Lloyd, the baby who survived the killings, stayed in Central Texas for some time. Then the father moved away and remarried. The same photograph will be found in the Houston *Daily Post*, July 15, 1906. (Courtesy Sam Beasley.)

Blacks and whites in the Conditt murder case in Jackson County (Chapter 12): from left to right: first position, Evy Davenport, future sheriff; second position, Sheriff Albert Egg; third position, Captain Bill McDonald; fourth position, Ranger Carl Ryan; fifth position, Henry Howard; sixth position, Felix Powell; seventh position, Monk Gibson; eight position, Ranger Sam McKenzie; ninth position, Will Asbeck, county convict guard. Gibson did gain weight during his incarceration. Yet his diminutive stature and the different weapons used in the murders pointed to other suspects like Howard and Powell. Gibson and Powell will be convicted and hanged. Puzzling questions, though, remain about Howard who went free. Did he receive information about the crimes from participants? Or was he a participant himself? McDonald believed all three black suspects were guilty. (Courtesy Photograph Collection, Victoria College/UH-Victoria Library, Victoria, Texas.)

A dramatic triple lynching in Henderson County (Chapter 9). The bodies of James Humphries, the father, and his two sons, John and George, dangled from the tree. Next to the main trunk was George; in the middle hung John; and James was placed at the outermost part of the stooping trunk. In another account, however, the feet of George were not pulled back and tied to his body. A third depiction had the middle person on the leaning tree with his legs extended and off the ground. No matter how the Humphries men died, Captain Bill, other Rangers, and state and local lawyers put eight Texans in prison for the crimes. Some historians believe that the Rangers arrested more people than were convicted in the courts. That did not happen in this case. (Dallas *Morning News*, May 29, 1899.)

The hanging of Felix Powell (1907). Sheriff R. S. Weisiger of Victoria County pulled the trap door. Sheriff Egg and Captain McDonald stood on the platform. The rope used in this execution was the same one that sent Monk Gibson to his death in Cuero in 1908. For years the board with the bloody handprint and a knife used in the crime were kept in a vault in the sheriff's office in Victoria. The deaths of Powell and Gibson resulted from legal means. No lynchers stormed the jail. "If you all try it," McDonald warned, "there will be crepe on many a door in Jackson County." The Ranger captain also prophesied in 1906 that "two men will yet swing for the crime." They did. (COURTESY PHOTOGRAPH COLLECTION, VICTORIA COLLEGE/UH-VICTORIA LIBRARY, VICTORIA, TEXAS.)

Bill McDonald with President Theodore Roosevelt's hunting party of cattlemen and soldiers in Oklahoma in 1905 (Chapter 11). Key figures in the photo would be as follows: from left to right: standing, second position, McDonald; third position, Jack Abernathy, noted wolf hunter; fifth position, Burk Burnett, cattle baron; sixth position, Roosevelt; sitting, fourth position, Chief Quanah Parker. The hunt took place on land owned by Burnett and W. T. Waggoner, who was not in the photo. The Democrat McDonald and the Republican Roosevelt became fast friends. (COURTESY WESTERN HISTORY COLLECTIONS, UNIVERSITY OF OKLAHOMA LIBRARIES.)

Bill McDonald in the twilight of his career as a peace officer. At this time he had a dapper look and a detective-like appearance. In McDonald's day Rangers had become capable police investigators. In this regard Captain Bill stood out for several reasons. First, he and the men in Company B took part in surveillance work, one of the ways the early Rangers defined a detective. Second, he especially took action against lynch mobs and rioters that threatened the peace of the community. Third, he developed a knack for protecting and questioning witnesses to a crime. And finally, he tried to evaluate evidence found at the scene of a crime and present his findings in a court of law. In doing these things, McDonald used more imagination than his fellow captains. But he also could rush headlong into action—even run amuck in the view of some. In the above photo, Captain Bill carried his guns in his coat pockets. (COURTESY TEXAS STATE LIBRARY AND ARCHIVES COMMISSION.)

An aging McDonald still had a flair for courting women. He entered into a second marriage after he turned sixty-two years old (Chapter 15). She outlived McDonald by several decades and remarried. Still, she is buried next to her first husband in the Quanah cemetery. (COURTESY, PHOTOGRAPH COLLECTION, VICTORIA COLLEGE/UH-VICTORIA LIBRARY, VICTORIA, TEXAS.)

After his career as a Ranger captain came to an end, Bill McDonald served with distinction as state revenue agent for several years. As a Ranger, he gained a reputation as a hard-nosed peace officer. As state revenue agent, he became an able administrative officer of the state of Texas. In the picture above, McDonald wrote reports and made telephone calls. (DENVER *POST*, OCT. 10, 1909.)

The passage of the Ranger tradition from old to new in the early 1900s: aging Bill McDonald (left) and the youthful Captain Francis A. "Frank" Hamer (right), the modern Ranger incarnate to many Texans. Born in Fairview, Texas, Hamer (1884–1955) stood six-feet-three-inches tall and weighed over 200 pounds. He served in the Rangers off and on for several decades. In between he worked as a cowboy, became a local peace officer, served in the federal prohibition service, and carried out orders from the Texas prison system. In these various endeavors, Ranger Hamer, tough, determined, even ruthless, tamed oil boom towns, went after smugglers, bootleggers, and bandits from the border to North Texas, and killed a number of lawbreakers, including Bonnie Parker and Clyde Barrow. In the early twentieth century Hamer joined three other peace officers to become the "Big Four" of the Ranger service: Manuel T. "Lone Wolf" Gonzaullas, Thomas R. "Tom" Hickman, and William L. "Will" Wright. (COURTESY HAROLD J. WEISS, JR.)

McDonald's burial site in Quanah, Texas. Engraved on his large tombstone is his motto with minor grammatical changes: "NO MAN IN THE WRONG CAN STAND UP AGAINST A FELLOW THAT'S IN THE RIGHT AND KEEP ON A COMIN'." Next to McDonald is the grave of his second wife: Pearl [Wilkirson] McDonald Williams (1881–1966). Near McDonald's grave stands a somewhat inaccurate historical marker erected by the State Historical Survey Committee of Texas in 1970:

> FEARLESS FRONTIER LAW OFFICER. KNOWN FOR CRACK MARKSMANSHIP AND LIGHTING-FAST DISARMING OF FOES. HIS LONG-TIME FRIEND GOV. JAMES HOGG MADE HIM CAPTAIN OF CO. B, FRONTIER BATTALION, IN 1891. THERE HE HANDLED THE "MURDER SOCIETY OF SAN SABA" AND WICHITA BANK ROBBERY. CONDUCTED PRES. THEODORE ROOSEVELT ON A WOLF HUNT IN 1904 [*SIC*]. WAS A U. S. MARSHAL UNDER PRES. WOODROW WILSON. FIRST WIFE WAS RHODA CARTER; SECOND WAS PEARL WILKERSON [*SIC*]. (COURTESY HAROLD J. WEISS, JR.)

Notes

The records of the adjutant general's office of the state of Texas contain five important sources for the study of Ranger history: l) a file of general correspondence—incoming mail from military and Ranger personnel and other people—in chronological order; 2) Letter Press Books of outgoing communications from the various adjutant generals; 3) service records of Ranger personnel; 4) the muster and pay rolls for the Ranger organization; and 5) a separate section of Ranger materials, including the Letter Press Books of outgoing messages of the quartermasters and the monthly returns of the companies in the field. For several decades the records of the adjutant general have been filed and refiled. Thus, any citations to folders and boxes are not always accurate.

Abbreviations and Short Titles Used in the Notes

AGR – Adjutant General Records (Archives Division, Texas State Library, Austin, Texas).

AHR – American Historical Review

AQ – American Quarterly

AW – American West

ETHJ – East Texas Historical Journal

GC-AGR – General Correspondence, Adjutant General Records (Archives Division, Texas State Library, Austin, Texas).

GR – Governor's Records (Archives Division, Texas State Library, Austin, Texas).

JAH – Journal of American History

JNH – Journal of Negro History

JSH – Journal of Sport History

JW – Journal of the West

LPB-AG-AGR – Letter Press Books, Adjutant General, Adjutant General Records (Archives Division, Texas State Library, Austin, Texas).

LPB-Q-RR-AGR – Letter Press Books, Quartermaster, Frontier Battalion or Ranger Force, Ranger Records, Adjutant General Records (Archives Division, Texas State Library, Austin, Texas).

McDonald, "RBO" – William J. McDonald, "Report of the Brownsville Outrage," General Correspondence, Adjutant General Records (Archives Division, Texas State Library, Austin, Texas).

MP – Mason (Madeline Mason Manheim McKesson) Papers (Center for American History, University of Texas at Austin, Austin, Texas).

MMWH – Montana: The Magazine of Western History

MPUS-1 – *Message from the President of the United States, Transmitting a Report from the Secretary of War, Together with Several Documents, Including a Letter of General Nettleton, and Memoranda as to Precedents for the Summary Discharge or Mustering Out of Regiments or Companies.* 59th Cong., 2nd Sess., Senate, Doc. No. 155, Pt. 1 (Washington, D.C.: Government Printing Office, 1907).

MPUS-2 – *Message from the President of the United States, Transmitting a Letter from the Secretary of War Containing Additional Testimony in the Brownsville Case.* 59th. Cong., 2nd Sess., Senate, Doc. No. 155, Pt. 2 (Washington, D.C.: Government Printing Office, 1907).

MRCB – Monthly Returns of Company B for the Years 1886-1907, Ranger Records, Adjutant General Records (Archives Division, Texas State Library, Austin, Texas).

MVHR – Mississippi Valley Historical Review

NMHR – New Mexico Historical Review

Paine, *McDonald* – Albert Bigelow Paine, *Captain Bill McDonald, Texas Ranger: A Story of Frontier Reform* (New York: J. J. Little & Ives, 1909).

PHR – Pacific Historical Review

PJF – Publius: The Journal of Federalism

PP – Albert Bigleow Paine Papers (Henry E. Huntington Library, San Marino, California).

PWW – Arthur S. Link, ed., *The Papers of Woodrow Wilson* (Princeton, N.J., 1966–1987).

RAGST – Reports of the Adjutant General of the State of Texas, 1889–1906 (Austin, 1890–1907).

RC-RR-AGR – Ranger Correspondence, Ranger Records, Adjutant General Records (Archives Division, Texas State Library, Austin, Texas).

RC-WP – Ranger Correspondence, Walter Prescott Webb Papers (Eugene C. Barker Texas History Collections, Center for American History, University of Texas at Austin, Austin, Texas).

RR-AGR – Ranger Records, Adjutant General Records (Archives Division, Texas State Library, Austin, Texas).

RRVHR – Red River Valley Historical Review

RSRA – Reports of the State Revenue Agent, 1906–1912 (Austin, 1908–1912).

SHQ – Southwestern Historical Quarterly

Seymour, *IPCH* – Charles Seymour, arr., *The Intimate Papers of Colonel House* (Boston: Houghton Mifflin, 1926).

SLJ – Southwestern Law Journal

Sullivan, *Twelve Years in the Saddle* – W. J. L. Sullivan, *Twelve Years in the Saddle for Law and Order on the Frontiers of Texas* (1909; repr., New York: Buffalo-Head Press, 1966).

TCHC – Texas Correspondence, E. M. House Collection, in Ramsdell Collection (Eugene C. Barker Texas History Collections, Center for American History, University of Texas at Austin, Austin, Texas).

TSCR-M-7747 – Case File M-7747, *W. A. Dunklin & Co. v. W. J. McDonald et al.*, Texas Supreme Court Records, Archives Division, Texas State Library, Austin, Texas.

TLR – Texas Law Review

VLR – Virginia Law Review

WHQ – Western Historical Quarterly

WP – Walter Prescott Webb Papers (Eugene C. Barker Texas History Collections, Center for American History, University of Texas at Austin, Austin, Texas).

WTHAYB – West Texas Historical Association Year Book

CHAPTER 1: BILL MCDONALD, THE HISTORICAL RECORD, AND THE POPULAR MIND

1. Will Wright, *Six Guns and Society: A Structural Study of the Western* (Berkeley: University of California Press, 1975), 4.

2. Rodger D. McGrath, *Gunfighters, Highwaymen, and Vigilantes: Violence on the Frontier* (Berkeley: University of California Press, 1984), 270.

3. Richard M. Brown, "Desperadoes and Lawmen: The Folk Hero," *Media Studies Journal* 6 (Winter 1992): 151–61, with folk quotations on p. 161; Brown, *No Duty to Retreat: Violence and Values in American History and Society* (New York: Oxford University Press, 1991); David T. Courtwright, *Violent Land: Single Men and Social Disorder from the Frontier to the Inner City* (Cambridge, MA: Harvard University Press, 1996); W. Eugene Hollon, *Frontier Violence: Another Look* (New York: Oxford University Press, 1974); Clare V. McKanna, Jr., "Alcohol, Handguns, and Homicide in the American West: A Tale of Three Counties, 1880–1920," *WHQ* 26 (Winter 1995): 455–82; McKanna, *Homicide, Race, and Justice in the American West, 1880–1920* (Tucson: University of Arizona Press, 1997); McKanna, *Race and Homicide in Nineteenth-Century California* (Reno: University of Nevada Press, 2002); Kevin J. Mullen, *Dangerous Strangers: Minority Newcomers and Criminal Violence in the Urban West, 1850–2000* (New York: Palgrave Macmillan, 2005); Richard Patterson, *Historical Atlas of the Outlaw West* (Boulder, CO: Johnson Printing, 1985); Frank R. Prassel, *The Great American Outlaw: A Legacy of Fact and Fiction* (Norman: University of Oklahoma Press, 1993); Prassel, *The Western Peace Officer: A Legacy of Law and Order* (Norman: University of Oklahoma Press, 1972). For the opposite viewpoint, see Robert R. Dykstra, "Field Notes: Overdosing on Dodge City," *WHQ* 27 (Winter 1996): 505–14. For a summary of the different views on a violent or not-so-violent American West, see McGrath, *Gunfighters, Highwaymen, and Vigilantes*, 261–71; and Harold J. Weiss, Jr., "Overdosing and Underestimating: A Look at a Violent and Not-So-Violent American West," *Quarterly* of the National Association for Outlaw and Lawman History 27 (Apr.–June 2003): 54–63.

Crime and violence in Texas in the late 1800s raise special questions. For coverage, see Richard M. Brown, *Strain of Violence: Historical Studies of American Violence and Vigilantism* (New York: Oxford University Press, 1975); Allen G. Hatley, *Bringing the Law to Texas: Crime and Violence in Nineteenth Century Texas* (La Grange, TX: Centex Press, 2002); William C. Holden, "Law and Lawlessness on the Texas Frontier, 1875–1890," *SHQ* 44 (Oct. 1940): 188–203; Rick Miller, *Sam Bass and Gang* (Austin: State House Press, 1999); Bill O'Neal, "Violence in Texas History," in *Texas: A Sesquicentennial Celebration*, ed. Donald W. Whisenhunt (Austin: Eakin Press, 1984), 353–69; C. C. Rister, "Outlaws and Vigilantes of the Southern Plains, 1865–1885," *MVHR* 19 (Mar. 1933): 537–54; and C. L. Sonnichsen, *I'll Die Before I'll Run: The Story of the Great Feuds of Texas* (New York: Harper & Bros., 1951).

4. William MacLeod Raine, *45-Caliber Law: The Way of Life of the Frontier Peace Officer* (Evanston, IL: Row, Peterson, 1941), 5.

5. Allan Silver, "The Demand for Order in Civil Society: A Review of Some Themes in the History of Urban Crime, Police, and Riot," in *The Police: Six Sociological Essays*, ed. David J. Bordua (New York: John Wiley & Sons, 1967), 6.

6. Besides the aforementioned work on policing in the west by Prassel, see Larry D. Ball, *Desert Lawmen: The High Sheriffs of New Mexico and Arizona, 1846–1912* (Albuquerque: University of New Mexico Press, 1992); Philip D. Jordan, *Frontier Law and Order: Ten Essays* (Lincoln: University of Nebraska Press, 1970); and two articles by Harold J. Weiss, Jr.: "Organized Constabularies: The Texas Rangers and the Early State Police Movement in the American Southwest," *JW* 34 (Jan. 1995): 27–33; and "Western Lawmen: Image and Reality," *JW* 24 (Jan. 1985): 23–32. For western justice in the context of American law and order, see Lawrence M. Friedman, *Crime and Punishment in American History* (New York: Basic Books, 1993); Friedman, *A History of American Law* (New York: Simon and Schuster, 1973); David R. Johnson, *American Law Enforcement: A History* (St. Louis: Forum, 1981); Mitchel Roth, *Crime and Punishment: A History of the Criminal Justice System* (Belmont, CA: Thomson Wadsworth, 2005); and Samuel Walker, *Popular Justice: A History of American Criminal Justice* (New York: Oxford University Press, 1980).

7. For key overviews of the Rangers, see Mike Cox, *The Texas Rangers: Wearing the Cinco Peso, 1821–1900*, vol. 1 (New York: Tom Doherty Assoc., 2008); Andrew R. Graybill, *Policing the Great Plains: Rangers, Mounties, and the North American Frontier, 1875–1910* (Lincoln: University of Nebraska Press, 2007); Stephen L. Hardin, *The Texas Rangers* (London: Osprey Pub., 1991); Ben Procter, "Texas Rangers," in *The New Handbook of Texas*, ed. Ron Tyler, et al. (Austin: Texas State Historical Association, 1996), VI, 393–95; Procter, "The Texas Rangers: An Overview," in *Texas Heritage*, ed. Ben Procter and Archie P. McDonald (St. Louis: Forum, 1980), 119–31; Charles M. Robinson III, *The Men Who Wear the Star: The Story of the Texas Rangers* (New York: Random House, 2000); Robert M. Utley, *Lone Star Justice: The First Century of the Texas Rangers* (New York: Oxford University Press, 2002); Utley, *Lone Star Lawmen: The Second Century of the Texas Rangers* (New York: Oxford University Press, 2007); Walter Prescott Webb, *The Texas Rangers: A Century of Frontier Defense* (Boston: Houghton Mifflin, 1935); and Harold J. Weiss, Jr., "The Texas Rangers Revisited: Old Themes and New Viewpoints," *SHQ* 97 (Apr. 1994): 621–40. National recognition of the Rangers came with their involvement in the U.S.-Mexican War from 1846 to 1848. In this struggle the bloody Texians killed Mexicans on and off the battlefields. For studies of key Ranger leaders in the war, see Thomas W. Cutrer, *Ben McCulloch and the Frontier Military Tradition* (Chapel Hill: University of North Carolina Press, 1993); James K. Greer, *Colonel Jack Hays: Texas Frontier Leader and California Builder* (New York: E. P. Dutton & Co., 1952); and W. J. Hughes, *Rebellious Ranger: Rip Ford and the Old Southwest* (Norman: University of Oklahoma Press, 1964). Alternating between policies of accommodation and aggression, Texan leaders, with the assistance of the Rangers, succeeded in pushing the Indian tribes beyond

the borders of the state by the late 1800s. In describing such events, one historical writer went so far as to say, "Rangers, then, could be brave defenders of the republic, rather harmless stay-at-home show-offs, or (more often than not) brutal murderers." Gary C. Anderson, *The Conquest of Texas: Ethnic Cleansing in the Promised Land, 1820–1875* (Norman: University of Oklahoma Press, 2005), 8–17, 226–27, with quotation on p. 9.

8. H. P. N. Gammel, comp., *The Laws of Texas: 1822–1897*...(Austin: Gammel Book Co., 1898), VIII, 89–91, with quotations on p. 91; Frederick Wilkins, *The Law Comes to Texas: The Texas Rangers, 1870–1901* (Austin: State House Press, 1999). During the 1870s two other law enforcement organizations were organized for brief periods of time: the Reconstruction State Police and a special force of citizen soldiers under Captain L. H. McNelly to suppress lawlessness along the Mexican border. See Ann P. Baenziger, "The Texas State Police During Reconstruction: A Reexamination," *SHQ* 72 (Apr. 1969): 470–91; Chuck Parsons and Marianne E. Hall Little, *Captain L. H. McNelly, Texas Ranger: The Life and Times of a Fighting Man* (Austin: State House Press, 2001); and Chuck Parsons, *John P. Armstrong: Texas Ranger and Pioneer Ranchman* (College Station: Texas A&M University Press, 2007).

9. See, for example, McDonald to Adj. Gen. W. H. Mabry, Apr. 2, 1891, GC-AGR. See also Walter Prescott Webb, *The Story of the Texas Rangers*, 2nd ed. (Austin: Encino, 1971), 112–13.

10. Carl T. Ryan to McDonald, Aug. 31, 1903, GC-AGR.

11. McDonald to Adj. Gen. John A. Hulen, Sept. 9, 1903, GC-AGR.

12. Hulen to McDonald, Sept. 11, 1903, GC-AGR.

13. James B. Gillett, *Six Years with the Texas Rangers, 1875 to 1881*, ed. M. M. Quaife (1921; repr., New Haven: Yale University Press, 1925), 19 (quotation).

14. Webb, *Story of the Texas Rangers*, 8.

15. Robinson, *Men Who Wear the Star*, xvii.

16. Brown, *No Duty to Retreat*, 3–37, 129–75; William M. Ravkind, "Comments: Justifiable Homicide in Texas," *SLJ* 13 (1959): 508–24; George W. Stumberg, "Defense of Person and Property under Texas Criminal Law," *TLR* 21 (1942–43): 17–35; Weiss, "Texas Rangers Revisited," 634 (second quotation); John P. White, *The Code of Criminal Procedure of the State of Texas, Adopted at the Regular Session of the Twenty-fourth Legislature, 1895*...(Austin: Gammel Book Co., 1900), 159 (first quotation). In a general order Adjutant General John B. Jones stressed that the Rangers in their new role as peace officers had only the powers as stated in the criminal procedure code. They had no authority to go beyond such powers in the "suppression of crime" and the "enforcement of the law." Adj. Gen. Jones, General Order No. 11, June 8, 1881, Ledger 401-984 (General Orders, 1870–1912), RC-RR-AGR.

17. Robinson, *Men Who Wear the Star*, 173.

18.Wilkins, *Law Comes to Texas*, 353–54. See also Charles Askins, *Texans, Guns and History* (New York: Winchester Press, 1970).

19. Bill O'Neal, *Encyclopedia of Western Gunfighters* (Norman: University of Oklahoma Press, 1979), 4–6, 160–63.

20. McMurry to Adj. Gen. W. H. King, Feb. 2, 1882, GC-ACR. See also Weiss, "Texas Rangers Revisited," 635.

21. For a look at the Ranger organization, see Weiss, "Texas Rangers Revisited," 630–32.

22. See the complimentary closing in McDonald to Mabry, Feb. 19, 1891, GC-AGR. See also Austin *Statesman*, July 14, 1906.

23. McDonald to Mabry, Feb. 7, 1891, GC-AGR.

24. Sullivan to Rogers, Feb. 13, 1897, typed transcript of message, RC-WP.

25. McDonald to Mabry, Mar. 6, 1897, typed transcript of message, RC-WP.

26.Sullivan to ibid., Mar. 17, 1897, typed transcript of message, RC-WP. See also Mabry to Rogers, Mar. 10, 1897, ibid. to Sullivan, Mar. 12, 1897, LPB-AG-AGR.

27. *A List of Fugitives from Justice* (Austin: Adjutant General's Office, 1878); Eric Rigler, "Frontier Justice in the Days Before NCIC," *FBI Law Enforcement Bulletin* 54 (July 1985): 16–22; William W. Sterling, *Trails and Trials of a Texan Ranger* (1959; repr., Norman: University of Oklahoma Press, 1968), 393–95, with quotations on p. 393. Major Jones started the process by sending out handwritten lists of wanted parties, giving names, counties, and types of crimes committed. Maj. Jones, General Order No. 2, July 15, 1874, General Order No. 3, Sept. 13, 1874, GC-AGR.

28. Harbert Davenport to Walter Prescott Webb, Dec. 26, 1934 (second quotation), Jan. 4, 1935 (first quotation), Box 2M260, WP. In writing his Ranger history Webb crossed out in a draft the second characterization of McDonald. Literary Productions, Box 2M281, WP. For a disparaging picture of McDonald and a critical view of the operations of the Rangers, see Julian Samora, et al., *Gunpowder Justice: A Reassessment of the Texas Rangers* (Notre Dame, IN: University of Notre Dame Press, 1979). An analysis of dichotomous relationships will be found in David H. Fischer, *Historians' Fallacies: Toward a Logic of Historical Thought* (New York: Harper & Row, 1970), 9–12, 276–77.

29. Ben Procter, *Just One Riot: Episodes of Texas Rangers in the 20th Century* (Austin: Eakin, 1991), 24.

30. Isaiah Berlin, *The Hedgehog and the Fox: An Essay on Tolstoy's View of History* (New York: Simon and Schuster, 1970), 1–4.

31. Webb, *Texas Rangers*, 460. See also Mike Cox, *Texas Ranger Tales II* (Plano, TX: Republic of Texas Press, 1999), 134–47 (Brooks and Rogers); Jack Martin, *Border Boss: Captain John R. Hughes—Texas Ranger* (1942; repr., Austin: State House Press, 1990); and two works by Paul H. Spellman: *Captain J. A. Brooks: Texas Ranger* (Denton: University of North Texas Press, 2007); and *Captain John H. Rogers: Texas Ranger* (Denton: University of North Texas Press, 2003). For the use of the expression, the "Four Great Captains," see Sterling, *Trails and Trials of a Texas Ranger*, 363. For an analysis of Webb's writ-

ings on the Rangers, see Llerena B. Friend, "W. P. Webb's Texas Rangers," *SHQ* 74 (Jan. 1971): 293–323. Webb's professional career is described in Necah Stewart Furman, *Walter Prescott Webb: His Life and Impact* (Albuquerque: University of New Mexico Press, 1976).

32. McDonald to Capt. G. A. Wheatley, Feb. 28, 1893, GC-AGR.

33. A Ranger captain characterized Sieker as an "honest gentleman" and "fearless officer," who was a "disciplinarian" and a believer in "good order." Capt. Frank Jones to Gov. James S. Hogg, Jan. 10, 1891, GR. For a brief look at Sieker's life, see Robert W. Stephens, *Texas Ranger Sketches* (Dallas: Privately printed, 1972), 144–46; and Harold J. Weiss, Jr., "Sieker, Lamartine Pemberton," in *New Handbook of Texas*, V, 1043.

34. This wording of McDonald's motto is taken from a copy of his letterhead paper. AP 1114, PP. The motto is often cited in official statements by the Texas Rangers. It even reached the White House during the administrations of Lyndon B. Johnson. A perceptive student of those years wrote, "He took the Texas Ranger myth and the Alamo too much to heart; it made him say foolish things such as 'When a Texas Ranger gets hit he just keeps on acomin' '—as if, literally, such men were bulletproof—or to beg his boys in Viet Nam to 'nail the coonskin to the wall.' " Larry L. King, "Bringing Up Lyndon," *Texas Monthly* 4 (Jan. 1976): 108.

35. Webb, *Texas Rangers*, 460.

36. Paine, *McDonald*, 79. See also Seymour, *IPCH*, I, 152.

37. Sterling, *Trails and Trials of a Texas Ranger*, 362.

38. McDonald to Hulen, Sept. 28, 1904, GC-AGR; ibid. to Mabry, June 23, 1897, typed transcript of message, RC-WP.

39. Paine, *McDonald*, 122–23. See also Seymour, *IPCH*, I, 22.

40. For example, see Mabry to McDonald, Jan. 18, 1896, LPB-AG-AGR. Event: El Paso prizefighting affair.

41. Although Adjutant General Wilburn H. King frowned upon the use of detectives in the 1880s, state officials still employed in that decade Rangers and the operatives of private detective agencies (like the Pinkerton National Detective Agency). They went underground to search for those committing illegal acts by cutting fences made of barbed wire. See Adj. Gen. King to Gov. O. M. Roberts, Apr. 11, 1882, GC-AGR; Frank Morn, *"The Eye That Never Sleeps": A History of the Pinkerton National Detective Agency* (Bloomington: Indiana University Press, 1982); and Utley, *Lone Star Justice*, 233–39. One of the better descriptions of the traits needed by an undercover agent came from the pen of Battalion Quartermaster Sieker. See Sieker to Sheriff N. H. Corder, Junction City, Mar. 24, 1891, LPB-Q-RR-AGR. The rise of the detective will be found in Friedman, *Crime and Punishment in American History*, 203–9.

42. Paine, *McDonald*, 329.

43. The changing nature of police work in this country is explored in William B. Secrest, *Dark and Tangled Threads of Crime: San Francisco's Famous Police*

Detective, Isaiah W. Lees (Sanger, CA: Word Dancer Press, 2003); and Samuel Walker, *A Critical History of Police Reform: The Emergence of Professionalism* (Lexington, MA: D. C. Heath, 1977).

44. Utley, *Lone Star Justice*, 280. Similar sentiments are expressed by other historical writers. See, for example, Evan Anders, *Boss Rule in South Texas: The Progressive Era* (Austin: University of Texas Press, 1982), 127. At one point McDonald showed compassion. He wrote the governor that a Panhandle convict should be pardoned. McDonald to Gov. Charles A. Culberson, July 8, 1896, GR.

45. McDonald to Capt. E. M. Phelps, Adjutant General's Office, Oct. 6, 1900 (quotation), GC-AGR.

46. Ibid. to Mabry, Sept. 30, 1891, GC-AGR. McDonald did not want to recruit a person who just wanted to carry a gun. Ibid., Feb. 10, 1897, GC-AGR. At one point he noted that a future replacement for a Ranger should understand the "mexican lingo." Ibid. to Hulen, July 5, 1905, GC-AGR.

47. MRCB for July 1891 (quotations), RR-AGR. Texans did complain about the actions of Company B. One critic wrote that McDonald "is so constituted that he thinks that a man who does not like the ranger force is a scoundrel and can't be too badly treated by them." E. G. Pendleton, Panhandle land agent, to Mabry, Jan. 28, 1893, GC-AGR. For the theory and practice of American intergovernmental relations, see H. Kenneth Bechtel, *State Police in the United States: A Socio-Historical Analysis* (Westport, CT: Greenwood, 1995); Edward S. Corwin, "The Passing of Dual Federalism," VLR 36 (Feb. 1950): 1–24; and Daniel J. Elazar, *The American Partnership: Intergovernmental Co-operation in the Nineteenth-Century United States* (Chicago: University of Chicago Press, 1962).

48. J. A. Rickard, *Famous Texans* (Dallas: Banks Upshaw and Co., 1955), 171.

49. Rufus R. Wilson, *A Noble Company of Adventurers* (New York: B. W. Dodge & Co., 1908), 111.

50. Webb, *Texas Rangers*, 458. For similar views about McDonald, see David G. McComb, *Texas: A Modern History* (Austin: University of Texas Press, 1989), 80–81; and Utley, *Lone Star Justice*, 257.

51. For the mention of Abilene or "one of its hard-boiled neighbors," see Thomas H. Rynning, *Gun Notches: A Saga of Frontier Lawman Thomas H. Rynning as Told to Al Cohn and Joe Chisholm* (San Diego, CA: Frontier Heritage Press, 1971), 44. The story of the prizefight has been retold in numerous works. See, for example, C. L. Douglas, *The Gentlemen in the White Hats: Dramatic Episodes in the History of the Texas Rangers* (Dallas: South-West Press, 1934), 155; Wayne Gard, *Frontier Justice* (Norman: University of Oklahoma Press, 1949), 231; and Tyler Mason and Edward M. House, *Riding for Texas: The True Adventures of Captain Bill McDonald of the Texas Rangers* (New York: Reynal & Hitchcock, 1936), 101–11. For the mob violence at Columbus, see William E. Syers, *Off the Beaten Trail* (Waco: Texian Press, 1971), 202. This intrepid tale has been attributed to other Rangers in the twentieth century, as, for example, Joe B. Brooks for an incident at Galveston in 1921 and Richard

R. "Bob" Crowder for involvement in a "riot-torn East Texas boomtown" in the late 1930s. Dallas *Times Herald*, Nov. 27, 1972 (Crowder), in M. T. Gonzaullas Scrapbooks (Texas Ranger Hall of Fame and Museum at Waco), Vol. 5, p. 403; Case Number 17 (Brooks), Texas Ranger Hall of Fame and Museum at Waco. This display might have been taken down. One work attributed the "one-Ranger-one-riot" story to Eugene Cunningham, the western novelist. Harry S. Drago, *The Legend Makers: Tales of the Old-Time Peace Officers and Desperadoes of the Frontier* (New York: Dodd, Mead & Co., 1975), 216.

52. Paine, *McDonald*, 219–20.

53. *MPUS*-1, p. 65. See also the chapter on Brownsville.

54. Leslie Scott, *Terror Stalks the Border: A Western Duo* (Waterville, ME: Five Star, 2002), 79–211, with quotations on pp. 93 (first) and 211 (second).

55. Laura L. McLemore, *Inventing Texas: Early Historians of the Lone Star State* (College Station: Texas A&M University Press, 2004), 94–100; Henry Nash Smith, *Virgin Land: The American West as Symbol and Myth* (Cambridge, MA: Harvard University Press, 1950).

56. Sidney Hook, *The Hero in History* (1943; repr. Boston: Beacon Press, 1955), 151–83.

CHAPTER 2: THE MAKING OF A TEXAS LAWMAN

1. Webb, *Texas Rangers*, 15.

2. Loren Baritz, "The Idea of the West," *AHR* 66 (Apr. 1961): 618–40.

3. Stephen Vincent Benét, *Western Star* (New York: Farrar & Rinehart, 1943), 3. For the influence of the "M-Factor," see George W. Pierson, "The M-Factor in American History," *AQ* 14 (Summer Supplement, 1962): 275–89.

4. The historical writings about the life and times of Bill McDonald can be grouped under five headings:

1) *Encyclopedic data:* as found, for example, in Walter Prescott Webb, et al., eds., *The Handbook of Texas* (Austin: Texas State Historical Association, 1952), II, 108–9.

2) *Brief references:* McDonald, probably the best-known captain of the Texas Rangers of his day, is mentioned in a minor way in numerous works on law enforcement, Texas, and the Old West, from several paragraphs like Gard, *Frontier Justice*, 231–32, to a few sentences, such as Glen Shirley, *Law West of Fort Smith: A History of Frontier Justice in the Indian Territory, 1834–1896* (New York: Henry Holt, 1957), 119.

3) *Episodes of dramatic lore:* the storied exploits of McDonald as a lawman have been retold with a mixture of myth and reality in a number of books about the Texas Rangers and the Lone Star State, as shown, for example, in a wild and woolly chapter in each of the following: Allyn Allen [pseud. of Irmengarde Eberle], *The Real Book About the Texas Rangers* (Garden City, NY: Doubleday, 1952), 145–69; Douglas, *Gentlemen in the White Hats*, 155–64; and Lee

McGiffin, *Ten Tall Texans* (New York: Lothrop, Lee and Shepard, 1956), 182–205.

4) *Interpretive sketches:* brief attempts at a mixture of narration and interpretation about the careers of McDonald will be found in Virgil E. Baugh, *A Pair of Texas Rangers: Bill McDonald and John Hughes* (Washington, D.C.: Potomac Corral, The Westerners, 1970), 1–12; Eugene Cunningham, *Triggernometry: A Gallery of Gunfighters* (1941; repr., Caldwell, ID: Caxton Printers,, 1971), 315–31; Robinson, *Men Who Wear the Star*, 247–48, 258, 261, 265–67; Sterling, *Trails and Trials of a Texas Ranger*, 334–62; Utley, *Lone Star Justice*, 256–63, 268–69, 272–73, 279–83, 285; Webb, *Texas Rangers*, 444–47, 457–61, 466–69; and Wilkins, *Law Comes to Texas*, 296–98, 318–30, 334–36, 338–39, 342–43, 347, 354.

5) *Full-length biographical studies:* an episodic account full of tall tales about the deeds of McDonald as a peace officer is Tyler Mason [pseud. of Madeline Mason Manheim McKesson] and Edward M. House, *Riding for Texas*. More informative yet equally romantic at times is the official biography of McDonald written by Albert Bigelow Paine entitled *Captain Bill McDonald, Texas Ranger: A Story of Frontier Reform*. Among Paine's papers is a summary of this book in printed form for sales promotion which bears the title "A Brief Synopsis of Some of the Leading Features of Captain McDonald's Memoirs." AP 1114, PP.

5. The flowery language of hero worshipers in the historiography of the American westward movement is well illustrated by the following lines by Paine about McDonald: "Two other features bespeak this man's character and career: his ears and his nose—the former, alert and extended—the ears of the wild creature, the hunter; the latter of that stately Roman architecture which goes with conquest, because it signifies courage, resolution and the peerless gift of command." Paine, *McDonald*, 13.

6. Ibid., 16–17; information about McDonald and his parents will be found in the following Bureau of Census Reports: 7th Census, 1850, Mississippi, Kemper County; 9th Census, 1870, Texas, Rusk County; 10th Census, 1880, Texas, Wood County; 12th Census, 1900, Texas, Hardeman County; 13th Census, 1910, Texas, Travis County.

7. Bureau of Census Reports: 7th Census, 1850, Mississippi, Slave Population, Kemper County; 8th Census, 1860, Mississippi, Slave Population, Kemper County; Paine, *McDonald*, 16 (second quotation); TSCR-M-7747, pp. 66 (first quotation), 81–85.

8. Dickson D. Bruce, Jr., *Violence and Culture in the Antebellum South* (Austin: University of Texas Press, 1979), 196–211; Paine, *McDonald*, 17–19.

9. Paine, *McDonald*, 17–19, 21.

10For an introduction to the history of the Old South, see two works by Clement Eaton: *The Growth of Southern Civilization, 1790–1860* (New York:Harper & Brothers, 1961); and *The Mind of the Old South* (Baton Rouge: Louisiana State University Press, 1964).

11. Janet B. Hewett, et al., eds., *Supplement to the Official Records of the Union and Confederate Armies* (Wilmington, NC: Broadfoot Publishing, 1994–1998), Vol. 34, pp. 163, 166; Paine, *McDonald*, 19–20; Dunbar Rowland, *History of Mississippi: The Heart of the South* (Chicago-Jackson: S. J. Clarke Publishing, 1925), I, 861–65, II, 86–87. Enoch McDonald was killed on October 4, not October 3, as stated by Paine. For the authoritative account of the Battle of Corinth, see Peter Cozzens, *The Darkest Days of the War: The Battles of Iuka and Corinth* (Chapel Hill: University of North Carolina Press, 1997).

12Bureau of Census Reports: 9th Census, 1870, Texas, Rusk County (Durham and McDonald); Tax Rolls of Texas Counties: Rusk, 1865–1871 (Durham); TSCR-M-7747, pp. 26–27, 34, 36, 61–65, 71 (quotations), 75, 77, 82–84.

13. Paine, *McDonald*, 21–22; TSCR-M-7747, pp. 27, 36, 63–66, 71–72, 82–85.

14Bureau of Census Reports: 9th Census, 1870, Texas, Rusk County (McDonald); Paine, *McDonald*, 22–25; TSCR-M-7747, p. 75.

15. Paul A. Hutton, "Phil Sheridan's Frontier," *MMWH* 38 (Winter 1988): 22.

16. For histories of Texas, see Robert A. Calvert and Arnoldo De León, *The History of Texas* (Arlington Heights, IL: Harlan Davidson, 1990); Randolph B. Campbell, *Gone to Texas: A History of the Lone Star* State (New York: Oxford University Press, 2003); James L. Haley, *Passionate Nation: The Epic Story of Texas* (New York: Free Press, 2006); McComb, *Texas: A Modern History*; and Archie P. McDonald, comp., *The Texas Experience* (College Station: Texas A&M University Press, 1986).

17. For the "mystique" of Texas, see Joe B. Frantz, "Lone Star Mystique," *AW* 5 (May 1968): 6–9. See also McComb, *Texas*, 147–84; and McDonald, *Texas Experience*, 177–79.

18. Campbell, *Gone to Texas*, 100–127, 187–238, 290–323; T. R. Fehrenbach, *Lone Star: A History of Texas and the Texans* (1968; repr., New York: American Legacy Press, 1983), 136–51, 279–324; Haley, *Passionate Nation*, 67–94, 271–81, 393–98.

19. H. C. Brearley, "The Pattern of Violence," in *Culture in the South*, ed. W. T. Couch (1934; repr., Westport, CT: Negro University Press, 1970), 678 (first quotation), 687 (second quotation).

20. Barry A. Crouch, *The Dance of Freedom: Texas African Americans During Reconstruction*, ed. Larry Madaras (Austin: University of Texas Press, 2007), 95–117; Carl H. Moneyhon, *Texas After the Civil War: The Struggle of Reconstruction* (College Station: Texas A&M University Press, 2004), 35–36, 59, 64–66, 77–82, 84, 115, 174–76, 182–83. For a comprehensive history of Reconstruction in America, see Eric Foner, *Reconstruction: America's Unfinished Revolution, 1863–1877* (New York: Harper & Row, 1988).

21. Barry A. Crouch Collection, Folder (Rusk Co./Henderson, 1869: Multiple Lynching of Freedmen), Victoria College, Victoria, Texas; Galveston *Daily News*, Apr. 14, 1869, Apr. 21, 1869, Apr. 23, 1869, May 7, 1869, Dec. 30, 1869; Letters Sent by the Department of Texas, the District of Texas, and the 5th Military District, Roll 3, Vol. 8, p. 83, Vol. 9, p. 201; Registers of Letters

Received and Letters Received of the Department of Texas, the District of Texas, and the 5th Military District, Roll 4, Vol. 10, pp. 15, 25, 188, Federal Archives and Records Center, Fort Worth, Texas.

22. Paine, *McDonald*, 26–30, with quotation on p. 29. Paine misspelled Green's name. For the impact of the Reconstruction years on the lives of Hardin and Longley, see Leon Metz, *John Wesley Hardin: Dark Angel of Texas* (El Paso: Mangan Books, 1996); and Rick Miller, *Bloody Bill Longley* (Wolfe City, TX: Henington Publishing, 1996).

23. William C. Holden, "Frontier Problems and Movements in West Texas, 1846–1900" (Ph.D. diss., University of Texas at Austin, 1928), 123, 349–54. See also Homer L. Kerr, "Migration into Texas, 1860–1880," *SHQ* 70 (Oct. 1966): 184–216.

24. Ty Cashion, *A Texas Frontier: The Clear Fork Country and Fort Griffin, 1849–1887* (Norman: University of Oklahoma Press, 1996); Cashion, "What's the Matter with Texas? The Great Enigma of the Lone Star State in the American West," *MMWH* 55 (Winter 2005): 2–15; Haley, *Passionate Nation*, 405–10; Frank E. Vandiver, *The Southwest: South or West?* (College Station: Texas A&M University Press, 1975), 37 (quotation). For the southern imprint on Texas, see the writings of Walter L. Buenger.

25. Ray Billington, *America's Frontier Heritage* (New York: Holt, Rinehart and Winston, 1966); Patricia N. Limerick, *The Legacy of Conquest: The Unbroken Past of the American West* (New York: W. W. Norton, 1987); Limerick and Clyde A. Milner II and Charles E. Rankin, eds., *Trails: Toward a New Western History* (Lawrence: University Press of Kansas, 1991), 85–87; Robert C. Ritchie and Paul A. Hutton, eds., *Frontier and Region: Essays in Honor of Martin Ridge* (San Marino, CA: Huntington Library Press, 1997); Richard White, *"It's Your Misfortune and None of My Own": A New History of the American West* (Norman: University of Oklahoma Press, 1991).

26. Paine, *McDonald*, 30–31; TSCR-M-7747, pp. 37–38, 62–64, 67, 76. For an advertisement about Soule's Commercial College, see New Orleans *Daily Picayune*, Sept. 15, 1872. McDonald's name appeared in a list of people who had not picked up their mail at the post office in New Orleans in the spring of 1872. Ibid., May 26, 1872.

27. Ora P. Bruner, "Mineola, Texas," in *New Handbook of Texas*, IV, 759; David Gilbreath, "Wood County," in ibid., VI, 1061–62. Paine incorrectly stated that McDonald became a grocer in Mineola in 1875. Paine, *McDonald*, 31. Newspaper advertisements for McDonald's grocery store appeared as early as September 1873. See, for example, Dallas *Weekly Herald*, Sept. 13, 1873. For mention of the year 1873 by McDonald, see TSCR-M-7747, p. 66.

28. Paine, *McDonald*, 31; TSCR-M-7747, pp. 34–35, 57, 66–67, 74–75, 85. For mention of McDonald as a businessman, see Lucille Jones, *History of Mineola, Texas* (Quanah, TX: Nortex Offset Publications, 1973), 6–7, 99; and [Mineola Centennial Corp.], comp., *Mineola: The First 100 Years* (Mineola, TX: Mineola Centennial Corp., 1973), 16.

29. John H. Newsom, MS Diary, privately owned, pp. 39–41. For a listing of Newsom among old pioneers of Mineola and Wood County, see Jones, *History of Mineola*, 101. This author added an "e" at the end of his name.

30. TSCR-M-7747, pp. 57–58, 67 (first quotation), 68 (second quotation), 69, 72–75, 85–87. The largest amount—$6,500—was owed J. T. Hardie & Company. Ibid.

31. Ibid., pp. 7, 11, 23–25, 25–41 (testimony of Eunice McDonald), 41–57 (testimony of McCauley), 58–60, 66–81 (testimony of Bill McDonald).

32. In the county court of Wood County in 1880, a case between Eunice McDonald (plaintiff) and T. G. Erwin and E. D. Burress (defendants) was settled out of court. Minutes, County Court, Vol. A, p. 128, Wood County, Texas. In another case in the same court in 1881, Howe Bitters Company won a judgment against McDonald and Carter for $335 plus interest and costs. The defendants appealed. Ibid., Vol. A, pp. 281–82. In a third case in the same court, another creditor, Louis Espencheid, sued McDonald and Carter in 1882. The court ruled in favor of the defendants because of the statute of limitations in filing cases. Ibid., Vol. A, p. 406. A fourth case arose in 1882 when the judge of the district court, county of Wood, ruled that McDonald and his mother owed J. W. Saxon $342.28. The monies had been used to buy a tract of land. The property would now be sold by the sheriff. Civil Minutes, District Court, Wood County, Texas, Vol. 1, pp. 292, 317, 337, 471, Vol. 2, pp. 43–44 (ruling).

33. Minutes, No. 201-104, p. 762, Texas Supreme Court Records, Archives Division, Texas State Library, Austin, Texas; TSCR-M-7747, pp. 1–22, 88–95.

34. TSCR-M-7747, pp. 27–28, 31 (quotation), 33, 35.

35. Bureau of Census Reports: 8th Census, 1860, Texas, Rusk County; 8th Census, 1860, Texas, Slave Populations, Rusk County.

36. Ibid., 9th Census, 1870, Texas, Rusk County; American *Statesman*, Sept. 22, 1909; Tax Rolls of Texan Counties: Rusk, 1865–1871. The Durham brothers, too, were in and out of the courts in East Texas for various reasons.

37. Tax Rolls of Texan Counties: Wood, 1874–1883.

38. TSCR-M-7747, pp. 78–81.

39. Mineola *Monitor*, Mar. 26, 1936. See also Jones, *History of Mineola*, 23, 100.

40. Austin *Statesman*, Mar, 10, 1906 (McDonald's statements on Hogg's death); Robert C. Cotner, *James Stephen Hogg: A Biography* (Austin: University of Texas Press, 1959), 83; Paine, *McDonald*, 31–32, 41–42. For mention of McDonald's interest in women and courtship of other ladies, see Paine, *McDonald*, 24–25, 31.

41. Ibid., 31 (quotation); TSCR-M-7747, pp. 68, 87.

42. Bureau of Census Reports: 8th Census, 1860, Texas, Wood County; 9th Census, 1870, Texas, Wood County; 10th Census, 1880, Texas, Wood County. In 1870 a black female with two small children kept house for the Carters. Ibid.

43. Paine, *McDonald*, 33–35, with first quotation on p. 33 and second quotation on p. 34. George Gordon appeared as a defendant in county court in 1883

and 1884. Minutes, County Court, Vol. B, pp. 70–71, 156, Wood County, Texas.

44. Jones, *History of Mineola*, 19, 100, 106–7; [Mineola Centennial Corp.], Mineola, 14, 16; Adele W. Vickery, *A Transcript of Centennial Edition, 1850–1950, Wood County Democrat* (Mineola: Adele W. Vickery, 1974), 24–25.

45. Paine, *McDonald*, 35–38.

46. Commissioner's Court Minutes, Wood County, Quitman, Texas, Vol. A, pp. 146, 158, 200, 214, 224–25, 240, 246–47, 291, 295–96, 306–07, 349. For a listing of the sheriffs of Wood County, see Vickery, *Transcript of Centennial Edition, Wood County Democrat*, 103.

47. Austin *Statesman* Mar. 10, 1906; Paine, *McDonald*, 38–42. An historical marker about McDonald's life has been erected in the town of Mineola.

48. Holden, "Frontier Problems and Movements in West Texas," 354; Paine, *McDonald*, 43–54, with quotation on p. 53; Tax Rolls of Texan Counties: Wood, 1880–84; Wichita, 1883–86; Webb, *Handbook of Texas*, II, 901–4. His official biographer said that McDonald moved to the Wichita area in 1883. Yet the rolls in Wood County showed that he still had taxable possessions in that year, but none in 1884.

49. Holden, "Frontier Problems and Movements in West Texas," 351; Paine, *McDonald* 55; Webb, *Handbook of Texas*, I, 767.

50. William R. Hunt, "Quanah, Texas," in *New Handbook of Texas*, V, 378; Christopher Long, "Hardeman County," in ibid., III, 451–52.

51. Tax Rolls of Texan Counties: Hardeman, 1885–1910.

52. Luke Gournay, *Texas Boundaries: Evolution of the State's Counties* (College Station: Texas A&M University Press, 1995); Walter Prescott Webb, *The Great Plains* (Boston: Ginn and Co., 1931), 487 (quotation).

53. Holden, "Frontier Problems and Movements in West Texas," 123, 134–36; Frederick W. Rathjen, *The Texas Panhandle Frontier* (Austin: University of Texas Press, 1973), 3–26, 228–49. For the impact of the railroads in the 1800s on the growth of Texas, see St. Clair Griffin Reed, *A History of the Texas Railroads . . .* (Houston: St. Clair Publishing, 1941).

54. John Miller Morris, *A Private in the Texas Rangers: A. T. Miller of Company B, Frontier Battalion* (College Station: Texas A&M University Press, 2001), 281.

55. William B. Ruggles, *Trails of Texas* (San Antonio: Naylor, 1972), 17.

56. Commissioner's Court Minutes, Hardeman County, Quanah, Texas, Vol. 1, pp. 160–61, 173–74, 215, 255. In 1890 the county seat was moved from Margaret to Quanah.

57. Morris, *A Private in the Texas Rangers*, 28 (first quotation), 60 (second quotation). Paine spelled the sheriff's name incorrectly—as "Alley." Paine, *McDonald*, 56.

58. Morris, *A Private in the Texas Rangers*, 16, 41, 47, 52–54, 66–68, 147 (quotation).

59. Ibid., 47.

60. Ibid., 16, 47–49, 58, 60–61, 116, 121–23, 125–26, 165–66; Paine, *McDonald*, 59–64.

61. Morris, *A Private in the Texas Rangers*, 4 ("boys"), 38 ("Soft Voice"), 51 ("McDonnell").

62. Ibid., 132 (diary story and editor's quotation); MRCB for May 1887, RR-AGR.

63. Samuel A. McMurry to Adj. Gen. W. H. King, Oct. 8, 1888, GC-AGR; Morris, *A Private in the Texas Rangers*, 50, 74–75, 105, 112–15, 130, 147.

64. MRCB for Dec. 1886, RR-AGR.

65. Morris, *A Private in the Texas Rangers*, 58.

66. Paine, *McDonald*, 66.

67. Frank McGhee to Gov. L. S, Ross, July 1, 1887 (with newspaper clipping), McMurry to King, July 2, 1887, Dec. 3, 1887, Jan. 31, 1888, GC-AGR; Morris, *A Private in the Texas Rangers*, 61, 70–72, 75, 78, 112–13, 125–27, 134–35, 146, 181–82, 199–201, 208–09, 239–40, 243–44; Paine, *McDonald*, 55–56, 58–59, 64–68.

68. Paine, *McDonald*, 68.

69. Morris, *A Private in the Texas Rangers*, 208.

70. Ibid., 47.

71. Ollie Perry, Service Records, AGR. McDonald informed a Panhandle resident that a Ranger captain had no "authority" to appoint Special Rangers: only the adjutant general could do that. McDonald to G. H. Eubank, Sept. 27, 1893, GC-AGR. The use of Special Rangers resulted from the actions of Adjutant General Wilburn H. King in the 1880s. He reasoned that the law creating the Ranger force in 1874 provided for 450 men. If the total number of paid Rangers in the regular companies dropped below this figure in financial emergencies, then unpaid, sworn-in Special Rangers could be appointed to take their place—as long as the total number of all men assigned to the companies did not exceed 450. King to George A. Helm, Apr. 11, 1889, LPB-AG-AGR.

72. McDonald to Adj. Gen. Thomas Scurry, May 27, 1901, GC-AGR. McDonald is listed in the muster and pay rolls of the Frontier Battalion as a Special Ranger from March 18, 1889, to Nov. 30, 1890. Paine stated that McDonald became a Special Ranger after an unsuccessful hunt with a posse for the Brooken gang. Paine, *McDonald*, 66. Another author has McDonald becoming a Special Ranger in the summer of 1887. Morris, *A Private in the Texas Rangers*, 60, 132. The records do not support either position.

73. Cotner, *Hogg*, 177, fn. 22; Hogg to McDonald, July 22, 1889, Letter Press Book, Attorney General Records, Archives Division, Texas State Library, Austin, Texas; MRCB for Dec. 1889, RR-AGR. For other correspondence with the attorney general, see John Craddock, office assistant, to McDonald, Dec. 12, 1889, Letter Press Book, Attorney General Records. In the summer

of 1890, McDonald requested requisition papers for a horse thief located in Oklahoma. The adjutant general sent him the proper forms to be filled out. King to McDonald, Aug. 4, 1890, LPB-AG-AGR; McDonald to King, July 21, 1890, GC-AGR.

74. McDonald to King, Nov. 9, 1889, GC-AGR.

75. Paine, *McDonald*, 87. This author stated that McDonald was also appointed a federal deputy marshal for the Southern District of Kansas. Ibid., 67.

76. Ibid., 69–125. Paine's account of McDonald confuses—not at all uncommonly—the Cherokee Outlet with the Cherokee Strip, a narrow piece of land above the Outlet in southern Kansas. Ibid., 99, 104–5, 115. See the definitions of these areas in Ramon F. Adams, *Western Words: A Dictionary of the American West* (1944; rev. ed., Norman: University of Oklahoma Press, 1968), 62.

77. Sheriff I. H. Lefors to Hogg, July 21, 1889, GC-AGR.

78. McMurry to King, Aug. 9, 1889, GC-AGR.

79. Paine, *McDonald*, 141.

80. Ibid., 139–42.

81. McDonald to Hogg, Dec. 12, 1890, GR.

82. Britton to Adj. Gen. William H. Mabry, Jan. 19, 1891, McMurry to Mabry, Jan. 18, 1891, petition to the adjutant general, Jan. 20, 1891, GC-AGR; Special Orders, 1870–1897, Ledger 401-1012, p. 256, RR-AGR. See also muster and pay rolls from December 1, 1890 to May 31, 1891, AGR. The acknowledgment of Britton's application for the captaincy by the adjutant general came in a letter to the Ranger dated Jan. 24, 1891 in LPB-AG-AGR. Mabry noted that McDonald would be the new captain. For short biographical accounts of McMurry, Britton, and the other members of Company B, see Morris, *A Private in the Texas Rangers*, 251–90; and Robert W. Stephens, *Texas Ranger Sketches* (Dallas: Privately printed, 1972).

83. G. Brown to Hogg, Jan. 12, 1891, GR. For views about the personal life of the new captain—hunting, gambling, and singing at a church service, see Morris, *A Private in the Texas Rangers*, 106, 111–12, 149, 175, 254.

CHAPTER 3: CAPTAIN BILL AND COMPANY B IN THE PANHANDLE

1. McDonald to Mabry, Feb. 19, 1891 (first quotation), Apr. 11, 1891 (second quotation), GC-AGR.

2. Summation of undated newspaper story, Card File Index 144, newspaper collection of Wichita Falls *Times*, WPA Historical Survey Project, Barker Texas History Collections, Center for American History, University of Texas at Austin. A similar account appeared in another newspaper. In this report McDonald apprehended the pickpocket but he could not find his valuables. The thief had passed them to a confederate. Austin *Statesman*, Oct. 15, 1910, Oct. 18, 1910.

3. Paine, *McDonald*, 95; Quanah *Tribune-Chief*, Oct. 14, 1909 (quotation).

4. Paine, *McDonald*, 149–51.

5. Ibid., 149–50; Bill Neal, *The Last Frontier: The Story of Hardeman County* (Quanah, TX: Quanah *Tribune-Chief* and Hardeman County Historical Society, 1966), 81. McDonald's cattle carried the brand 2/Mc (left jaw under tail). Neal, *Last Frontier*, 277.

6. W. D. Powell (as told to Rupert Richardson), "A Baptist Preacher on the Texas Frontier," *WTHAYB* 9 (Oct. 1933): 51–52.

7. Paine, *McDonald*, 192–93.

8. J. Evetts Haley and William C. Holden, eds., *The Flamboyant Judge: James D. Hamlin* (Canyon, TX: Palo Duro Press, 1972), 79.

9. McDonald to Mabry, Nov. 29, 1892, GC-AGR; Quanah *Chief*, Jan. 5, 1893.

10. R. H. Bruce to Tyler Mason, Mar. 14, 1935, MP; Haley and Holden, *Flamboyant Judge*, 78; Paine, *McDonald*, 14, 24.

11. McDonald to Hogg, Dec. 12, 1890, GR.

12. Cotner, *Hogg*, 211

13. Ibid., 300; Alwyn Barr, *Reconstruction to Reform: Texas Politics, 1876–1906* (Austin: University of Texas Press, 1971), 134; Paine, *McDonald*, 151–53.

14. McDonald to Mabry, Apr. 12, 1892, GC-AGR. See similar sentiments in ibid., June 18, 1892, Nov. 5, 1892, GC-AGR.

15. Paine, *McDonald*, 323; *State Topics*, V (Feb. 28, 1914), 10.

16. Barr, *Reconstruction to Reform*, 111–42; Cotner, *Hogg, passim*; Rupert N. Richardson, *Texas: The Lone Star State* (New York: Prentice-Hall, 1943), 346–63.

17. Cotner, *Hogg*, 353–91.

18. Ibid., 226. Still useful for a study of Texas at the turn of the twentieth century would be James A. Tinsley, "The Progressive Movement in Texas" (Ph.D. diss., University of Wisconsin, 1953).

19. McDonald to Mabry, Jan. 25, 1895, Jan. 31, 1895, GC-AGR.

20. Ibid. to Lamartine P. Sieker, Ranger quartermaster, Dec. 14, 1901, GC-AGR.

21. The dispute over Greer County between Texas and the central government ended in 1896 when the United States Supreme Court declared that Greer County fell under the jurisdiction of the United States. Although administered by Texas for decades, this area now became a territory of the United States and after the turn of the twentieth century was combined with the state of Oklahoma.

22. *RAGST* for 1890–1891, pp. 8–11, Appendix, 99.

23. Mabry to McDonald, May 5, 1891, LPB-AG-AGR; Muster and Pay Rolls from Dec. 1890 through Nov. 1891, AGR.

24. Adj. Gen. Mabry, General Order No. 2 (revocation), Feb. 21, 1891, Ledger 401-984, RR-AGR; ibid., Special Order No. 6 (new regulations), Mar. 6, 1891, Ledger 401-1012, RR-AGR.

25. McDonald to Mabry, Feb. 1, 1891 (first gun quote), Feb. 7, 1891 (other quotations); McDonald to Sieker, Feb. 3, 1891, GC-AGR. See also MRCB for Jan. 1891, RR-AGR.

26. Paine, *McDonald*, 143–44 (quotation on p. 144).

27. Sieker to McDonald, Feb. 11, 1891, Feb. 19, 1891, Feb. 23, 1891, Feb. 24, 1891, Mar. 16, 1891, Mar. 17, 1891, Mar. 18, 1891, LPB-Q-RR-AGR.

28. Ibid., Feb. 12, 1891, LPB-Q-RR-AGR; sworn statement by McDonald and others, Feb. 21, 1891, RC-RR-AGR.

29. Sieker to McDonald, Feb. 21, 1891, Feb. 23, 1891, Mar. 18, 1891, LPB-Q-RR-AGR.

30. McDonald to Mabry, Jan. 30, 1891, GC-AGR.

31. Hogg to McDonald, Jan. 30, 1891, GC-AGR.

32. McDonald to Mabry, Jan. 30, 1891 (quotation), GC-AGR; MRCB for Feb. 1891, RR-AGR. See also Paine, *McDonald*, 145–48. For the impact of the Indian scare on Potter County, see Della T. Key, *In the Cattle Country: History of Potter County, 1887–1966*, 2nd ed. (Quanah-Wichita Falls, TX: Nortex Offset Publications, 1972), 97.

33. Mabry to McDonald, Feb. 10, 1891, LPB-AG-AGR. The adjutant general informed the governor that the Indian scare was a "false alarm" and that the "excitement" about the affair had "subsided." Mabry to Hogg, Jan. 31, 1891, GR. Another Indian scare took place in several Texan counties along the line with Oklahoma at the end of 1890. Both Rangers of Company B and militiamen investigated the doings. Judge G. S. Huling of Greer County to Gov. Lawrence S. Ross, Dec. 15, 1890, Judge W. P. Jones of Childress County to Capt. W. T. Levy, Panhandle Cavalry, Dec. 14, 1890, Levy to Ross, Dec. 16, 1890, Ranger Sgt. Tom Platt to Adj. Gen. King, Dec. 20, 1890, Dec. 23, 1890, GC-AGR.

34. Key, *In the Cattle Country*, 63.

35 McDonald to Mabry, Feb. 14, 1891, GC-AGR; MRCB for Feb. 1891, RR-AGR.

36. MRCB for June and Aug. 1891, RR-AGR.

37. See, for example, McDonald to Mabry, Feb. 19, 1891, Feb. 21, 1891, Mar. 19, 1891, May 23, 1891, Aug. 14, 1891, GC-AGR.

38. Ibid., Feb. 19, 1891, Apr. 11, 1891, GC-AGR.

39. MRCB for Jan. through Dec. 1891, RR-AGR.

40. McDonald to Mabry, Feb. 14, 1891, Feb. 21, 1891, Feb. 23, 1891, Mar. 19, 1891, GC-AGR; MRCB for Feb. 1891 (second quotation), Mar. 1891, July 1891, Nov. 1891 (first quotation), RR-AGR.

41. Aten to Mabry, May 31, 1891, GC-AGR.

42. Hogg to J. W. Aikin, May 16, 1891, ibid. to McDonald, June 24, 1891 (quotation), June 29, 1891, R. B. Levy, private secretary, to McDonald, July 2, 1891, McDonald to Hogg, two telegrams dated June 24, 1891, telegram (last

quotation) and letter, June 26, 1891, letter and report, June 30, 1891, with attached telegrams: Knight to McDonald (quotation) and Gov. John L. Routt to Sheriff J. F. Bradley (quotation), June 24, 1891, R. C. McPhaill to Hogg, May 1891, GR; MRCB for June 1891, RR-AGR.

43. Hogg to Routt, June 25, 1891, GR. A copy, dated Mar. 17, 1891, of the indictment in Aug. 1889 of Marlow for murder by a grand jury will be found in the governor's records. For a biography of the Marlow brothers, see Glenn Shirley, *The Fighting Marlows: Men Who Wouldn't Be Lynched* (Fort Worth: Texas Christian University Press, 1994).

44. Mabry to McDonald, Sept. 26, 1891, LPB-AG-AGR; McDonald to Mabry, Aug. 14, 1891, Sept. 22, 1891, Sept. 30, 1891, Dec. 3, 1891, Dec. 8, 1891 (quotation), GC-AGR; MRCB from Aug. through Dec. 1891, RR-AGR.

45. MRCB from Oct. through Dec. 1891, RR-AGR; "Report of Affairs in Hartley County," Dec. 2, 1891, GR.

46. Mabry to McDonald, Dec. 7, 1891 (quotation), Dec. 15, 1891, LPB-AG-AGR.

47. McDonald to Mabry, Dec. 10, 1891 (quotation), Dec. 18, 1891, Dec. 19, 1891, GC-AGR; MRCB for Dec. 1891, RR-AGR. The battalion quartermaster wrote, "Hope you will like your new station." Sieker to McDonald, Dec. 24, 1891, LPB-Q-RR-AGR. As early as February 1891, McDonald sought advice from Sieker about moving his command and dispatching Rangers to different places. Ibid., Feb. 10, 1891, LPB-Q-RR-AGR.

48. H. Allen Anderson, "Amarillo, Texas," in *New Handbook of Texas*, I, 140–42; ibid., and John Leffler, "Potter County," in ibid., V, 299–301.

49. McDonald to Mabry, Apr. 2, 1891, Sept. 30, 1891, GC-AGR; MRCB for Apr. 1891, July 1891, Sept. 1891, RR-AGR.

50. MRCB for Aug. 1891, RR-AGR.

51. Ibid., for Dec. 1891, RR-AGR; McDonald to Mabry, Dec. 11, 1891, Dec. 18, 1891, GC-AGR.

52. *RAGST* for 1892, pp. 9–10, 13, Appendix, 96.

53. MRCB from Jan. through Dec. 1892, RR-AGR.

54. County Attorney of Greer County to McDonald, Apr. 6, 1892, Louis Dumas. trustee of the Panhandle Townsite Company, to ibid., June 12, 1892, S. H. Tittle, sheriff of Greer County, to ibid., Apr. 7, 1892, GC-AGR.

55. E. R. Fletcher, justice of the peace in Greer County, to ibid., Apr. 7, 1892, GC-AGR.

56. MRCB from Jan. through Dec. 1892, RR-AGR; Sullivan to Mabry, Aug. 23, 1892 (quotations), GC-AGR. The idea of going south in Texas affected other members of Company B. A. M. Lewis wrote the adjutant general that he was "dissatisfied" with the "country" in northern Texas and that he and another Ranger desired a transfer to a ranging force stationed in the southern part of the state. Lewis to Mabry, Jan. 19, 1892, GC-AGR.

57. MRCB for Feb. 1892, RR-AGR.

58. Ibid. for Mar. 1892, RR-AGR.

59. G. A. Brown, judge of the 46th Judicial District, to McDonald, May 14, 1892 (quotation), McDonald to Mabry, May 18, 1892, GC-AGR.

60. Fletcher to McDonald, Apr. 7, 1892, McDonald to Mabry, Apr. 12, 1892, Apr. 16, 1892, Apr. 27, 1892 (first quotation), May 18, 1892 (second quotation), Tittle to McDonald, Apr. 7, 1892, GC-AGR; MRCB for Apr. 1892, RR-AGR.

61. McDonald to Mabry, June 18, 1892, June 24, 1892 (last two quotations), July 11, 1892, Sept. 10, 1892, Sept. 15, 1892, GC-AGR; MRCB for Jan. 1892, June 1892 (first two quotations), July 1892, Oct. 1892 (quotation), RR-AGR.

62. Dumas to McDonald, June 12, 1892, GC-AGR; MRCB for July 1892 (quotation), RR-AGR. See also James A. Schellenberg, "County Seat Wars: A Preliminary Analysis," *Journal of Conflict Resolution* 14 (Sept. 1970): 345–52. For McDonald's involvement in the relocation of the county seat in Hardeman County before he became a Ranger captain, see Neal, *Last Frontier*, 49–50. In the election for the county seat in early 1890, residents of Margaret requested the presence of Rangers to keep the peace. Company B was so ordered. *RAGST* for 1889–1890, Appendix, 93.

63. Evans to Hogg, July 12, 1892 (second quotation), GR; ibid. to McDonald, July 12, 1892 (first quotation), Hogg to McDonald, July 19, 1892 (third quotation), McDonald to Mabry, July 19, 1892, GC-AGR.

64. Britton to McDonald, July 22, 1892, McDonald to Mabry, July 19, 1892 (first quotation), Nov. 5, 1892, GC-AGR; ibid. to Hogg, July 19, 1892 (second quotation), GR. Amazingly, soon after this episode Evans wrote central headquarters and asked that he be considered for an appointment to the adjutant general's staff in order to achieve his career ambitions. Evans also believed that he should be made second sergeant of Company B. Evans to Mabry, Sept. 22, 1892, GC-AGR.

65. *RAGST* for 1893–1894, Appendix, 66; Spellman, *Captain John H. Rogers*, 72–73; Utley, *Lone Star Justice*, 264–66. See also McNeel to Hogg, Dec. 23, 1892, GR.

66. Charles H. Harris III, and Louis R. Sadler, *The Texas Rangers and the Mexican Revolution: The Bloodiest Decade, 1910–1920* (Albuquerque: University of New Mexico Press, 2004); Benjamin H. Johnson, *Revolution in Texas: How a Forgotten Rebellion and Its Bloody Suppression Turned Mexicans into Americans* (New Haven: Yale University Press, 2003); *RAGST* for 1893–1894, pp. 5–8, Appendix, 9–11, 66; Utley, *Lone Star Lawmen*, 8–67, with quotation on p. 38.

67. McDonald still found time to request that he be allowed to go to Dallas and enter livestock in a fair. McDonald to Mabry, Sept. 27, 1893, GC-AGR.

68. Ibid. to Mabry, Jan. 19, 1893 (first quotation), Jan. 25, 1893, Feb. 14, 1893, Feb. 16, 1893, E. G. Pendleton, Panhandle land agent, to ibid., Jan. 28, 1893, GC-AGR; Mabry to McDonald, Jan. 23, 1893 (second quotation), LPB-AG-AGR.

69. McDonald to Mabry, July 20, 1893, ibid. to Capt. G. A. Wheatley, Feb. 28, 1893, Oct. 4, 1893, GC-AGR; Ration Return of Co. B for Sept. 1893, RR-AGR; Wheatley to McDonald, Feb. 24, 1893, May 12, 1893, Sept. 25, 1893, Dec. 9, 1893, LPB-Q-RR-AGR.

70. McDonald to Mabry, Feb. 28, 1893 (quotation), GC-AGR; MRCB from Jan. 1893 through Dec. 1893, RR-AGR. Knighten will be mentioned in the monthly returns for Feb., Mar., and May. Special Ranger Aten reported a number of arrests, including an extradited criminal, in 1893. Aten to Mabry, Sept. 30, 1893, Oct. 31, 1893, GC-AGR. In the middle of 1893 McDonald supported the efforts of the adjutant general to suppress train robbers through the cooperation of the railroads and the county sheriffs. In the pursuit of such criminals, a sheriff's posse, not to exceed six men, would be given by the state a daily allowance of five dollars per person for ten days. McDonald to Mabry, June 10, 1893, GC-AGR.

71. Ibid., July 20, 1893, Aug. 24, 1893, McDonald to Wheatley, Oct. 4, 1893, GC-AGR.

72. McDonald to Mabry, Jan. 25, 1893, Apr. 24, 1893 (quotation), June 17, 1893, GC-AGR.

73. The Ranger private wrote his name in two ways: O'Hare and OHare. Service Records, AGR. Other people, then and now, have spelled the name several other ways.

74. Newspaper clipping, E1 Reno *Globe*, Oklahoma Territory, n.d., attached to a document dated Dec. 16, 1894, GC-AGR. O'Hare was removed to a jail in E1 Reno, Canadian County, Oklahoma Territory, and was brought to trial in that district a year after the death of the Indian. Since there were no witnesses to the shooting, the jurors accepted the evidence in favor of O'Hare and returned a verdict of not guilty. Ibid. This newspaper clipping was attached to a letter from W. L. Lyon, an inspector and detective for the Cattle Raisers Association of Texas. Lyon wrote the adjutant general that a deputy US marshal in the Territory contacted him for assistance and he told this federal lawman to write O'Hare at Higgins. The Ranger private and the sheriff of Lipscomb County had tried to catch outlaws in the Oklahoma Territory once before. Lyon to Mabry, Dec. 16, 1894, typed transcript of message, RC-WP. Temple Houston defended O'Hare at his trial and praised his character. Houston to ibid., Dec. 12, 1894, typed transcript of message, RC-WP.

75. McDonald to Mabry, Nov. 22, 1893 (first telegram), ibid., Nov. 22, 1893 (quotations from second telegram), ibid., Nov. 22, 1893 (letter), GC-AGR; Mabry to McDonald, Nov. 22, 1893 (quotations), LPB-AG-AGR. The telegram by Mabry will also be found in GC-AGR. This dialogue between the adjutant general and Captain Bill had happened before. In September 1893 Mabry wired McDonald, "Do not go. Best for you not to leave the State, in which your authority is always unquestioned." Mabry to McDonald, Sept. 13, 1893, LPB-AG-AGR.

76. McDonald to Mabry, Nov. 22, 1893 (letter and first two quotations), ibid. to Wheatley, Nov. 24, 1893 (last quotation), GC-AGR.

77. Ibid. to Mabry, Jan. 19, 1893 (quotation), GC-AGR; Mabry to McDonald, Jan. 9, 1894 (quotation), LPB-AG-AGR. McDonald asked the adjutant general whether O'Hare should be paid to the end of the year. He said that he had "neglected" to put "discharged" on O'Hare's last voucher. McDonald to Mabry, Jan. 5, 1893 [1894], GC-AGR.

78. Wheatley to McDonald, Jan. 11, 1894, LPB-Q-RR-AGR.

79. B. M. Baker to Mabry, Jan. 2, 1894, typed transcript of message, RC-WP.

80. Chief Clerk to Britton, Jan. 4, 1894, Chief Clerk to McDonald, Jan. 4, 1894, Mabry to Baker, Jan. 8, 1894, Mabry to McDonald, Jan. 8, 1894, LPB-AG-AGR.

81. Britton to McDonald, Jan. 1, 1894 (quotations), McDonald to Mabry, Jan. 5, 1893 [1894], GC-AGR.

82. Baker to Mabry, Jan. 4, 1894, typed transcript of message, RC-WP; McDonald to Capt. Henry Orsay, Jan. 8, 1893 [1894] (first quotation), Thomas F. Turner to Mabry, Mar. 31, 1894 (last two quotations), GC-AGR; MRCB for Jan. 1894, RR-AGR.

83. MRCB from Jan. through Dec. 1894, RR-AGR. Quotations have been taken from Fullerton's report in March.

84. Andrew Graybill, "Texas Rangers, Canadian Mounties, and the Policing of the Transnational Industrial Frontier, 1885–1910," *WHQ* 35 (Summer 2004): 167–91; Marilyn D. Rhinehart, *A Way of Work and a Way of Life: Coal Mining in Thurber, Texas, 1888–1926* (College Station: Texas A&M University Press, 1992), 6–7 (first quotation), 11–12, 113 (second quotation).

85. Marilyn D. Rhinehart, " 'Underground Patriots': Thurber Coal Miners and the Struggle for Individual Freedom, 1888–1903," *SHQ* 92 (Apr. 1989): 520–21 (first quotation), 522 (second quotations); Utley, *Lone Star Justice*, 230–33, 259–60, 277–78.

86. Henry M. Furman, attorney at law, to Mabry, June 6, 1894, June 8, 1894, sworn statement of W. K. Gordon, superintendent of the coal company, June 16, 1894, sworn statement of R. D. Hunter, president of the Texas & Pacific Coal Company, June 18, 1894, sworn statement of William Lightfoot, undercover agent of the coal company, June 18, 1894, and affidavits from more than twenty people living in or around Thurber, GC-AGR.

87. Hunter to Mabry, June 5, 1894, sworn statements by Gordon, June 16, 1894, and Lightfoot, June 18, 1894, GC-AGR.

88. Mabry to McDonald, June 7, 1894, LPB-AG-AGR.

89. McDonald to Mabry, June 8, 1894, GC-AGR.

90. Mabry to McDonald, June 11, 1894, LPB-AG-AGR.

91. Ibid., June 12, 1894, LPB-AG-AGR; McDonald to Mabry, June 10, 1894, GC-AGR.

92. Mabry to McDonald, June 16, 1894, LPB-AG-AGR; McDonald to Mabry, June 13, 1894, GC-AGR.

93. Hunter to Mabry, June 10, 1894, GC-AGR. See also McDonald to ibid., June 11, 1894, June 16, 1894, July 1, 1894. McDonald even forwarded to headquarters affidavits from people living in or around Thurber. Ibid., June 20, 1894, GC-AGR.

94. Mabry to McDonald, June 16, 1894, LPB-AG-AGR; MRCB for June (quotation), Oct., and Nov. 1894, RR-AGR.

95. Hunter to Mabry, Oct. 1, 1893, Oct. 19, 1893, Nov. 1, 1893, McDonald to ibid., Sept. 28, 1893, Price to ibid., Nov. 30, 1893, GC-AGR; MRCB for Nov. and Dec. 1893, RR-AGR; Robert W. Stephens, *Bullets and Buckshot in Texas* (Dallas: Privately printed, 2002), 300–4.

96. Lightfoot to Mabry, July 7, 1894, ibid. to Capt. Owen, Aug. 6, 1894, GC-AGR; MRCB for Sept., Nov., and Dec. 1894, RR-AGR. Another newly appointed Special Ranger attached to Company B in 1894 would be G. W. Arrington, ex-Ranger captain of note. Arrington to Mabry, June 9, 1894, GC-AGR.

97. McDonald to ibid., July 15, 1894 (second quotations), GC-AGR; MRCB for July 1894, RR-AGR; Utley, *Lone Star Justice*, 259–60 (first quote). Paine interpreted McDonald's role at Thurber and Wichita Falls in terms of the "one-Ranger-one-riot" story. Paine, *McDonald*, 214–20. In McDonald's day, keeping order in railroad construction camps became an important part of the developing tradition of using hard-nosed Rangers in labor-management relations. Utley, *Lone Star Justice*, 226–28.

98. Edward Herring, "The Hunt for the Hughes Boys," *Old West* 1 (Summer 2000): 60–65; Herring, *Sam Baker: Winston County's Gunfighter* (Mt. Hope, AL: Privately printed, 1998), 22–36, 102–06; McDonald to Mabry, Oct. 27, 1894, Nov. 7, 1894, Nov. 22, 1894, May 29, 1895, Sullivan to McDonald, Nov. 3, 1894, typed transcripts of messages, RC-WP; MRCB for Oct. and Nov. 1894, RR-AGR; Sullivan to Mabry, Nov. 2, 1894, Nov. 3, 1894, GC-AGR; ibid., *Twelve Years in the Saddle*, 98–106, with quotation on p. 106. In May 1895 McDonald and his Rangers arrested Jim Hughes on suspicion that he took part in the Gordon train robbery. But that was not the case. MRCB for May 1895, RR-AGR.

99. Galveston *Daily News*, Dec. 8, 1894; McDonald to Mabry, Dec. 5, 1894, GC-AGR; ibid., Dec. 21, 1894 (quotation), typed transcript of message, RC-WP; MRCB for Dec. 1894, RR-AGR.

100. Shirley, *Law West of Fort Smith*, 111–37; Shirley, *Marauders of the Indian Nations: The Bill Cook Gang and Cherokee Bill* (Stillwater, OK: Barbed Wire Press, 1994); Lonnie E. Underhill, *Outlaws in the Indian Territory: The Bill Cook Gang, 1894–1895* (Tucson, AZ: Roan Horse Press, 1985).

101. Bob Alexander, " 'An Outlaw Tripped Up by Love,' " *Quarterly* of the National Association for Outlaw and Lawman History 26 (July–Sept. 2002): 7–16; Austin *Daily Statesman*, Nov. 23, 1894; McDonald to Mabry, Nov. 19, 1894, Nov. 24, 1894, Dec. 3, 1894, GC-AGR; ibid., Dec. 17, 1894, Dec. 27,

1894, original telegrams, Dec. 21, 1894, typed transcript of message, RC-WP; MRCB for Nov. 1894, RR-AGR; Paine, *McDonald*, 123–25; Sullivan, *Twelve Years in the Saddle*, 107–12.

102. Alexander, " 'An Outlaw Tripped Up by Love,' " 9–14.

103. MRCB for Jan. 1895 (quotation), RR-AGR; Sullivan, *Twelve Years in the Saddle*, 113–24.

104. *RAGST* for 1895–96, pp. 8–13, Appendix, 15–17.

105. Deputy United States Marshal William Banks to McDonald, Dec. 13, 1895, McDonald to Mabry, May 19, 1895, May 25, 1895, May 29, 1895, Aug. 2, 1895, Dec. 16, 1895; Sheriff N. N. Rogers, Kent County, to McDonald, Dec. 7, 1895 (first quotation); Sullivan to Adj. Gen., Dec. 31, 1895 (second quotation), typed transcripts of messages, RC-WP; McDonald to Mabry, Oct. 3, 1895, ibid. to Owen, Sept. 9, 1895, GC-AGR. In May 1895 McDonald reported that he and other Rangers assisted a sheriff in trying to capture members of the Bill Doolin gang. MRCB for May 1895, RR-AGR. At one point McDonald sent for two copies of "Barnard's Criminal Cipher Code" for sending messages that was adopted at a sheriff's convention. He asked his superiors if they would pay the bill of $9.00. The adjutant general told McDonald that with the cut in the expense budget by the legislature, the request could not be approved. Mabry to McDonald, Aug. 30, 1895, LPB-AG-AGR; McDonald to Mabry, Aug. 29, 1895, GC-AGR.

106. Mabry to McDonald (and other company commanders), Apr. 30, 1895 (quotation), LPB-AG-AGR; Muster and Pay Rolls from May 1895 to Jan. 1896, AGR. Mabry also ordered that Aten, Arrington, and three other Special Rangers be dropped from the rolls of Company B for failure to turn in monthly reports. Mabry to McDonald, May 25, 1895, LPB-AG-AGR.

107. Paine, *McDonald*, 163–64.

CHAPTER 4: A GUNFIGHT BETWEEN TWO GUARDIANS OF THE LAW

1. Paine, *McDonald*, 165.

2. Capt. Neal Coldwell to Maj. Jones, June 30, 1877 (quotation), Special Order No. 97, July 8, 1877, GC-AGR; Jones to Coldwell, July 8, 1877, RC-RR-AGR.

3. Capt. G. W. Baylor to Adj. Gen., Feb. 19, 1882, RC-RR-AGR; King to Baylor, Feb. 27, 1882, LPB-AG-AGR; Monthly Return of Co. A for Feb. 1882, RR-AGR.

4. MRCB for Sept. 1886, RR-AGR; Stephens, *Bullets and Buckshot in Texas*, 300–1.

5. Capt. Hughes to Mabry, Apr. 6, 1894 (telegram and letter), GC-AGR; O'Neal, *Encyclopedia of Western Gunfighters*, 248–49, 278.

6. Buck Guise [Guyse] Folder, Extradition Papers (1837–1899), Secretary of State, Archives Division, Texas State Library, Austin, Texas; Sgt. J. T. Gillespie

to King, Oct. 30, 1881, Capt. C. L. Nevill to Battalion Quartermaster Coldwell, Aug. 1, 1882, GC-AGR; ibid., Mar. 8, 1882, Special Order No. 12, Co. E, Nov. 6, 1881, RC-RR-AGR; Monthly Return of Co. E for Oct. and Nov. 1881 and July 1882, RR-AGR. See also J. Evetts Haley, *Jeff Milton: A Good Man with a Gun* (Norman: University of Oklahoma Press, 1948), 79–80. In another case, Sheriff J. T. Morris of Reeves County, drunk and brandishing his weapon, shot and killed Private T. P. Nigh. Other Rangers gunned down the sheriff while trying to arrest him. Capt. J. T. Gillespie to King, Aug. 19, 1885, GC-AGR; Monthly Return of Co. E for Aug. 1885, RR-AGR.

7. McDonald to King, Nov. 9, 1889, GC-AGR.

8. An attorney wrote the adjutant general that the McDonald-Matthews shootout "will greatly tend to increase the war on the force" by those who oppose the Rangers. W. W. Turney to Mabry, Dec. 14, 1893, GC-AGR.

9. J. P. Beckham to Hogg, July 27, 1893, J. L. Moore to Hogg (with attached court record), July 26, 1893, GR.

10. H. H. Campbell, county judge of Motley County, to Hogg, Sept. 10, 1893, GR.

11. J. S. Harkey, sheriff of Dickens County, to Hogg, Aug. 11, 1893, Matthews to Hogg, Aug. 4, 1893, GR; McDonald to Mabry, Aug. 17, 1893, Aug. 21, 1893 (quotation), GC-AGR.

12. McDonald to Mabry, Jan. 10, 1893 [1894], Aug. 17, 1893 (quotations), Aug. 21, 1893, GC-AGR.

13. Ibid., Aug. 17, 1893, GC-AGR; MRCB for Aug. 1893, RR-AGR; Paine, *McDonald*, 168–69 (quotation).

14. Michael G. Ehrle, comp., *The Childress County Story* (Childress, TX: Ox Bow Printing, 1971), 59–60 (second quotation); MRCB for Dec. 1893 (first quotation), RR-AGR.

15. McDonald to Mabry, Jan. 10, 1893 [1894], citation for "abuse," "branded," "coward," and "usefulness," Aug. 21, 1893, citation for "domineering," "mad," and "rather sore," GC-AGR.

16. Duncan Smith to ibid., Mar. 13, 1894, typed transcript of message, RC-WP.

17. McDonald to ibid., Jan. 10, 1893 [1894], GC-AGR.

18. Britton to ibid., Dec. 11, 1893 (first quotation), GC-AGR; Stephens, *Bullets and Buckshot in Texas*, 140 (second quotation).

19. McDonald to Mabry, Jan. 10, 1893 [1894], GC-AGR.

20. Ibid.; Quanah *Chief*, Dec. 14, 1893 (quotation).

21. Ehrle, *Childress County Story*, 61 (quotation); Paine, *McDonald*, 165–69.

22. Adjutant General's Office to Matthews, June 26, 1893, LPB-AG-AGR; Matthews to Mabry, May 31, 1892, GC-AGR.

23. Ehrle, *Childress County Story*, 246; Paul Ord, ed., *They Followed the Rails: A History of Childress County* (Childress, TX: Childress *Reporter*, 1970), 369. Ehrle's work stated incorrectly that Matthews was first elected sheriff in 1892.

24. Ehrle, *Childress County Story*, 61–62, 246–49.

25. Hogg to Matthews, Sept. 10, 1891 (quotations), R. B. Levy, private secretary, to ibid., Sept. 22, 1891, Oct. 2, 1891 (a statement about rewards), May 20, 1892, Matthews to Hogg, Sept. 7, 1891, May 14, 1892, GR. These messages from the governor's office stressed the use of state funds in capital cases.

26. Ehrle, *Childress County Story*, 62.

27. Britton to Mabry, Dec. 11, 1893 (first quotations), GC-AGR; Coffer's statement in Ehrle, *Childress County Story*, 59–60, with second quotation on p. 60.

28. Crutcher's statement in Ehrle, *Childress County Story*, 60–61.

29. Britton to Mabry, Dec. 11, 1893, McDonald to ibid., Jan. 10, 1893 [1894], GC-AGR; Coffer's statement, p. 60 (quotations), and Crutcher's statement, p. 61, in Ehrle, *Childress County Story*; Quanah *Chief*, Dec, 14, 1893.

30. Britton to Mabry (with attached newspaper clipping including a statement and quotations by Matthews), Dec. 11, 1893, McDonald to ibid., Jan. 10, 1893 [1894], Dec. 10, 1893, Dec. 26, 1893, Jan. 1, 1894, GC-AGR; Coffer's statement, p. 60, Crutcher's statement, p. 61, and statement by Judge Fires, p. 61, in Ehrle, *Childress County Story*; Quanah *Chief*, Dec. 14, 1893.

31. Britton to Mabry (with attached newspaper statement by Matthews), Dec. 11, 1893, GC-AGR.

32. McDonald to ibid., Dec. 10, 1893 (quotation), Jan. 10, 1893 [1894], GC-AGR.

33. Ehrle, *Childress County Story*, 60; Quanah *Chief*, Dec. 14, 1893.

34. Ehrle, *Childress County Story*, 61.

35. Britton to Mabry, Dec. 11, 1893, GC-AGR.

36. Ehrle, *Childress County Story*, 58, 61; McDonald to Mabry, Jan. 1, 1894 (second quotation), GC-AGR; Quanah *Chief*, Dec. 21, 1893, Jan. 4, 1894 (first quotations). Percy Roberts, a deputy sheriff under Matthews, took over as the third sheriff of Childress County after Matthews' death.

37. Britton to Mabry, Dec. 16, 1893, Feb. 9, 1894 (third quotations), Feb. 11, 1894, McDonald to ibid., Dec. 26, 1893 (first quotation), Jan. 1, 1894, ibid. to Wheatley, Jan. 20, 1894 (second quotation), GC-AGR.

38. Mabry to McDonald, Dec. 28, 1893, Jan. 8, 1894 (quotation), Jan. 12, 1894, LPB-AG-AGR; Quanah *Chief*, Dec. 14, 1893. The battalion quartermaster allowed doctor bills to be attached to McDonald's incidental expenses for April. But the bills needed to be put in proper form. Wheatley to McDonald, June 8, 1894, LPB-Q-RR-AGR.

39. Britton to Mabry, Dec. 11, 1893, McDonald to ibid., Jan. 1, 1894, GC-AGR; Criminal Minutes, District Court, Hardeman County, Vol. 2, pp. 31–32, 38–39, 49; Ehrle, *Childress County Story*, 61.

40. Ehrle, *Childress County Story*, 61.

41. Britton to Mabry, Dec. 11, 1893, GC-AGR.

42. MRCB for Dec. 1893, RR-AGR.

43. Britton to Mabry, Dec. 11, 1893, GC-AGR.

44. MRCB for Dec. 1893, RR-AGR.

45. Ibid. for Aug. 1894, RR-AGR.

46. McDonald to Mabry, Jan. 1, 1895 [1896] (quotations), GC-AGR; ibid., May 29, 1895, typed transcript of message, RC-WP; MRCB for May 1895, RR-AGR.

47. McDonald to Mabry, Jan. 1, 1895 [1896], GC-AGR; MRCB for Dec. 1896 [1895]; Paine, *McDonald*, 176–78; Sullivan, *Twelve Years in the Saddle*, 144–45. See also Glenn Shirley, *West of Hell's Fringe: Crime, Criminals, and the Federal Peace Officer in Oklahoma Territory, 1889–1907* (Norman: University of Oklahoma Press, 1978), 341–47. McDonald wrote his superiors, "The boys buried the body of Beckham without holding an inquest & I telegraphed to the sheriff of Wichita Co & to Sullivan to have inquest held which was done." McDonald to Mabry, Jan. 4, 1896, GC-AGR.

48. *National Police Gazette*, Sept. 17, 1904. The most important work in the historiography of the Matthews-McDonald gunfight has been Paine, *McDonald*, 165–75. Paine's account contains factual mistakes, like having the shootout in 1895, and gives a derogatory picture of the sheriff of Childress County. Paine also includes dialogue by Captain Bill not found in other records. For example, McDonald responded to one question after being wounded with the statement, "Well, I think I'm a dead rabbit" (p. 173). Other secondary writings have followed the romanticized story by McDonald's official biographer. These include the following: Baugh, *Pair of Texas Rangers*, 9–10; McGiffin, *Ten Tall Texans*, 186–91; Stephens, *Bullets and Buckshot in Texas*, 139–47; and Bob St. John, "He Just Kept a-Comin'," *Texas Parade* 25 (Apr. 1965): 46–48. Neal, *Last Frontier*, 67–69, gave several different versions of the gun battle. For the ups and downs in the life of Beckham, see Bob Alexander, Lawmen, Outlaws, and S.O.Bs.—Volume 2: *Gunfighters of the Old Southwest* (Silver City, NM: High-Lonesome, 2007), 250–66.

CHAPTER 5: PROCEED TO EL PASO: THE RANGERS AND PRIZEFIGHTING

1. Douglas, *Gentlemen in the White Hats*, 155.

2. Culberson to Mabry, Feb. 19, 1896, original telegram, RC-WP.

3. For the art and science of prizefighting in the United States, see John R. Betts, *America's Sporting Heritage: 1850–1950* (Reading, MA: Addison-Wesley, 1974); Elliott J. Gorn, *The Manly Art: Bare-Knuckle Prize Fighting in America* (Ithaca, NY: Cornell University Press, 1986); John D. McCallum, *The World Heavyweight Boxing Championship: A History* (Radnor, PA: Chilton Book Co., 1974); Donald J. Mrozek, *Sport and American Mentality, 1880–1910* (Knoxville: University of Tennessee Press, 1983); Jeffrey T. Sammons, *Beyond the Ring: The Role of Boxing in American Society* (Urban: University of Illinois Press,

1988); and Nancy Struna, "Puritans and Sport: The Irretrievable Tide of Change," *JSH* 4 (Spring 1977): 1–21.

4. Larry D. Ball, " 'Redeemed, Regenerated and Disenthralled': Arkansas Resists the Pugilists," *The Record* (annual of the Garland County [Arkansas] Historical Society) 18 (1977): 15–25. See also Gov. James P. Clarke of Arkansas to Culberson, Oct. 25, 1895, GR. For a recent popular account of Stuart's attempt to hold the prizefight in Arkansas and Texas, see Leo H. Miletich, *Dan Stuart's Fistic Carnival* (College Station: Texas A&M University Press, 1994). See also Steve Bogener, "The World Heavyweight Boxing Championship Bout, 1896, at Langtry, Texas," *WTHAYB* 74 (1998): 47–56.

5. Harry Jebsen, Jr., "The Public Acceptance of Sports in Dallas, 1880–1930," *JSH* 6 (Winter 1979): 5–19.

6. Elmer M. Million, "History of the Texas Prize Fight Statute," *TLR* 17 (Feb. 1939): 152–53.

7. Ibid., 154–55; Austin *Daily Statesman*, Aug. 24, 1895, Aug. 28, 1895; Sheriff Ben E. Cabell of Dallas County to Culberson, Aug. 20, 1895, Attorney General M. M. Crane to ibid., Aug. 26, 1895, GR.

8. Million, "History of the Texas Prize Fight Statute," 155–57. For the legal reasoning of Judge Hurt, see Austin *Daily Statesman*, Sept. 23, 1895. For Culberson's interest in a similar case, see Culberson to Dallas County Judge T. F. Nash, July 26, 1895, Letter Press Book, GR; Nash to Culberson, July 27, 1895 (filed under the year 1898), GR.

9. Austin *Daily Statesman*, Sept. 15, 1895.

10. Ibid., Aug. 24, 1895, Sept. 19, 1895, Sept. 27, 1895 (quotations); Million, "History of the Texas Prize Fight Statute," 157. For different views of Culberson's role in this affair, see Frank H. Bushick, *Glamorous Days* (San Antonio: Naylor, 1934), 117–19; James J. Corbett, *The Roar of the Crowd: The True Tale of the Rise and Fall of a Champion* (1925; repr., New York: Arno Press, 1976), 245–47; and Robert L. Wagner, "The Gubernatorial Career of Charles Allen Culberson" (M.A. Thesis, University of Texas at Austin, 1954), 103. In an out-of-state interview the governor's wife was quoted as saying that she did not agree with her husband's stand against prizefighting. She declared, "At least nine men out of every ten in Texas want the prize fight, and after all he was elected to carry out the will of the people and the people want the fight. I don't care what they say they want or pretend to say, they would every one of them go to it." Austin *Daily Statesman*, Sept. 28, 1895. Later she denied these statements. Ibid., Sept. 30, 1895. The supporters of Culberson called him the "young Christian governor." John W. Rogers, *The Lusty Texans of Dallas* (1951; repr., New York: E. P. Dutton, 1960), 192.

11. Austin *Daily Statesman*, Oct. 3, 1895. For the views of legislators on this subject, see ibid., Sept. 30, 1895, Oct. 1, 1895. For the legislative proceedings leading to the new law prohibiting prizefights, see ibid., Oct. 2, 1895. For a Texan court case upholding the new prohibition law over the former license law, see ibid., Oct. 15, 1895.

12. Ibid., Nov. 26, 1895.

13. The history of E1 Paso over the centuries can be explored in the following works: Conrey Bryson, *Down Went McGinty: El Paso in the Wonderful Nineties* (El Paso: Texas Western Press, 1977); Cleofas Calleros (collaboration with Marjorie F. Graham), *El Paso—Then and Now* (El Paso: American Printing Co., 1954); and Charles L. Sonnichsen, *Pass of the North: Four Centuries on the Rio Grande* (El Paso: Texas Western Press, 1968).

14. El Paso *Daily Times*, Jan. 16, 1896.

15. Austin *Daily Statesman*, Oct. 8, 1895. On the issue of where the fight would be held, see Pastor L. R. Millican of El Paso to Culberson, Jan. 11, 1896, GR.

16. Stuart to Culberson, Jan. 27, 1896, GR.

17. Culberson to Stuart, Jan. 29, 1896, Letter Press Book, GR. For those who praised Culberson's actions and talked about boundary lines, see Millican to Culberson, Feb. 1, 1896, Ministers' Union to ibid., Feb. 1, 1896, Feb. 6, 1896, GR.

18. *RAGST* for 1895–96, p. 11.

19. Ibid.

20. El Paso *Daily Times*, Feb. 5, 1896.

21. Hughes to Mabry, Jan. 21, 1896, typed transcript of message, RC-WP.

22. Mabry to McDonald, Jan. 18, 1896 (quotation), LPB-AG-AGR; McDonald to Mabry, Jan. 25, 1896, original telegram and typed transcript of message, RC-WP; ibid., Feb. 4, 1896, GC-AGR; MRCB for Feb. 1896, RR-AGR. The Rangers sent to El Paso to work as undercover agents were Privates Edward Connell and Arthur Jones.

23. Brooks to Mabry, Feb. 3, 1896, Hughes to ibid., Feb. 5, 1896, Rogers to ibid., Feb. 3, 1896, GC-AGR; Monthly Return of Co. F for Feb. 1896, RR-AGR. From Brooks' company came Privates W. A. Evetts and A. D. Settle. Captain Rogers sent Sergeant Tupper Harris and Private Tom Ross.

24. Monthly Return of Co. D for Feb. 1896, RR-AGR.

25. Austin *Daily Statesman*, Feb. 10, 1896; El Paso *Daily Times*, Feb. 11, 1896; Monthly Return of Co. E for Feb. 1896, Monthly Return of Co. F for Feb. 1896, RR-AGR.

26. Austin *Daily Statesman*, Feb. 11, 1896; Mabry to McDonald, Feb. 6, 1896 (first quotation), Feb. 8, 1896 (second quotation), Sullivan to ibid., Feb. 8, 1896, GC-AGR; McDonald to Mabry, Feb. 6, 1896, original telegram, RC-WP; MRCB for Feb. 1896, RR-AGR.

27. Sonnichsen, *Pass of the North*, 345–78.

28. McDonald to Mabry, Jan. 25, 1896, typed transcript of message, RC-WP. For mention of the Rangers being spectators, see Austin *Daily Statesman*, Feb. 10, 1896; Sullivan, *Twelve Years in the Saddle*, 181.

29. El Paso *Daily Times*, Feb. 13, 1896 (quotation), Feb. 20, 1896, Mar, 18, 1896.

30. For mention of the wooded areas around El Paso, see ibid., Feb. 8, 1896. The use of the opera house was recorded in an interview with the adjutant

general. Ibid., Mar, 1, 1896. For the boxing exhibition, see ibid., Jan, 18, 1896, Jan. 19, 1896. See also Bryson, *Down Went McGinty*, 71–72.

31 Mabry to Culberson, Feb. 11, 1896, GR. See also Austin *Daily Statesman*, Feb. 11, 1896; El Paso *Daily Times*, Feb. 11, 1896.

32. Mabry to Culberson, Feb. 10, 1896 (last quotation), Feb. 11, 1896 (first quotation), Feb. 12, 1896 (other quotations), GR. See also *RAGST* for 1895–96, p. 11. For the coverage of the federal marshals in this affair, see Larry D. Ball, *The United States Marshals of New Mexico and Arizona Territories, 1846–1912* (Albuquerque: University of New Mexico Press, 1978), 145–46.

33. Hughes to Mabry, Feb. 6, 1896, GC-AGR.

34. El Paso *Daily Times*, Feb. 13, 1896; Monthly Return of Co. F for Feb. 1896 (quotation), RR-AGR; Paine, *McDonald*, 196. See also Austin *Daily Statesman*, Feb. 15, 1896.

35. Ibid., Feb. 21, 1896.

36. El Paso *Daily Times*, Feb. 14, 1896.

37. *RAGST* for 1895–96, p. 11.

38. Culberson to Mabry, Feb. 12, 1896, GC-AGR; El Paso *Daily Times*, Feb. 14, 1896. One writer has Fitzsimmons saying, "And to cap it all [Mabry] said he would shoot the principals first and fire on the spectators after he had settled our hash." Miletich, *Dan Stuart's Fistic Carnival*, 157–58.

39. El Paso *Daily Times*, Feb. 15, 1896. Later the ministers in the city passed resolutions condemning the violations of the law by gamblers, prostitutes, and those keeping their places of business open on Sunday. Ibid., Feb. 19, 1896.

40. Larry D. Ball, "Lawman in Disgrace: Sheriff Charles C. Perry of Chaves County, New Mexico," *NMHR* 61 (Apr. 1986): 131–32; Sullivan, *Twelve Years in the Saddle*, 178–81 (quotation on p. 180).

41. El Paso *Daily Times*, Feb. 19, 1896.

42. Ibid., Feb. 13, 1896 (quotation); Hughes to Mabry, Feb. 5, 1896, GC-AGR; Martin, *Border Boss*, 164; MRCB for Feb. 1896, Monthly Return of Co. E for Feb. 1896, RR-AGR; Sullivan, *Twelve Years in the Saddle*, 179 (quotation).

43. El Paso *Daily Times*, Feb. 8, 1896, Feb. 15, 1896, Feb. 18, 1896; Mabry to Culberson, Feb. 17, 1896, GR.

44. MRCB for Feb. 1896, RR-AGR; *RAGST* for 1895–96, pp. 11–12; Sullivan, *Twelve Years in the Saddle*, 181.

45. Austin *Daily Statesman*, Feb. 21, 1896.

46. [Mabry] to Culberson, Feb. 19, 1896, GR; Monthly Return of Co. D for Feb. 1896, RR-AGR; Jack Skiles, *Judge Roy Bean Country* (Lubbock: Texas Tech University Press, 1996), 31–36; Charles L. Sonnichsen, *The Story of Roy Bean: Law West of the Pecos* (1943; repr., Greenwich, CT: Fawcett Pub., 1972), 172–76.

47. Austin *Daily Statesman*, Feb. 6, 1896, Feb. 11, 1896, Feb. 21, 1896 (quotation); El Paso *Daily Times*, Jan. 19, 1896, Feb. 5, 1896, Feb. 6, 1896, Feb. 7,

1896, Feb. 9, 1896, Feb. 12, 1896, Mar. 1, 1896; Martin, *Border Boss*, 164; Paine, *McDonald*, 195; *RAGST* for 1895–96, p. 12.

48. Paine, *McDonald*, 197–98. For Masterson's denial of the incident, see New York *Morning Telegraph*, May 18, 1919. A valuable sketch of this encounter will be found in Robert K. DeArment, "That Masterson-McDonald Standoff," *True West* 45 (Jan. 1998): 12–15. See also DeArment, *Bat Masterson: The Man and the Legend* (Norman: University of Oklahoma Press, 1979), 348–49; and Boyce House, *Cowtown Columnist* (San Antonio: Naylor, 1946), 234. One family tale has a different ending: "The Rogers family has always related this story differently. According to them it was Rogers who responded to Masterson as McDonald gripped the gunfighter's arm, 'He don took it up.' " Spellman, *Captain John H. Rogers*, 86.

49. Austin *Daily Statesman*, Feb. 22, 1896; DeArment, *Bat Masterson*, 349–50; El Paso *Daily Times*, Feb. 23, 1896, Mar. 1, 1896; Monthly Return of Co. E for Feb. 1896, Monthly Return of Co. F for Feb. 1896, RR-AGR; *RAGST* for 1895–96, p. 12. For Stuart the heavyweight prizefight was a financial bust. After the boxing match, Maher suffered from depression. And Corbett tried to reclaim the heavyweight title. Dallas *Morning News*, Feb. 26, 1896, Feb. 27, 1896, Mar. 1, 1896. Although Mexican officials requested that the United States take criminal action against the pugilists in this affair, American authorities realized that federal laws about prizefighting applied to territories and the District of Columbia, not the states in the Union, and that no national or state law applied to the jurisdictions of other countries. Secretary of State Richard Olney to the Governor of Texas, Mar. 13, 1896, ibid. to the Mexican Minister, Mar. 12, 1896, GR. The Mexican government decided to "dismiss the case" against Fitzsimmons and Maher for the violation of Mexican laws. Ibid. to the Governor of Texas, Apr. 30, 1896, GR.

50. Enforcing the prizefight law in Galveston would be part of Culberson's program in 1898. For an introduction to the use of the anti-prizefight law by Governor Joseph D. Sayers and the Texas Rangers to stop a contest in Galveston in 1901, see Randy Roberts, "Galveston's Jack Johnson: Flourishing in the Dark," *SHQ* 87 (July 1983): 52–56.

51. Hughes to Mabry, Jan. 21, 1896, typed transcript of message, RC-WP. For an interview of Mabry about this affair and reaction of residents in El Paso to his statements, see Dallas *Morning News*, Feb. 28, 1896, Mar. 1, 1896. For the interplay among Culberson, Hogg, and James H. Robertson about legal services and the use of state funds in the prizefight affair, see the James Stephen Hogg Papers (Sept. 1895) and the governor's records (Oct. 1895 and Sept. 1896).

CHAPTER 6: A BANK ROBBERY IN WICHITA FALLS

1. [McDonald] to Mabry, Apr. 4, 1896, GC-AGR.

2. Brian Hart, "Wichita County," in *New Handbook of Texas*, VI, 952–53; Donovan L. Hofsommer, "Wichita Falls, Texas," in ibid., VI, 955–56.

3. Adams, *Western Words*, 56 (quotation); Morn, "*Eye That Never Sleeps*," 86–87, 116–20, 142–44, 174–75; Prassel, *Great American Outlaw*, 114–15, 128–42, 174–75.

4. A. N. Dexter to King, Mar. 26, 1884, Schmitt to ibid., Mar. 28, 1884 (quotation), GC-AGR; Louise Kelly, comp., *Wichita County Beginnings* (Burnet, TX: Eakin Press, 1982), 43; Monthly Return of Company C for Mar. 1884, RR-AGR.

5. Kelly, *Wichita County Beginnings*, 43 (quotation).

6. Ibid., 44; Austin *Daily Statesman*, Feb. 26, 1896; Dallas *Morning News*, Feb. 27, 1896, Feb. 28, 1896; Galveston *Daily News*, Feb. 26, 1896; Houston *Daily Post*, Feb. 26, 1896 (quotation from Langford's statement); Quanah *Tribune*, Feb. 27, 1896.

7. Dallas *Morning News*, Feb. 27, 1896; Galveston *Daily News*, Feb. 26, 1896; Houston *Daily Post*, Feb. 26, 1896; Kelly, *Wichita County Beginnings*, 44 (quotation).

8. Dallas *Morning News*, Feb. 28, 1896; Kelly, *Wichita County Beginnings*, 44.

9. MRCB for Aug. and Sept. 1895, RR-AGR; Sullivan, *Twelve Years in the Saddle*, 183–84.

10. JVG (Fort Worth & Denver City Railway) to Sullivan, Feb. 25, 1896, McDonald to Mabry, Feb. 26, 1896, GC-AGR; MRCB for Feb. 1896, RR-AGR; Sullivan, *Twelve Years in the Saddle*, 182–83.

11. Dallas *Morning News*, Feb. 27, 1896 (first quotation), Mar. 2, 1896 (interview of McDonald); McDonald to Mabry, Feb. 26, 1896, telegram and letter (second quotation), Feb. 28, 1896, GC-AGR; MRCB for Feb. 1896, RR-AGR.

12. Dallas *Morning News*, Mar. 2, 1896.

13. Madsen to Sheriff [of Wichita County], Feb. 25, 1896, ibid. to Sullivan, Feb. 25, 1896, Feb. 26, 1896, Feb. 27, 1896, GC-AGR.

14. Dallas *Morning News*, Mar. 2, 1896.

15. Sullivan, *Twelve Years in the Saddle*, 185–86.

16. Dallas *Morning News*, Feb. 27, 1896; Kelly, *Wichita County Beginnings* 44. For the details of the role of the local populace in the robbery, chase, capture, and incarceration of the bandits, see the accounts by John Gould in the Wichita *Daily Times*, June 10, 1951, June 17, 1951.

17. Dallas *Morning News*, Feb. 27, 1896.

18. McDonald to Mabry, Feb. 27, 1896, GC-AGR.

19. Dallas *Morning News*, Feb. 27, 1896, Feb. 28, 1896 (quotation).

20. Ibid., Feb. 27, 1896 (quotations); Wichita *Daily Times*, June 24, 1951.

21. Dallas *Morning News*, Feb. 27, 1896 (quotations), Feb. 28, 1896; Wichita *Daily Times*, June 24, 1951, July 1, 1951.

22. Wichita *Daily Times*, June 24, 1951.

23. Ibid., June 10, 1951, June 24, 1951, July 1, 1951; Dallas *Morning News*, Feb. 27, 1896.

24. Dallas *Morning News*, Feb. 28, 1896 (quotation); Houston *Daily Post*, Feb. 28, 1896; Wichita *Daily Times*, July 1, 1951.

25. Austin *Daily Statesman*, Feb. 28, 1896 (quotation); Houston *Daily Post*, Feb. 28, 1896.

26. Wichita *Daily Times*, June 24, 1951.

27. McDonald to Mabry, morning telegram and afternoon telegram (first quotation), Feb. 27, 1896, Feb. 28, 1896 (second quotation), GC-AGR.

28. Ibid., afternoon telegram (quotation), Feb. 27, 1896, Apr. 4, 1896, GC-AGR.

29. Ibid., Apr. 4, 1896, GC-AGR. Upon behalf of the governor, Mabry asked McDonald for information about why the bank robbers were left in the "hands of the citizens" in the absence of the sheriff. Mabry to McDonald, Mar. 31, 1896, LPB-AG-AGR.

30. McDonald to Mabry, Apr. 4, 1896, GC-AGR. For congratulations for their efforts, see J. R. C. (railroad president) to McDonald, Feb. 27, 1896, GC-AGR.

31. Kelly, *Wichita County Beginnings*, 45; Wichita *Daily Times*, July 1, 1951. Both the Rangers ($800) and members of the posse shared in the reward money established by local banks for the capture of Crawford and Lewis. Ibid.

32. Dallas *Morning News*, Feb. 28, 1896. The same editorial appeared in the Galveston *Daily News*, Feb. 28, 1896.

33. Wichita *Daily Times*, July 1, 1896.

34. Ibid. In the historiography of the bank robbery a common source has been the extensive coverage of the crime in the Dallas *Morning News*. Historical accounts of the affair have differed on the role played by the Rangers. Some writers, as, for example, Kelly, *Wichita County Beginnings*, 43–45, have downplayed the actions of Company B in the manhunt. On the other hand, McDonald's official biographer magnified the efforts of Captain Bill and his men in the chase and capture of the bandits (Paine, *McDonald*, 199–213). Paine's book even has dialogue by the Ranger captain not found in other records. The most extensive treatment of the robbery murder, with emphasis on the role of the locals, will be found in a series of newspaper articles by John Gould in the Wichita *Daily Times*: June 7, 1951 (introduction), June 10, 1951 (bank robbery), June 17, 1951 (capture of the robbers), June 24, 1951 (hanging of Lewis), July 1, 1951 (hanging of Crawford). These accounts by Gould, though, depend too much on information in Paine's biography of McDonald. The role of Captain Bill in the affair will be portrayed more accurately in the correspondence in the records of the adjutant general's office. Other works about the robbery murder, sometimes factual, sometimes not, include the following: Donald R. Hale, "The Double Lynching of Crawford and 'The Kid'," *Quarterly* of the National Association for Outlaw and Lawman History 22 (Jan.–Mar. 1998): 8–12; Jonnie R. Morgan, *The History of Wichita Falls* (1931; repr., Wichita Fails: Nortex Publications, 1971), 87–90; and Sullivan, *Twelve Years in the Saddle*, 182–88. For a popular account with emphasis on the legal issues, see Bill Neal, *Getting Away with Murder on the Texas Frontier: Notorious Killings and Celebrated Trials* (Lubbock: Texas Tech University Press, 2006), 49–73.

CHAPTER 7: SAN SABA MOB: A MURDER SOCIETY

1. Sonnichsen, *I'll Die Before I'll Run*, 185.

2. Calvert and De León, *History of Texas*, 211–13, 254–55; Richardson, Texas, 360–70. See also Fred Gantt, Jr., *The Chief Executive in Texas: A Study in Gubernatorial Leadership* (Austin: University of Texas Press, 1964).

3. Daniel P. Greene, "San Saba, Texas," in *New Handbook of Texas*, V, 877; Victoria S. Murphy, "San Saba County," in ibid., V, 877–78. See also Alma W. Hamrick, *The Call of the San Saba: A History of San Saba County*, 2nd ed. (Austin: Jenkins Publishing, 1969); and [n. a.], *San Saba County History, 1856–1983* (San Saba, TX: San Saba County Historical Commission, 1983).

4. David Grimsted, *American Mobbing, 1828–1861: Toward Civil War* (New York: Oxford University Press, 1998); Robert B. Shoemaker, *The London Mob: Violence and Disorder in Eighteenth-Century England* (London: Hambledon and London, 2004); Sonnichsen, *I'll Die Before I'll Run*, 164–70, 287. See also Austin *Daily Statesman*, Feb. 28, 1897.

5. Sullivan to Mabry, Aug. 26, 1896, typed transcript of message, RC-WP.

6. McDonald to ibid., Sept. 26, 1897, GC-AGR.

7. Ibid.

8. Sonnichsen, *I'll Die Before I'll Run*, 170–76, with quotation on p. 171. See also Notes on the San Saba Mob in Sonnichsen Collection (University of Texas at El Paso, El Paso, Texas).

9. District Judge to King, Dec. 2, 1889, GC-AGR.

10 P. C. Jackson to Mabry, July 4, 1896, typed transcript of message, RC-WP. See also John Poe to Culberson, July 2, 1896, GR.

11. W. M. Allison to Mabry, Nov. 21, 1895, GC-AGR.

12. Ibid., June 29, 1896, typed transcript of message, RC-WP.

13. Ibid., July 17, 1896, typed transcript of message, RC-WP.

14. Allison to Culberson, July 22, 1896, GR.

15. Mabry to McDonald, July 30, 1896, LPB-AG-AGR.

16. Ibid., Aug. 6, 1896, Mabry to Sheriff S. E. W. Hudson, Aug. 6, 1896 (quotations), LPB-AG-AGR.

17. Hamrick, *Call of the San Saba*, 102; MRCB for Aug. 1896, RR-AGR; San Saba *County News*, Aug. 21, 1896, in Sonnichsen Collection; Sullivan, *Twelve Years in the Saddle*, 197–98. In time Neal would become sheriff of San Saba County and do a creditable job. Barker, an admirer of McDonald, would also become a local sheriff. A person who was shot by Barker was "Barkerized" in popular accounts. Sterling, *Trails and Trials of a Texas Ranger*, 338. For biographical accounts of Barker, Maddox, and Neal, see Stephens, *Texas Ranger Sketches*, 22–23, 90–91, 102–03.

18. Sullivan, *Twelve Years in the Saddle*, 198–99.

19. Sonnichsen, *I'll Die Before I'll Run*, 178. The conflict in the chain of command between Sullivan and Rogers is covered in Chapter 1.

20. McDonald to Mabry, Sept. 26, 1897, Sullivan to Mabry, Sept. 17, 1896, GC-AGR; ibid., Oct. 2, 1896, typed transcript of message, RC-WP.

21. Sonnichsen, *I'll Die Before I'll Run*, 178–79.

22. [W. C. Linden] to Mabry, Nov. 30, 1896, typed transcript of message, RC-WP. Linden was less flattering to Hawkins. "The sheriff of this county," he noted, "was elected at the late election and has had absolutely no experience in the duties of the office. He seems to be willing and in earnest, but he received almost the unanimous support of that element [the Mob] in this county." Ibid.

23. MRCB for Sept. 1896, RR-AGR.

24. Ibid. for Nov. 1896, RR-AGR.

25. Ibid. for Jan. 1897, Mar. 1897, Apr. 1897, RR-AGR.

26. Sullivan to Mabry, Aug. 26, 1896, typed transcript of message, RC-WP.

27. San Saba *County News*, Aug. 14, 1896, Aug. 28, 1896, Sept. 4, 1896 (quotation), Sept. 11, 1896, Sept. 18, 1896, Sept. 25, 1896, Oct. 2, 1896, Oct, 30, 1896, in Sonnichsen Collection; Sonnichsen, *I'll Die Before I'll Run*, 176–77.

28. For Sullivan attending district court in April and May 1896, see MRCB for those months, RR-AGR.

29. Ibid. for Oct. and Nov. 1896, RR-AGR.

30. Sullivan to Mabry, Oct. 20, 1896, GC-AGR.

31. MRCB for Mar. 1897, RR-AGR.

32. [Linden] to Mabry, Nov. 30, 1896, typed transcript of message, RC-WP.

33. Austin *Daily Statesman*, June 9, 1897, June 10, 1897; Sullivan to Mabry, Sept. 17, 1896, Oct. 2, 1896, Oct. 13, 1896, Oct. 20, 1896, Nov. 13, 1896, GC-AGR; ibid., Aug. 26, 1896, typed transcript of message, RC-WP.

34. Ibid., Sept. 17, 1896, GC-AGR.

35. Sonnichsen, *I'll Die Before I'll Run* 179.

36. Sullivan to Mabry, Nov. 30, 1896, GC-AGR.

37. [Linden] to ibid., Nov. 30, 1896, typed transcript of message, RC-WP.

38. Sullivan to ibid., Dec. 27, 1896, GC-AGR.

39. Allison to Culberson, Dec. 16, 1896 (quotation), Jan. 7, 1897, GR.

40. Sullivan to Mabry, Feb. 7, 1897, typed transcript of message, RC-WP.

41. James P. Hart, clerk of the district courts of Travis County, to Culberson, June 29, 1897, GR.

42. MRCB for June 1897, RR-AGR.

43. For the testimony at the trial of Ford in February and its aftermath, see San Saba *County News*, Mar. 5, 1897, Mar. 12, 1897, June 4, 1897, June 25, 1897, in Sonnichsen Collection. Extensive coverage of the testimony at both trials in June will be found in the Austin *Daily Statesman*, June 9, 1897, June

10, 1897 (quotation), June 11, 1897, June 15, 1897, June 16, 1897, June 17, 1897, June 18, 1897. For the basic elements of the criminal cases in the June court term, see *State of Texas vs. George Trowbridge* (No. 11154) and *State of Texas vs. Mat Ford* (No. 11155), Microfilm No. 44, District Clerk's Office, Austin, Texas.

44. San Saba *County News*, Mar. 12, 1897, June 25, 1897, in Sonnichsen Collection.

45. Allison to W. T. Melton, May 8, 1897, Linden to Mabry, May 11, 1897 (quotations), typed transcripts of messages, RC-WP.

46. Mabry to Linden, May 17, 1897, ibid. to McDonald, Apr. 29, 1897, May 17, 1897 (quotation), May 25, 1897, LPB-AG-AGR.

47. McDonald to Mabry, May 5, 1897 (first quotation), typed transcript of message, RC-WP; ibid., May 6, 1897, May 14, 1897, May 15, 1897, May 18, 1897 (second quotation), May 29, 1897, GC-AGR; MRCB for May 1897, RR-AGR.

48. McDonald to Mabry, July 3, 1897, GC-AGR. See also ibid., June 23, 1897, typed transcript of message, RC-WP.

49. MRCB for July 1897, RR-AGR; Sullivan to Mabry, July 4, 1897, GC-AGR.

50. McDonald would continue to have problems with Sullivan's ambition to replace him as captain of Company B. Chief Clerk to McDonald, Sept. 30, 1897, LPB-AG-AGR; McDonald to Mabry, Sept. 27, 1897, GC-AGR. Sometimes the adjutant general supported Sullivan and not McDonald on some issue. For an example of such a case dealing with company finances, see Mabry to McDonald, Sept. 26, 1896, LPB-AG-AGR; McDonald to Mabry, Sept. 24, 1896, Oct. 1, 1896, Sullivan to McDonald, Sept. 15, 1896, typed transcripts of messages, RC-WP. Throughout 1896 and 1897 Sullivan's work as a Ranger would be praised. Chief Clerk to District Attorney, San Saba, Dec. 7, 1896, LPB-AG-AGR; Hawkins to Adjutant General, Dec. 24, 1896, GC-AGR; G. T. Monk to Sullivan, Feb. 8, 1897, in Sonnichsen Collection.

51. Mabry to D. D. Dodd, Oct. 9, 1897, ibid. to S. J. Morris, Oct. 9, 1897, ibid. to A. C. Oliver, Oct. 9, 1897, LPB-AG-AGR. For an assessment of Sullivan at the end of his Ranger career, see Utley, *Lone Star Justice*, 262.

52. McDonald to Mabry, Aug. 7, 1897 (first quotation), Aug. 12, 1897, Nov. 1, 1897, Nov. 13, 1897, Jan. 16, 1898, Mob to McDonald, Jan. 9, 1898 (quotations), GC-AGR; McDonald to Capt. W. H. Owen, July 1, 1897, July 2, 1897, July 6, 1897, July 27, 1897, Jan. 8, 1898, Quartermaster Returns, RR-AGR; MRCB from July 1897 to Dec. 1898, RR-AGR.

53. McDonald's correspondence with central headquarters and letters from other people about the San Saba Mob is extensive. See McDonald to Mabry, July 19, 1897, July 23, 1897, Aug. 7, 1897, Aug. 12, 1897, Sept. 10, 1897, Sept. 29, 1897, Oct. 19, 1897, Oct. 27, 1897, Nov. 1, 1897, Nov. 6, 1897, Nov. 13, 1897, Mar. 26, 1898, Apr. 11, 1898, GC-AGR; and Leigh Burleson, attorney at law, to ibid., Nov. 11, 1897, typed transcript of message, RC-WP.

54. MRCB for July 1897 (quotations) and Mar. 1898, RR-AGR.

55. McDonald to Mabry, Dec. 12, 1897 (quotations), GC-AGR; ibid., Dec. 19, 1897, Dec. 23, 1897, Nov. 24, 1898, typed transcripts of messages, RC-WP. See also Sonnichsen, *I'll Die Before I'll Run*, 181–82.

56. Mabry to McDonald, Sept. 24, 1897, LPB-AG-AGR.

57. MRCB for Jan. 1898, Apr. 1898, June 1898, RR-AGR.

58. Ibid., July 1898, Aug. 1898, Sept. 1898, Nov. 1898, Dec. 1898, RR-AGR.

59. Ibid., Oct. 1898, RR-AGR.

60. Ibid., Aug. 1897, RR-AGR. See also McDonald to Capt. Owen, Sept. 2, 1897, Sept. 16, 1897, Quartermaster Returns, RR-AGR; and San Saba *County News*, Sept. 3, 1897, in Sonnichsen Collection.

61. Paine, *McDonald*, 228–39.

62. McDonald to Capt. Henry Orsay, Sept. 6, 1897, GC-AGR.

63. Ibid. to Mabry, Sept. 26, 1897, Sept. 29, 1897, GC-AGR. In time the court clerk would claim that the indictment against Ogle was "stolen." Ibid., Feb. 9, 1898, GC-AGR.

64. San Antonio *Daily Express*, Sept. 11, 1897.

65. See, for example, the statements about Mills County in San Saba *County News*, July 31, 1896.

66. For Ogle's convict data form, see Convict Record of the Texas State Penitentiaries, Book G, p. 132.

67. Court of Criminal Appeals, Docket, April Term, 1900, Austin, Vol. 211-118, p. 2; Court of Criminal Appeals, Minutes, 1900, Austin, Vol. 211-077, pp. 801, 808, 829; *Ogle v. State*, 58 *Southwestern Reporter* 1004 (1900).

68. Paine, *McDonald*, 240–42, with quotation on p. 241.

69. Executive Record: Pardons and Remissions, State Department, Ledger 4-20/692 (1909–11), p. 178.

70. Sonnichsen, *I'll Die Before I'll Run*, 182.

71. Austin *Daily Statesman*, May 31, 1899 (quotation); McDonald to Mabry, Apr. 11, 1898, GC-AGR.

72. San Angelo *Morning Times*, Dec. 21, 1934, in Sonnichsen Collection; Sonnichsen, *I'll Die Before I'll Run*, 182–85. Sullivan exaggerated when he wrote, "The two factions in San Saba finally made peace with each other and buried the hatchet. The last time I was with them they were going to church and visiting each other, and all signs of former strife and bad feeling had faded away." Sullivan, *Twelve Years in the Saddle*, 200.

73. Burleson to Adj. Gen. A. P. Wozencraft, Nov. 4, 1898, McCauley to ibid., Nov. 4, 1898 (quotation), McDonald to ibid., Nov. 24, 1898, typed transcripts of messages, McDonald to ibid., Nov. 7, 1898, original telegram, RC-WP; MRCB for Nov. 1898, RR-AGR. For secondary accounts of the shootout between Barker and Boren, with a mixture of fact and fiction, see Stephens, *Texas Ranger Sketches*, 22–23; and Sterling, *Trails and Trials of a Texas Ranger*, 337–38. In

another shooting incident McDonald reported to central headquarters from San Saba in December 1897 that Eugene Bell of Company E got drunk and shot off his gun. McDonald to Mabry, Dec. 5, 1897, GC-AGR; MRCB for Dec. 1897, RR-AGR. The adjutant general informed McDonald that the "conduct" of Bell was "very reprehensible." The Ranger captain should "allow the law to take its course." Mabry to McDonald, Dec. 7, 1897, LPB-AG-AGR.

74. Allison to Gov. Joseph D. Sayers, Feb. 25, 1899, Hawkins to ibid., Mar. 12, 1899, N. D. Lidstone, et al. to ibid., Feb. 25, 1899 (quotation), typed transcripts of messages, RC-WP.

75. McCauley to McDonald, June 3, 1899, ibid. to Capt. W. H. Owen, Oct. 15, 1898, ibid. to Adj. Gen. Thomas Scurry, Mar. 4, 1899 (quotation), McDonald to Scurry, Jan. 31, 1899, Feb. 6, 1899, Mar. 19, 1899, May 19, 1899, May 31, 1899, Sheriff Edgar T. Neal to ibid., May 17, 1899, GC-AGR; McDonald to ibid., Mar. 4, 1899, typed transcript of message, RC-WP; MRCB from Jan. 1899 to June 1899, RR-AGR.

76. Scurry to McDonald, July 24, 1899, LPB-AG-AGR.

77. Sullivan, *Twelve Years in the Saddle*, 197–200; with the quotation (p. xiii) from the introduction written by John Miller Morris for the reprint of this volume by the University of Nebraska Press in 2001. For other statements by the Ranger sergeant, see Sullivan to Capt. Owen, Jan. 14, 1897, May 27, 1897, Quartermaster Returns, RR-AGR. The saga of Sullivan and the Ranger service continued. On July 20, 1898, Adj. Gen. Wozencraft notified Sullivan of his appointment as a Special Ranger attached to Company B under McDonald. Wozencraft to Sullivan, July 20, 1898, LPB-AG-AGR. When told about this arrangement, Captain Bill wrote his superiors: " . . . I was sorry he was attached to my company as he is very unfriendly to me & has been a long time & has recently written to an ally at San Saba that represents the mob element that is not at all complimentary to me & for a year before I discharged him he said many things derogatory to myself & men & to the service." McDonald to Wozencraft, July 25, 1898, typed transcript of message, RC-WP. Two days later the adjutant general replied by saying that if he had known about McDonald's poor relationship with Sullivan he would not have appointed him. If Sullivan "does not conduct himself properly," Wozencraft continued, "I shall revoke his commission." Wozencraft to McDonald, July 27, 1898, LPB-AG-AGR. At the start of 1899 Sullivan enlisted the aid of Sheriff Ben Cabell of Dallas County to help him rejoin the Rangers with pay. This never happened. Sullivan to Cabell, Feb. 22, 1899, typed transcript of message, RC-WP. This whining letter prompted C. L. Sonnichsen to think that "Capt. Bill was right." Sonnichsen Collection.

78. Utley, *Lone Star Justice*, 262.

79. Paine, *McDonald*, 221–42.

80. McDonald to Scurry, Mar. 4, 1899, typed transcript of message, RC-WP. One of the last communications about the San Saba Mob came from Linden. He did not want the Ford-Trowbridge cases, still pending in the court, to be

dismissed. Although no longer district attorney, Linden told the governor that he would still work on these cases for a retainer of $250. Linden to Sayers, Jan. 3, 1900, GR. District Attorney Warren W. Moore informed the governor's office that he wanted the legal assistance of Linden. Moore to Sayers, Jan. 12, 1900, GR. For Linden's response to Moore and the governor, see Linden to ibid., Feb. 5, 1900, GR. See also Sayers to Linden, Feb. 15, 1900, Letter Press Book, GR.

81. Ross J. Cox, Sr., *The Texas Rangers and the San Saba Mob* (San Saba, TX: C&S Farm Press, 2005), I, 46. This reliable account of the Mob has been divided into two parts. The first volume gave an overview of Mob operations. Here the author stressed that the Mob began as a vigilante force in Mills County; and that the efforts of Linden, McDonald, Sanderson, and Sullivan brought an end to the murderous society. The second volume contained a compilation of newspaper reports, court records, and other documents pertinent to Mob killings. This part ended with a listing of the names of local citizens and the Rangers who were involved in the affair. The author even noted the changes McDonald made in his Masonic membership as he moved from locality to locality. Cox, in addition, has been instrumental in erecting an historical marker about the Mob at the courthouse in San Saba.

82. Ibid. An interview with the wife of Ranger Neal has been printed in the Houston *Chronicle*, June 30, 1929.

CHAPTER 8: REESE–TOWNSEND FEUD AT COLUMBUS

1. *RAGST* for 1899–1900, p. 21.

2. Don Allon Hinton, "Columbus, Texas," in *New Handbook of Texas*, II, 235–36; Mark Odintz, "Colorado County," in ibid., II, 224–26.

3. Sonnichsen, *I'll Die Before I'll Run*, 243.

4. Ibid., 242–45; Bill Stein, "Consider the Lily: The Ungilded History of Colorado County, Texas," *Nesbitt Memorial Library Journal* 10 (Jan. 2000): Pt. 8, pp. 23–24.

5. Colorado County Historical Commission, comp., *Colorado County Chronicles* (Austin: Eakin Pub., 1986), I, 208; Sonnichsen, *I'll Die Before I'll Run*, 245–49. One of the better examinations of the coming feud will be found in a series of news stories by Bill Stein. See Colorado County *Citizen*, Jan. 21, 1988, Jan. 28, 1988, Feb. 4, 1988, Feb. 11, 1988, Feb. 18, 1988, Feb. 25, 1988, Mar. 3, 1988, Mar. 10, 1988, Mar. 17, 1988, Mar. 31, 1988.

6. Sonnichsen, *I'll Die Before I'll Run*, 250.

7. Bill Stein to author, Mar. 16, 2000. County Judge J. J. Mansfield believed that "much of the bitter feeling" between the Reese-Townsend factions can be traced back to the "old feud" between the Staffords and the Townsends. See the judge's statement attached to the report of the adjutant general to the governor dated June 10, 1899, in GR.

8. Colorado County *Citizen*, Feb. 4, 1988.

9. Stein to author, Mar. 16, 2000.

10. Colorado County *Citizen*, Feb. 11, 1988.

11. Ibid., Mar. 23, 1899, Feb. 18, 1988; Galveston *Daily News*, Mar. 17, 1899, Mar. 24, 1899, Mar. 25, 1899, Mar. 29, 1899; Houston *Post*, Mar. 17, 1899, Mar. 19, 1899; Sonnichsen, *I'll Die Before I'll Run*, 250–52; quotations taken from a statement attached to a report, Scurry to Sayers, June 10, 1899, GR. The statement by the physician also mentioned that Reese took part in deceptive financial practices while sheriff and that Clements fired first in the gun battle that killed Reese. In addition, Scurry's report included a summary of the feud by Judge Mansfield. For a brief but useful outline of the feud, see Bill Stein, "Colorado County Feud," *New Handbook of Texas*, II, 227. For a controversial, one-sided view of the feuding parties, see John W. Reese and Lillian E. Reese, *Flaming Feuds of Colorado County* (Salado, TX: Anson Jones, 1962). This helter-skelter account includes not only tales about the Reeses, but also sketches of other people and events. At one point this work noted that Walter Reese ran through a hail of lead to where his father fell, found his weapon empty, laid the dead man's head in his lap, and vowed to get the killer. Ibid., 80–81. Bill Stein has written a valuable critique of this volume. Colorado County *Citizen*, Mar. 31, 1988.

12. Statement of Judge Mansfield attached to report, Scurry to Sayers, June 10, 1899, GR.

13. Reese and Reese, *Flaming Feuds of Colorado County*, 127–28.

14. M. Kennon to Sayers, Mar. 20, 1899, George McCormack to ibid., Mar. 20, 1899, GR; Sayers to Kennon, Mar. 20, 1899, ibid. to McCormack, Mar. 20, 1899, Letter Press Book, GR.

15. Sayers to Scurry, two messages, Mar. 20, 1899, Letter Press Book, GR; Scurry to Sayers, Mar. 20, 1899, Mar. 21, 1899, GR.

16. Galveston *Daily News*, Mar. 22, 1899, Mar. 23, 1899, Mar. 24, 1899; McDonald to Scurry, Mar. 22, 1899, GC-AGR; ibid., Feb. 23, 1899 [*sic*], original telegram, RC-WP.

17. Galveston *Daily News*, Mar. 31, 1899; MRCB for Mar. 1899 (quotations), RR-AGR.

18. Galveston *Daily News*, Mar. 23, 1899, Mar. 24, 1899; McDonald to Scurry, Mar. 22, 1899 (quotations), GC-AGR.

19. Galveston *Daily News*, Mar. 25, 1899; Scurry to McDonald, Mar. 25, 1899 (quotation), LPB-AG-AGR.

20. Galveston *Daily News*, Mar. 29, 1899.

21. Paine, *McDonald*, 243–49. Paine's brief account incorrectly stated that the murder of a boy brought McDonald to Columbus, mentioned only two other Rangers in his text, and stressed how Captain Bill confused the sheriff with a foxy argument. See also Sonnichsen, *I'll Die Before I'll Run*, 252–53.

22. Quotation in statement attached to report, Scurry to Sayers, June 10, 1899, GR.

23. Kennon, et al. to Sayers, Mar. 30, 1899, GR.

24. Colorado County *Citizen*, Feb. 18, 1988; Galveston *Daily News*, May 19, 1899 (quotation), May 20, 1899; Houston *Post*, May 19, 1899, May 20, 1899; statement by Judge Mansfield attached to report, Scurry to Sayers, June 10, 1899, GR. The story by the Reese family of the killing of their kinsman will be found in Reese and Reese, *Flaming Feuds of Colorado County*, 94–97.

25. Houston *Post*, May 19, 1899; Mansfield to Sayers, May 18, 1899, GR.

26. Scurry to Sayers, June 10, 1899, GR.

27. Ibid.

28. Ibid.; Houston *Post*, May 23, 1899; MRCB for May 1899, RR-AGR; Scurry to McDonald, May 22, 1899, LPB-AG-AGR. Captain Brooks tried to find out if he would be ordered to Columbus. Brooks to E. M. Phelps, central headquarters, May 23, 1899, GC-AGR.

29. Scurry to Sayers, May 23, 1899, GR.

30. Ibid., June 10, 1899, GR.

31. McDonald to Scurry, May 31, 1899, GC-AGR.

32. Scurry to Sayers, June 16, 1899, GR.

33. Ibid.

34. Statements by Scurry and Ranger T. C. Taylor attached to ibid. The adjutant general kept the governor informed about the situation in the town in June. Ibid., June 12, 1899, GC-AGR.

35. McDonald to Scurry, June 6, 1899, June 19, 1899 (quotation), GC-AGR; Scurry to McDonald, May 27, 1899, June 1, 1899, June 3, 1899, June 5, 1899, LPB-AG-AGR.

36. Rogers to Scurry, May 18, 1899, GC-AGR.

37. The extensive correspondence between Wright and his superiors (an unusual undertaking for a private) included the following: Wright to Rogers, June 10, 1899 (second quotations), ibid. to Scurry, June 9, 1899 (first quotations), June 18, 1899, June 19, 1899, June 28, 1899, July 13, 1899, July 22, 1899, July 26, 1899, GC-AGR. In the middle of June Wright requested that two additional Rangers should be sent to Columbus. Scurry told Captain Rogers to send his sergeant and one "reliable" man to the town on the next train. Rogers dispatched Sergeant Dubose and Private A. Y. Old. E. M. Phelps, chief clerk, to Scurry, June 11, 1899, June 12, 1899, Rogers to ibid., June 12, 1899, Scurry to Rogers, June 11, 1899 (quotation), Wright to Scurry, June 11, 1899, GC-AGR.

38 Attached statement by Taylor, dated June 14, 1899, to a report from Scurry to Sayers, June 16, 1899, GR. A statement by Wright dated June 14 was also attached to this report by the adjutant general.

39. MRCB for May 1899, RR-AGR.

40. Monthly Return of Co. E for May 1899, RR-AGR.

41. MRCB for June 1899, RR-AGR.

42. Monthly Return of Co. E for June 1899, RR-AGR. This record also showed that Private A. Y. Old arrested a person for aggravated assault in Colorado County.

43. Ibid. for July 1899, RR-AGR.

44. Ibid. for Sept. 1899, RR-AGR.

45. Monthly Returns of Company F for Aug. and Sept. 1899, RR-AGR.

46. *RAGST* for 1899–1900, p. 24.

47. MRCB for Sept. 1899, RR-AGR.

48. Sonnichsen, *I'll Die Before I'll Run*, 254.

49 Ibid., 254–55; Austin *Daily Statesman*, Jan. 22, 1900; Colorado County *Citizen*, Feb. 25, 1988; Galveston *Daily News*, Jan. 16, 1900 (quotation), Jan. 17, 1900; Houston *Post*, Jan. 16, 1900, Jan. 17, 1900.

50. Houston *Post*, Jan. 20, 1900 (quotations); *RAGST* for 1899–1900, p. 24.

51. Monthly Return of Co. E for Jan. 1900, RR-AGR; Monthly Return of Co. F for Jan. 1900, RR-AGR.

52. Colorado County *Citizen*, Feb. 25, 1988.

53. Galveston *Daily News*, Jan. 23, 1900.

54. Scurry to McCauley, Jan. 15, 1900, Jan. 17, 1900 (quotation), LPB-AG-AGR.

55. MRCB for Jan. 1900, RR-AGR.

56. Houston *Post*, Jan. 19, 1900, Jan. 20, 1900, Jan. 21, 1900, Jan. 23, 1900 (quotation).

57. *RAGST* for 1899–1900, p. 24.

58. Houston *Post*, Jan. 23, 1900.

59. Ibid.

60. Ibid., Jan. 24, 1900, Jan. 25, 1900, Jan. 26, 1900; Sonnichsen, *I'll Die Before I'll Run*, 254–55. The account of the feud by the Reese family noted that Captain Rogers searched for weapons on the trip to Bastrop, The Ranger captain was surprised when he discovered a handkerchief with the blood of Sam Reese on it in the possession of one of Reese's daughters. This book also contained the statement that at one point the widow of Sam Reese had to be protected by the Rangers from Will Clements. Reese and Reese, *Flaming Feuds of Colorado County*, 100–3. In another work a story appeared that members of the Reese faction, "unwilling to be caught without weapons, tied strings to their pistols and let them down their pants legs. In that way they passed inspection by the Rangers and were able to leave their hardware at a convenient barber shop." Sonnichsen, *I'll Die Before I'll Run*, 254.

61. Colorado County *Citizen*, Feb. 25, 1988; Houston *Post*, Aug. 1, 1900, Aug. 2, 1900.

62. Colorado County *Citizen*, Mar. 3, 1988.

63. MRCB for Nov. and Dec. (quotation) 1900, RR-AGR.

64. Colorado County *Citizen* Mar. 3, 1988; Galveston *Daily News*, July 1, 1906; Houston *Post*, July 1, 1906, July 2, 1906.

65. Monthly Return of Co. D for July 1906, RR-AGR.

66. Hughes to Hulen, July 18, 1906 (two letters, morning and evening), GC-AGR.

67. Kennon to Gov. S. W. T. Lanham, Aug. 21, 1906, GC-AGR.

68. Monthly Return of Co. D for Sept. 1906, RR-AGR.

69. Adjutant General to J. W. Towell, July 23, 1906, Towell to Lanham, July 21, 1906, GC-AGR; Colorado County *Citizen*, Mar. 10, 1988; Monthly Return of Co. D for Oct. 1906, RR-AGR, See also Colorado County Historical Commission, *Colorado County Chronicles*, I, 211–14.

70. Colorado County *Citizen*, Mar. 17, 1988; San Antonio *Express*, May 18, 1907.

71. Colorado County *Citizen*, Mar. 17, 1988.

72. Houston *Post*, Jan. 25, 1900.

73. Colorado County Historical Commission, *Colorado County Chronicles* I, 214. For another look at some of the stages in the feud (with a few names misspelled), see Wilkins, *Law Comes to Texas*, 334–36, 343. See also Sonnichsen, *I'll Die Before I'll Run*, 254–56.

CHAPTER 9: HUMPHRIES CASE: AN EAST TEXAS LYNCHING

1. Letter from N. B. Morris, former assistant attorney general, to Scurry, quoted in *RAGST* for 1899–1900, pp. 21–22.

2. Information about vigilantes and lynchers in Texas and the nation will be found in Brown, *Strain of Violence*; William D. Carrigan, *The Making of a Lynching Culture: Violence and Vigilantism in Central Texas, 1836–1916* (Urbana: University of Illinois Press, 2004); and Michael J. Pfeifer, *Rough Justice: Lynching and American Society, 1874–1947* (Urbana: University of Illinois Press, 2004). The most extensive record of the lynching of the men in the Humphries family will be found in the Dallas *Morning News*. For the mind set of one of the lynchers and his diatribe against others, see J. L. Wilkinson, *The Trans-Cedar Lynching and the Texas Penitentiary* . . . (Dallas: Johnston Printing, [n. d.]). The secondary literature includes the following: Mark Busby, "An East Texas Lynching: The Humphries/ Wilkinson-Greenhaw Feud," in *Corners of Texas*, ed. Francis E. Abernethy (Denton, TX: University of North Texas Press, 1993), 147–58; and Paine, *McDonald*, 250–60.

3. J. J. Faulk, *History of Henderson County, Texas* (Athens, TX: Athens Review Printing, 1929); Linda S. Hudson, "Henderson County," in *New Handbook of Texas*, III, 556–59, with quotation on p. 558.

4. Dallas *Morning News*, Dec. 18, 1899.

5. Ibid., May 26, 1899, May 27, 1899, May 29, 1899, June 27, 1899, June 28, 1899, June 29, 1899.

6. Ibid., Aug. 11, 1899.

7. Ibid., May 27, 1899.

8. Ibid., May 29, 1899.

9. Wilkinson, *Trans-Cedar Lynching*, opposite p. 9 (Chapter 1). See also Austin *Daily Statesman*, Dec. 16, 1899.

10. Dallas *Morning News*, May 27, 1899.

11. Ibid., May 29, 1899, June 29, 1899; Convict Record at the Texas State Penitentiaries, Book G, p. 122 (data sheet). In this document his name was spelled Wilkerson.

12. Wilkinson, *Trans-Cedar Lynching*, 33–38.

13. Dallas *Morning News*, June 27, 1899.

14. Ibid. During the planning stage two other methods of doing away with the Humphries besides hanging them were proposed: either hire an assassin or seize the men of the Humphries family and shoot them. Ibid., Aug. 12, 1899.

15. Mention of the slaying of the constable will be found in ibid., May 26, 1899, May 27, 1899, May 29, 1899, June 12, 1899, June 27, 1899, June 29, 1899 (quotation), Aug. 11, 1899 (Patterson returns), Aug. 12, 1899, Dec. 17, 1899, Dec. 19, 1899, Dec. 20, 1899, Dec. 31, 1899, Aug. 3, 1900, Aug. 4, 1900. For the death of Rhodes and subsequent events through the eyes of Wilkinson, see Wilkinson, *Trans-Cedar Lynching*, 42–58.

16. Mention of hog stealing will be found in Dallas *Morning News*, May 27, 1899, May 29, 1899, June 12, 1899, June 28, 1899, June 29, 1899, Dec. 17, 1899 (quotation), Dec. 19, 1899, Aug. 3, 1900.

17. Wilkinson, *Trans-Cedar Lynching*, 38–41, with quotation on p. 40.

18. Dallas *Morning News*, June 4, 1899. See also ibid., Dec. 29, 1899.

19. Paine, *McDonald*, 253, 256 (quotation).

20. Busby, "An East Texas Lynching," 157. This statement came from the pen of Jim Monaghan who edited a work entitled *The Trans-Cedar Tragedy: Triple Lynching in Henderson County, Texas* (Dallas: Homemade Pub., 1989). This volume contained transcribed newspaper stories and reprints of the accounts of the crime by Paine and Wilkinson.

21. Busby, "An East Texas Lynching," 157.

22. Dallas *Morning News*, May 29, 1899, June 30, 1899 (quotation), Aug. 11, 1899, Dec. 17, 1899, Dec. 18, 1899, Dec. 20, 1899, Jan. 14, 1900; Houston *Daily Post*, May 27, 1899.

23. Dallas *Morning News*, May 27, 1899, May 28, 1899.

24. Houston *Daily Post*, May 27, 1899.

25. Dallas *Morning News*, June 7, 1899, June 8, 1899, June 12, 1899, June 28, 1899, June 30, 1899, Aug. 10, 1899.

26. Ibid., June 12, 1899.

27. Ibid., June 28, 1899.

28. Ibid., May 30, 1899. A lawyer in Athens asked the governor would he be eligible for the reward if he intervened in the case. L. W. Meredith to Sayers, June 12, 1899, GR.

29. Dallas *Morning News*, May 31, 1899, June 1, 1899; Sayers to N. B. Morris, May 31, 1899, Letter Press Book, GR.

30. Dallas *Morning News*, May 30, 1899.

31. Sayers to J. M. Crook, June 3, 1899, Letter Press Book, GR. At the same time the governor informed the attorney general of his actions. Dallas *Morning News*, June 4, 1899.

32. Ibid., June 7, 1899; McDonald to Scurry, June 6, 1899 (quotation), GC-AGR; Scurry to McDonald, June 5, 1899, LPB-AG-AGR.

33. MRCB for June and August 1899, RR-AGR. Since Old's transfer involved two Ranger captains, the adjutant general took his time in approving this change of command. McDonald to Scurry, June 19, 1899, GC-AGR; Scurry to McDonald, June 17, 1899, June 21, 1899, LPB-AG-AGR.

34. Busby, "An East Texas Lynching," 150.

35. *RAGST* for 1899–1900, pp. 21–22.

36. Another lyncher mentioned in the records was Ed Mahan. Dallas *Morning News*, June 29, 1899, Dec. 17, 1899, Aug. 2, 1900.

37. Ibid., June 8, 1899; MRCB for June 1899, RR-AGR.

38. Dallas *Morning News*, June 12, 1899; MRCB for June 1899, RR-AGR.

39. McDonald to Scurry, June 13, 1899, June 25, 1899, GC-AGR.

40. Ibid., June 13, 1899, GC-AGR.

41. Dallas *Morning News*, June 29, 1899.

42. McDonald to Scurry, June 13, 1899, GC-AGR.

43. Ibid.

44. Ibid., June 25, 1899, GC-AGR. See also ibid., June 23, 1899, GC-AGR.

45. Morris to Sayers, June 6, 1899, GR.

46. Ibid., June 10, 1899, GR. Another letter by Morris asked questions about the reward offered by the state for the capture of Patterson and stressed the need to hire a "good stenographer" for the court proceedings. Ibid., June 23, 1899, GR.

47. Crook to Sayers, July 7, 1899, GR. This letter contained Crook's expenses of $73.85, to be reimbursed by the state.

48. Data sheets on those put on trial will be found in Convict Record of the Texas State Penitentiaries, Book G, p. 121 (Wilkerson), p. 122 (Brooks), p. 136 (Cain and Stevens).

49. Dallas *Morning News*, Dec. 31, 1899. See also ibid., May 29, 1899, June 29, 1899. For the employment of Guy Green to assist in the prosecution of the cases, see Morris to Sayers, Sept. 7, 1899, GR.

50. Paine, *McDonald*, 255.

51. Dallas *Morning News*, Aug. 11, 1899, Aug. 12, 1899, Dec. 16, 1899, Dec. 19, 1899, Dec. 31, 1899, Aug. 14, 1900, Aug. 17, 1900.

52. Paine, *McDonald*, 255.

53. Dallas *Morning News*, Aug. 11, 1899.

54. Ibid., June 28, 1899, June 29, 1899, June 30, 1899, Aug. 9, 1899, Aug. 10, 1899, Dec. 22, 1899, Dec. 23, 1899, Jan. 14, 1900; McDonald to Scurry, July 10, 1899 (letter and telegram), Nov. 22, 1899, July 30, 1900, GC-AGR. At one point McDonald requested that handcuffs and leg irons be sent to Palestine. Ibid. to Sieker, Dec. 8, 1899, GC-AGR; Sieker to McDonald, Dec. 6, 1899, LPB-Q-RR-AGR.

55. Dallas *Morning News*, Dec. 29, 1899.

56. Ibid., Dec. 14, 1899.

57. Ibid., June 27, 1899. Private Old resigned from the Ranger service on Jan. 7, 1900. MRCB for Jan. 1900, RR-AGR.

58. Dallas *Morning News*, June 29, 1899.

59. MRCB from July 1899 through Aug. 1900, RR-AGR.

60. Dallas *Morning News*, Aug. 22, 1900. For the payment of a $1,000 reward to the sheriff of Henderson County for the convictions of the lynchers and other legal aspects, see N. A. Cravens, private secretary, to Morris, Sept. 18, 1899, A. P. Gardner to Sayers, Oct. 23, 1900, Morris to ibid., Sept. 8, 1899, Dec. 21, 1899, Feb. 3, 1900, and Sheriff K. Richardson to ibid., Sept. 8, 1900, GR; Cravens to Morris, Sept. 13, 1899, Feb. 16, 1900, ibid. to Gardner, Oct. 26, 1900, ibid. to Richardson, Sept. 1, 1900, and Sayers to Morris, Feb. 26, 1900, Letter Press Book, GR.

61. MRCB for Aug. 1900, RR-AGR.

62. McDonald to Scurry, July 30, 1900, GC-AGR.

63. *Ed Cain v. The State*, 42 *Texas Criminal Reports* 210 (1900); *Ex Parte John Greenhaw*, 41 *Texas Criminal Reports* 278 (1899); *Bob Stevens v. The State*, 42 *Texas Criminal Reports* 154, 175 (quotation) (1900). For the thinking of McDonald about lawyers and the use of alibis, see McDonald to Scurry, Nov. 9, 1899, Dec. 2, 1899, GC-AGR.

64. Morris to Sayers, Dec. 27, 1902, GR.

65. Dodge Mason and W. A. Watkins to ibid., Jan. 8, 1903, GR.

66. Campbell to J. M. Edwards, Aug. 5, 1907, Edwards to Campbell, June 19, 1907, GR.

67. Executive Board: Pardons and Remissions, State Department, Ledger 4-20/691 (1906–1909), p. 481, ibid., Ledger 4-20/692 (1909–1911), pp. 85, 221, 419–20, 423–24, ibid., Ledger 4-20/693 (1911–1912), p. 61 (Joe Wilkinson), Archives Division, Texas State Library, Austin, Texas. For prison records of the lynchers, see Conduct Register, Nos. 19578–19583, 19877–19878, State Penitentiary, Huntsville, Texas, and Convict Record of the Texas State Penitentiaries, Book G, Archives Division, Texas State Library, Austin, Texas.

68. Wilkinson, *Trans-Cedar Lynching*, 60.

69. Ibid., 52.

70. Ibid., 59.

71. Ibid., 54.

72. Crook to Sayers, Sept. 6, 1900, GR.

CHAPTER 10: FINALE OF THE FRONTIER BATTALION

1. *RAGST* for 1899–1900, Appendix, 33.

2. McCauley to Sieker, May 24, 1901, McDonald to Scurry, Oct. 14, 1899, Mar. 14, 1900, ibid. to Sieker, Nov. 22, 1899, Dec. 8, 1899, Jan. 14, 1900, Mar. 17, 1900, May 25, 1901, Ration Return of Company B, Frontier Battalion, for Month Ending Feb. 28, 1900, GC-AGR; Phelps to McDonald, Feb. 16, 1899, Feb. 18, 1899, Feb. 21, 1899, Sieker to ibid., June 19, 1899, July 3, 1899, Aug. 10, 1899, Nov. 18, 1899, Jan. 3, 1900, Apr. 24, 1900, May 22, 1900, LPB-Q-RR-AGR. McDonald noted that railroad fares and hotel bills add up quickly when you have to pay them yourself. McDonald to Scurry, May 14, 1900, GC-AGR. McDonald was still drawing pay of $300 per quarter as captain. Sieker to American National Bank, Austin, Texas, June 7, 1901, GC-AGR.

3. *RAGST* for 1897–98, pp. 12–13.

4. Ibid. for 1899–1900, pp. 27, Appendix, 32.

5. McDonald to Mabry, Jan. 4, 1896, Mar. 2, 1896, Apr. 3, 1896, Apr. 8, 1896, Apr. 14, 1896, July 7, 1896, July 27, 1896, Sept. 2, 1896 (second quotation), Nov. 9, 1896, Dec. 14, 1896, GC-AGR; ibid., Oct. 16, 1896, typed transcript of message, RC-WP; MRCB from Jan. through Dec. 1896, with the first quotation in Apr. 1896 and George Knighten mentioned in June and Dec. 1896, RR-AGR. Former Ranger Ira Aten noted that, besides cattle and horse thieving, setting grass fires was a "frequent" occurrence. Aten to McDonald, Jan. 2, 1896, GC-AGR. In the previous year the governor offered a $200 reward for the arrest and conviction of George Knighten. Culberson to McDonald, July 2, 1895, Letter Press Book, GR.

6. Dale L. Walker, *The Boys of '98: Theodore Roosevelt and the Rough Riders* (New York: Tom Doherty, 1998).

7. Austin *Statesman*, May 19, 1898.

8. J. W. Cottrell to Culberson, Apr. 22, 1898, R. J. Kleberg, manager of the King Ranch, to ibid., Apr. 26, 1898, O. O. Perry to ibid., Apr. 27, 1898, L. P. Sieker to ibid., Apr. 27, 1898, Frank C. Smith to ibid., Apr. 25, 1898, Charles F. Stevens to ibid., Apr. 23, 1898, W. H. Van Riper to ibid., Apr. 28, 1898, James B. Wells to ibid., May 1, 1898 (quotations), GR. Several Texans asked permission to raise a cavalry force, like "Terry's Texas Rangers" in the American Civil War, to go and fight outside the state. John M. Claiborne to Culberson, Apr. 25, 1898 (quotation), James Wells to ibid., May 1, 1898 (in support of a company from Laredo to fight outside the country), GR. One company

was to be called the "Culberson Carbineers," in honor of the father of the governor. H. F. O'Beirne to ibid., May 26, 1898, GR. Two petitioners asked for permission to raise volunteer companies of Tejanos, so that they could show their "loyalty to the Stars and Stripes." W. A. Old to Culberson, May 30, 1898 (quotation), Taylor Thompson to ibid., May 30, 1898, GR. Captain Rogers wrote a recommendation for W. B. Bates, an acquaintance, to lead a volunteer company. Rogers to ibid., May 30, 1898, GR. A lawyer expressed his desire to have the name, "The Texas Rangers" be "perpetuated by a regiment in this war." Eugene Williams to ibid., July 11, 1898, GR.

9. MRCB for Apr. 1898, RR-AGR; Muster and Pay Rolls of Company B, from the beginning of Mar. 1898 to the end of Aug. 1898, AGR.

10. MRCB for Apr. (quotation), May, and June 1898, RR-AGR.

11. Austin *Statesman*, May 19, 1898; Porfirio Diaz to Culberson, May 13, 1898 (quotation), GR. See also McDonald to Mabry, May 1, 1898, typed transcript of message, RC-WP.

12. Culberson to McDonald, May 17, 1898, Letter Press Book, GR. Similar messages went to the other captains.

13. McDonald to Culberson, May 19, 1898, GR. Captain Hughes wrote his superiors that he would try to meet with Mexican officials and "have an understanding with them." Hughes also noted that his Rangers, with deputy sheriffs, scouted the borderlands for armed Mexicans without success. He concluded that the Mexicans along the river seemed to be just as "quiet as before the war trouble commenced." Hughes to ibid., May 19, 1898 (first quotation), May 20, 1898 (second quotation), GR.

14. Austin *Statesman*, Aug. 4, 1898.

15. Muster and Pay Rolls of Company B, 1899–1900, AGR.

16. McDonald to Mabry, Dec. 25, 1897, Dec. 28, 1897 (quotations), GC-AGR; MRCB for Dec. 1897, RR-AGR. See also Nancy B. Samuelson, *The Dalton Gang Story: Lawmen to Outlaws* (Eastford, CT: Shooting Star Press, 1992), 137–48. During December 1897 the Longview Rifles, an officer and eighteen men, guarded the county jail to stop a "rescue" by the "friends" of Nite, the "bank robber, pending his trial." *RAGST* for 1897–98, p. 4. See also Capt. R. B. Levy to Mabry, Dec. 26, 1897, typed transcript of message, RC-WP.

17. McDonald to Wozencraft, Aug. 4, 1898, Aug. 5, 1898 (first quotation), Aug. 9, 1898 (second quotation), GC-AGR; MRCB for Aug. 1898, RR-AGR.

18. McDonald to Culberson, Aug. 5, 1898, GR.

19. Crane to Culberson, Dec. 17, 1898 (first quotation), Gillaspie to ibid., Sept. 29, 1898, Oct. 13, 1898, Nov. 27, 1898, GR; Culberson to Gillaspie, Sept. 28, 1898, Sept. 30, 1898, Oct. 12, 1898, Oct. 14, 1898, ibid. to Thomas, Nov. 30, 1898, Dec. 5, 1898, Dec. 20, 1898, Dec. 21, 1898 (second quotation), Letter Press Book, GR.

20. Galveston *Daily News*, Jan. 19, 1899, Jan. 20, 1899; McDonald to Wozencraft, Jan. 17, 1899 (quotation), original telegram, RC-WP; MRCB for Jan.

1899, RR-AGR. Later that year a businessman and president of the Galveston Athletic Association asked the governor to approve a contest with boxing gloves to aid the victims of a flood. Charles Davis to Sayers, July 15, 1899, GR. At the start of 1901, a prizefight between Choynski and Jack Johnson in Galveston came to an end in an unusual way. One fighter not only went down in the early rounds, but also Ranger Captain Brooks entered the ring and arrested the pugilists. This happened after local police failed to intervene. Brooks to Scurry, Feb. 25, 1901, Attorney John Lovejoy to Sayers, Feb. 27, 1901, Mar. 5, 1901, Mar. 8, 1901, Mar. 9, 1901, Mar. 10, 1901, May 28, 1901, June 9, 1901, GR. Rangers, as well as military forces, also helped to maintain order and assist residents after the disastrous hurricane which struck Galveston in 1900. *RAGST* for 1899–1900, pp. 10–11, 25; Scurry to Sayers, Sept. 11, 1900, Sieker to ibid., Oct. 8, 1900, GR.

21. S. W. Blunt to Sayers, June 4, 1900, District Judge to ibid., Aug. 29, 1900, W. C. Donley to ibid., Sept. 7, 1900, Attorney G. C. Greer to ibid., June 3, 1900 (letter and telegram), June 4, 1900 (quotation), Scurry to ibid., June 7–8, 1900, GR; MRCB for June, July, and Aug. 1900 (reports by Bates included), RR-AGR; *RAGST* for 1899–1900, pp. 10, 23, 25. In early 1900 McDonald went to Hunt County to investigate the stealing of cattle. Sheriff R. Patton of Hunt Co. to McDonald, Feb. 26, 1900, McDonald to Scurry, Feb. 28, 1900, Mar. 3, 1900, GC-AGR. In late 1900 state officials learned about partisan politics and racial attacks on blacks in Grimes County. Sheriff G. L. Scott of Grimes County to Sayers, Oct. 1, 1900, Deputy Sheriff J. H. Scott to ibid., Oct. 11, 1900, GR.

22. McDonald to Mabry, Mar. 4, 1897, Apr. 11, 1898, ibid. to Scurry, Feb. 6, 1899, Mar. 19, 1899, Apr. 2, 1899, July 22, 1899, Mar. 4, 1900 (two letters), Mar. 6, 1900, Mar. 11, 1900, Mar. 19, 1900, Apr. 5, 1900, May 18, 1901, June 3, 1901, GC-AGR; MRCB from Jan. 1897 to July 1901, with first quotation in July 1898, RR-AGR; Scurry to McDonald, Aug. 27, 1900 (last quotations), LPG-AG-AGR. Special Order #3, which dealt with Special Rangers, was issued by Adjutant General Scurry, with the authority of the governor, on February 10, 1899. These regulations were similar to the previously mentioned rules of 1891. Scurry especially pointed out that the authority of a Special Ranger would be revoked for unbecoming conduct, drunkenness, unnecessary show of authority, and performing duties without just cause. See GC-AGR. Early in 1899 McDonald submitted some names for appointments as Special Rangers, including former Ranger Captain Arrington and two former members of Company B, Forest Edwards and Oliver Perry. McDonald to Scurry, Feb. 25, 1899, Feb. 26, 1899, GC-AGR. In 1899 Adjutant General Scurry received requests from the Panhandle to appoint former Sergeant Sullivan a Special Ranger. He replied that he would not do this, as Sullivan had been "discharged" for "insubordination" and "intemperance." Scurry to McDonald, Dec. 7, 1899 (quotations), Dec. 11, 1899, LPB-AG-AGR.

23. For a description of the extradition process with Mexico, see P. Clayton to Sayers, June 5, 1899, June 12, 1899, GR.

24. Acting Secretary, Department of State, to Culberson, Jan. 28, 1895, Feb. 6, 1895, Brice requisition papers (Mar. 1898), Folder 102, Box 301-160, GR; Culberson to Department of State, Jan. 21, 1895, ibid. to McDonald, Jan. 21, 1895, W. F. Bowman, private secretary, to ibid., early Mar. 1895, Mar. 29, 1895, Sept. 22, 1895, Letter Press Book, GR; MRCB for Jan. 1895 (quotation), RR-AGR.

25. Scurry to McDonald, Mar. 9, 1900, LPB-AG-AGR.

26 Diana J. Kleiner, "Orange, Texas," in *New Handbook of Texas*, IV, 1160–61; Alan S. Mason, "Orange County," in ibid., IV, 1161–62.

27. Austin *Statesman*, Aug. 19, 1899, Aug. 20, 1899; Sheriff P. F. Eastin, Orange County, et al. to Sayers, Aug. 18, 1899 (quotations), GR; Paine, *McDonald*, 260–61; *RAGST* for 1899–1900, pp. 9–10, 22–23. Whitecapping was a virulent form of local violence aimed at white ne'er-do-wells, blacks, and Spanish-Mexicans in the late nineteenth and early twentieth centuries.

28. "Report of Conditions at Orange, Texas," Oct. 11, 1899, GR. Key documents will be attached to Adjutant General Scurry's report to the governor.

29. Ibid. A lawyer recommended that at "least two rangers" should be kept at Orange for "several months." They would help in stopping a "veritable reign of terror." C. A. Teagle to Sayers, Aug. 21, 1899, GR.

30. Sheriff Eastin and County Judge George F. Poole to Sayers, Sept. 18, 1899 (quotation), Teagle to Hon. J. M. Browning, Sept. 19, 1899, GR.

31. Scurry to McDonald, Sept. 20, 1899, Sept. 21, 1899, LPB-AG-AGR.

32. MRCB for Sept. 1899, RR-AGR.

33. Ibid. for Oct. 1899, RR-AGR.

34. McDonald to Scurry, Oct. 2, 1899, GC-AGR.

35. Ibid., Oct. 14, 1899, GC-AGR; MRCB for Oct. 1899, RR-AGR. McDonald told the governor about the doings of Judge Poole, the county attorney, and the sheriff that hindered the investigation and prosecution of criminals. Due to this state of affairs, the Ranger captain did not make complaint against two men who were arrested. The sheriff asked the governor about the length of time he could hold those arrested without a complaint being made. The governor replied by saying that the complaint should be made out immediately and a warrant obtained. Eastin to Sayers, Oct. 6, 1899, McDonald to ibid., Oct. 6, 1899, GR.

36. "Report of Conditions at Orange, Texas," Oct. 11, 1899, GR.

37. Houston *Post*, Oct. 1, 1899.

38. McDonald to Capt. Phelps, Nov. 26, 1899, ibid. to Scurry, Nov. 9, 1899, GC-AGR; MRCB for Nov. and Dec. 1899, RR-AGR; Scurry to McDonald, Dec. 6, 1899, Dec. 7, 1899, Dec. 9, 1899, Dec. 11, 1899, LPB-AG-AGR.

39. MRCB from Jan. 1900 through June 1901, RR-AGR.

40. Fuller to Scurry, May 1, 1900, GC-AGR; MRCB for June 1899, RR-AGR; *RAGST* for 1899–1900, p. 23 (quotation).

41. Austin *Statesman*, Dec. 22, 1899, Dec. 24, 1899; Galveston *Daily News*, Dec. 22, 1899; MRCB for Dec. 1899 (quotation), Jan. 1900, Apr. 1900, RR-AGR; Paine, *McDonald*, 261; *RAGST* for 1899–1900, Appendix, 33; Scurry to McCauley, Dec. 21, 1899, Dec. 24, 1899; Scurry to McDonald, Dec. 25, 1899, Dec. 26, 1899, Dec. 29, 1899, Jan. 4, 1900, Jan. 11, 1900, Feb. 23, 1900, Mar. 17, 1900, Mar. 26, 1900, Phelps to McDonald, Dec. 22, 1899, LPB-AG-AGR.

42. McDonald to Scurry, Apr. 12, 1900, GC-AGR; Scurry to McDonald, Dec. 29, 1899, LPB-AG-AGR.

43. Galveston *Daily News*, Oct. 17, 1900; Houston *Post*, Oct. 16, 1900 (quotation); MRCB for Oct. 1900, RR-AGR; Paine, *McDonald*, 261–62; *RAGST* for 1899-1900, pp. 23, Appendix, 33; Sterling, *Trails and Trials of a Texas Ranger*, 339.

44. MRCB for Oct. 1900, RR-AGR. George H. Poole had several scrapes with the law. Officials in Orange County tried to extradite him from Louisiana in 1896 and 1898 for burglary of two different dwellings and from Missouri in 1899 for filing a forged instrument. In the case in 1898 Samuel Poole was an accomplice. Secretary of State, Extradition Papers, Box 2-10/407. See also Sheriff Eastin to Private Secretary Cravens, Dec. 3, 1899, Office of the Sheriff, Orange County (with expense attachments) to Sayers, Dec. 21, 1899, GR. At one point McDonald reported to his superiors that Judge Poole lost the case files on George Poole. The Ranger captain thought that this was in line with the judge's "way of doing business." McDonald to Scurry, Apr. 18, 1900, GC-AGR.

45. Sterling, *Trails and Trials of a Texas Ranger*, 339.

46. Utley, *Lone Star Justice*, 272. On October 17, 1900, McDonald and Saxon took Fuller's body, with the coffin and other expenses paid for by the state, to Fulshear, Texas, for burial. In time, his financial debts (nearly sixty-five dollars) were handled by the central office of the Frontier Battalion. His unpaid salary and other monies covered the debts. MRCB for Oct. 1900, RR-AGR; Scurry to McDonald, Oct. 16, 1900, LPB-AG-AGR; Sieker to McCauley, Jan. 22, 1901, Jan. 23, 1901, Feb. 6, 1901, LPB-Q-RR-AGR.

47. Lieut. Gov. J. N. Browning to District Attorney W. L. Douglas, Oct. 18, 1900, Letter Press Book, GR; Douglas to Browning, Oct. 20, 1900 (quotations), GR; Scurry to McDonald, Oct. 26, 1900, LPB-AG-AGR.

48. Criminal Minutes, District Court, Orange County, Vol. J, pp. 17, 21. The records showed that in early 1902 a case against George H. Poole was dismissed for lack of evidence. Ibid., Vol. J, p. 53.

49. Utley, *Lone Star Justice*, 272 (quotation).

50. MRCB for Nov. 1899, RR-AGR.

51. McDonald to Scurry, Nov. 22, 1899, GC-AGR.

52. Ibid., May 8, 1900 (quotation), GC-AGR; MRCB for May 1900, RR-AGR.

53. McDonald to Scurry, Apr. 12, 1900, GC-AGR.

54. Ibid., Mar. 4, 1900, Mar. 6, 1900, Mar. 11, 1900, May 21, 1900 (first quotation), May 22, 1900 (second quotation), May 28, 1900, May 31, 1900, GC-

AGR; Amarillo *Weekly News*, June 8, 1900; MRCB for Mar., May, and Dec. 1900, RR-AGR. The Ranger records contain a poster about a mass meeting in Memphis in Hall County on May 29, 1900 to consider statements by McDonald against the "good people of Hall County" and pass resolutions denouncing such remarks. See GC-AGR. In December 1900, the battalion quartermaster sent a warrant to McDonald to pay for a judgment against Saxon. Sieker to McDonald, Dec. 4, 1900, LPB-Q-RR-AGR.

55. J. B. Daniel to Sayers, June 6, 1900, GR.

56. Executive Board, Pardons and Remissions, State Department, Pardon Register, S. W. T. Lanham (1899–1900), Reel 3490, p. 588.

57. MRCB for Apr. 1901, RR-AGR; Scurry to McDonald, Apr. 5, 1901, LPB-AG-AGR.

58. Presiding Judge W. L. Davidson to Sayers, Feb. 11, 1901, GR; Scurry to McDonald, Feb. 16, 1901, LPB-AG-AGR.

59. T. S. Smith to Sayers, May 24, 1900, GC-AGR. See also ibid., May 25, 1900, GR.

60. Haley, *Jeff Milton*, 49–54, 88–92.

61. *Report of the Adjutant-General of the State of Texas, Dec. 31, 1882*, pp. 27–28.

62. King to Lieut. George H. Schmitt, Co. C, Jan. 4, 1884, LPB-AG-AGR.

63. Amarillo *Weekly News*, June 8, 1900.

64. McDonald to Scurry, May 28, 1900, GC-AGR.

65. Smith to ibid., May 25, 1900, GC-AGR.

66. *RAGST* for 1899–1900, Appendix, 127–30, with quotations on p. 130.

67. Scurry to McDonald, July 3, 1900, Aug. 27, 1900, LPB-AG-AGR; Special Orders, Ledger 401-1013, 1897–1901, p. 104, RR-AGR.

68. Monthly Returns of Co. C from July 1900 through June 1901, RR-AGR.

69. Ibid., Jan. 1901, RR-AGR.

70. McDonald to Scurry, Mar. 19, 1900, Apr. 5, 1900, May 27, 1901, June 3, 1901, GC-AGR; MRCB for Mar. 1900, RR-AGR; Scurry to McCauley, Feb. 25, 1901, LPB-AG-AGR.

71. *RAGST* for 1899–1900, p. 27.

72. As the end of the Frontier Battalion drew near, McDonald had an accident. He was riding in a carriage with his wife. The horse became "unmanageable" and both were thrown to the ground and bruised. The Ranger captain's hip was "hurt" the worst. McDonald to Scurry, June 10, 1901 (quotations), June 21, 1901, GC-AGR. For the steadfast opposition of Governor Sayers to holding prizefights, see Sayers to John Lovejoy, Mar. 1, 1901, Mar. 3, 1901, Mar. 6, 1901, Mar. 8, 1901, June 6, 1901, ibid. to Scurry, Feb. 22, 1901, Letter Press Book, GR. Aficionados of the Wild West will be interested in the service of James B. "Deacon" Miller as a Special Ranger attached to Company B. Miller served in this capacity from the end of August 1898 to the close of February 1899. McDonald to Scurry, Feb. 25, 1899, Feb. 26, 1899, Mar. 4, 1900, GC-

AGR; MRCB for Feb. 1899, RR-AGR; Muster and Pay Rolls, Co. B, Box 401-749, AGR; Service Records, Box 401-164, AGR; Scurry to McDonald, Feb. 27, 1900, LPB-AG-AGR.

CHAPTER 11: FORMING A NEW RANGER FORCE

1. McDonald to Hulen, Feb. 19, 1904, GC-AGR.

2. *General Laws of the State of Texas, Passed at the Regular Session of the Twenty-Seventh Legislature, Convened at the City of Austin, January 8, 1901, and Adjourned April 9, 1901* (Austin: State Printers, 1901), 41–43, with quotations on p. 41.

3. *RAGST* for 1901–1902, Appendix, 126–27. For other copies of this order, see General Order No. 62, July 3, 1901, Ledger 401-984, p. 651, RC-RR-AGR; and ibid., RC-WP. Section 10 of the legislative act detailed the amounts of rations and forage.

4. *General Laws of the State of Texas*, 1901, pp. 42–43; *RAGST* for 1901–1902, Appendix, 127–28, with quotations on p. 128.

5. *RAGST* for 1901–1902, pp. 28–30, Appendix, 128–29.

6. Muster and Pay Rolls, Co. B, from July 9, 1901 to the end of July 1903, AGR; MRCB for July 1901, RR-AGR.

7. Calvert and De León, *History of Texas*, 215–89; Campbell, *Gone to Texas*, 324–48.

8. McDonald to Scurry, Nov. 10, 1901, Jan. 10, 1902, Jan. 14, 1902, Feb. 1, 1902, Mar. 20, 1902, Mar. 31, 1902, Aug. 17, 1902, Aug. 19, 1902, GC-AGR; MRCB from July 1901 through Dec. 1902, RR-AGR; *RAGST* for 1901–1902, Appendix, 40. Opposition to the operations of the Rangers in the Panhandle still existed. And Captain McDonald still viewed these people as the "ones that stand in with the lawless element." McDonald to Scurry, Aug. 24, 1902, GC-AGR.

9. County Judge V. E. Middlebrook to Sayers, July 27, 1901, GR.

10. Ibid., July 28, 1901, Aug. 5, 1901, Wozencraft to Sayers, July 29, 1901 (quotation), July 30, 1901, GR; MRCB for July and Aug. 1901, RR-AGR; *RAGST* for 1901–1902, p. 32; Scurry to McDonald, July 27, 1901, LPB-AG-AGR.

11. MRCB for Mar. 1902, RR-AGR.

12. Ibid. for Aug. 1902, RR-AGR.

13. Ibid. for Sept. 1902, RR-AGR; *RAGST* for 1903–1904, Appendix, 156 (quotation).

14. MRCB for Oct. 1902, RR-AGR; *RAGST* for 1903–1904, Appendix, 156 (quotation).

15. Scurry to McDonald, Feb. 28, 1902, LPB-AG-AGR.

16. Ibid. to Sayers, Mar. 7, 1902, GR.

17 MRCB for Mar. 1902, RR-AGR.

18. *RAGST* for 1901–1902, p. 33. McDonald's official biographer told a story about the Ranger captain and his small detachment meeting a mob on the street in the town. In an exchange of words both sides realized that a fight would be unequal: five Rangers versus four hundred men. McDonald was ready for a showdown. But the leader of the mob said, "I think these Rangers are all right. Let's all have a drink!" Paine, *McDonald*, 262–64, with quotation on p. 264.

19. McDonald to Scurry, Aug. 17, 1902 (quotations), Aug. 19, 1902, GC-AGR; MRCB for July 1902, RR-AGR; Scurry to McDonald, Aug. 16, 1902, Aug. 19, 1902, LPB-AG-AGR.

20. McDonald to Scurry, Aug. 19, 1902 (quotations), GC-AGR; Muster and Pay Rolls for Sept. 1902, AGR. In 1902 McDonald had to house prisoners who committed crimes in Hutchison County in safe jails outside the county lines. Some judicial officials in Hutchison County supported this effort, while other officers opposed the Ranger captain. McDonald to Scurry, Feb. 1, 1902, GC-AGR; Scurry to McDonald, Jan. 29, 1902, Feb. 3, 1902, LPB-AG-AGR.

21. McDonald to Scurry, Aug. 19, 1902 (quotation), GC-AGR; Scurry to McDonald, Aug. 16, 1902, LPB-AG-AGR.

22. Arnoldo De León, "The Tejano Experience in Six Texas Regions," *WTHAYB* 65 (1989): 36–49.

23. Elmer Kelton, *Jericho's Road* (New York: Forge, 2004), 15.

24. A brief look at the doings of Cortez will be found in Cynthia E. Orozco, "Cortez Lira, Gregorio," in *New Handbook of Texas*, II, 342–43. For a more detailed account of the Cortez affair, see Richard J. Mertz, " 'No One Can Arrest Me': The Story of Gregorio Cortez," *Journal of South Texas* 1 (1974): 1–17.

25. Américo Paredes, *"With His Pistol in His Hand": A Border Ballad and Its Hero* (Austin: University of Texas Press, 1958), 171–72.

26. Utley, *Lone Star Justice*, 275.

27. MRCB for Sept. 1902 (quotations), RR-AGR; *RAGST* for 1901–1902, p. 34. More records on the Cortez affair will be found in the papers of the governor than in the records of the adjutant general. More than one individual requested that the governor send Rangers to stop mob rule. A Tejano organization even asked that the Rangers be dispatched to aid local officers in keeping Cortez in "safe custody." This petition from Laredo, with seventy-five names, and a covering letter dated Sept. 11, 1901, will be found in GR.

28. Scurry to Sayers, report plus attachments, Nov. 11, 1902, GR.

29. *RAGST* for 1901–1902, pp. 33–34; Spellman, *Captain J. A. Brooks*, 138–50; Utley, *Lone Star Justice*, 275–77; William V., Wilkinson, "Lawlessness in Cameron County and the City of Brownsville: 1900 to 1912," in *More Studies in Brownsville History*, ed. Milo Kearney (Brownsville, TX: Pan American University at Brownsville, 1989), 295–304. See also Laura Caldwell, "Baker,

Anderson Yancey," in *New Handbook of Texas*, I, 342–43; Juan O. Sanchez, "Cerda, Alfredo De La," in ibid., II, 21–22; and Sterling, *Trails and Trials of a Texas Ranger*, 321–25.

30. Sayers to Scurry, Oct. 27, 1902, Letter Press Book, GR. See also ibid. to Cecil Lyon, Oct. 27, 1902, ibid., GR.

31. Scurry to Sayers, Nov. 11, 1902, GR. Baker was acquitted of the killings of the Cerda brothers. This violence made people believe that Baker "bore a charmed life." Sterling, *Trails and Trials of a Texas Ranger*, 323.

32. *RAGST* for the Years 1903 and 1904, App., 154, 156, 160, 162; Scurry to Sayers, Nov. 12, 1902 (quotations), GR. A lawyer informed the governor that he opposed the move of Captain Hughes and Company D from West Texas. W. W. Turney to Sayers, Nov. 5, 1902, GR. Prominent individuals in South Texas requested that the governor keep Brooks and his Rangers in Cameron County. Robert Kleberg, John Kenedy, and John B. Armstrong to Sayers, Nov. 8, 1902, Judge Stanley Welch to ibid., Nov. 8, 1902, GR.

33. McDonald to Edward M. House, Dec. 6, 1902, Dec. 15, 1902, Jan. 29, 1903, Feb. 13, 1903, TCHC, Microfilm roll 112A, No. 7. McDonald penned additional letters to House about Texas affairs at the turn of the century. Ibid., Oct. 19, 1896, Dec. 5, 1898, Dec. 30, 1898.

34. Sayers to W. W. Turney, Nov. 8, 1902, Letter Press Book, GR.

35. MRCB for Dec. 1902, RR-AGR.

36. Scurry to McDonald, Nov. 29, 1902, Dec. 2, 1902, Dec. 22, 1902, LPB-AG-AGR.

37. Hulen to McDonald, Sept. 5, 1903, Sept. 8, 1903, Sept. 21, 1903, McDonald to Hulen, June 6, 1903, Sept. 11, 1903, Sept. 19, 1903, Sept. 25, 1903, Oct. 1, 1903, Nov. 12, 1903, Dec. 13, 1903, ibid. to Scurry, May 24, 1903, Phelps to McDonald July 11, 1903, GC-AGR; MRCB from Jan. through Dec. 1903, RR-AGR; *RAGST* for the Years 1903 and 1904, Appendix, 156–58, with quotations on p. 157. At the start of 1903, the adjutant general informed McDonald that an inventory, to be made out in duplicate, of all state property in the possession of Company B must be filed with his office by state law. Scurry to McDonald, Jan. 22, 1903, LPB-AG-AGR. McDonald traveled from Texas to Mangum in the Oklahoma Territory in early 1903 to testify at the trial of several individuals charged with stealing his horses. The Ranger captain had trailed the thieves, notorious for their activities along the Texas-Oklahoma border, and the result was that they were sent to the penitentiary. McDonald to Hulen, Sept. 3, 1903, ibid. to Scurry, Feb. 16, 1903, ibid. to Sieker, Sept. 1, 1903, GC-AGR; *RAGST* for the Years 1903 and 1904, Appendix, 156. In the middle of 1903 in the coal fields at Thurber, Rangers from Captain Rogers' company entered that area during labor-management troubles. At one point in the labor dispute the local sheriff requested that McDonald be sent to Thurber to "look the situation over," since the Ranger captain was "acquainted with the town and conditions" there. Mark Creswell, sheriff of Erath County, to Gov. Lanham,

Sept. 1, 1903, GC-AGR. At the end of December 1903, McDonald learned that Private Bean killed a black porter during a scuffle at El Paso. The Ranger was hit over the head with a poker by the black man; Bean, in turn, took the life of his assailant. Placed under bond, the Ranger was acquitted in court. The position of justifiable homicide was supported in the records by those at the scene. McCauley to McDonald, Dec. 30, 1903, McDonald to Hulen, Dec. 31, 1903, GC-AGR; *RAGST* for the Years 1903 and 1904, Appendix, 158.

38. Paine, *McDonald*, 266.

39. McDonald to Hulen, Mar. 17, 1904, Mar. 19, 1904, Apr. 4, 1904 (quotation), Oct. 3, 1904, Phelps to McDonald, Apr. 6, 1904, H. L. Robb, county attorney of Trinity County, to ibid., Nov. 10, 1904, GC-AGR.

40. Galveston *Daily News*, Dec. 5, 1903, Dec. 15, 1903, Dec. 17, 1903; McDonald to Hulen, Dec. 25, 1903 (all quotations except second), Jan. 30, 1904, Mar. 4, 1904, Mar. 19, 1904, Mar. 29, 1904, Apr. 4, 1904, June 16, 1904, Sept. 28, 1904, Oct. 3, 1904, Mar. 28, 1905, Aug. 29, 1905, GC-AGR; MRCB for Dec. 1903 and Jan., Feb., Mar. 1904, RR-AGR; Paine, *McDonald*, 266–67; *RAGST* for the Years 1903 and 1904, Appendix, 158 (second quotation).

41. Phelps to McDonald, Dec. 29, 1903, GC-AGR.

42. For the confession of Albert Angle, see Paine, *McDonald*, 267–71.

43. McDonald to Hulen, Feb. 14, 1904, GC-AGR.

44. Ibid., Jan. 31, 1904, Feb. 6, 1904, Feb. 8, 1904, Feb. 14, 1904, Feb. 19, 1904, Mar. 4, 1904, Mar. 12, 1904, Apr. 4, 1904, Apr. 15, 1904, Aug. 6, 1904, Phelps to McDonald, Apr. 6, 1904, GC-AGR; MRCB for Feb., Mar., Apr., and Aug. 1904, RR-AGR; Paine, *McDonald*, 270; *RAGST* for the Years 1903 and 1904, Appendix, 158.

45. Conduct Register, No. 24625, State Penitentiary, Huntsville, Texas; Convict Record of the Texas State Penitentiaries, Book H, Archives Division, Texas State Library, Austin, Texas.

46. Morris to Lanham, Mar. 24, 1904 (misfiled in Oct. folder), GR.

47. Ibid., Apr. 18, 1904 (quotation and misfiled in Oct. folder), GR; McDonald to Hulen, Apr. 15, 1904, GC-AGR.

48. McDonald to Hulen, Oct. 3, 1904, GC-AGR; Morris to N. A. Cravens, private secretary, Oct. 11, 1904 (quotations), GR. See also Morris to Cravens, Mar. 18, 1904, Mar. 22, 1904 (misfiled), Mar. 26, 1904 (misfiled), ibid. to Lanham, Oct. 19, 1904, GR. The cases of the other defendants were dismissed for lack of evidence.

49. Morris to Cravens, Oct. 11, 1904, GR.

50. Robb to Lanham, Feb. 20, 1904, GR.

51. J. A. Elkins, county judge of Walker County, to ibid., Jan. 12, 1904, GR.

52. Hayne Nelms to ibid., Apr. 2, 1904, GR.

53. McDonald to Hulen, June 16, 1904, GC-AGR.

54. Ibid., May 5, 1904, July 26, 1904, July 28, 1904, Aug. 29, 1904, Dec. 29, 1904, McCauley to McDonald, Nov. 28, 1904, GC-AGR; MRCB from Jan. 1904 through Dec. 1904, RR-AGR; *RAGST* for the Years 1903 and 1904, Appendix, 158–59.

55. McDonald to Hulen, Mar. 4, 1904, Mar. 12, 1904, GC-AGR.

56. Ibid., May 25, 1904, GC-AGR.

57. Ibid., Sept. 19, 1904, Sept. 28, 1904 (quotations), GC-AGR.

58. Ibid., Jan. 5, 1904 (first two quotations), GC-AGR; MRCB for Jan. and July, 1904, RR-AGR; *RAGST* for the Years 1903 and 1904, Appendix, 158 (last quotation).

59. MRCB for May 1904, RR-AGR; *RAGST* for the Years 1903 and 1904, Appendix, 159 (quotation).

60. McDonald to Hulen, Mar. 29, 1904 (quotation), GC-AGR; MRCB for Mar. 1904, RR-AGR.

61. McDonald to Hulen, Oct. 3, 1904, GC-AGR.

62. Ibid., May 25, 1904, GC-AGR. An interesting point in the records dealt with blacks in East Texas "selling questions" to "teachers" involved in public education. Ibid., Dec. 11, 1904 (first quotation), Hulen to McDonald, Dec. 23, 1904, McDonald to Sieker, Sept. 6, 1904 (second quotation), GC-AGR; MRCB for Sept. 1904, RR-AGR.

63. Austin *Statesman*, Apr. 2, 1905, Apr. 3, 1905, Apr. 4, 1905, Apr. 5, 1905, Apr. 6, 1905, Apr. 7, 1905, Apr. 8, 1905. Coverage of the trip from various newspaper files will be found in Edward H. Phillips, "Teddy Roosevelt in Texas, 1905," *WTHAYB* 56 (1980): 58–67.

64. Austin *Statesman*, Apr. 9, 1905, Apr. 11, 1905; Hulen to McDonald, Apr. 1, 1905, GC-AGR; MRCB for Apr. 1905, RR-AGR; Paine, *McDonald*, 273–78. Newspapermen, Secret Service agents, and the president's secretary returned to Fort Worth, the temporary seat of government. Austin *Statesman*, Apr. 10, 1905, Apr. 11, 1905.

65. Ibid., Apr. 15, 1905 (quotation), Apr. 16, 1905; Paine, *McDonald*, 278–89. One account noted that the camp swarmed with people, horses, and dogs. The hunters left the site in the morning, went for lunch to a conveniently located chuck wagon, eating such foods as calf brains and sweetbreads, and had another chase in the evening before winding up at Camp Roosevelt, the permanent site. Austin *Statesman*, Apr. 15, 1905.

66. McDonald to Hulen, Apr. 13, 1905, GC-AGR.

67. Paine, *McDonald*, 11 (reprint of letter); Roosevelt to McDonald, Dec. 19, 1908, TCHC, Microfilm roll 112A, No. 7. McDonald wrote back, "The recollection of the wolf hunt in Oklahoma will always be a bright spot in my memory." McDonald to Roosevelt, Dec. 22, 1908, in ibid. The president's account of the events will be found in "A Wolf Hunt in Oklahoma," *Scribner's Magazine* 38 (Nov. 1905): 513–32. See also John R. Abernathy, *In Camp with Theodore Roosevelt; or The Life of John R. (Jack) Abernathy* (Oklahoma City:

Times-Journal Publishing Co., 1933); and Brian L. Smith, "Theodore Roosevelt Visits Oklahoma," *Chronicles of Oklahoma* 51 (Fall 1973): 263–79.

68. T. S. Hubbell, sheriff of Bernalillo County, New Mexico, to McDonald, Apr. 15, 1905, Hulen to Dunaway, Apr. 20, 1905, ibid, to McDonald, Jan. 4, 1905, John T. Lytle, secretary of the Cattle Raisers Association of Texas, to ibid., Aug. 1, 1905, McDonald to Hulen, Jan. 4, 1905, Feb. 28, 1905, Mar. 21, 1905, Mar. 27, 1905, Mar. 28, 1905, Apr. 13, 1905, Apr. 18, 1905, June 3, 1905, June 30, 1905, July 1, 1905, July 19, 1905, Aug. 14, 1905, Aug. 29, 1905, Sept. 4, 1905, Sept. 8, 1905, Sept. 22, 1905, Nov. 6, 1905, Nov. 7, 1905, Nov. 14, 1905, Nov. 16, 1905, Nov. 21, 1905, Sieker to McDonald, June 2, 1905, GC-AGR; MRCB from Jan. through Dec. 1905, with quotations in the Jan. report, RR-AGR.

69. McDonald to Hulen, July 1, 1905, GC-AGR.

70. Muster and Pay Rolls, Co. B, from Jan. 1905 through Aug. 1905, AGR. See also the letterhead paper dated July 5, 1905 and Nov. 14, 1905, GC-AGR.

71. McDonald to Hulen, July 5, 1905, GC-AGR.

72. Asst. Quartermaster Gen. to McDonald, Aug. 23, 1905, GC-AGR; *RAGST* for the Period Ending December 31, 1906, Appendix, 170–71.

73. MRCB from Jan. 1906 through Dec. 1906, RR-AGR.

74. Austin *Statesman*, Mar. 10, 1906.

75. Paine, *McDonald* 304–7.

CHAPTER 12: CONDITT MURDER CASE: A STUDY IN DETECTION

1. Austin *Statesman*, Oct. 12, 1905.

2. Various newspapers reported the crime. See, for example, ibid., Sept. 29, 1905, Sept. 30, 1905. See also Jackson County *Herald-Tribune*, July 6, 1998. For secondary accounts of this murder case, see Paine, *McDonald*, 290-314; and Sterling, *Trails and Trials of a Texas Ranger*, 340–47.

3. Austin *Statesman*, Oct. 1, 1905 (quotation), Oct. 2, 1905. See also Hallettsville *Herald*, Oct. 5, 1905; and Victoria *Daily Advocate*, Sept. 30, 1905. For a sketch of the life of Sheriff Egg, see Twin Centennial Committee, *Twin Centennial Commemorative History: Edna—Ganado, 1882–1982* (Edna: Texana Foundation, 1982), 43.

4. *RAGST* for the Period Ending December 31, 1906, p. 28. See also Austin *Statesman*, Oct. 3, 1905; and Special Order No. 45, Oct. 2, 1905, GC-AGR.

5. McDonald to Hulen, Oct. 4, 1905, GC-AGR. See also MRCB for Oct. 1905, RR-AGR. Captain Hughes and two Rangers from Company D accompanied the adjutant general to Edna. Days later Ranger Privates W. O. Dale and J. C. White followed. From this Ranger company, Sergeant Tom Ross also played an important role in the Conditt case. "Monthly Return of Co. D for Oct. 1905," "Monthly Return of Co. D for July 1906," RR-AGR.

6. For the history of Edna and Jackson County, see Ira T. Taylor, *The Cavalcade of Jackson County* (San Antonio: Naylor, 1938).

7. S. R. Weisiger to Edward Kilman, Sept. 26, 1965, Box 3, File 52, Sidney Roper Weisiger Collection, Victoria College, Victoria, Texas.

8. Austin *Statesman*, Oct. 4, 1905.

9. Ibid., Oct. 8, 1905, Oct. 9, 1905, Oct. 10, 1905; Victoria *Weekly Advocate*, Oct. 14, 1905.

10. MRCB for Oct. 1905, RR-AGR; Paine, *McDonald*, 298–303; Sterling, *Trails and Trials of a Texas Ranger*, 345–47. Powell was also questioned as a witness in the case. Austin *Statesman*, Oct. 14, 1905.

11. Ibid., Oct. 14, 1905; Victoria *Weekly Advocate*, Oct. 21, 1905. See also McDonald to Hulen, Oct. 18, [1905], GC-AGR. This message is filed under the year 1906. During his stay in Edna, a local newspaper reported that Captain McDonald allowed a black convict to escape. The story told was that the prisoner had been released, given a head start, and tracked by McDonald's dogs. The purpose of this exercise was to better train his animals. But the convict got away. This episode, as reported, showed poor judgment by Captain Bill. Victoria *Weekly Advocate*, Oct. 21, 1905.

12. Austin *Statesman*, Dec. 8, 1905 (quotations); MRCB for Dec. 1905, RR-AGR.

13.Houston *Post*, Dec. 11, 1905, Dec. 12, 1905, Dec. 13, 1905, Dec. 14, 1905, Dec. 15, 1905, Dec. 16, 1905, Dec. 17, 1905, Dec. 18, 1905, Dec. 19, 1905, Dec. 20, 1905, Dec. 21, 1905, Dec. 22, 1905, Dec. 24, 1905.

14. Austin *Statesman*, Dec. 24, 1905. For the questioning of Gibson by law officers at one point, see ibid., Oct. 29, 1905.

15 H. S. Crawford to Lanham, May 21, 1906, GC-AGR.

16. Adj. Gen. to Crawford, Apr. 28, 1906, ibid. to J. V. Vandenberge, July 18, 1906, ibid. to L. Ward, July 23, 1906, Crawford to Hulen, May 16, 1906, ibid. to Lanham, Apr. 20, 1906, Vandenberge to Hulen, July 7, 1906, Ward to Lanham (petition attached), July 20, 1906, GC-AGR.

17. Adj. Gen. to McDonald, Apr. 28, 1906, GC-AGR.

18. McDonald to Hulen, Mar. 12, 1906, GC-AGR. See also ibid., Apr. 13, 1906, Apr. 30, 1906, May 5, 1906, GC-AGR.

19. Ibid., received May 12, 1906 (first quotations), May 15, 1906 (second quotations), GC-AGR; MRCB for May 1906, RR-AGR.

20. MRCB for June and July 1906, RR-AGR. See also Victoria *Weekly Advocate*, June 30, 1906. For grand jury and district court actions that set various criminal charges against Diggs, Gibson, Henry Howard, Felix Powell, and Reed; that showed the change of venues in cases against these defendants; and that ordered the setting of bail for Diggs ($750), Howard ($1,500), and Reed ($750), see Criminal Minutes, District Court, Jackson County, Vol. F, pp. 573–74, 597, 614–16, 622–23, Vol. G, pp. 136–37. Felix Powell was held without bail.

21. Weisiger to Kilman, Sept. 26, 1965, Box 3, File 52, Weisiger Collection.

22. Houston *Post*, July 15, 1906. See also Galveston *Daily News*, July 8, 1906, for the various combinations of motives.

23. Of the numerous works on Victoria and Victoria County, see Roy Grimes, ed., *300 Years in Victoria County* (Victoria, TX: Victoria Advocate Pub., 1968); Robert W. Shook and Charles D. Spurlin, *Victoria: A Pictorial History* (Norfolk, VA: Donning Co., 1985); and R. W. Shook, "Year of Transition: Victoria, Texas, 1880–1920," *SHQ* 78 (Oct. 1974): 155–82.

24. Austin *Statesman*, July 24, 1906, July 25, 1906.

25. MRCB for Oct. and Nov. 1906, RR-AGR.

26. McDonald to Hulen, July 7, 1906, GC-AGR.

27. Ibid., Oct. 17, 1906, GC-AGR.

28. Houston *Post*, Dec. 6, 1906, Dec. 7, 1906, Dec. 8, 1906, Dec. 9, 1906, Dec. 11, 1906, Dec. 12, 1906, Dec. 13, 1906. See also Austin *Statesman*, Dec. 7, 1906, Dec. 8, 1906, Dec. 10, 1906; MRCB for Dec. 1906, RR-AGR; Victoria *Daily Advocate*, Dec. 8, 1906, Dec. 10, 1906, Dec. 11, 1906, Dec. 12, 1906.

29. Victoria *Daily Advocate*, Dec. 11, 1906.

30. Houston *Post*, Dec. 9, 1906.

31. Ibid., Dec. 11, 1906 (quotation); Victoria *Daily Advocate*, Dec. 10, 1906. For a look at the presentation of evidence about Powell's deformed finger at his examining hearing, see Galveston *Daily News*, July 7, 1906.

32. *Felix Powell v. State of Texas*, 99 *Southwestern Reporter* 1005 (1907); 50 *Texas Criminal Reports* 592, 597 (first quotation), 599 (second quotation) (1907); McDonald to Hulen, Dec. 12, 1906, GC-AGR.

33. Criminal Minutes, District Court, Victoria County, Vol. 13, pp. 341, 348–49; Victoria *Daily Advocate*, Mar. 2, 1907; Victoria *Weekly Advocate*, Mar. 9, 1907. For an interview of Powell in the jail, see Victoria *Weekly Advocate*, Mar. 2, 1907. See also ibid., Mar. 16, 1907.

34. Austin *Statesman*, Apr. 3, 1907; Houston *Post*, Apr. 3, 1907; Victoria *Daily Advocate*, Apr. 2, 1907.

35. See the legal opinion in Victoria *Daily Advocate*, Dec. 13, 1906.

36. Cuero *Daily Record*, June 11, 1907, June 17, 1907, June 19, 1907, June 21, 1907, June 23, 1907, June 24, 1907, June 25, 1907, June 26, 1907, June 28, 1907, July 8, 1907.

37. *Monk Gibson v. State of Texas*, 110 *Southwestern Reporter* 41 (1908); 53 *Texas Criminal Reports* 349, 372 (quotation) (1908). For some of the aspects of the Gibson case, see Victoria *Daily Advocate*, June 28, 1907, June 29, 1907; Victoria *Weekly Advocate*, May 16, 1908, May 30, 1908.

38. Cuero *Daily Record*, May 13, 1908, May 25, 1908; Victoria *Weekly Advocate*, Dec. 21, 1907, July 4, 1908 (quotation), July 11, 1908. See also Austin *Statesman*, July 12, 1908; Victoria *Daily Advocate*, June 29, 1908, July 3, 1908. For a

look at Cuero and DeWitt County, see Nellie Murphree, *A History of DeWitt County*, ed. R. W. Shook (Victoria: Graham Printing, 1962).

39. Criminal Minutes, District Court, Guadalupe County, Vol. K, p. 167 (quotation); Criminal Minutes, District Court, Jackson County, Vol. G, pp. 136–37; Criminal Minutes, District Court, Victoria County, Vol. 13, pp. 392, 416; Victoria *Daily Advocate*, Dec. 19, 1906, Mar. 18, 1909; Victoria *Weekly Advocate*, Sept. 28, 1907.

40. County Attorney W. W. McCrory to Gov. Thomas M. Campbell, Apr. 24, 1908, May 9, 1908, County Judge Guy Mitchell to ibid., May 4, 1908, GR; Jackson County *Herald-Tribune*, July 6, 1998.

41. Criminal Minutes, District Court, Jackson County, Vol. G, pp. 53–54; Cuero *Daily Record*, Nov. 1, 1907; M. C. Shelby Collection, Crimes, Tragedies, Murders, Book 5 (covers testimony of those involved); Sterling, *Trails and Trials of a Texas Ranger*, 347 (which names Warren instead of Arthur).

42. Weisiger to Kilman, Sept. 26, 1965, Box 3, File 52, Weisiger Collection.

43. Houston *Post*, July 15, 1906. This author learned about the beliefs of the descendants of the Powell family from correspondence with residents of Edna. Descendants of J. F. Conditt mentioned to this author several familial beliefs about the crime, one being that the husband committed the murders and blamed someone else.

44. Austin *Statesman*, Oct. 1, 1905.

45. Newspaper Collection—Conditt Murder, Texana Museum, Edna, Texas.

46. McDonald to Hulen, May 15, 1906, GC-AGR.

47. Victoria *Weekly Advocate* Dec. 15, 1906. Through the twentieth century newspapermen have written columns about the Conditt murders. These included Ed Kilman (Houston *Post*, Dec. 20, 1964); Bert West (Jackson County *Herald-Tribune*, July 6, 1998); and Henry Wolff (Victoria *Advocate*, Feb. 18, 1998). Pat Hathcock also has an account in the Victoria *Advocate*, Mar. 8, 2004. Another narrative of the murder case, based upon newspaper reports and including a diagram of the bloody handprint, appeared in Gary D. Hall, *Murder and Malice: Crimes of Passion from Victoria County, Texas (1891–1913)* (Austin: Nortex Publishing, 2006), 145–64.

CHAPTER 13: BROWNSVILLE AFFAIR: A MUDDLED INCIDENT

1. Austin *Statesman*, Aug. 26, 1906.

2. The basic documents about the affair have been collected in *MPUS*-1 and *MPUS*-2. Equally important would be the volumes of testimony published after the hearings by the Committee on Military Affairs of the United States Senate and by the Court of Inquiry endorsed by Congress and carried out by army officers. The historical literature on the raid and its aftermath has become extensive. Works on the presidential years of Theodore Roosevelt, as, for example, those by H. W. Brands, Edmund Morris, and Henry Pringle,

mention the incident. Histories of the Texas Rangers, such as those by Robert Utley and Walter Prescott Webb, cover the law-and-order angle. For a complete understanding of the local, state, and national aspects of the Brownsville raid, four works have become essential: Garna Christian, *Black Soldiers in Jim Crow Texas, 1899–1917* (College Station: Texas A&M University Press, 1995); Ann Lane, *The Brownsville Affair; National Crisis and Black Reaction* (Port Washington, NY: Kennikat Press, 1971); and two books by John Weaver: *The Brownsville Raid* (New York: W. W. Norton, 1970); and *The Senator and the Sharecropper's Son: Exoneration of the Brownsville Soldiers* (College Station: Texas A&M University Press, 1997). Other works of note include James Leiker, *Racial Borders: Black Soldiers Along the Rio Grande* (College Station: Texas A&M University Press, 2002); Quintard Taylor, *In Search of the Racial Frontier: African Americans in the American West, 1528–1990* (New York: W. W. Norton, 1998); James Tinsley, "The Brownsville Affray" (M.A. Thesis, University of North Carolina at Chapel Hill, 1948); and Weiss, " 'Yours to Command'." For a look at various studies of the raid, see Walter Pierce, "The Brownsville Raid: A Historiographical Assessment," in *Studies in Brownsville History*, ed. Milo Kearney (Brownsville, TX: Pan American University at Brownsville, 1986), 219–28.

3. *MPUS*-1, p. 65. This bit of phrase-making has been incorrectly attributed to Major Charles W. Penrose, commanding officer at Fort Brown. Sterling, *Trails and Trials of a Texas Ranger*, 351; and Webb, *Texas Rangers*, 467. Webb wrongly noted in another work that the phrase came from the pen of a newsman. Webb, *Story of the Texas Rangers*, 135. One newspaper printed in error in McDonald's obituary that the coiner of the "charge-hell-with-one-bucket-of-water" phrase could be either President Theodore Roosevelt or a congressman from the state of Texas. San Antonio *Express*, Jan. 16, 1918.

4. Alicia A. Garza and Christopher Long, "Brownsville, Texas," in *New Handbook of Texas*, I, 776–79; ibid., "Cameron County," in ibid., I, 918–21.

5. For examples of the typical account of the Brownsville Affray, see Austin *Statesman*, Aug. 15, 1906; Brownsville *Daily Herald*, Aug. 14, 1906; and San Antonio *Express*, Aug. 15, 1906. Histories of the fort and the black regiment will be found in Richard T. Marcum, "Fort Brown, Texas: The History of a Border Post" (Ph.D. diss., Texas Technological College, 1964); and John H. Nankivell, ed., *The History of the Twenty-Fifth Regiment, United States Infantry, 1869–1926* (Ft. Collins, CO: Old Army Press, 1972). For a more devastating raid on Brownsville and the surrounding countryside by Juan Nepomuceno Cortina in the 1850s, see Robinson, *Men Who Wear the Star*, 121–37.

6. Lane, *Brownsville Affair*, 33 (quotation). Summaries of the events in the raid and its aftermath will be found in Garna L. Christian, "Brownsville Raid," in *New Handbook of Texas*, I, 779–80; and Marvin Fletcher, *The Black Soldier and Officer in the United States Army, 1891–1917* (Columbia: University of Missouri Press, 1974), 119–52.

7. *MPUS*-1, pp. 62–63, 163–74, 177, 182–83, 291–97; *MPUS*-2, p. 198; Weaver, *Brownsville Raid*, 34–42, 162–64, 166–69.

8. Lane, *Brownsville Affair*, 6 (quotation); Tinsley, "Brownsville Affray," iii–xv.

9. Extensive coverage of these events will be found in four articles by Garna L. Christian: "The El Paso Racial Crisis of 1900," *RRVHR* 6 (Spring 1981): 28–41; "Rio Grande City: Prelude to the Brownsville Raid," *WTHAYB* 57 (1981): 118–32; "The Twenty-Fifth Regiment at Fort McIntosh: Precursor to Retaliatory Racial Violence," *WTHAYB* 55 (1979): 149–61; and "The Violent Possibility: The Tenth Cavalry at Texarkana," *ETHJ* 23 (Spring 1985): 3–15. For Christian's most recent statements about these happenings and Brownsville, see his *Black Soldiers in Jim Crow Texas*.

10. Austin *Statesman*, July 10, 1906, July 26, 1906, Aug. 16, 1906; Thomas R. Buecker, "Prelude to Brownsville: The Twenty-Fifth Infantry at Fort Niobrara, Nebraska, 1902–06," *Great Plains Quarterly* 16 (Spring 1996): 95–106; Lane, *Brownsville Affair*, 12–14; *MPUS*-1, pp. 19, 61; Weaver, *Brownsville Raid*, 18–19, with quotation on p. 19.

11. *MPUS*-1, pp. 61, 71, 116, 139–63, 165, 210; *MPUS*-2, pp. 100, 150. For a description of the saloons in the town, see *Report of the Proceedings of the Court of Inquiry* . . . , 61st Cong., 3rd Sess., Senate, Doc. No. 701, Vol. 6, pp. 1477–78.

12. Austin *Statesman*, Aug. 14, 1906; Brownsville *Daily Herald*, Aug. 13, 1906; Lane, *Brownsville Affair*, 15–17; *MPUS*-1, pp. 61–62, 68–69, 89–90 (first quotation), 113, 133–34, 222–23; *MPUS*-2, pp. 150–51, 195–97; Weaver, *Brownsville Raid*, 26–27, 29–31, 161–62.

13. Weaver, *Brownsville Raid*, 70 (quotation).

14. Paine, *McDonald*, 321.

15. *Report of the Proceedings of the Court of Inquiry* . . . , 61st Cong., 3rd Sess., Senate, Doc. No. 701, Vol. 4, p. 884.

16. Ibid., Vol. 5, pp. 1271–73. During the court-martial of Major Penrose an attempt was made to show that the "Mexican policemen of Brownsville were guilty of shooting up the town and not the negro soldiers." This charge made the news media. Austin *Statesman*. Feb. 12, 1907.

17. *Report of the Proceedings of the Court of Inquiry* . . . , 61st Cong., 3rd Sess., Senate, Doc. No. 701, Vol. 10, p. 1820.

18. Lane, *Brownsville Affair*, 16–17; *MPUS*-1, pp. 61 (quotations), 90, 113, 179–80; Weaver, *Brownsville Raid*, 27–28.

19. *The Brownsville Affray* . . . , 60th Cong., 1st Sess., Senate, Doc. No. 389, p. 105. See also Christian, *Black Soldiers in Jim Crow Texas*, 83; and Weaver, *Brownsville Raid* 260–61.

20. *Report of the Proceedings of the Court of Inquiry* . . . , 61st Cong., 3rd Sess., Senate, Doc. No. 701, Vol. 4, p. 1063 (first quotation), Vol. 5, p. 1107 (second quotation).

21. *MPUS*-1, pp. 62–63, 67–68, 75–88; *MPUS*-2, pp. 7–201.

22. *MPUS*-1, pp. 196–243.

23. Ibid., pp. 73–74, 116–17 (with quotation on p. 116), 203–04, 228, 232, 235; *Hearings before the Committee on Military Affairs, United States Senate* . . . , 60th Cong., 1st Sess., Senate, Doc. No. 402, Pt. 4, pp. 437–40, 449–54, 471–76, 480–85; Weaver, *Brownsville Raid*, 39–41, 71, 124–25, 136, 241.

24. *Report of the Proceedings of the Court of Inquiry* . . . , 61st Cong., 3rd Sess., Senate, Doc. No. 701, Vol. 6, pp. 1466–1624. A black lawyer from Texas hired to investigate the affair reported that the "soldiers were entirely to blame." Brownsville *Daily Herald*, Dec. 5, 1906.

25. For a noteworthy attempt to fix the blame for the raid on the townspeople, see Weaver, *Brownsville Raid*, 23–24, 35–38, 67, 70, 89–90, 128, 150–53, 165–66, 175–76, 186–89, 193–96, 228, 238–40, 249–78. See also Brownsville *Daily Herald*, Aug. 17, 1906, Nov. 24, 1906, Dec. 11, 1906, Dec. 15, 1906, Dec. 18, 1906; and *MPUS*-1, pp. 163–74, 204–22, 236–37. For a defense of the black soldiers by a US senator, see James B. Foraker, "A Review of the Testimony in the Brownsville Investigation," *North American Review* 187 (Apr. 1908): 550–58. Both the killing of Natus and the wounding of Paulno Preciado, a newspaperman, who received "a slight flesh wound on the left hand," will be found in the Brownsville *Daily Herald*, Aug. 14, 1906, Aug. 15, 1906; *MPUS*-1, pp. 62–63; and *MPUS*-2, pp. xv–xvi, xix (quotation), 100–7.

26. For further elaboration, see Lane, *Brownsville Affair*, 166–67; and Leiker, *Racial Borders*, 143–45.

27. *Hearings before the Committee on Military Affairs, United States Senate* . . . , 60th Cong., 1st Sess., Senate, Doc. No. 402, Pt. 6, pp. 2138–55, 2224–41, 2564–65, 3293–99; *MPUS*-1, pp. 62, 85–88; *MPUS*-2, pp. 46–47, 49, 57–65, 107–8, 144–51; Weaver, *Brownsville Raid*, 44, 48–50, 55, 57, 87, 154–56, 255, 257–58. During the two years before the raid the mayor tried to dress up the town police and instill a feeling of professionalism in the force. Weaver, *Brownsville Raid*, 43–44. Before the raid the local police department received instructions from the mayor to give the same treatment to white and black troops. *MPUS*-2, p. 149. In about a month the left-handed Dominguez returned to duty. The citizens of Brownsville raised over $200 to give to Dominguez for his brave actions. Brownsville *Daily Herald*, Sept. 11, 1906, Sept. 25, 1906, Oct. 3, 1906, Oct. 9, 1906, Nov. 2, 1906, Dec. 28, 1906.

28. Austin *Statesman*, Aug. 15, 1906, Aug. 16, 1906, Aug. 17, 1906, Aug. 18, 1906, Aug. 19, 1906; Brownsville *Daily Herald*, Aug. 14, 1906, Aug. 15, 1906; Citizens' Committee to Gov. Lanham, Aug. 15, 1906, Aug. 18, 1906, GC-AGR; *MPUS*-1, pp. 19–29, 66–71.

29. Austin *Statesman*, Aug. 15, 1906, Aug. 16, 1906, Aug. 17, 1906, Aug. 18, 1906, Aug. 19, 1906; Brownsville *Daily Herald*, Aug. 15, 1906, Aug. 16, 1906 (quotation), Aug. 17, 1906; *MPUS*-1, pp. 19–42.

30. Austin *Statesman*, Aug. 21, 1906, Aug. 22, 1906; Brownsville *Daily Herald*, Aug. 22, 1906; *MPUS*-1, pp. 19–45, with quotation on p. 39.

31. Brownsville *Daily Herald*, Aug. 18, 1906.

32. Austin *Statesman*, Aug. 15, 1906, Aug. 16, 1906, Aug. 17, 1906, Aug. 18, 1906, Aug. 19, 1906; Brownsville *Daily Herald* Aug. 18, 1906, Aug. 20, 1906, Aug. 21, 1906; County Judge John Bartlett, et al. to Adj. Gen. Hulen, Aug. 14, 1906, Hulen to Bartlett, Aug. 14, 1906, Hulen to Commanding Officer, Fort Brown, Aug. 14, 1906, Hulen to Kelly, Aug. 18, 1906, Kelly to Gov. Lanham, Aug. 17, 1906, Penrose to Adjutant General, State of Texas, Aug. 14, 1906, James B. Wells to Hulen, Aug. 20, [1906], GC-AGR; Bartlett, et al. to Lanham, Aug. 17, 1906, Wells to ibid., Aug. 20, [1906], GR. Wells called for troops or Rangers.

33. Harbert Davenport to Walter Prescott Webb, Dec. 26, 1934, Box 2M260, WP. See also Webb, *Texas Rangers*, 469.

34. *MPUS*-1, p. 88. From Harlingen, Texas, Delling wired Austin: "Have request from sheriff Brownsville for assistance trouble negro soldiers." Dulling [*sic*] to Hulen, Aug. 14, 1906, GC-AGR.

35. Austin *Statesman*, Aug. 16, 1906, Aug. 17, 1906; Brownsville *Daily Herald*, Aug. 22, 1906; McDonald, "RBO," p. 1; MRCB for Aug. 1906, RR-AGR; Paine, *McDonald*, 322–25; San Antonio *Express*, Aug. 17, 1906, Aug. 21, 1906, Aug. 22, 1906; Weaver, *Brownsville Raid*, 79–81. At the time of the raid McDonald had been serving as sergeant at arms at the state convention of the Democratic Party in Dallas, Texas. San Antonio *Express*, Aug. 18, 1906. McDonald submitted his "Report on the Brownsville Outrage" to the governor and the adjutant general at the end of August 1906. McDonald to Lanham and Hulen, Aug. 30, 1906, GC-AGR.

36. Weaver, *Brownsville Raid*, 80.

37. Procter, *Just One Riot*, 36.

38. *MPUS*-1, pp. 42–43, 61 (second quotation), 70 (first quotation), 72.

39. McDonald, "RBO," pp. 1–2, with quotations on p. 1; Weaver, *Brownsville Raid*, 81–82, 255–57. McDonald's official biographer noted that Delling and McKenzie told the Ranger captain that Spanish-Mexican residents would testify to shots being fired from the fort, that Captain Lyons' squad of black soldiers were looking for Macklin and Miller in the town after the raid, and that a black saloon closed early on the night of the violence—a "suspicious circumstance" to the Rangers (but not in light of the curfew). Paine, *McDonald*, 326–27, with quotation on p. 326.

40. McDonald, "RBO," p. 2.

41. Paine, *McDonald*, 327–28, with quotation on p. 328. See also Procter, *Just One Riot*, 37–38; and Weaver, *Brownsville Raid*, 82.

42. McDonald to US Senator C. A. Culberson, Dec. 15, 1906, GC-AGR; ibid., "RBO," pp. 2–4, with quotation about Askew on p. 3 and quotation about Macklin on p. 4; Paine, *McDonald*, 329–38; Weaver, *Brownsville Raid*, 82–83. Culberson had requested a report on the raid from McDonald. He wanted a "brief and clear statement" of the evidence McDonald had of the "guilt of the negro soldiers." Culberson to Lanham, Dec. 7, 1906, Hulen to McDonald, Dec. 7, 1906, GC-AGR. Paine's account is marred by flowery

phrases to describe McDonald's performance: "fox," "ears alert," "nose sharp," "eyes needle-pointed," and "X-ray eyes." Paine, *McDonald*, 330, 333. A black sergeant testified at another time that he saw Askew inside Fort Brown before the firing had stopped on August 13. *MPUS*-1, p. 116.

43. McDonald, "RBO," pp. 4–5, with all quotations on p. 5. If Allison and Hollomon were the ringleaders, they went against a basic desire: to protect their financial interest in their saloon. Weaver, *Brownsville Raid*, 241.

44. McDonald, "RBO," p. 5 (quotation); Weaver, *Brownsville Raid*, 81–82.

45. Austin *Statesman*, Aug. 24, 1906; Brownsville *Daily Herald*, Aug. 23, 1906; McDonald to Culberson, Dec. 15, 1906, GC-AGR; *MPUS*-1, pp. 64, 73–75, 169, 175–77, 216 (quotation), 232, 457–58; MRCB for Aug. 1906, RR-AGR; Tinsley, "Brownsville Affray," 32–33; Weaver, *Brownsville Raid*, 27–28, 37–39, 65, 71, 116, 157–60, 238–41. McDonald's official biographer had the twelve arrested soldiers coming from Company B. Paine, *McDonald*, 338.

46. McDonald to Culberson, Dec. 15, 1906, GC-AGR.

47. Ibid. to Hulen, Aug. 23, 1906, GC-AGR.

48. *MPUS*-1, pp. 46, 56 (first quotation), 61, 64, 66 (second quotation); Paine, *McDonald*, 338–40; Weaver, *Brownsville Raid*, 83–84. McDonald's official biographer again had Captain Bill in an armed confrontation with the military guard at the entrance to the fort. Paine, *McDonald*, 338–39.

49. Anders, *Boss Rule in South Texas*, 128. At one point McDonald told the governor that Penrose and another official "admitted we had six of the right men but the others were not in it . . . ." McDonald to Lanham, Aug. 25, 1906, GR.

50. *MPUS*-1, pp. 47–49.

51. Ibid., pp. 49–53 (quotation on pp. 50–51), 100–1.

52. McDonald, "RBO," p. 9 (quotation); Paine, *McDonald*, 341–42. Blocksom and Penrose recognized that McDonald got information about military matters through a "leak in the telegraph office." *MPUS*-1, pp. 103–4.

53. McDonald, "RBO," p. 9 (quotation); Paine, *McDonald*, 342.

54. *MPUS*-1, pp. 102–3; Paine, *McDonald*, 344–46. The War Department sought clarification of Penrose's disobeying orders. *MPUS*-1, pp. 99–100. Previously Captain Preston had been sent by Penrose to see Judge Welch about the "safety" and "fair trial" for the black soldiers under arrest if left at the fort. The judge noted that "he could insure a fair trial, but as to safety, he was not prepared to say." McDonald was present. Ibid., p. 102.

55. Ibid., pp. 102, 104; Brownsville *Daily Herald*, Aug. 25, 1906; McDonald, "RBO," p. 9 (quotation).

56. Brownsville *Daily Herald*, Aug. 25, 1906; McDonald, "RBO," p. 10; *MPUS*-1, p. 70 (quotations). Major Penrose told Sheriff Garza late in the evening that he could not surrender the prisoners to him either. This event when reported surprised the War Department. *MPUS*-1. pp. 65, 70, 97–98, 103.

57. Brownsville *Daily Herald*, Aug. 25, 1906; McDonald, "RBO," p. 10 (quotation); Paine, *McDonald*, 346–47.

58. Austin *Statesman*, Aug. 25, 1906, Aug. 26, 1906; Brownsville *Daily Herald*, Aug. 25, 1906; San Antonio *Express*, Aug. 25, 1906.

59. Austin *Statesman*, Aug. 26, 1906 (quotation); McCaskey to Lanham, Aug. 25, [1906], GR.

60. *MPUS*-1, p. 103.

61. Ibid., p. 65.

62. Brownsville *Daily Herald*, Aug. 25, 1906; McDonald to Lanham and Hulen, [Aug.] 24, [1906] (quotation), GR. McDonald also telegraphed US Senator J. W. Bailey about the removal of the prisoners and his call for assistance from the governor. Brownsville *Daily Herald*, Aug. 25, 1906.

63. *MPUS*-1, p. 104.

64. Austin *Statesman*, Aug. 26, 1906 (second quotation), Mar. 10, 1907 (first quotation); Brownsville *Daily Herald*, Aug. 25, 1906; Paine, *McDonald*, 344, 354–55; Weaver, *Brownsville Raid*, 86.

65. Paine, *McDonald*, 343, 348–49; Weaver, *Brownsville Raid*, 86.

66. Anders, *Boss Rule in South Texas*, 128–29.

67. For the irony in the situation in Brownsville, see Weaver, *Brownsville Raid*, 85.

68. Brownsville *Daily Herald*, Aug. 25, 1906 (quotation); McDonald to Lanham, Aug. 25, 1906, GR.

69. McDonald to Lanham and Hulen, Aug. 30, 1906, GC-AGR; ibid., "RBO," p. 6; *MPUS*-1, p. 65; Paine, *McDonald*, 347–55; San Antonio *Express*, Aug. 25, 1906; Weaver, *Brownsville Raid*, 86.

70. Paine, *McDonald*, 351.

71. Ibid., 354; Brownsville *Daily Herald*, Aug. 25, 1906; Lanham to McDonald, Aug. 24, 1906 (quotation), Letter Press Book, GR; McDonald, "RB0," p. 6.

72. McDonald, "RBO," p. 6.

73. Ibid. See also MRCB for Aug. 1906, RR-AGR.

74. Brownsville *Daily Herald*, Aug. 25, 1906; *MPUS*-1, pp. 53–54; MRCB for Aug. 1906, RR-AGR; Weaver, *Brownsville Raid*, 87.

75. *MPUS*-1, p. 55.

76. Ibid., pp. 54–58, with quotations on p. 58; Brownsville *Daily Herald*, Aug. 28, 1906.

77. *MPUS*-1, p. 59.

78. Ibid., pp. 107–8; Asst. Adj. Gen. to McDonald, Sept. 3, 1906, McDonald to E. M. Phelps, Sept. 11, 1906, GC-AGR; Austin *Statesman*, Oct. 2, 1906 (quotation); Brownsville *Daily Herald*, Sept. 4, 1906, Sept. 28, 1906, Oct. 2, 1906; Paine, *McDonald*, 355–59, n.; Weaver, *Brownsville Raid*, 91–92.

79. Austin *Statesman*, Nov. 8, 1906 (quotation); MPUS-1, pp. 178–85; Tinsley, "Brownsville Affray," 39. For reports of these happenings in a local newspaper,

see Brownsville *Daily Herald*, Oct. 19, 1906, Nov. 7, 1906, Nov. 8, 1906, Nov. 12, 1906, Nov. 14, 1906. The differences between a discharge without honor and a dishonorable discharge will be found in Weaver, *Brownsville Raid*, 133–34. For what happened to Allison in the years after the raid, see ibid., 252–54.

80. Coverage of the happenings between the president and Congress, besides the histories of Roosevelt's presidency and the works by Lane and Weaver, will be found in Joseph B. Foraker, *Notes of a Busy Life*, 2 vols. (Cincinnati: Stewart & Kid Co., 1916); James A. Tinsley, "Roosevelt, Foraker, and the Brownsville Affray," *JNH* 41 (Jan. 1956): 43–65; and Everett Walters, *Joseph Benson Foraker: An Uncompromising Republican* (Columbus: Ohio University Press, 1948).

81. Austin *Statesman*, Mar. 9, 1907, Mar. 10, 1907 (quotations), Mar. 11, 1907. In 1907 Penrose and Macklin were court-martialed. One study described the results thus:

> Major Penrose was charged with neglect of duty, with two specifications: (1) having been informed that his soldiers were guilty of the raid he failed to take the measures necessary to detect the guilty men; and (2) knowing of the feeling in the town toward the soldiers he failed to order Captain Macklin to inspect frequently the men under his command. He was found not guilty on the charge and first specification; he was found guilty of the second specification, but the court added that it did not attach any criminality to the officer's failure to give Captain Macklin more explicit orders. He was thus acquitted of any responsibility for the affray.
>
> Captain Macklin was also charged with neglect of duty, with one specification, that he retired to his quarters from which it was found impossible to arouse him for some time. He was judged not guilty of both charge and specification. Each court, however, held that though the officers were not responsible, men of their command had committed the midnight attack. (Lane, *Brownsville Affair*, 38–39)

Another mystifying event occurred in December 1906 when an intruder shot and wounded Macklin in his quarters at Fort Reno. Robbery and/or assault were the likely motives. Garner L. Christian, "The Brownsville Raid's 168th Man: The Court-Martial of Corporal Knowles," *SHQ* 93 (July 1989): 45–59.

82. Brownsville *Daily Herald*, Dec. 24, 1906.

83. Sterling, *Trails and Trials of a Texas Ranger*, 351.

84. Austin *Statesman*, Apr. 8, 1910.

85. Ibid., Mar. 10, 1907.

86. Ibid., Aug. 28, 1906; San Antonio *Express*, Sept. 4, 1906.

87. Adj. Gen. to W. E. Caldwell, ibid. to H. W. Garrett, Jr., ibid. to James Gibson, Sept. 20, 1906, Caldwell to Hulen, Sept. 8, 1906, Garrett to ibid., Sept. 7, 1906, Gibson to ibid., received Sept. 10, 1906 (quotation), GC-AGR.

88. Brownsville *Daily Herald*, Sept. 12, 1906. Another resolution dealt with the offering of a reward by the governor for the arrest and delivery to the sheriff of those who attacked Brownsville. The reward totaled $500. Ibid., Sept. 5, 1906, Sept. 12, 1906.

89. San Antonio *Express*, Sept. 4, 1906; Weaver, *Brownsville Raid*, 88.

90. McDonald, "RBO," pp. 6, 9.

91. Weaver, *Brownsville Raid*, 86.

92. Brownsville *Daily Herald*, Oct. 2, 1906. The next day the editors of the newspaper wrote that they did "not wish to cast aspersions on the bravery of Capt. McDonald or on his efficiency as an officer of the law . . . ." Ibid., Oct. 3, 1906.

93. Anders, *Boss Rule in South Texas*, 127–28. Another historian concluded, "McDonald could see nothing beyond the laws of Texas, the color of the offenders' skin, and his duty to bring the lawbreakers to justice. His imperious and belligerent investigation played no constructive part in the process. Until the governor finally intervened, Captain Bill played the fellow in the right who 'just keeps acomin'.' " Utley, *Lone Star Justice*, 281.

94. Procter, *Just One Riot*, 39. In the writing of his historical study of the Texas Rangers, Webb initially talked about the "courageous investigation" that McDonald made in the Brownsville affair. Then in the draft that went to print he crossed out the adjective. Webb also drew a pencil line in the draft through the characterizations of McDonald by Harbert Davenport quoted elsewhere in this biography. Literary Productions, WP. Webb also eliminated a statement by Davenport, who arrived in Brownsville a few years after the raid, that the attack on the town "afforded Bill McDonald the greatest possible opportunity for his favorite diversion of talking to the reporters, because he was, for once, absolutely safe in so doing. There was no chance that the negroes would read what he said or that even the most incompetent military officers would permit a repetition of the riot." Ibid.; Davenport to Webb, Dec. 26, 1934, WP. At the turn of the twenty-first century local public opinion still blames the black soldiers for the raid on Brownsville in 1906. Pierce, "Brownsville Raid: A Historiographical Assessment," 226–27.

CHAPTER 14: RIO GRANDE CITY: THE LAST STAND

1. W. E. Caldwell to Hulen, Sept. 8, 1906, GC-AGR.

2. Ibid.

3. Garna L. Christian, "Rio Grande City, Texas," in *New Handbook of Texas*, V, 584–85; Alicia A. Garza, "Starr County," in ibid., VI, 67–69.

4. Anders, *Boss Rule in South Texas*, 48.

5. Cynthia E. Orozco, "Reds and Blues," in *New Handbook of Texas*, V, 499–500.

6. Evan Anders, "Boss Rule," in ibid., I, 656–57; ibid., "Wells, James Babbage, Jr.," in ibid., VI, 877; ibid., *Boss Rule in South Texas*, 43–64; Dale Lasater, *Falfurrias: Ed C. Lasater and the Development of South Texas* (College Station: Texas A&M University Press, 1985); ibid., "Lasater, Edward Cunningham," in *New Handbook of Texas*, IV, 88.

7. Anders, *Boss Rule in South Texas*, 49 (quotation); Austin Statesman, Nov. 10, 1906; Brownsville *Daily Herald*, Nov. 12, 1906.

8. Austin *Statesman*, Nov. 10, 1906 (first quotations); Brownsville *Daily Herald*, Nov. 6, 1906, Nov. 12, 1906, Nov. 16, 1906 (second quotation), Dec. 4, 1906. See also Paine, *McDonald*, 357–61. Wells expressed his concern to the governor about finding the right person to replace Welch on the bench. "No man should be appointed who is not above reproach as a man and lawyer," Wells concluded his telegram, "and who also has the courage to enforce the law." Wells to Lanham, Nov. 6, 1906, GR. Eventually, Judge W. B. Hopkins of Corpus Christi was selected to replace Welch after consultation between the governor and other interested parties. Austin *Statesman*, Nov. 10, 1906.

9. Joe Baulch, "The Murder of Stanley Welch and the 1906 Starr County Election," *Journal of South Texas* 4 (Spring 1991): 33–38, with quotation on p. 33.

10. T. B. Skidmore to Hulen, Nov. 12, 1906, GC-AGR.

11. Guerra to Lanham, Nov. 8, [1906], GR; Seabury to Hulen, [Nov.] 7, [1906] (first quotation), Nov. 8, [1906] (second quotation), Wells to ibid., Nov. 6, 1906, GC-AGR. See also Paine, *McDonald*, 361–62, 426–29.

12. *RAGST* for the Period Ending Dec. 31, 1906, p. 29.

13. Asst. Adj. Gen. to McDonald, Oct. 8, 1906, R. W. Dowe, Collector of Customs, to Hulen, Oct. 11, 1906, Hulen to Dowe, Oct. 11, [1906], ibid. to McCauley, Oct. 11, 1906, McDonald to Hulen, Oct. 3, 1906 (quotations), ibid. to Phelps, Oct. 10, 1906, GC-AGR; MRCB for Oct. 1906, RR-AGR.

14. Paine, *McDonald*, 362–64, with first quotation on p. 363 and second quotation on p. 364.

15. Ibid., 364–65; Brownsville *Daily Herald*, Nov. 7, 1906, Nov. 8, 1906; McDonald to Hulen, Nov. 7, 1906, GC-AGR; MRCB for Oct. and Nov. 1906, RR-AGR; Muster and Pay Rolls of Co. B for Oct., Nov., and Dec. 1906, AGR.

16. Sterling, *Trails and Trials of a Texas Ranger*, 354–55.

17. Paine, *McDonald*, 367.

18. Ibid., 368.

19. Asst. Adj. Gen. to Rogers, Nov. 10, 1906, GC-AGR. Rogers would be the only Ranger captain not ordered to Rio Grande City. He stayed at Del Rio. Reports of the gun battle will be found in Brownsville *Daily Herald*, Nov. 9, 1906; McDonald to Lanham, Nov. 9, [1906], Seabury to ibid., Nov. 8–9, 1906, GR; MRCB for Nov. 1906, RR-AGR. For examples of the story of the shootout, see Paine, *McDonald*, 365–72; and Sterling, *Trails and Trials of a Texas Ranger*, 356–57.

20. Brownsville *Daily Herald*, Nov. 13, 1906; MRCB for Nov. 1906, RR-AGR.

21. McDonald and his contemporaries in their various statements did not always correctly identify those who were gunned down. Ever since, historians have misspelled names and misidentified bodies.

22. Brownsville *Daily Herald*, Nov. 13, 1906.

23. Ibid. See also ibid., Nov. 24, 1906.

24. Anders, *Boss Rule in South Texas*, 50.

25. Sterling, *Trails and Trials of a Texas Ranger*, 356.

26. Ibid.

27. Ibid., 357.

28. Ibid. For another view of the planned-attack approach, see Paine, *McDonald*, 365–72. See also Brownsville *Daily Herald*, Nov. 9, 1906.

29. Skidmore to Hulen, Nov. 12, 1906, GR.

30. The best overview of the gun battle from a political angle, even with factual mistakes, will be found in Baulch, "Murder of Stanley Welch and the 1906 Starr County Election," 38. Another author stressed the political aspects of the gun battle. But he viewed the intoxication factor as being more important. This writer also has McDonald and his men in Rio Grande City two days before the shootout. But that is factually incorrect. Anders, *Boss Rule in South Texas*, 50–51.

31. Brownsville *Daily Herald*, Nov. 15, 1906.

32. McDonald to Lanham, Nov. 9, [1906], GR; Paine, *McDonald*, 370.

33. McDonald to Lanham, Nov. 9, [1906], GR.

34. Paine, *McDonald*, 370.

35. Brooks to Lanham, Nov. 7, 1906, Nov. 9, [1906], GR. Seabury believed that a "larger force" than McDonald and his four Rangers was needed. Seabury to Lanham, Nov. 8–9, 1906, GR. Central headquarters notified Sergeant J. D. Dunaway of Company A that McDonald was involved in a shootout. Asst. Adj. Gen. to Dunaway, Nov. 10, 1906, GC-AGR.

36. Brownsville *Daily Herald*, Nov. 10, 1906, Nov. 13, 1906; *RAGST* for the Period Ending Dec. 31, 1906, p. 29 (quotation).

37. Brownsville *Daily Herald*, Nov. 13, 1906.

38. Paine, *McDonald*, 371.

39. Ibid., 393–94, with second quotation on p. 394; Sterling, *Trails and Trials of a Texas Ranger*, 357–58, with first quotation on p. 358.

40. MRCB for Nov. 1906, RR-AGR.

41. Brownsville *Daily Herald*, Nov. 14, 1906. In August 1906, McKenzie arrested a Texan for disorderly conduct and calling him a damned "S of B____." The Ranger private "hit him for it with his gun." MRCB for Aug. 1906, RR-AGR.

42. McDonald to Lanham, Nov. 9, 1906, GR.

43. MRCB for Nov. 1906, RR-AGR; *RAGST* for the Period Ending Dec. 31, 1906, p. 29.

44. Hughes to Hulen, Nov. 17, 1906, Nov. 20, 1906, Nov. 22, 1906, Nov. 29, 1906, ibid. to Phelps, Nov. 13, 1906, Nov. 30, 1906, Dec. 23, 1906, GC-AGR.

45. Anders, *Boss Rule in South Texas*, 51–64; Baulch, "Murder of Stanley Welch and the 1906 Starr County Election," 39–42.

46. McDonald to Lanham, Nov. 9, 1906, GR.

CHAPTER 15: THE END COMES: STATE REVENUE AGENT AND OTHER ROLES

1. Paine, *McDonald*, 390.

2. Ibid., 374.

3. Brooks to Hulen, Nov. 14, 1906, Hulen to Brooks, Nov. 17, 1906, GC-AGR.

4. Tom M. Ross replaced McDonald as officer in charge of Company B. Frank Johnson replaced Brooks as captain of Company A.

5. Austin *Statesman*, Jan. 17, 1907; *RSRA, 1906–08*, p. 3; Paine, *McDonald*, 373.

6. Paine, *McDonald*, 374–76, with quotation on p. 375.

7. Austin *Statesman*, Jan. 17, 1907.

8. *General Laws of the State of Texas Passed at the Regular Session of the Thirtieth Legislature Convened at the City of Austin, January 8, 1907, and Adjourned April 12, 1907* (Austin: Von Boeckmann-Jones, 1907), 357.

9. For a statement of instructions to county assessors by the state comptroller, see Austin *Statesman*, Dec. 26, 1907.

10. Paine, *McDonald*, 376–77.

11. Ibid., 378–80; *RSRA, 1906–08*, pp. 3–5, with quotations on p. 3, except for the last one on p. 4.

12. Paine, *McDonald*, 380–83.

13. Ibid., 383–85; Austin *Statesman*, Mar. 29, 1907, Mar. 30, 1907 (quotation).

14. Paine, *McDonald*, 384–85, with quotations on p. 385.

15. Austin *Statesman*, Apr. 1, 1907.

16. Ibid., Apr. 7, 1907.

17. Ibid., Apr. 22, 1907, May 6, 1907, May 25, 1907, June 16, 1907, June 26, 1907.

18. Ibid., Apr. 1, 1907.

19. Paine, *McDonald*, 383–84.

20. Austin *Statesman*, July 2, 1908, July 21, 1908, Aug. 12, 1908.

21. Ibid., Feb. 2, 1909; *RSRA, 1906–08*, p. 5.

22. Austin Statesman, Aug. 5, 1907.

23. *RSRA, 1906–08*, p. 7 (quotation).

24. Ibid., 9–24.

25. Ibid., 25–29. McDonald also wrote, "Your attention is further directed to the fact that there are a large number of women in the State who annually secure internal revenue license [*sic*] to sell beer and liquor, and who pay no license fees to the State for engaging in that character of business. For the current year there are over 100 of such persons engaged in this character of business." Ibid., 30.

26. Austin *Statesman*, Oct. 29, 1907.

27. Ibid., Sept. 30, 1907, Oct. 9, 1907, Nov. 15, 1907; *RSRA,1906–08*, p. 31.

28. Austin *Statesman*, Sept. 14, 1907.

29. McDonald summarized these evasive tactics in his letter to Attorney General R. V. Davidson, Sept. 8, 1908, Correspondence, Attorney General Records, Archives Division, Texas State Library, Austin, Texas.

30. *RSRA, 1906–08*, pp. 7–8.

31. Asst. Atty. Gen. James D. Walthall to McDonald, Sept. 11, 1908, ibid. to Comptroller J. W. Stephens, Sept. 11, 1908 (quotations), Letter Press Opinions, Attorney General Records. Barnum and Bailey sent a letter to state officials about setting up procedures for one continuous performance. Ibid. to Stephens, Sept. 19, 1908, Letter Press Opinions, Attorney General Records.

32. Austin *Statesman*, Sept. 12, 1908, Sept. 14, 1908.

33. Ibid., Feb. 21, 1909, Apr. 29, 1909 (quotation). For correspondence between Cody's staff, with definitions of exhibitions and circuses, and a few legal documents, see Cody (William F.) Lawsuit Papers, Manuscript Collections, Archives Division, Texas State Library, Austin, Texas.

34. *State of Texas, et al. vs. W. F. Cody* (1908), No. 25727, 53rd Judicial District, District Clerk's Office, Travis County, with quotation on p. 40.

35. Ibid., 2–17, 39–40, with the quotation on p. 14.

36. Ibid., 4.

37. Ibid., 6.

38. Ibid.

39. Ibid., 13.

40. Ibid., 15.

41. *State of Texas, et al. vs. W. F. Cody* (1909), No. 4515, Court of Civil Appeals, Opinion Record, Book 18, Vol. 223-1088, pp. 109–111, with quotation on p. 111, Archives Division, Texas State Library, Austin, Texas.

42. Ibid., 110. See also Austin *Statesman*, Apr. 29, 1909. To follow the appellate case through the judicial process, see Court of Civil Appeals (Third Supreme Judicial District), Austin, Texas, Trial Docket, 1907–1913, Vol. 223-1058, Case No. 4515; and ibid., Minutes, Book 5, Vol. 223-1071, pp. 341, 352, 359, Archives Division, Texas State Library, Austin, Texas.

43. Austin *Statesman*, Apr. 29, 1909.

44. Ibid., Dec. 17, 1907.

45. *RSRA, 1906–08*, pp. 29–32, with quotation on p. 32. For McDonald's effort to collect the occupation tax in one local area, see McDonald to Gov. Campbell, Sept. 27, 1907, GR.

46. Austin *Statesman*, Jan. 7, 1909.

47. Ibid., Jan. 23, 1909.

48. *RSRA, 1908–1910*, pp. 4–5. For McDonald going after those who undervalued cash, notes, mortgages, and other property, see Austin *Statesman*, Feb. 19, 1910, Apr. 22, 1910.

49. *RSRA, 1908–1910*, pp. 12–13.

50. Asst. Atty. Gen. R. E. Crawford to McDonald, Aug. 4, 1909, McDonald to Gov. Campbell, Aug. 25, 1909 (quotations), GR; Asst. Atty. Gen. J. W. Brady to McDonald, Apr. 31, 1910, Crawford to ibid., July 30, 1909, Aug. 10, 1909, Asst. Atty. Gen. C. A. Leddy to ibid., Mar. 5, 1910, Letter Press Opinions, Attorney General Records; McDonald to Atty. Gen. Davidson, Apr. 16, 1909, July 30, 1909, Aug. 4, 1909, Aug. 10, 1909, Nov. 17, 1909, Nov. 22, 1909, ibid. to Atty. Gen. J. P. Lightfoot, Feb. 23, 1910, Attorney General Records.

51. Austin *Statesman*, Sept. 14, 1909, Nov. 10, 1909, Nov. 28, 1909, Feb. 22, 1910; Asst. Atty. Gen. Leddy to McDonald, Feb. 2, 1910, Feb. 12, 1910, Mar. 26, 1910, June 22, 1910, Letter Press Opinions, Attorney General Records; McDonald to Atty. Gen. Davidson, July 24, 1909, ibid. to Atty. Gen. Lightfoot, Mar. 24, 1910, Mar. 30, 1910, Attorney General Records.

52. *RSRA, 1908–1910*, pp. 16–17.

53. Ibid. to Atty. Gen. Davidson, Sept. 18, 1909, Attorney General Records; Asst. Atty. Gen. Leddy to McDonald, Sept. 27, 1909, private secretary of the governor to W. F. Swift, Oct. 4, 1909, Swift to Gov. Campbell, Oct. 2, 1909, GR.

54. *RSRA, 1908–1910*, p. 17.

55. Ibid., 13–15; McDonald to Atty. Gen. Davidson, Aug. 9, 1909, ibid. to Atty. Gen. Lightfoot, Aug. 1, 1910, Attorney General Records; Asst. Atty. Gen. Lightfoot to McDonald, Aug. 13, 1909, Letter Press Opinions, Attorney General Records.

56. Austin *Statesman*, Dec. 4, 1909. The state revenue agent challenged the fees charged by county or district attorneys in the collection of the occupation tax. McDonald to Atty. Gen. Davidson, Nov. 29, 1909, Attorney General Records. McDonald also questioned the selling of cider with alcoholic contents. Ibid. to Atty. Gen. Lightfoot, Apr. 16, 1910, Apr. 25, 1910, Attorney General Records.

57. Austin *Statesman*, Oct. 14, 1909, Oct. 22, 1909 (quotation), Oct. 25, 1909, Oct. 29, 1909, Nov. 7, 1909. For another letter to a state official on the deceptive practices of the circuses, see McDonald to Atty. Gen. Davidson, Sept. 14, 1909, Attorney General Records. The attorney general's office advised McDonald that suits against the circuses could be filed in the counties where the shows were held or in the district court of Travis County. Asst. Atty. Gen.

Leddy to McDonald, Oct. 23, 1909, Letter Press Opinions, Attorney General Records. The attorney general, in addition, told McDonald to employ counsel to bring lawsuits to collect occupation taxes against Ringling Brothers. Atty. Gen. Davidson to ibid., Oct. 21, 1909, Letter Press Opinions, Attorney General Records.

58. Austin *Statesman*, Sept. 11, 1910, Sept. 24, 1910, Sept. 29, 1910. The monies were divided between the state and various counties. Atty. Gen. Lightfoot to McDonald, Nov. 28, 1910, Letter Press Opinions, Attorney General Records. See also Asst. Atty. Gen. Leddy to ibid., May 13, 1910, Letter Press Opinions, Attorney General Records.

59. *RSRA, 1908–1910*, pp. 6–8, with quotation on p. 8.

60. Austin *Statesman*, Sept. 30, 1910, Oct. 5, 1910, Oct. 15, 1910, Oct. 18, 1910.

61. Ibid., Oct. 20, 1910.

62. Ibid., Oct. 29, 1910. See also ibid., Oct. 31, 1910, Nov. 27, 1910.

63. Ibid., Dec. 8, 1910; *RSRA, 1908–1910*, pp. 9 (quotation), 11–12.

64. Seymour, *IPCH*, I, pp. 20–22, with quotation on p. 21. William Sidney Porter (pseud. O. Henry) was House's first choice to write a biography of McDonald. Ibid.

65. Austin *Statesman*, Feb. 23, 1909.

66. Ibid., June 2, 1908 (quotations), June 4, 1908. See also Paine, *McDonald*, 394–95. In January 1909 McDonald returned from another trip to Washington, D.C. Here he again met the president and, reportedly, spent time dealing with the Brownsville affair. Austin *Statesman*, Jan. 7, 1909. By then McDonald had thanked Roosevelt for his prompt action in the Brownsville raid in removing the black soldiers from military service. McDonald to Roosevelt, Dec. 22, 1908, TCHC, Microfilm Roll 112A, No. 7. In 1907 the Texas House of Representatives passed a concurrent resolution that supported the stand taken by President Roosevelt and the "Texas delegation in Congress" in discharging without honor the black soldiers stationed at Fort Brown. *General Laws of the State of Texas Passed at the Regular Session of the Thirtieth Legislature*, 421.

67. Albert Bigelow Paine, "Captain 'Bill' McDonald of Texas," *Pearson's Magazine* 20 (Oct. 1908): 421–28. Other sketches of events in the life of the Ranger captain appeared in volumes 20, 21, and 22 (Sept. 1908–Sept. 1909).

68. House to Paine, Apr. 26, [1908], May 6, 1908, June 14, 1908, June 27, 1908, [Aug. ?, 1908], Nov. 2, 1908, [Nov. ?, 1908], Dec. 8, 1908, Dec. 11, 1908, Dec. 13, [1908], Dec. 18, [1908], Jan. 2, 1909, Jan. 16, 1909, AP 748 to AP 760, PP; Paine to House, June 16, 1908, June 25, 1908, July 11, 1908, Nov. 5, 1908, Dec. 1, 1908, Dec. 9, 1908, Dec. 16, 1908, Dec. 17, 1908, Jan. 22, 1909, Feb. 2, 1909, Apr. 5, 1909, Sept. 27, 1909, Dec. 6, 1909, and two undated letters (1909–1910), TCHC, Microfilm Roll 112A, No. 13. For other correspondence by McDonald with House in appreciation of his assistance, see McDonald to House, Jan. 27, 1906, Feb. 13, 1906, ibid., Microfilm Roll 112A, No. 7. President Roosevelt was

"glad" to see McDonald published his "memorials." Roosevelt to McDonald, Dec. 19, 1908, ibid., Microfilm Roll, 112A, No. 7. The president received a synopsis of Paine's book. William Loeb, sec. to the President, to Paine, Jan. 7, 1909, ibid., Microfilm Roll, 112A, No. 7.

69. Paine, *McDonald*, 394.

70. Austin *Statesman*, Jan. 20, 1911. See also ibid., Sept. 19, 1910, Nov. 12, 1910.

71. Ibid., Aug. 28, 1910.

72. Ibid., Aug. 20, 1911, Aug. 22, 1911.

73. Seymour, *IPCH*, I, 77–79, with quotations on p. 79. See also Arthur D. Howden Smith, *Mr. House of Texas* (New York: Funk & Wagnalls, 1940), 56–57; William Manners, *TR and Will: A Friendship that Split the Republican Party* (New York: Harcourt, Brace & World, 1969), 287–88; and Catherine O. Peare, *The Woodrow Wilson Story: An Idealist in Politics* (New York: Thomas Y. Crowell Co., 1963), 156–57. For the use of Secret Service agents, other police forces, and private guards for the protection of the candidates in the presidential election of 1912, see Washington *Post*, Oct. 17, 1912, Oct. 18, 1912, Oct. 20, 1912, Oct. 23, 1912, Oct. 26, 1912.

74. Seymour, *IPCH*, I, 79–80.

75. Ibid., I, 80. See also Arthur D. Howden Smith, *The Real Colonel House* (New York: George H. Doran Co., 1918), 123–25. Important information about McDonald's role as a bodyguard to Wilson will be found in Arthur S. Link, ed., *The Papers of Woodrow Wilson* (multivolume, Princeton, NJ: Princeton University Press, 1966 to present), Volumes 25, 27, 40, 41, 46.

76. John W. Davidson, ed., *A Crossroads of Freedom: The 1912 Campaign Speeches of Woodrow Wilson* (New Haven, CT: Yale University Press, 1956), 468, 479.

77. Austin *Statesman*, Oct. 25, 1912.

78. Seymour, *IPCH*, I, 80. For other mention of McDonald as a bodyguard, see Link, *Papers of Woodrow Wilson*, Vol. 25, pp. 423–24, 448, 507.

79. Ibid., Vol. 25, pp. 508–10, Vol. 27, p. 238; Austin *Statesman*, Nov. 4, 1912; Washington *Post*, Nov. 4, 1912 (quotation).

80. Davidson, *Crossroads of Freedom*, 523–24, with quotation on p. 524. See also Washington *Post*, Nov. 6, 1912.

81. Ibid., Nov. 7, 1912; Austin *Statesman*, Nov. 7, 1912; Link, *Papers of Woodrow Wilson*, Vol. 25, pp. 525–26.

82. Seymour, *IPCH*, I, 81. See also Link, *Papers of Woodrow Wilson*, Vol. 25, p. 532.

83. Austin *Statesman*, Nov. 9, 1912; Washington *Post*, Nov. 9, 1912 (quotation).

84. Seymour, *IPCH*, I, 80–81.

85. Ibid., I, 81.

86. David F. Houston, *Eight Years with Wilson's Cabinet, 1913 to 1920* (2 vols., Garden City, NY: Doubleday, Page & Co., 1926), I, 239.

87. Arthur Walworth, *Woodrow Wilson* (2 vols., New York: Longmans, Green & Co., 1958), I, 428, fn. 1.

88. Seymour, *IPCH*, I, 360. See also Link, *Papers of Woodrow Wilson*, Vol. 27, p. 414, Vol. 40, p. 133, Vol. 41, p. 340. For other accounts that mention the 1912 election and McDonald, see Ruth Cranston, *The Story of Woodrow Wilson* (New York: Simon and Schuster, 1945), 114; and Walworth, *Wilson*, I, 250, 258. For an account of Texas during the Wilson years, see Lewis L. Gould, *Progressives and Prohibitionists: Texas Democrats in the Wilson Era* (Austin: University of Texas Press, 1973).

89. Howden Smith, *Mr. House of Texas*, 57–58

90. *Register of the Department of Justice and the Courts of the United States . . . 1914* (Washington, D.C.: Government Printing Office, 1914), 183; Virgil D. White, transcriber, *Index of U. S. Marshals, 1789–1960* (Waynesboro, TN: National Historical Publishing, 1988), 58. These sources do not agree on dates. His commission was dated March 28, 1913.

91. Minutes, U. S. District Court, Ft. Worth, Vol. 3, File Box 22-5-18, p. 504, Federal Archives and Records Center, Fort Worth, Texas.

92. New York *Times*, Mar. 12, 1913.

93. Link, *Papers of Woodrow Wilson*, Vol. 27, p. 223. In March of 1913, McDonald again returned from a trip to the "effete East." " 'I'm goin' back to Texas,' he said at the White House yesterday. 'I don't like these here rugs you got 'round this place. My feet's gettin' tired, and I want to plant them in an acre of plowed ground.' " Washington *Post*, Mar. 11, 1913.

94. See, for example, *Register of the Department of Justice and the Courts of the United States . . . 1916* (Washington, D.C.: Government Printing Office, 1916), 185.

95. Minutes, U. S. District Court, Ft. Worth, Vol. 3, File Box 22-5-18, pp. 503, 505, 525, 529, 568–71, 629–32; Minutes, U. S. District Court, Dallas, Vol. 7, File Box 30-5-12, pp. 581–83, 590–92; Minutes, U. S. District Court, Dallas, Vol. 8, File Box 30-6-1, pp. 13–15, 45–46, 65–70, 180–81, 193–201, 315–27, 435–49, 599–614, 617–18, 623–26.

96. *Annual Report of the Attorney General of the United States for the Year 1914* (Washington, D.C.: Government Printing Office, 1914), 224; *Annual Report of the Attorney General of the United States for the Year 1917* (Washington, D.C.: Government Printing Office, 1917), 358–59. For a look at the history of federal marshals, see Ball, *The United States Marshals of New Mexico and Arizona Territories, 1846–1912*; and Frederick S. Calhoun, *Lawmen: United States Marshals and Their Deputies, 1789–1989* (Washington, D.C.: Smithsonian Institution Press, 1989).

97. See fn. 95. Marshal McDonald's name was linked to the investigation of a murder case. Wichita *Daily Times*, Jan. 16, 1918.

98. Marriage Record, Vol. 3, No. 2029, county clerk, Hardeman County, Quanah, Texas.

99. Pearl Williams (after her remarriage) to Madeline Mason Manheim, July 16, 1930, Box 2.325/W7, Feb. 12, 1931 (quotation), Box 2.325/W9, MP. McDonald even asked Pearl's father for her hand in marriage. Ibid.

100. See, for example, *Annual Report of the Attorney General of the United States for the Year 1915* (Washington, D. C.: Government Printing Office, 1915), 230.

101. Williams to Manheim, Feb. 12, 1931, MP.

102. Link, *Papers of Woodrow Wilson*, Vol. 46, p. 5. Obituaries appeared in numerous newspapers, as, for example, Austin *American*, Jan. 16, 1918; Dallas *Morning News*, Jan. 16, 1918; Houston *Post*, Jan. 16, 1918; Lampasas *Leader*, Jan. 18, 1918; New York *Times*, Jan. 16, 1918; San Antonio *Express*, Jan. 16, 1918; Washington *Post*, Jan. 16, 1918; and Wichita *Daily Times*, Jan. 16, 1918.

103. Newspaper clipping, 1918, Scrapbook #3, Box 3L431, Texas Ranger Papers, Center for American History, University of Texas at Austin, Austin, Texas.

104. Mason and House, *Riding for Texas.*

105. Tyler Mason, "Hell in Boots," *Liberty* 12 (Mar. 23, 1935): 7–11. This continuing story appeared in articles in this volume under the following dates: Mar. 30, 1935, Apr. 6, 1935, Apr. 13, 1935, and Apr. 20, 1935. The correspondence about contracts for publishing the book and the articles will be found in Mason's papers (MP).

106. Williams to Manheim, July 16, 1930, MP.

107. Ibid., Feb. 12, 1931, MP.

108. Featured news stories with bylines about McDonald and other Rangers appeared in the Denver *Post*, Oct. 10, 1909, and the San Antonio *Express*, Sept. 13, 1936.

Bibliography

MANUSCRIPTS

Adjutant General Records. Archives Division, Texas State Library, Austin, Texas.

Attorney General Records. Archives Division, Texas State Library, Austin, Texas.

Cameron County Scrapbook. Center for American History, University of Texas at Austin, Austin, Texas.

Cody, William F. Lawsuit Papers. Archives Division, Texas State Library, Austin, Texas.

Crouch, Barry A. Collection. Victoria College, Victoria, Texas.

Davenport, Harbert. Collection. Archives Division, Texas State Library, Austin, Texas.

Gonzaullas, M. T. Scrapbooks. 5 vols. Texas Ranger Hall of Fame and Museum, Waco, Texas.

Governor's Records. Archives Division, Texas State Library, Austin, Texas.

Hogg, James S. Papers. Center for American History, University of Texas at Austin, Austin, Texas.

Mason (Madeline Mason Manheim McKesson). Papers. Center for American History, University of Texas at Austin, Austin, Texas.

McDonald, William J. Scrapbook. Former Texas Rangers Foundation, Kerrville, Texas.

Newsom, John H. MSS Diary. Privately Owned, Mineola, Texas.

Orsay, Henry. Papers. Center for American History, University of Texas at Austin, Austin, Texas.

Paine, Albert B. Papers. Henry E. Huntington Library, San Marino, California.

Shelby, M. C. Collection. Texana Museum, Edna, Texas.

Sonnichsen, C. L. Collection. University of Texas at El Paso, El Paso, Texas.

Sullivan, W. J. L. Collection. Texas Ranger Hall of Fame and Museum, Waco, Texas.

Texas Correspondence (Early). E. M. House Collection, Yale University Library, in Ramsdell Collection, Center for American History, University of Texas at Austin, Austin, Texas.

Texas Rangers Papers. 1835-1940. Center for American History, University of Texas at Austin, Austin, Texas.

Webb, Walter P. Papers. Center for American History, University of Texas at Austin, Austin, Texas.

Weisiger, Sidney R. Collection. Victoria College, Victoria, Texas.

Wells, James B. Papers. Center for American History, University of Texas at Austin, Austin, Texas.

GOVERNMENT DOCUMENTS

General

Annual Reports of the Attorney General of the United States, 1914–1919. Washington, D.C.: Government Printing Office, 1914–1919.

Bureau of Census Reports. Population Schedules of the United States, 7th-13th Censuses, 1850–1910. Texas State Library, Austin, Texas.

Department of Texas and the 5th Military District: Letters Sent and Received. Federal Archives and Records Center, Fort Worth, Texas.

Gammel, H. P. N., comp. *The Laws of Texas: 1822–1897* . . . . 10 vols. Austin: Gammel Book Co., 1898.

General Laws of the State of Texas, Passed at the Regular Session of the Twenty-Seventh Legislature . . . . Austin: State Printers, 1901.

General Laws of the State of Texas, Passed at the Regular Session of the Thirtieth Legislature . . . . Austin: Von Boeckmann-Jones Co., 1907.

General Laws of the State of Texas, Passed at the Thirty-First Legislature . . . . Austin: Von Boeckmann-Jones Co., 1909.

Hewett, Janet B., et al., eds. *Supplement to the Official Records of the Union and Confederate Armies*. 80 vols. Wilmington, N.C.: Broadfoot Publishing Co., 1994–1998.

List of Fugitives from Justice. Austin: Adjutant General's Office, State of Texas, 1878.

List of Fugitives from Justice: 1891—Part VII. Austin: Henry Hutchings, State Printer, 1891.

McDonald, William J. *Biennial Report of the State Revenue Agent, 1906–08*. Austin: Von Boeckmann-Jones Co., 1908.

______. *Biennial Report of the State Revenue Agent, 1908–1910*. Austin: Austin Printing Co., 1910.

Registers of the Department of Justice and the Courts of the United States, 1913–1919. Washington, D.C.: Government Printing Office, 1913–1919.

Registers of the Department of Justice and the Judicial Officers of the United States . . . , 1886–1891. Washington, D.C.: Government Printing Office, 1886–1891.

Reports of the Adjutant General of the State of Texas, 1889–1906. Austin: State Printers, 1890–1907.

Tax Rolls of Texas Counties: Hardeman, Potter, Rusk, Wichita, Wilbarger, Wood. Austin: Texas State Library, Austin, Texas.

White, John P. *The Code of Criminal Procedure of the State of Texas, Adopted at the Regular Session of the Twenty-Fourth Legislature, 1895 . . . .* Austin: Gammel Book Co., 1900.

White, Virgil D., trans. *Index of U.S. Marshals, 1789–1960*. Waynesboro, TN: National Historical Publishing Co., 1988.

Court and Prision Records

Ed Cain v. The State, 42 Texas Criminal Reports 210 (1900).

Civil Minutes, Vols. 1 and 2, District Court, Wood County, Quitman, Texas.

Commissioner's Court Minutes, Vol. 1, Hardeman County, Quanah, Texas.

Commissioner's Court Minutes, Vol. A, Wood County, Quitman, Texas.

Conduct Register, State Penitentiary, Huntsville, Texas. Archives Division, Texas State Library, Austin, Texas.

Convict Record of the Texas State Penitentiaries. Archives Division, Texas State Library, Austin, Texas.

Court of Civil Appeals, Trial Dockets, Minutes, and Opinion Records. Archives Division, Texas State Library, Austin, Texas.

Court of Criminal Appeals, Docket and Minutes, 1900, Austin. Archives Division, Texas State Library, Austin, Texas.

Criminal Minutes, Vol. K, District Court, Guadalupe County. District Clerk's Office, Seguin, Texas.

Criminal Minutes, Vol. 2, District Court, Hardeman County. District Clerk's Office, Quanah, Texas.

Criminal Minutes, Vols. F and G, District Court, Jackson County. District Clerk's Office, Edna, Texas.

Criminal Minutes, Vol. J, District Court, Orange County. District Clerk's Office, Orange, Texas.

Criminal Minutes, Microfilm No. 44, District Court, Travis County. District Clerk's Office, Austin, Texas.

Criminal Minutes, Vol. 13, District Court, Victoria County. District Clerk's Office, Victoria, Texas.

W. A. Dunklin & Co. v. W. J. McDonald et al. Case File M-7747, Texas Supreme Court Records. Archives Division, Texas State Library, Austin, Texas.

Executive Board: Pardons and Remissions, State Department. Archives Division, Texas State Library, Austin, Texas.

Monk Gibson v. State of Texas, 110 *Southwestern Reporter* 41 (1908); 53 *Texas Criminal Reports* 349 (1908).

Index to Commissioner's Court, Vol. M-Z, Wood County, Quitman, Texas.

Minutes, County Court, Vols. A and B, Wood County, Quitman, Texas.

Minutes, United States District Court, Dallas and Fort Worth, Texas, Vols. 2, 3, 7, and 8, 1883–1916. Federal Archives and Records Center, Fort Worth, Texas.

Ogle v. State, 58 Southwestern Reporter 1004 (1900).

Ex Parte John Greenhaw, 41 *Texas Criminal Reports* 278 (1899).

Felix Powell v. State of Texas, 99 Southwestern Reporter 1005 (1907); 50 *Texas Criminal Reports* 592 (1907).

Secretary of State, Extradition Papers. Archives Division, Texas State Library, Austin, Texas.

State of Texas, et al. vs. W. F. Cody (1908). No. 25727, 53rd Judicial District. District Clerk's Office, Travis County, Texas.

State of Texas, et al. vs. W. F. Cody (1909). No. 4515, Court of Civil Appeals, Opinion Record Book 18, Vol. 223-1088, pp. 109–111. Archives Division, Texas State Library, Austin, Texas.

Bob Stevens v. The State, 42 Texas Criminal Reports 154 (1900).

Texas Supreme Court Records. Archives Division, Texas State Library, Austin, Texas.

Brownsville Affray

The Brownsville Affray: Report of the Inspector-General of the Army; Order of the President Discharging Enlisted Men of Companies B, C, and D, Twenty-fifth Infantry; Messages of the President to the Senate; and Majority and Minority Reports of the Senate Committee on Military Affairs. 60th Cong., 1st Sess., Senate, Doc. No. 389. Serial 5252. Washington, D.C.: Government Printing Office, 1908.

Congressional Record. 59th Cong., 2nd Sess.; 60th Cong., 1st Sess.; 61st Cong., 2nd Sess. Washington, D.C.: Government Printing Office, 1907–1910.

Hearings before the Committee on Military Affairs United States Senate Concerning the Affray at Brownsville, Tex. on the Night of August 13 and 14, 1906. 60th Cong., 1st Sess., Senate, Vols. 1–3, Doc. No. 402, Pts. 4–6. Serials 5254–5256. Washington, D.C.: Government Printing Office, 1908.

Letter from the Acting Secretary of War, Transmitting, Pursuant to a Senate Resolution of April 6, 1908, the Names of the Enlisted Men of the Twenty-fifth Infantry Discharged Without Honor on Account of the Brownsville, Tex., Shooting Affray, Who Have Applied for Reenlistment under the Order of the Secretary of War, and the Statements Submitted by Them. 60th Cong., 1st Sess., Senate, Doc. No. 430. Serial 5256. Washington, D.C.: Government Printing Office, 1908.

Message from the President of the United States, Transmitting a Report from the Secretary of War, Together with Several Documents, Including a Letter of General Nettleton, and Memoranda as to Precedents for the Summary Discharge or Mustering Out of Regiments or Companies. 59th Cong., 2nd Sess., Senate, Doc. No. 155, Pt. 1. Serial 5078. Washington, D.C.: Government Printing Office, 1907.

Message from the President of the United States, Transmitting a Letter from the Secretary of War Containing Additional Testimony in the Brownsville Case. 59th Cong., 2nd Sess., Senate, Doc. No. 155, Pt. 2. Serial 5078. Washington, D.C.: Government Printing Office, 1907.

(The basic reports and documents in No. 155 have been reprinted in 60th Cong., 1st Sess., Senate, Doc. No. 402, Pts. 1 and 2. Serial 5252. Washington, D.C.: Government Printing Office, 1908.)

Proceedings of a General Court-Martial . . . in the Case of Capt. Edgar A. Macklin. 60th Cong., 1st Sess., Senate, Doc. No. 402, Pt. 3. Serial 5254. Washington, D.C.: Government Printing Office, 1908.

Proceedings of a General Court-Martial . . . in the Case of Maj. Charles W. Penrose. 60th Cong. 1st Sess., Senate, Doc. No. 402, Pt. 2. Serial 5253. Washington, D.C.: Government Printing Office, 1908.

Report of the Proceedings of the Court of Inquiry Relative to the Shooting Affray at Brownsville, Tex. . . . . 61st Cong., 3rd Sess., Senate, Doc. No. 701, Vols. 1–12. Serials 5888–5891. Washington, D.C.: Government Printing Office, 1911.

PRIMARY PUBLISHED SOURCES

Abernathy, John R. *In Camp with Theodore Roosevelt; or The Life of John R. (Jack) Abernathy.* Oklahoma City: Times-Journal Publishing Co., 1933.

Corbett, James J. *The Roar of the Crowd: The True Tale of the Rise and Fall of a Champion.* 1925. Repr., New York: Arno Press, 1976.

Davidson, John W., ed. *A Crossroads of Freedom: The 1912 Campaign Speeches of Woodrow Wilson.* New Haven, CT: Yale University Press, 1956.

Durham, George (as told to Clyde Wantland). *Taming the Nueces Strip: The Story of McNelly's Rangers.* Austin: University of Texas Press, 1962.

Foraker, Joseph B. *Notes of a Busy Life.* 2 vols. Cincinnati, OH: Stewart & Kid Co., 1916.

_____. "A Review of the Testimony in the Brownsville Investigation." *North American Review* 187 (Apr. 1908): 550–58.

Ford, John S. *Rip Ford's Texas*. Ed. Stephen B. Oates. Austin: University of Texas Press, 1963.

Gillett, James B. *Six Years with the Texas Rangers, 1875 to 1881*. Ed. M. M. Quaife. 1921. Repr., New Haven, CT: Yale University Press, 1925.

Gober, Jim. *Cowboy Justice: Tale of a Texas Lawman*. Ed. James R. Gober and B. Byron Price. Lubbock: Texas Tech University Press, 1997.

Haley, J. Evetts, and William C. Holden, eds. *The Flamboyant Judge: James D. Hamlin*. Canyon, TX: Palo Duro Press, 1972.

Houston, David F. *Eight Years with Wilson's Cabinet, 1913 to 1920*. 2 vols. Garden City, NY: Doubleday, Page & Co., 1926.

King, W. H. "The Texas Ranger Service and History of the Rangers with Observations on Their Value as a Police Protection." *A Comprehensive History of Texas, 1685 to 1897*. Ed. Dudley G. Wooten, pp. 329–67. 2 vols. Dallas: William G. Scarff, 1898.

Link, Arthur S., ed. *The Papers of Woodrow Wilson*. Multivolume. Princeton, NJ: Princeton University Press, 1966–Present.

Morris, John Miller. *A Private in the Texas Rangers: A. T. Miller of Company B, Frontier Battalion*. College Station: Texas A&M University Press, 2001.

Powell, W. D. (as told to Rupert Richardson). "A Baptist Preacher on the Texas Frontier." *WTHAYB* 9 (Oct. 1933): 48–59.

Reese, John W., and Lillian E. Reese. *Flaming Feuds of Colorado County*. Salado, TX: Anson Jones Press, 1962.

Roosevelt, Theodore. "A Wolf Hunt in Oklahoma." *Scribner's Magazine* 38 (Nov. 1905): 513–32.

Rynning, Thomas H. *Gun Notches: A Saga of Frontier Lawman Captain Thomas H. Rynning as Told to Al Cohn and Joe Chisholm*. San Diego, CA: Frontier Heritage Press, 1971.

Seymour, Charles, ed. *The Intimate Papers of Colonel House*. 2 vols. Boston: Houghton Mifflin Co., 1926.

Sterling, William W. *Trails and Trials of a Texas Ranger*. 1959. Repr., Norman: University of Oklahoma Press, 1968.

Sullivan, W. J. L. *Twelve Years in the Saddle for Law and Order on the Frontiers of Texas*. 1909. Repr., New York: Buffalo-Head Press, 1966.

Sutton, Fred E., and A. B. MacDonald. *Hands Up! Stories of the Six-Gun Fighters of the Old Wild West*. Indianapolis, IN: Bobbs-Merrill Co., 1927.

Wilkinson, J. L. *The Trans-Cedar Lynching and the Texas Penitentiary . . . .* Dallas: Johnston Printing & Adv Co., [n.d.].

Newspapers and Periodicals

Amarillo *Daily News.*
Amarillo *Daily Panhandle.*
Amarillo *Evening News.*
Amarillo *News.*
Amarillo *Star.*
Amarillo *Weekly News.*
Austin *American.*
Austin *Statesman.*
Brownsville *Daily Herald.*
Colorado County *Citizen.*
Cuero *Daily Record.*
Dallas *Morning News.*
Dallas *Weekly Herald.*
Denver *Post.*
El Paso *Daily Times.*
Galveston *Daily News.*
Halletsville *Herald.*
Houston *Chronicle.*
Houston *Post.*
Jackson County *Herald-Tribune.*
Lampasas *Leader.*
Mineola *Monitor.*
National Police Gazette.
Newspaper Collection—Conditt Murder. Texana Museum, Edna, Texas.
New Orleans *Daily Picayune.*
New York *Morning Telegraph.*
New York *Times.*
Quanah *Chief.*
Quanah *Quirt.*
Quanah *Tribune.*
Quanah *Tribune-Chief.*
San Antonio *Express.*
San Saba *County News.*
State Topics.
Texas Volunteer.
Victoria *Daily Advocate.*
Victoria *Weekly Advocate.*

Washington *Post*.
Wichita *Daily Times*.

SECONDARY PUBLISHED SOURCES

Books

Adams, Ramon F., comp. *Burs Under the Saddle: A Second Look at Books and Histories of the West*. Norman: University of Oklahoma Press, 1964.

_______. *Six-Guns and Saddle Leather: A Bibliography of Books and Pamphlets on Western Outlaws and Gunmen*. 1954. Rev. ed., Norman: University of Oklahoma Press, 1969.

_______. *Western Words: A Dictionary of the American West*. 1944. Rev. ed., Norman: University of Oklahoma Press, 1968.

Alexander, Bob. *Lawmen, Outlaws, and S.O.Bs—Vol. 2: Gunfighters of the Old Southwest*. Silver City, NM: High-Lonesome Books, 2007.

Allen, Allyn [pseud. of Irmengarde Eberle]. *The Real Book About the Texas Rangers*. Garden City, NY: Doubleday & Co., 1952.

Anders, Evan. *Boss Rule in South Texas: The Progressive Era*. Austin: University of Texas Press, 1982.

Anderson, Gary C. *The Conquest of Texas: Ethnic Cleansing in the Promised Land, 1820–1875*. Norman: University of Oklahoma Press, 2005.

Askins, Charles. *Texans, Guns and History*. New York: Winchester Press, 1970.

Ball, Larry D. *Desert Lawmen: The High Sheriffs of New Mexico and Arizona, 1846–1912*. Albuquerque: University of New Mexico Press, 1992.

______. *United States Marshals of New Mexico and Arizona Territories, 1846–1912*. Albuquerque: University of New Mexico Press, 1978.

Barr, Alwyn. *Reconstruction to Reform: Texas Politics, 1876–1906*. Austin: University of Texas Press, 1971.

Bartlett, Richard A. *The New Country: A Social History of the American Frontier, 1776–1890*. New York: Oxford University Press, 1974.

Baugh, Virgil E. *A Pair of Texas Rangers: Bill McDonald and John Hughes*. Washington, D.C.: Potomac Corral, The Westerners, 1970.

Bechtel, H. Kenneth. *State Police in the United States: A Socio-Historical Analysis*. Westport, CT: Greenwood Press, 1995.

Benét, Stephen Vincent. *Western Star*. New York: Farrar & Rinehart, 1943.

Berlin, Isaiah. *The Hedgehog and the Fox: An Essay on Tolstoy's View of History*. New York: Simon and Schuster, 1970.

Betts, John R. *America's Sporting Heritage: 1850–1950*. Reading, MA: Addison-Wesley Publishing Co., 1974.

Billington, Ray A. *America's Frontier Heritage*. New York: Holt, Rinehart and Winston, 1966.

______, and Martin Ridge. *Westward Expansion: A History of the American Frontier.* 1949. 5th ed., New York: Macmillan Publishing Co., 1982.

Boessenecker, John. *Badge and Buckshot: Lawlessness in Old California.* Norman: University of Oklahoma Press, 1988.

Braudy, Leo. *The Frenzy of Renown: Fame and Its History.* New York: Oxford University Press, 1986.

Brearley, H. C. "The Pattern of Violence." *Culture in the South.* Ed. W. T. Couch, pp. 678–92. 1934. Repr., Westport, CT: Negro University Press, 1970.

Breihan, Carl W. *Great Lawmen of the West.* London: John Long, 1963.

Brice, Donaly E. *The Great Comanche Raid: Boldest Indian Attack of the Texas Republic.* Austin: Eakin Press, 1987.

Brown, Richard M. "The American Vigilante Tradition." *Violence in America: Historical and Comparative Perspectives.* Ed. Hugh D. Graham and Ted R. Gurr, pp. 144–218. New York: New American Library, 1969.

______. "Historical Patterns of Violence in America." Ibid., pp. 43–80. New York: New American Library, 1969.

______. "Historiography of Violence in the American West." *Historians and the American West.* Ed. Michael P. Malone, pp. 234–69. Lincoln: University of Nebraska Press, 1983.

______. *No Duty to Retreat: Violence and Values in American History and Society.* New York: Oxford University Press, 1991.

______. *Strain of Violence: Historical Studies of American Violence and Vigilantism.* New York: Oxford University Press, 1975.

______. "Violence." *Oxford History of the American West.* Ed. Clyde A. Milner II, et al., pp. 393–425. New York: Oxford University Press, 1994.

Bruce, Dickson D., Jr. *Violence and Culture in the Antebellum South.* Austin: University of Texas Press, 1979.

Bryce, James. *The American Commonwealth.* 2 vols. 1893. Rev. ed., New York: Macmillan Co., 1910.

Bryson, Conrey. *Down Went McGinty: El Paso in the Wonderful Nineties.* El Paso: Texas Western Press, 1977.

Buenger, Walter L. *The Path to a Modern South: Northeast Texas between Reconstruction and the Great Depression.* Austin: University of Texas Press, 2001.

______, and Robert A. Calvert, eds. *Texas through Time: Evolving Interpretations.* College Station: Texas A&M University Press, 1991.

Busby, Mark. "An East Texas Lynching: The Humphries/Wilkinson-Greenhaw Feud." *Corners of Texas.* Ed. Francis E. Abernethy, pp. 147–58. Denton: University of North Texas Press, 1993.

Bushick, Frank H. *Glamorous Days.* San Antonio: Naylor Co., 1934.

Calhoun, Frederick S. *Lawmen: United States Marshals and Their Deputies, 1789–1989.* Washington, D.C.: Smithsonian Institution Press, 1989.

Calleros, Cleofas (collaboration with Marjorie F. Graham). *El Paso—Then and Now*. El Paso: American Printing Co., 1954.

Calvert, Robert A., and Arnoldo De León. *The History of Texas*. Arlington Heights, IL: Harlan Davidson, 1990.

Campbell, Randolph B. *Gone to Texas: A History of the Lone Star State*. New York: Oxford University Press, 2003.

Carrigan, William D. *The Making of a Lynching Culture: Violence and Vigilantism in Central Texas, 1836–1916*. Urbana: University of Illinois Press, 2004.

Cash, W. J. *The Mind of the South*. New York: Alfred A. Knopf, 1941.

Cashion, Ty. *A Texas Frontier: The Clear Fork Country and Fort Griffin, 1849–1887*. Norman: University of Oklahoma Press, 1996.

Christian, Garna L. *Black Soldiers in Jim Crow Texas, 1899–1917*. College Station: Texas A&M University Press, 1995.

Clark, Dan E. *The West in American History*. New York: Thomas Y. Crowell Co., 1937.

Colorado County Historical Commission, comp. *Colorado County Chronicles*. 2 vols. Austin: Eakin Publications, 1986.

Connor, Seymour V. *Texas: A History*. New York: Thomas Y. Crowell Co., 1971.

Cotner, Robert C. *James Stephen Hogg: A Biography*. Austin: University of Texas Press, 1959.

Courtwright, David T. *Violent Land: Single Men and Social Disorder from the Frontier to the Inner City*. Cambridge, MA: Harvard University Press, 1996.

Cox, Mike. *The Texas Rangers: Wearing the Cinco Peso, 1821–1900*. Vol. 1. New York: Tom Doherty Associates, 2008.

______. *Texas Ranger Tales: Stories That Need Telling*. Plano, TX: Republic of Texas Press, 1997.

______. *Texas Ranger Tales II*. Plano, TX: Republic of Texas Press, 1999.

Cox, Ross J., Sr. *The Texas Rangers and the San Saba Mob*. 2 vols. San Saba, TX: C&S Farm Press, 2005.

Cozzens, Peter. *The Darkest Days of the War: The Battles of Iuka and Corinth*. Chapel Hill: University of North Carolina Press, 1997.

Cranston, Ruth. *The Story of Woodrow Wilson*. New York: Simon and Schuster, 1945.

Crouch, Barry A. *The Dance of Freedom: Texas African Americans During Reconstruction*. Ed. Larry Madaras. Austin: University of Texas Press, 2007.

Cunningham, Eugene. *Triggernometry: A Gallery of Gunfighters*. 1941. Repr., Caldwell, ID: Caxton Printers, Ltd., 1971.

Cutrer, Thomas W. *Ben McCulloch and the Frontier Military Tradition*. Chapel Hill: University of North Carolina Press, 1993.

Darnton, Robert. *The Great Cat Massacre and Other Episodes in French Cultural History*. New York: Basic Books, 1984.

Davis, John L. *The Texas Rangers: Images and Incidents*. San Antonio: Institute of Texan Cultures, 1991.

DeArment, Robert K. *Bat Masterson: The Man and the Legend*. Norman: University of Oklahoma Press, 1979.

_______. *Deadly Dozen: Twelve Forgotten Gunfighters of the Old West*. Vol. 2. Norman: University of Oklahoma Press, 2007.

Douglas, C. L. *Famous Texas Feuds*. Dallas: Turner Co., 1936.

_______. *The Gentlemen in the White Hats: Dramatic Episodes in the History of the Texas Rangers*. Dallas: South-West Press, 1934.

Drago, Harry S. *The Legend Makers: Tales of the Old-Time Peace Officers and Desperadoes of the Frontier*. New York: Dodd, Mead & Co., 1975.

Dyer, Thomas G. *Theodore Roosevelt and the Idea of Race*. Baton Rouge: Louisiana State University Press, 1980.

Dykstra, Robert R. *The Cattle Towns*. New York: Alfred A. Knopf, 1968.

Eaton, Clement. *The Growth of Southern Civilization, 1790–1860*. New York: Harper & Brothers, 1961.

_______. *The Mind of the Old South*. Baton Rouge: Louisiana State University Press, 1964.

Ehrle, Michael G., comp. *The Childress County Story*. Childress, TX: Ox Bow Printing, 1971.

Elazar, Daniel J. *The American Partnership: Intergovernmental Co-operation in the Nineteenth-Century United States*. Chicago: University of Chicago Press, 1962.

Faulk, J. J. *History of Henderson County, Texas*. Athens, TX: Athens Review Printing, 1929.

Faulk, Odie B. *Land of Many Frontiers: A History of the American Southwest*. New York: Oxford University Press, 1968.

Fehrenbach, T. R. *Lone Star: A History of Texas and the Texans*. 1968. Repr., New York: American Legacy Press, 1983.

Fischer, David H. *Historians' Fallacies: Toward a Logic of Historical Thought*. New York: Harper & Row, 1970.

Fletcher, Marvin. *The Black Soldier and Officer in the United States Army, 1891–1917*. Columbia: University of Missouri Press, 1974.

Foner, Eric. *Reconstruction: America's Unfinished Revolution, 1863–1877*. New York: Harper & Row, 1988.

Foner, Jack D. *Blacks and the Military in American History: A New Perspective*. New York: Praeger, 1974.

Frantz, Joe B. "Leander H. McNelly." *Rangers of Texas*, Roger N. Conger, et al., pp. 135–46. Waco: Texian Press, 1969.

_______. *Texas: A Bicentennial History.* New York: W. W. Norton & Co., 1976.

Friedman, Lawrence M. *Crime and Punishment in American History.* New York: Basic Books, 1993.

_______. *A History of American Law.* New York: Simon and Schuster, 1973.

Fuermann, George. *Reluctant Empire.* Garden City, NY: Doubleday & Co., 1957.

Furman, Necah S. *Walter Prescott Webb: His Life and Impact.* Albuquerque: University of New Mexico Press, 1976.

Gantt, Fred, Jr. *The Chief Executive in Texas: A Study in Gubernatorial Leadership.* Austin: University of Texas Press, 1964.

Gard, Wayne. *Frontier Justice.* Norman: University of Oklahoma Press, 1949.

_______. *Rawhide Texas.* Norman: University of Oklahoma Press, 1965.

Goldstein, Kenneth S. " 'The Texas Rangers' in Aberdeenshire." *A Good Tale and a Bonnie Tune.* Ed. Mody C. Boatright, et al., pp. 188–98. Dallas: Southern Methodist University Press, 1964.

Gorn, Elliott J. *The Manly Art: Bare-Knuckle Prize Fighting in America.* Ithaca, NY: Cornell University Press, 1986.

Gould, Lewis L. *The Presidency of Theodore Roosevelt.* Lawrence: University Press of Kansas, 1991.

_______. *Progressives and Prohibitionists: Texas Democrats in the Wilson Era.* Austin: University of Texas Press, 1973.

Gournay, Luke. *Texas Boundaries: Evolution of the State's Counties.* College Station: Texas A&M University Press, 1995.

Graves, W. Brooke. *American Intergovernmental Relations: Their Origins, Historical Development, and Current Status.* New York: Charles Scribner's Sons, 1964.

Graybill, Andrew R. *Policing the Great Plains: Rangers, Mounties, and the North American Frontier, 1875–1910.* Lincoln: University of Nebraska Press, 2007.

Greer, James K. *Colonel Jack Hays: Texas Frontier Leader and California Builder.* New York: E. P. Dutton & Co., 1952.

Grimes, Roy, ed. *300 Years in Victoria County.* Victoria: Victoria Advocate Publishing Co., 1968.

Grimsted, David. *American Mobbing, 1828–1861: Toward Civil War.* New York: Oxford University Press, 1998.

Grodzins, Morton. *The American System: A New View of Government in the United States.* Ed. Daniel J. Elazar. Chicago: Rand McNally & Co., 1966.

Haley, James L. *Passionate Nation: The Epic History of Texas.* New York: Free Press, 2006.

Haley, J. Evetts. *Jeff Milton: A Good Man with a Gun.* Norman: University of Oklahoma Press, 1948.

Hall, Gary D. *Murder & Malice: Crimes of Passion from Victoria County, Texas (1891–1913)*. Austin: Nortex Press (for Victoria Preservation), 2006.

Hamrick, Alma W. *The Call of the San Saba: A History of San Saba County*. 1941. 2nd ed., Austin: Jenkins Publishing Co., 1969.

Harbaugh, William H. *The Life and Times of Theodore Roosevelt*. 1961. Rev. ed., New York: Collier Books, 1966.

Hardin, Stephen L. *The Texas Rangers*. London: Osprey Publishing Ltd, 1991.

________. *Texian Iliad: A Military History of the Texas Revolution, 1835–1836*. Austin: University of Texas Press, 1994.

Harris, Charles H. III, and Louis R. Sadler. *The Texas Rangers and the Mexican Revolution: The Bloodiest Decade, 1910–1920*. Albuquerque: University of New Mexico Press, 2004.

Hatley, Allen G. *Bringing the Law to Texas: Crime and Violence in Nineteenth Century Texas*. La Grange, TX: Centex Press, 2002.

________. "Keeping Score: A New Look at the Frontier Battalion." *Revenge! And Other True Tales of the Old West*. Ed. Sharon Cunningham and Mark Boardman, pp. 97–111. [n.p.]: Scarlet Mask Enterprises, 2004.

Hendricks, George D. *The Bad Man of the West*. 1942. Repr., San Antonio: Naylor Co., 1950.

Henry, Will. *The Texas Rangers*. New York: Random House, 1957.

Herring, Edward. *Sam Baker: Winston County's Gunfighter*. Mt. Hope, AL: Privately Printed, 1998.

Hine, Robert V., and John Mack Faragher, *The American West: A New Interpretive History*. New Haven, CT: Yale University Press, 2000.

Hollon, W. Eugene. *Frontier Violence: Another Look*. New York: Oxford University Press, 1974.

________. *The Southwest: Old and New*. New York: Alfred A. Knopf, 1961.

Hook, Sidney. *The Hero in History*. 1943. Repr., Boston: Beacon Press, 1955.

Horan, James D. *The Pinkertons: The Detective Dynasty That Made History*. New York: Crown Publishers, 1967.

Horgan, John J. *Criminal Investigation*. New York: McGraw-Hill Book Co., 1974.

Hornung, Chuck. *Fullerton's Rangers: A History of the New Mexico Territorial Mounted Police*. Jefferson, NC: McFarland & Co., 2005.

House, Boyce. *Cowtown Columnist*. San Antonio: Naylor Co., 1946.

Howden Smith, Arthur D. *Mr. House of Texas*. New York: Funk & Wagnalls Co., 1940.

________. *The Real Colonel House*. New York: George H. Doran Co., 1918.

Hughes, W. J. *Rebellious Ranger: Rip Ford and the Old Southwest*. Norman: University of Oklahoma Press, 1964.

Johnson, Benjamin H. *Revolution in Texas: How a Forgotten Rebellion and Its Bloody Suppression Turned Mexicans into Americans.* New Haven, CT: Yale Univ. Press, 2003.

Johnson, David R. *American Law Enforcement: A History.* St. Louis: Forum Press, 1981.

Johnson, Herbert A. *History of Criminal Justice.* Cincinnati, OH: Anderson Publishing Co., 1988.

Jones, Lucille. *History of Mineola, Texas.* Quanah, TX: Nortex Offset Publications, 1973.

Jordan, Philip D. *Frontier Law and Order: Ten Essays.* Lincoln: University of Nebraska Press, 1970.

Keating, Bern. *An Illustrated History of the Texas Rangers.* New York: Promontory Press, 1980.

Kelly, Louise, comp. (published in cooperation with the Wichita County Historical Commission). *Wichita County Beginnings.* Burnet, TX: Eakin Press, 1982.

Kelton, Elmer. *Jericho's Road.* New York: Forge, 2004.

Key, Della T. *In the Cattle Country: History of Potter County, 1867–1966.* 1961. Rev. ed., Quanah-Wichita Falls, TX: Nortex Offset Publications, 1972.

Knowles, Thomas W. *They Rode for the Lone Star: The Saga of the Texas Rangers—The Birth of Texas—The Civil War.* Dallas: Taylor Publishing Co., 1999.

Lamar, Howard R., ed. *The New Encyclopedia of the American West.* 1977. Rev. ed., New Haven, CT: Yale University Press, 1998.

Lane, Ann J. *The Brownsville Affair; National Crisis and Black Reaction.* Port Washington, NY: Kennikat Press, 1971.

Lasater, Dale. *Falfurrias: Ed C. Lasater and the Development of South Texas.* College Station: Texas A&M University Press, 1985.

Lavender, David. *The Southwest.* Albuquerque: University of New Mexico Press, 1984.

Leiker, James. *Racial Borders: Black Soldiers Along the Rio Grande.* College Station: Texas A&M University Press, 2002.

Limerick, Patricia N. *The Legacy of Conquest: The Unbroken Past of the American West.* New York: W. W. Norton, 1987.

________, and Clyde A. Milner II and Charles E. Rankin, eds. *Trails: Toward a New Western History.* Lawrence: University Press of Kansas, 1991.

Link, Arthur. *Wilson: The New Freedom.* Princeton, NJ: Princeton University Press, 1956.

________. *Wilson: The Road to the White House.* Princeton, NJ: Princeton University Press, 1947.

Lowenthal, David. *The Past Is a Foreign Country.* Cambridge, Eng.: Cambridge University Press, 1985.

McCallum, John D. *The World Heavyweight Boxing Championship: A History.* Radnor, PA: Chilton Book Co., 1974.

McComb, David G. *Texas: A Modern History.* Austin: University of Texas Press, 1989.

McDonald, Archie P., comp. *The Texas Experience.* College Station: Texas A&M University Press, 1986.

McGiffin, Lee. *Ten Tall Texans.* New York: Lothrop, Lee and Shepard Co., 1956.

McGrath, Roger D. *Gunfighters, Highwaymen and Vigilantes: Violence on the Frontier.* Berkeley: University of California Press, 1984.

McKanna, Clare V., Jr. *Homicide, Race, and Justice in the American West, 1880–1920.* Tucson: University of Arizona Press, 1997.

_______. *Race and Homicide in Nineteenth-Century California.* Reno: University of Nevada Press, 2002.

McLemore, Laura L. *Inventing Texas: Early Historians of the Lone Star* State. College Station: Texas A&M University Press, 2004.

McReynolds, Edwin C. *Oklahoma: A History of the Sooner State.* Norman: University of Oklahoma Press, 1954.

McWhiney, Grady (with a prologue by Forrest McDonald). *Cracker Culture: Celtic Ways in the Old South.* Tuscaloosa: University of Alabama Press, 1988.

McWilliams, Carey. *North from Mexico: The Spanish-Speaking People of the United States.* Philadelphia: J. B. Lippincott Co., 1949.

Madden, James W. *Charles Allen Culberson: His Life, Character and Public Service.* Austin: Gammel's Book Store, 1929.

Manners, William. *TR and Will: A Friendship That Split the Republican Party.* New York: Harcourt, Brace & World, 1969.

Martin, Jack. *Border Boss: Captain John R. Hughes—Texas Ranger.* 1942. Repr., Austin: State House Press, 1990.

Mason, Herbert M., Jr. *The Texas Rangers.* New York: Meredith Press, 1967.

Mason, Tyler [pseud. of Madeline Mason Manheim McKesson], and Edward M. House. *Riding for Texas: The True Adventures of Captain Bill McDonald of the Texas Rangers.* New York: Reynal & Hitchcock, 1936.

Meinig, D. W. *Imperial Texas: An Interpretive Essay in Cultural Geography.* Austin: University of Texas Press, 1975.

Merk, Frederick. *History of the Westward Movement.* New York: Alfred A. Knopf, 1978.

Metz, Leon. *John Wesley Hardin: Dark Angel of Texas.* El Paso: Mangan Books, 1996.

Miletich, Leo N. *Dan Stuart's Fistic Carnival.* College Station: Texas A&M University Press, 1994.

Miller, Rick. *Sam Bass and Gang.* Austin: State House Press, 1999.

______. *Bloody Bill Longley*. Wolfe City, TX: Henington Publishing Co., 1996.

[Mineola Centennial Corp.], comp. *Mineola: The First 100 Years*. Mineola, TX: Mineola Centennial Corp., 1973.

Monaghan, Jim, ed. *The Trans-Cedar Tragedy: Triple Lynching in Henderson County, Texas*. Dallas: Homemade Publishers, 1989.

Moneyhon, Carl H. *Texas after the Civil War: The Struggle of Reconstruction*. College Station: Texas A&M University Press, 2004.

Moore, Stephen L. *Savage Frontier: Rangers, Riflemen, and Indian Wars in Texas, Vol. I, 1835–1837*. Plano, TX: Republic of Texas Press, 2002.

______. *Savage Frontier: Rangers, Riflemen, and Indian Wars in Texas, Vol. II, 1838–1839*. Denton: University of North Texas Press, 2006.

______. *Savage Frontier: Rangers, Riflemen, and Indian Wars in Texas, Vol. III, 1840–1841*. Denton: University of North Texas Press, 2007.

Morgan, Jonnie R. *The History of Wichita Falls*. 1931. Repr., Wichita Falls, TX: Nortex Publications, 1971.

Morn, Frank. "*The Eye That Never Sleeps*": *A History of the Pinkerton National Detective Agency*. Bloomington: Indiana University Press, 1982.

Morris, Edmund. *Theodore Rex*. New York: Random House, 2001.

Mowry, George E. *The Era of Theodore Roosevelt and the Birth of Modern America, 1900–1912*. New York: Harper & Row, 1962.

Mrozek, Donald J. *Sport and American Mentality, 1880–1910*. Knoxville: University of Tennessee Press, 1983.

Mullen, Kevin J. *Dangerous Strangers: Minority Newcomers and Criminal Violence in the Urban West, 1850–2000*. New York: Palgrave Macmillan, 2005.

Murphree, Nellie. *A History of DeWitt County*. Ed. R. W. Shook. Victoria, TX: Graham Printing Co., 1962.

[n. a.]. *San Saba County History, 1856–1983*. San Saba, TX: San Saba County Historical Commission, 1983.

Nankivell, John H., ed. *The History of the Twenty-Fifth Regiment, United States Infantry, 1869–1926*. Ft. Collins, CO: Old Army Press, 1972.

Neal, Bill. *Getting Away with Murder on the Texas Frontier: Notorious Killings and Celebrated Trials*. Lubbock: Texas Tech University Press, 2006.

Neal, Bill. *The Last Frontier: The Story of Hardeman County*. Quanah, TX: Quanah *Tribune-Chief* and Hardeman County Historical Society, 1966.

Nevin, David. *The Texans: What They Are—And Why*. New York: Bonanza Books, 1968.

Oates, Stephen B. *Visions of Glory: Texans on the Southwestern Frontier*. Norman: University of Oklahoma Press, 1970.

O'Connor, Robert F., ed. *Texas Myths*. College Station: Texas A&M University Press, 1986.

O'Neal, Bill. *The Arizona Rangers*. Austin, TX: Eakin Press, 1987.

_______. *Encyclopedia of Western Gunfighters.* Norman: University of Oklahoma Press, 1979.

_______. "Violence in Texas History." *Texas: A Sesquicentennial Celebration.* Ed. Donald W. Whisenhunt, pp. 353–69. Austin: Eakin Press, 1984.

Ord, Paul, ed. *They Followed the Rails: A History of Childress County.* Childress, TX: Childress *Reporter*, 1970.

Paddock, B. B. *A History of Central and Western Texas . . . .* 2 vols. Chicago: Lewis Publishing Co., 1911.

Paine, Albert B. *Captain Bill McDonald, Texas Ranger: A Story of Frontier Reform.* New York: J. J. Little & Ives Co., 1909. Readability: excellent. Style: flowery. Factual information: some mistakes. Result: a romantic story of a two-gun western hero. Superior, though, to the work by Tyler Mason.

Paredes, Américo. *"With His Pistol in His Hand": A Border Ballad and Its Hero.* Austin: University of Texas Press, 1958.

Parsons, Chuck. *John B. Armstrong: Texas Ranger and Pioneer Ranchman.* College Station: Texas A&M University Press, 2007.

_______. and Marianne E. Hall Little. *Captain L. H. McNelly, Texas Ranger: The Life and Times of a Fighting Man.* Austin: State House Press, 2001.

Paterson, Richard. *Historical Atlas of the Outlaw West.* Boulder, CO: Johnson Publishing Co., 1985.

Peare, Catherine O. *The Woodrow Wilson Story: An Idealist in Politics.* New York: Thomas Y. Crowell Co., 1963.

Pfeifer, Michael J. *Rough Justice: Lynching and American Society, 1874–1947.* Urbana: University of Illinois Press, 2004.

Pierce, Walter. "The Brownsville Raid: A Historiographical Assessment." *Studies in Brownsville History*, ed. Milo Kearney, pp. 219–28. Brownsville, TX: Pan American University at Brownsville, 1986.

Prassel, Frank R. *The Great American Outlaw: A Legacy of Fact and Fiction.* Norman: University of Oklahoma Press, 1993.

_______. *The Western Peace Officer: A Legacy of Law and Order.* Norman: University of Oklahoma Press, 1972.

Preece, Harold. *Lone Star Man: Ira Aten, Last of the Old Texas Rangers.* New York: Hastings House, 1960.

Pringle, Henry F. *Theodore Roosevelt: A Biography.* New York: Harcourt, Brace & Co., 1931.

Procter, Ben H. *Just One Riot: Episodes of Texas Rangers in the 20th Century.* Austin: Eakin Press, 1991.

_______. "The Texas Rangers: An Overview." *The Texas Heritage.* Ed. Ben Procter and Archie P. McDonald, pp. 119–31. St. Louis: Forum Press, 1980.

Raine, William M. *45-Caliber Law: The Way of Life of the Frontier Peace Officer.* Evanston, IL: Row, Peterson and Co., 1941.

Rathjen, Frederick W. *The Texas Panhandle Frontier.* Austin: University of Texas Press, 1973.

Raymond, Dora N. *Captain Lee Hall of Texas*. Norman: University of Oklahoma Press, 1940.

Reed, St. Clair Griffin. *A History of the Texas Railroads*. Houston: St. Clair Publishing Co., 1941.

Rhinehart, Marilyn D. *A Way of Work and a Way of Life: Coal Mining in Thurber, Texas, 1888–1926*. College Station: Texas A&M University Press, 1992.

Richardson, Rupert N. *Colonel Edward M. House: The Texas Years, 1858–1912.* Abilene, TX: Abilene Printing & Stationery Co., 1964.

_______. *Texas: The Lone Star State.* New York: Prentice-Hall, 1943.

Rickard, J. A. *Famous Texans.* Dallas: Banks Upshaw and Co., 1955.

Ritchie, Robert C., and Paul A. Hutton, eds. *Frontier and Region: Essays in Honor of Martin Ridge*. San Marino, CA: Huntington Library Press, 1997.

Roberts, Gary L. "Violence and the Frontier Tradition." *Kansas and the West: Bicentennial Essays in Honor of Nyle H. Miller.* Ed. Forrest R. Blackburn, et al., pp. 96–111. Topeka: Kansas State Historical Society, 1976.

Robinson, Charles M. III. *The Men Who Wear the Star: The Story of the Texas Rangers.* New York: Random House, 2000.

Rogers, John W. *The Lusty Texans of Dallas.* 1951. Repr., New York: E. P. Dutton and Co., 1960.

Roller, David C., and Robert W. Twyman, eds. *The Encyclopedia of Southern History*. Baton Rouge: Louisiana State University Press, 1979.

Rosa, Joseph G. *The Gunfighter: Man or Myth?* Norman: University of Oklahoma Press, 1969.

Roth, Mitchel. *Crime and Punishment: A History of the Criminal Justice System.* Belmont, CA: Thomson Wadsworth, 2005.

________. "History of the DPS." *Courtesy, Service, Protection: The Texas Department of Public Safety's Sixtieth Anniversary*. Ed. Mike Cox, et al., pp. 8–86. Dallas: Taylor Publishing Co., 1995.

Rowland, Dunbar. *History of Mississippi: The Heart of the South*. 2 vols. Chicago-Jackson: S. J. Clarke Publishing Co., 1925.

Ruggles, William B. *Trails of Texas.* San Antonio: Naylor Co., 1972.

Sammons, Jeffrey T. *Beyond the Ring: The Role of Boxing in American Society.* Urbana: University of Illinois Press, 1988.

Samora, Julian, et al. *Gunpowder Justice: A Reassessment of the Texas Rangers.* Notre Dame, IN: University of Notre Dame Press, 1979.

Samuelson, Nancy B. *The Dalton Gang Story: Lawmen to Outlaws.* Eastford, CT: Shooting Star Press, 1992.

Scheiber, Harry N. "The Condition of American Federalism: An Historian's View." *American Intergovernmental Relations* . . . . Ed. Laurence J. O'Toole, Jr., pp. 51–57. Washington, D.C.: Congressional Quarterly, 1985.

Scott, Leslie. *Terror Stalks the Border: A Western Duo*. Waterville, ME: Five Star, 2002.

Secrest, William B. *Dark and Tangled Threads of Crime: San Francisco's Famous Police Detective, Isaiah W. Lees*. Sanger, CA: Word Dancer Press, 2003.

Shirley, Glenn. *The Fighting Marlows: Men Who Wouldn't Be Lynched*. Fort Worth: Texas Christian University Press, 1994.

———. *Law West of Fort Smith: A History of Frontier Justice in the Indian Territory, 1834–1896*. New York: Henry Holt and Co., 1957.

———. *Marauders of the Indian Nations: The Bill Cook Gang and Cherokee Bill*. Stillwater, OK: Barbed Wire Press, 1994.

———. *Six-gun and Silver Star*. Albuquerque: University of New Mexico Press, 1955.

———. *West of Hell's Fringe: Crime, Criminals, and the Federal Peace Officer in Oklahoma Territory, 1889–1907*. Norman: University of Oklahoma Press, 1978.

Shoemaker, Robert B. *The London Mob: Violence and Disorder in Eighteenth-Century England*. London: Hambledon and London, 2004.

Shook, Robert W., and Charles D. Spurlin. *Victoria: A Pictorial History*. Norfolk, VA: Donning Co., 1985.

Silver, Allan. "The Demand for Order in Civil Society: A Review of Some Themes in the History of Urban Crime, Police, and Riot." *The Police: Six Sociological Essays*. Ed. David J. Bordua, pp. 1–24. New York: John Wiley & Sons, 1967.

Sinise, Jerry. *George Washington Arrington* . . . . Burnet, TX: Eakin Press, 1979.

Skiles, Jack. *Judge Roy Bean Country*. Lubbock: Texas Tech University Press, 1996.

Slotkin, Richard. *The Fatal Environment: The Myth of the Frontier in the Age of Industrialization, 1800–1890*. New York: Atheneum, 1985.

Smith, Bruce. *Police Systems in the United States*. 1940. Rev. ed., New York: Harper & Row, 1960.

———. *The State Police: Organization and Administration*. 1925. Repr., Montclair, NJ: Patterson Smith, 1969.

Smith, David P. *Frontier Defense in the Civil War: Texas' Rangers and Rebels*. College Station: Texas A&M University Press, 1992.

Smith, Henry N. *Virgin Land: The American West as Symbol and Myth*. Cambridge: Harvard University Press, 1950.

Sonnichsen, C. L. *I'll Die Before I'll Run: The Story of the Great Feuds of Texas*. New York: Harper & Brothers, 1951.

———. *Pass of the North: Four Centuries on the Rio Grande*. El Paso: Texas Western Press, 1968.

———. *The Story of Roy Bean: Law West of the Pecos*. 1943. Repr., Greenwich, CT: Fawcett Publications, 1972.

_______. *Ten Texas Feuds.* 1957. Repr., Albuquerque: University of New Mexico Press, 1971.

Spellman, Paul N. *Captain J. A. Brooks: Texas Ranger.* Denton: University of North Texas Press, 2007.

______. *Captain John H. Rogers, Texas Ranger.* Denton: University of North Texas Press, 2003.

Spratt, John S. *The Road to Spindletop: Economic Change in Texas, 1875–1901.* Austin: University of Texas Press, 1970.

Spurlin, Charles D. *Texas Volunteers in the Mexican War.* Austin: Eakin Press, 1998.

Steckmesser, Kent L. *The Western Hero in History and Legend.* Norman: University of Oklahoma Press, 1965.

Stephens, Robert W. *Bullets and Buckshot in Texas.* Dallas: Privately Printed, 2002.

_______. *Texas Ranger Sketches.* Dallas: Privately Printed, 1972.

Syers, William E. *Off the Beaten Trail.* Waco: Texian Press, 1971.

Taylor, Ira T. The *Cavalcade of Jackson County.* San Antonio: Naylor Co., 1938.

Taylor, Quintard. *In Search of the Racial Frontier: African Americans in the American West, 1528–1990.* New York: W. W. Norton, 1998.

Thayer, William R. *Theodore Roosevelt: An Intimate Biography.* New York: Grosset & Dunlap, 1919.

Thrapp, Dan L. *Encyclopedia of Frontier Biography.* 3 vols. 1988. Repr., Lincoln: University of Nebraska Press, 1991.

Tijerina, Andrés. *Tejanos and Texas under the Mexican Flag, 1821–1836.* College Station: Texas A&M University Press, 1994.

Twin Centennial Committee. *Twin Centennial Commemorative History: Edna-Ganado, 1882–1982.* Edna: Texana Foundation, 1982.

Underhill, Lonnie E. *Outlaws in the Indian Territory: The Bill Cook Gang, 1894–1895.* Tucson, AZ: Roan Horse Press, 1985.

Utley, Robert M. *Lone Star Justice: The First Century of the Texas Rangers.* New York: Oxford University Press, 2002.

_______. *Lone Star Lawmen: The Second Century of the Texas Rangers.* New York: Oxford University Press, 2007.

Vandiver, Frank E. *The Southwest: South or West?* College Station: Texas A&M University Press, 1975.

Vickery, Adele W., comp. *Chips of Wood County, Texas.* Mineola, TX: Adele W. Vickery, 1969.

_______. *A Transcript of Centennial Edition, 1850–1950, Wood County Democrat.* Mineola, TX: Adele W. Vickery, 1974.

Walker, Dale L. *The Boys of '98: Theodore Roosevelt and the Rough Riders.* New York: Tom Doherty Associates, 1998.

Walker, David B. *Toward a Functioning Federalism.* Cambridge, MA: Winthrop Publishers, 1981.

Walker, Samuel. *A Critical History of Police Reform: The Emergence of Professionalism.* Lexington, MA: D. C. Heath and Co., 1977.

———. *Popular Justice: A History of American Criminal Justice.* New York: Oxford University Press, 1980.

Walters, Everett. *Joseph Benson Foraker: An Uncompromising Republican.* Columbus: Ohio University Press, 1948.

Walworth, Arthur. *Woodrow Wilson.* 2 vols. New York: Longmans, Green and Co., 1958.

Weaver, John D. *The Brownsville Raid.* New York: W. W. Norton & Co., 1970.

———. *The Senator and the Sharecropper's Son: Exoneration of the Brownsville Soldiers.* College Station: Texas A&M University Press, 1997.

Webb. Walter P. *The Great Plains.* Boston: Ginn and Co., 1931.

———, et al., eds. *The Handbook of Texas.* 2 vols. Austin: Texas State Historical Association, 1952.

———. *The Story of the Texas Rangers.* 1957. 2nd ed., Austin: Encino Press, 1971.

———. *The Texas Rangers: A Century of Frontier Defense.* Boston: Houghton Mifflin Co., 1935.

Weiss, Harold J., Jr. "Texas Rangers." *Violence in America: An Encyclopedia.* Ed. Ronald Gottesman and Richard Maxwell Brown, Vol. III, pp. 288–90. 3 vols. New York: Charles Scribner's Sons, 1999.

White, Richard. *"It's Your Misfortune and None of My Own": A New History of the American West.* Norman: University of Oklahoma Press, 1991.

Wiebe, Robert H. *The Search for Order: 1877–1920.* New York: Hill and Wang, 1967.

Wilkins, Frederick. *Defending the Borders: The Texas Rangers, 1848–1861.* Austin: State House Press, 2001.

———. *The Highly Irregular Irregulars: Texas Rangers in the Mexican War.* Austin: Eakin Press, 1990.

———. *The Law Comes to Texas: The Texas Rangers, 1870–1901.* Austin: State House Press, 1999.

———. *The Legend Begins: The Texas Rangers, 1823–1845.* Austin: State House Press, 1996.

Wilkinson, William V. "Lawlessness in Cameron County and the City of Brownsville: 1900 to 1912." *More Studies in Brownsville History.* Ed. Milo Kearney, pp. 295–304. Brownsville, TX: Pan American University at Brownsville, 1989.

Wilson, Charles R., and William Ferris, et al., eds. *Encyclopedia of Southern Culture.* Chapel Hill: University of North Carolina Press, 1989.

Wilson, Rufus R. *A Noble Company of Adventurers*. New York: B. W. Dodge & Co., 1908.

Wood County Historical Society. *Wood County, 1850–1900*. Quitman, TX: Wood County Historical Society, 1976.

Wright, Will. *Six Guns and Society: A Structural Study of the Western*. Berkeley: University of California Press, 1975.

Young, Elliott. *Catarino Garza's Revolution on the Texas-Mexican Border*. Durham: Duke University Press, 2004.

Encyclopedia Entries

Tyler, Ron, et al., eds. *The New Handbook of Texas*. 6 vols. Austin: Texas State Historical Association, 1996. Entries cited in the chapters are as follows:

Anders, Evan. "Boss Rule," I, 656–57.

_______. "Wells, James Babbage, Jr.," VI, 877.

Anderson, H. Allen. "Amarillo, Texas," I, 140–42.

_______, and John Leffler. "Potter County," V, 299–301.

Bruner, Ora P. "Mineola, Texas," IV, 759.

Caldwell, Laura. "Baker, Anderson Yancey," I, 342–43.

Christian, Garna L. "Brownsville Raid," I, 779–80.

_______. "Rio Grande City, Texas," V, 584–85.

Garza, Alicia A. "Starr County," VI, 67–69.

_______, and Christopher Long. "Brownsville, Texas," I, 776–79.

_______, and _______. "Cameron County," I, 918–21.

Gilbreath, David. "Wood County," VI, 1061–62.

Greene, Daniel P. "San Saba, Texas," V, 877.

Hart, Brian. "Wichita County," VI, 952–53.

Hinton, Don A. "Columbus, Texas," II, 235–36.

Hofsommer, Donovan L. "Wichita Falls, Texas," VI, 955–56.

Hudson, Linda S. "Henderson County," III, 556–59.

Hunt, William R. "Quanah, Texas," V, 378.

Kleiner, Diana J. "Orange, Texas," IV, 1160–61.

Lasater, Dale. "Lasater, Edward Cunningham," IV, 88.

Long, Christopher. "Hardeman County," III, 451–52.

Mason, Alan S. "Orange County," IV, 1161–62.

Murphy, Victoria S. "San Saba County," V, 877–78.

Odintz, Mark. "Colorado County," II, 224–26.

Orozco, Cynthia E. "Cortez Lira, Gregorio," II, 342–43.

_______. "Reds and Blues," V, 499–500.

Procter, Ben. "Texas Rangers," VI, 393–95.

Sanchez, Juan O. "Cerda, Alfredo De La," II, 21–22.

Stein, Bill. "Colorado County Feud," II, 227.

Weiss, Harold J., Jr. "Brooks, John [James] Abijah," I, 750.

_______. "Chevallie, Michael H.," II, 66.

_______. "Hays, John Coffee," III, 519.

_______. "McCulloch, Henry Eustace," IV, 385–86.

_______. "Rogers, John Harris," V, 664.

_______. "Sieker, Lamartine Pemberton," V, 1043.

_______. "Wright, William Lee," VI, 1093.

_______, and Rie Jarratt. "McDonald, William Jesse," IV, 392–93.

Periodical Articles

Alexander, Bob. " 'An Outlaw Tripped Up by Love.' " *Quarterly* of the National Association for Outlaw and Lawman History 26 (July–Sept. 2002): 7–16.

Baenziger, Ann P. "The Texas State Police During Reconstruction: A Reexamination." *SHQ* 72 (Apr. 1969): 470–91.

Ball, Larry D. "Lawman in Disgrace: Sheriff Charles C. Perry of Chaves County, New Mexico." *NMHR* 61 (Apr. 1986): 124–36.

________. " 'Redeemed, Regenerated, and Disenthralled': Arkansas Resists the Pugilists." *The Record* (annual of the Garland County [Arkansas] Historical Society) 18 (1977): 15–25.

Baritz, Loren. "The Idea of the West." *AHR* 66 (Apr. 1961): 618–40.

Barton, Henry W. "The United States Cavalry and the Texas Rangers." *SHQ* 63 (Apr. 1960): 495–510.

Baulch, Joe. "The Murder of Stanley Welch and the 1906 Starr County Election." *Journal of South Texas* 4 (Spring 1991): 33–46.

Bogener, Steve. "The World Heavyweight Boxing Championship Bout, 1896, at Langtry, Texas." *WTHAYB* 74 (1998): 47–56.

Brown, Richard M. "Desperadoes and Lawmen: The Folk Hero." *Media Studies Journal* 6 (Winter 1992): 151–61.

_______. "Western Violence: Structure, Values, Myth." *WHQ* 24 (Feb. 1993): 5–20.

Buecker, Thomas R. "Prelude to Brownsville: The Twenty-Fifth Infantry at Fort Niobrara, Nebraska, 1902–06." *Great Plains Quarterly* 16 (Spring 1996): 95–106.

Carter, Keith. "The Texas Court of Criminal Appeals." *TLR* 11 (Dec. 1932): 1–27; 11 (Feb. 1933): 185–203; 11 (Apr. 1933): 301–34; 11 (June 1933): 455–76.

Cashion, Ty. "What's the Matter with Texas? The Great Enigma of the Lone Star State in the American West." *MMWH* 55 (Winter 2005): 2–15.

Christian, Garna L. "The Brownsville Raid's 168th Man: The Court-Martial of Corporal Knowles." *SHQ* 93 (July 1989): 45–59.

_______. "The El Paso Racial Crisis of 1900." *RRVHR* 6 (Spring 1981): 28–41.

_______. "Rio Grande City: Prelude to the Brownsville Raid." *WTHAYB* 57 (1981): 118–32.

_______. "The Twenty-Fifth Regiment at Fort McIntosh: Precursor to Retaliatory Racial Violence." *WTHAYB* 55 (1979): 149–61.

_______. "The Violent Possibility: The Tenth Cavalry at Texarkana." *ETHJ* 23 (Spring 1985): 3–15.

Corwin, Edward S. "The Passing of Dual Federalism." *VLR* 36 (Feb. 1950): 1–24.

DeArment, Robert K. "That Masterson-McDonald Stand Off." *True West* 45 (Jan. 1998): 12–15.

De León, Arnoldo. "The Tejano Experience in Six Texas Regions." *WTHAYB* 65 (1989): 36–49.

DeMattos, Jack. "Bill McDonald—Bullheaded Ranger." *Real West* (Spring 1984): 44–49.

Denman, Clarence P. "The Office of Adjutant General in Texas, 1835–1881." *SHQ* 28 (Apr. 1925): 302–22.

Dykstra, Robert R. "Field Notes: Overdosing on Dodge City." *WHQ* 27 (Winter 1996): 505–14.

Ethington, Philip J. "Vigilantes and the Police: The Creation of a Professional Police Bureaucracy in San Francisco, 1847–1900." *Journal of Social History* 21 (Winter 1987): 197–227.

Frantz, Joe B. "Lone Star Mystique." *AW* 5 (May 1968): 6–9.

Friend, Llerena B. "W. P. Webb's Texas Rangers." *SHQ* 74 (Jan. 1971): 293–323.

Fritschler, A. Lee, and Morley Segal. "Intergovernmental Relations and Contemporary Political Science: Developing an Integrative Typology." *PJF* 1 (Winter 1972): 95–122.

Graybill, Andrew R. "Rangers, Mounties, and the Subjugation of Indigenous Peoples, 1870–1885." *Great Plains Quarterly* 24 (Spring 2004): 83–100.

________. "Texas Rangers, Canadian Mounties, and the Policing of the Transnational Industrial Frontier, 1885–1910." *WHQ* 35 (Summer 2004): 167–91.

Hackney, Sheldon. "Southern Violence." *AHR* 74 (Feb. 1969): 906–25.

Hale, Donald R. "The Double Lynching of Crawford and 'The Kid'." *Quarterly* of the National Association for Outlaw and Lawman History 22 (Jan.–Mar. 1998): 8–12.

Herring, Edward. "The Hunt for the Hughes Boys." *Old West* 1 (Summer 2000): 60–65.

Holden, William C. "Law and Lawlessness on the Texas Frontier, 1875–1890." *SHQ* 44 (Oct. 1940): 188–203.

Hutton, Paul A. "Phil Sheridan's Frontier." *MMWH* 38 (Winter 1988): 16–31.

Jebsen, Harry, Jr. "The Public Acceptance of Sports in Dallas, 1880–1930." *JSH* 6 (Winter 1979): 5–19.

Jordan, Terry G. "A Century and a Half of Ethnic Change in Texas, 1836–1986." *SHQ* 89 (Apr. 1986): 385–422.

Kerr, Homer L. "Migration into Texas, 1860–1880." *SHQ* 70 (Oct. 1966): 184–216.

King, Larry L. "Bringing Up Lyndon." *Texas Monthly* 4 (Jan. 1976): 78–85, 107–9.

McKanna, Clare V., Jr. "Alcohol, Handguns, and Homicide in the American West: A Tale of Three Counties, 1880–1920." *WHQ* 26 (Winter 1995): 455–82.

Mason, Tyler. "Hell in Boots." *Liberty* 12 (Mar. 23, 1935): 7–11. This continuing story about McDonald appeared in four other issues in Vol. 12 dated as follows: Mar. 30, 1935; Apr. 6, 1935; Apr. 13, 1935; and Apr. 20, 1935.

Mertz, Richard J. " 'No One Can Arrest Me': The Story of Gregorio Cortez." *Journal of South Texas* 1 (1974): 1–17.

Million, Elmer M. "History of the Texas Prize Fight Statute." *TLR* 17 (Feb. 1939): 152–59.

Oates, Stephen B. "*Los Diablos Tejanos!*" *AW* 2 (Summer 1965): 41–50.

Paine, Albert B. "Captain 'Bill' McDonald of Texas." *Pearson's Magazine* 20 (Oct. 1908): 421–28. Other sketches of events in McDonald's life appeared in volumes 20, 21, and 22 (Sept. 1908–Sept. 1909).

Phillips, Edward H. "Teddy Roosevelt in Texas, 1905." *WTHAYB* 56 (1980): 58–67.

Pierson, George W. "The M-Factor in American History." *AQ* 14 (Summer Supplement 1962): 275–89.

Ravkind, William M. "Comments: Justifiable Homicide in Texas." *SLJ* 13 (1959): 508–24.

Rhinehart, Marilyn D. " 'Underground Patriots': Thurber Coal Miners and the Struggle for Individual Freedom, 1888–1903." *SHQ* 92 (Apr. 1989): 509–42.

Richardson, Rupert N. "Edward M. House and the Governors." *SHQ* 61 (July 1957): 51–65.

Ridge, Martin. "The American West: From Frontier to Region." *NMHR* 64 (Apr. 1989): 125–41.

Rigler, Erik. "Frontier Justice in the Days Before NCIC." *FBI Law Enforcement Bulletin* 54 (July 1985): 16–22.

Rister, C. C. "Outlaws and Vigilantes of the Southern Plains, 1865–1885." *MVHR* 19 (Mar. 1933): 537–54.

Roberts, Gary L. "The West's Gunmen: I." *AW* 8 (Jan. 1971): 10–15, 64.

_______. "The West's Gunmen: II." *AW* 8 (Mar. 1971): 18–23.

Roberts, Randy. "Galveston's Jack Johnson: Flourishing in the Dark." *SHQ* 87 (July 1983): 37–56.

Rosenthal, Donald B., and James M. Hoefler. "Competing Approaches to the Study of Federalism and Intergovernmental Relations." *PJF* 19 (Winter 1989): 1–23.

Scheiner, Seth M. "President Theodore Roosevelt and the Negro, 1901–1908." *JNH* 47 (July 1962): 169–82.

Schellenberg, James A. "County Seat Wars: A Preliminary Analysis." *Journal of Conflict Resolution* 14 (Sept. 1970): 345–52.

_______. "Courthouse Coups D'Etat: County Seat Wars in the Old West." *AW* 10 (Mar. 1973): 33–37, 62–63.

Shook, R. W. "Year of Transition: Victoria, Texas, 1880–1920." *SHQ* 78 (Oct. 1974): 155–82.

Smith, Brian L. "Theodore Roosevelt Visits Oklahoma." *Chronicles of Oklahoma* 51 (Fall 1973): 263–79.

St. John, Bob. "He Just Kept a-Comin'." *Texas Parade* 25 (Apr. 1965): 46–48.

Stein, Bill. "Consider the Lily: The Ungilded History of Colorado County, Texas." *Nesbitt Memorial Library Journal* 10 (Jan. 2000): Pt. 8, pp. 3–62.

Steiner, Michael. "From Frontier to Region: Frederick Jackson Turner and the New Western History." *PHR* 64 (Nov. 1995): 479–501.

Struna, Nancy. "Puritans and Sport: The Irretrievable Tide of Change." *JSH* 4 (Spring 1977): 1–21.

Stumberg, George W. "Defense of Person and Property under Texas Criminal Law." *TLR* 21 (1942–43): 17–35.

Tinsley, James A. "Roosevelt, Foraker, and the Brownsville Affray." *JNH* 41 (Jan. 1956): 43–65.

Traub, Stuart H. "Rewards, Bounty Hunting, and Criminal Justice in the West, 1865–1900." *WHQ* 19 (Aug. 1988): 287–301.

Weiss, Harold J., Jr. "Hedgehogs and Foxes: Texas Ranger Captains and Their Transition to Mounted Constables." *Quarterly* of the National Association for Outlaw and Lawman History 19 (Oct.–Dec. 1995): 1, 3–6, 8–9.

_______. "Organized Constabularies: The Texas Rangers and the Early State Police Movement in the American Southwest." *JW* 34 (Jan. 1995): 27–33.

_______. "Overdosing and Underestimating: A Look at a Violent and Not-So-Violent American West." *Quarterly* of the National Association for Outlaw and Lawman History 27 (Apr.–June 2003): 54–63.

_______. "The Texas Rangers and Captain Bill McDonald in General—And the Conditt Murder Case in Particular." *South Texas Studies* (Victoria College), 1998, pp. 52–70.

———. "The Texas Rangers Revisited: Old Themes and New Viewpoints." *SHQ* 97 (Apr. 1994): 621–40.

———. "Western Lawmen: Image and Reality." *JW* 24 (Jan. 1985): 23–32.

Young, Richard. "The Brownsville Affray." *American History Illustrated* 21 (Oct. 1986): 10–17.

THESES AND DISSERTATIONS

Barton, Henry W. "Texas Volunteers under General Taylor in 1846." Master's thesis, University of Texas at Austin, 1962.

Boaz, Sallie R. "A History of Amarillo, Texas." Master's thesis, University of Texas at Austin, 1950.

Bonner, Helen F. "Major John B. Jones: The Defender of the Texas Frontier." Master's thesis, University of Texas at Austin, 1950.

Charlton, Thomas L. "The Texas Department of Public Safety, 1935–1957." Master's thesis, University of Texas at Austin, 1961.

Gunn, Jack W. "Life of Ben McCulloch." Master's thesis, University of Texas at Austin, 1947.

Holden, William C. "Frontier Problems and Movements in West Texas, 1846–1900." Ph.D. diss., University of Texas at Austin, 1928.

Kennedy, Mizell F. "A Study of James Stephen Hogg, Attorney-General and Governor." Master's thesis, University of Texas at Austin, 1919.

Marcum, Richard T. "Fort Brown, Texas: The History of a Border Post." Ph.D. diss., Texas Technological College, 1964.

McClung, John B. "Texas Rangers Along the Rio Grande, 1910–1919." Ph.D. diss., Texas Christian University, 1981.

Nunn, William C. "A Study of the State Police During the E. J. Davis Administration." Master's thesis, University of Texas at Austin, 1931.

Rigler, Erick T. "A Descriptive Study of the Texas Ranger: Historical Overtones on Minority Attitudes." Master's thesis, Sam Houston State University, 1971.

Schuster, Stephen W. IV. "The Modernization of the Texas Rangers, 1930–1936." Master's thesis, Texas Christian University, 1964.

Shearer, Ernest C. "A Survey History of Potter County." Master's thesis, University of Colorado, 1933.

St. Clair, Grady S. "The Hogg-Clark Campaign." Master's thesis, University of Texas at Austin, 1927.

Tinsley, James A. "The Brownsville Affray." Master's thesis, University of North Carolina at Chapel Hill, 1948.

———. "The Progressive Movement in Texas." Ph.D. diss., University of Wisconsin, 1953.

Wagner, Robert L. "The Gubernatorial Career of Charles Allen Culberson." Master's thesis, University of Texas at Austin, 1954.

Ward, James R. "The Texas Rangers, 1919–1935: A Study in Law Enforcement." Ph.D. diss., Texas Christian University, 1972.

Webb, Walter P. "The Texas Rangers in the Mexican War." Master's thesis, University of Texas at Austin, 1920.

Weiss, Harold J., Jr. " 'Yours to Command': Captain William J. 'Bill' McDonald and the Panhandle Rangers of Texas." Ph.D. diss., Indiana University at Bloomington, 1980.

Williamson, Robert L. "A History of Company E of the Texas Frontier Battalion, 1874–1879." Master's thesis, University of Texas at Austin, 1952.

Winfrey, Dorman H. "A History of Rusk County, Texas." Master's thesis, University of Texas at Austin, 1951.

Scholarly Papers

Weiss, Harold J., Jr. "Flying Forces: The Origins of the Texas Rangers." Paper read at the annual meeting of the Texas State Historical Association, March 1997, at Austin, Texas.

________. "A Hedgehog and a Fox: Texas Ranger Captain Bill McDonald in Fact and Fiction." Paper presented at a symposium at the Texas Ranger Hall of Fame and Museum, August 1998, at Waco, Texas.

Correspondence

Sam Beasley to author. Sept. 10, 2001; Sept. 13, 2001; Sept. 25, 2001.

Harrell Cherry to author. Mar. 25, 1998.

Brenda L. Fisseler to author. Jan. 8, 2001.

Tiffany Karkhoff to author. Feb. 14, 2001; Feb. 26, 2001.

Bill Stein to author. Mar. 16, 2000.

Index

A

C

D

G

H

N

O

P

Q

R

S

U

V

W

Y